THE LINES BETWEEN US

THE LINES
BETWEEN US

*Two Families and a Quest to Cross
Baltimore's Racial Divide*

LAWRENCE LANAHAN

NEW YORK
LONDON

Requests for permission to reproduce selections from this book should be mailed to: Permissions Department, The New Press, 120 Wall Street, 31st floor, New York, NY 10005.

Published in the United States by The New Press, New York, 2019
Distributed by Two Rivers Distribution

ISBN 978-1-62097-344-8 (hc)
ISBN 978-1-62097-345-5 (ebook)
CIP data is available

The New Press publishes books that promote and enrich public discussion and understanding of the issues vital to our democracy and to a more equitable world. These books are made possible by the enthusiasm of our readers; the support of a committed group of donors, large and small; the collaboration of our many partners in the independent media and the not-for-profit sector; booksellers, who often hand-sell New Press books; librarians; and above all by our authors.

www.thenewpress.com

Book design and composition by Bookbright Media
This book was set in Minion and Filosofia

Printed in the United States of America

10 9 8 7 6 5 4 3 2 1

For Theo, Emil, Andrea, Mom, Dad, and Mary Gibson

It's in the way their curtains open and close.

—"Respectable Street," XTC

I don't even have to do nothing to you.

—"Big Brother," Stevie Wonder

CONTENTS

PREFACE

THIS BOOK GREW OUT OF MY WORK AS A PRODUCER FOR WYPR, A BALTIMORE public radio station. We covered a broad range of topics, but race and class were frequently the backstory. Residential segregation in the region had created separate worlds, and racial inequality touched seemingly every aspect of people's lives, right down to how long they lived. In 2012, I launched a year-long multimedia series about regional inequality called *The Lines Between Us*.

We produced fifty episodes, but racial inequality in Baltimore is so complex and deeply rooted that much remained unexplored. As I considered writing a book about segregation and racial inequality in Baltimore, events elsewhere—particularly the death in 2014 of Michael Brown in Ferguson, Missouri—revealed similar dynamics at work in other regions. Across America, wealth and health followed whiteness, and people and places were penalized for blackness. For the book I had in mind, I thought, now is the time.

And Baltimore was the place. As a civil rights lawyer once put it to me, Baltimore was a "petri dish." Segregation and inequality flourished in the Baltimore region, and several major experiments to abate those conditions had been conducted.

Soon after I began planning the book in earnest, Freddie Gray died of injuries sustained while in police custody. The book seemed more urgent than ever.

In *The Lines Between Us: Two Families and a Quest to Cross Baltimore's Racial Divide*, I have attempted to vivisect the region and expose some of the pathologies that maintain segregation and inequality. I have grounded the story in the lives of real people, including a black mother in a poor city neighborhood trying to find better opportunities for her son; a white evangelical couple trying to reconcile their faith with their privilege in the suburbs; and a civil rights lawyer fighting for fair housing on both sides of the city's border. In their stories, I hope not only to make clear how forces in this region created its black spaces and white spaces, its poor spaces and rich spaces, but also to illuminate the obstacles and breakthroughs that await people who try to break down the lines between us. There are no easy answers in the book, but I hope you'll see how urgent the questions are.

This book is not an attempt to convey "the black experience" in Baltimore. Society and institutions regard me as white and place me in different circumstances than people who are not white. What I can try to do as a white journalist is to write about *the entire region* and the forces that divide it. Segregation pays dividends to white Americans, in the wealth their homes generate, how they are policed, the resources in their schools, and many other ways. I have been a witness to whiteness in this region my whole life. I grew up in a small suburban town outside Baltimore that was 95 percent white, the kind of place where white strangers felt perfectly comfortable making racist comments in front of me. As a young person, despite feeling like I knew who the "real" racists and bigots were, I casually indulged in racist jokes, stereotypes, and slurs. It's easy to tell yourself that you're "not actually racist" in a place that is so white. Leaving town for more heterogeneous places—in particular, a state college—disabused me of that notion and fostered a conviction that I needed to combat the culture that had polluted my youth. I eventually moved back to the region to live in Baltimore City. I have lived here for fourteen of the past eighteen years and have reported on the dynamics of segregation and racial inequality for over a decade.

Although notorious for hypersegregation, the Baltimore region is not unique. The song remains the same, even if other regions change the tune a little. This book is a lens for looking at a place. Wherever you live, I hope it helps you understand where you fit in the deeply American story I am telling.

Some notes on the book's format and sources: Many books have detailed the roots of American segregation during the first two-thirds of the twentieth century. Arnold Hirsch's *Making the Second Ghetto: Race and Housing in Chicago 1940–1960* and Thomas Sugrue's *The Origins of the Urban Crisis: Race and Inequality in Postwar Detroit* are two of them. In *Not in My Neighborhood: How Bigotry Shaped a Great American City*, Antero Pietila lays out how Baltimore's civic leaders created a landscape of inequality through segregation ordinances, redlining, blockbusting, and other policies that mostly preceded the Fair Housing Act of 1968. *The Lines Between Us* focuses on the five decades since the passage of that legislation, during which time the "truly integrated and balanced living patterns" envisioned by its architects failed to materialize. I spend only as much time on the early twentieth century as is necessary to establish the context for this depiction of a metropolitan region taking on the unfinished business of the civil rights movement.

To reconstruct the last five decades, I conducted over two hundred interviews; collected over seven hundred newspaper and magazine articles; read scores of research articles and other secondary sources; scoured stacks of filings and court transcripts at a federal courthouse; plodded through copious pages of legislation; unearthed audio and video recordings and transcripts to put myself in the room as I wrote scenes from the past; digitally scanned hundreds of memos, letters, and other primary sources from several local archives; resuscitated relevant reporting of my own from years past; and took my pen, pad, audio recorder, and camera on reporting trips to capture scenes in person.

A number of names have been changed to protect individuals' privacy, sometimes because of stated safety concerns. I printed "the N word" in full when a black person used it in the context of fighting oppression, but not when white people used it to further oppression. Dialogue appears within quotation marks. Some dialogue I witnessed; other dialogue comes from transcripts, recordings, and journalistic accounts. I occasionally use dialogue taken from sources' recollections. I followed up with sources months after their original interviews to ensure they were confident enough in their recollections that I could use the dialogue, and, where I could, I triangulated with other sources who were present. I was present to report on many of the scenes from 2014 onward, both in the lives of the book's main characters and at public events.

Some authors place themselves in the story when writing narrative nonfiction. I felt that my experience in this region was not sufficiently illuminating to do so. Because I was out reporting so often, I occasionally step into the narrative, but it happens infrequently. It would have been jarring to leave myself in. You'll see several disclosures in the endnotes, mostly in part six, about where I chose to excise myself.

Narrative nonfiction demands a large degree of compression and omission. That can give short shrift to people and institutions that are integral to the history that a writer tries to convey. I often describe characters who appear briefly in the book only by their roles (e.g., "another advocate," "Nicole's aunt"). Too many proper names can distract and confuse the reader, and this became apparent during the editing process. Entirely absent from the book are dozens of organizations— many of them black-led—that fought for fair housing alongside Barbara Samuels, and many public housing residents and attorneys who volunteered their time.

Likewise, legions of neighborhood leaders and activists who have dedicated their lives to community development in Sandtown and other parts of Baltimore did not make it into the book. I regret that there wasn't room for everything and everyone I wanted to include.

There are many stories left to tell.

THE LINES BETWEEN US

Prologue

Nicole

Nicole Smith sat in her living room and flipped through the afternoon's television talk shows.

A thin, easygoing twenty-five-year-old with warm dark eyes, Nicole savored the rare peace and quiet in the house. She was enrolled at Baltimore City Community College, but she didn't have class this day. Her younger sister was not at home. Her mother was out running errands. Her son, Joe, was at the after-school program at his elementary school a few blocks away.

Outside on this winter afternoon in 2007, the sky was gray, the air was cold, and on the ground lay the remnant of a typical Baltimore "wintry mix": a frustrating slush that turns the color of ash when it hits the street and piles up alongside the curb, Styrofoam cups and plastic miniatures of vodka protruding from it.

From her living room window, Nicole saw students walking past brick row-houses with missing steps and boarded-up windows. Across the street, the corner "package goods" liquor store with a little bar in the back—a staple along the major east–west North Avenue corridor—did steady business.

Around 4:30 p.m., Nicole's mother, Melinda, came through the door. She stayed long enough to say hello, and then left to run more errands.

After Melinda walked out the door, Nicole heard what sounded like a gunshot from out in front of the house.

Then four more: *pop-pop-pop-pop.*

Despite its grime and abandonment, this neighborhood had been a step up for the Smiths. Nicole, her mother, and her two younger sisters had lived in some of the most violent parts of West Baltimore, including Murphy Homes, a notorious public housing high-rise. Their new neighborhood still made the news for poverty, drug dealing, and violence, but trouble seemed to elude the Smiths here. People called them "the Huxtables" after the family on *The Cosby Show*. Nicole's father had left when she was three, but her mother still ran a tight ship. Melinda hadn't tolerated cigarettes or cursing. She knew who the girls' friends were and where they hung out. Even the roughest neighbors left the Smiths alone. Sometimes they sat on the Smiths' steps, but they moved on when someone came out the door—a sign of respect.

Melinda had purchased the rowhouse for $16,000 in the mid-1990s when Nicole was in middle school. It was the first home she'd ever owned. After lining up a mortgage through the previous owner for almost no money down and $219 per month, Melinda moved her family into the spacious home. It was fifteen feet across and three windows wide in front (many Baltimore rowhouses are only two windows wide). Just three blocks away, the pulsing crossroads of West Baltimore—Pennsylvania Avenue and North Avenue—offered a library, a CVS pharmacy, and a subway stop. "Formstone," the faux-stone overlay that defined Baltimore's housing stock after World War II, covered the front of Melinda's house. (In the 1990s, you could tell a gentrifying neighborhood by the crews peeling off Formstone to reveal the original red brick. Nicole's block remained mostly Formstone.) Melinda refinanced, and then renovated the house, including the wood floors and the green walls in the living room where Nicole was watching television.

Nicole felt that the neighborhood had deteriorated in the twelve years since their arrival. Frequent commotion and nighttime fights erupted around the bar across the street. The cops and corner boys regularly faced off up and down the block. One time a cop threw a suspect on the hood of Nicole's car, leaving a big dent. (Nicole was ready to give the cop an earful. Melinda had to talk her down.) A neighborhood troublemaker once slashed Nicole's car tire. A few years earlier, Nicole had watched from the window with her young son in her arms as someone jumped out of a car and shot a man.

But nothing had hit this close to home. After she heard the gunshots, Nicole ran to the door in a panic. As she scanned up and down the block for her mother, she saw someone run out of the corner bar. She picked up the landline and called her mother's cell phone, but no one answered. Then she noticed that her mother's car was no longer parked on the street. A sense of relief washed over Nicole as she realized her mother must have already driven away.

Then the police knocked. Someone had been fatally shot in the head inside the bar, and the police were canvassing the block for witnesses.

"Did you hear the shots or see anything?" an officer asked.

"I heard shots," Nicole said, "and then someone came running out of the bar."

"We might have to get you down to the station to question you," the officer said.

Nicole blanched. She wished the police could just use her answers without making her testify. "No, don't come back and ask me nothing," she said. "I don't want to be part of that—I'm not going to no police station or court!"

The police moved on, and after about an hour, Melinda came back through the door. Normalcy returned—at least what was normal for this part of town. But the incident remained with Nicole. She wanted out.

Nicole's entire family had long entertained thoughts of living out "in the county," as Baltimoreans referred to suburbs beyond the city line, but her mother had fallen behind on payments for the house. Melinda wasn't likely to go anywhere—at least willingly.

A few years earlier, Nicole's sister Jessica had gotten pregnant, dropped out of college, and moved home. When Jessica's baby was born, three-year-old Joe, who had been in his own room, crammed into a bedroom with Nicole and her other sister, Kelly. Jessica and her son took over Joe's old room.

Nicole dreamed of an apartment for just Joe and her herself. Columbia, a planned community thirty minutes away, had a good reputation, particularly when it came to its schools. (At now six-year-old Joe's West Baltimore elementary school, fourth and fifth graders had jumped him and taken his hat and gloves.) Searching online, Nicole found some apartments in a part of Columbia called Running Brook for $800 to $900 a month. Nicole had been working at a Safeway supermarket for a few years, making what she considered to be good money, but it wasn't enough to move to Columbia.

Nicole longed to be independent, but it was hard to make it very far. She was close to her mother and sisters, and she had missed them during her three semesters at West Virginia State University. West Baltimore, not West Virginia, was what she knew, and with her job and the boy to take care of, it was all she could afford right now.

Every effort Nicole took to get out seemed to be met with an obstacle. She enrolled at Baltimore City Community College, hoping to transfer to a four-year college and become a teacher, but BCCC administrators kept placing her in classes that didn't count toward her degree. She put in an application to the Housing Authority of Baltimore City for a rental unit in public housing or a "Section 8" voucher, named for a federal program under which low-income households paid 30 percent of their income toward a rental in the private market and the government paid the rest. A voucher offered the possibility of moving outside of the city. The housing authority's waiting list, however, included nearly thirty thousand people. When her aunt told her about special vouchers you could use in the county, she applied but was rejected.

Still, Nicole kept dreaming of getting herself and Joe out of the house and out of the neighborhood and into a community with safe streets and good schools.

It was just a matter of how.

Mark

Mark Lange and his next-door neighbor Kenny chatted on the sidewalk along Hunter's Run Drive, a long stretch of single-family homes amid the growing sprawl of the small town of Bel Air, Maryland. Mark's house and Kenny's house were nearly identical: a garage on the left side, a gabled roof with a louvered vent, a short concrete driveway wide enough for two cars, a square front lawn bisected by a sidewalk, rows of vinyl siding, and crisp gray shingles. Each house was an island of right angles in a sea of right angles, helping the neighborhood achieve a sense of order and propriety.

Down the street and just four doors away, however, was a complete aberration: a house with half the square footage of its neighbors. Only one story tall, it looked like someone had shoved half of it into the ground. Not only that, but the owner was building an addition in the back with siding that didn't match the siding in the front. This, of course, had invited the threat of a lawsuit from the homeowners association.

"That house doesn't belong here," Mark said.

Kenny agreed.

Mark was born just after his parents moved out of his maternal grandfather's home in the working-class neighborhood of Brooklyn, about thirty minutes down Interstate 95 from Bel Air, just inside Baltimore City's southern border. That move, made in the late 1950s, was the first chapter in an uninterrupted story of upward mobility for Mark. The story was reaching its climax here on Hunter's Run Drive. Mark and his wife, Betty, had bought the house in 1987 and now, a decade later, he had finally started his own business. Mark had achieved the American Dream.

And it could only get better. A nice house in a safe, affluent neighborhood, zoned for good schools? A home like that was sure to appreciate in value.

The nuisance house with the mismatched siding wasn't helping, though.

Mark thought it was worth 60 percent of what his or Kenny's house could sell for—70 percent, tops.

Back in the early 1980s, the company that built the houses on Mark's street had built a massive subdivision a few exits up Interstate 95. There was a wide range of houses there, including the smaller, more affordable model currently earning scorn from Mark and Kenny. Perhaps the developer wanted at least one family of modest means to be able to live among the upper-middle-class families on Hunter's Run Drive.

Affordability was not what was on Mark's or Kenny's mind.

"It's not helping our property values," Mark said.

Kenny agreed.

Not long after that conversation, cognitive dissonance overcame Mark. An evangelical Christian, he knew what his very namesake had written in the Bible. According to Jesus, Mark 12:31 read, the most important commandment after loving the Lord God with all your heart was "Thou shalt love thy neighbor as thyself."

Mark considered what he'd said about his neighbor's little house.

That, he decided, was not what Christ would be thinking.

Mark didn't aspire to be Christlike in a casual, "What Would Jesus Do?" bumper-sticker kind of way. You could see it in his intense, boxy face. He wanted his actions to be guided by the exact truth. If you misrepresented the truth or failed to live by what you claimed as your truth, Mark's estimation of you withered.

It had always been that way. His mother said about his birth, "I didn't have a boy or a girl, Mark. I had a little man." His first word was not yes or no, she said. It was *why*. This attitude first created trouble for him in fourth grade. Mark was excited about a filmstrip his teacher planned to show about how the earth was made. In his Lutheran household and at St. John's School in Brooklyn, little Mark had learned that God made the earth. But now he was in public school: Johnnycake Elementary, in which his family had enrolled him when they moved to the growing suburb of Woodlawn in Baltimore County, a large jurisdiction that nearly encircled Baltimore City and stretched up through miles of farmland to the Pennsylvania line.

His teacher, Mrs. Spector, put on the record, and as the beeps came, she turned the knob on the projector. It was not what Mark was expecting. When the filmstrip was over, he raised his hand and told his teacher that he thought God had made everything. Mrs. Spector tried to explain the difference between science and religion.

Mark turned to Richard Gooner, who sat next to him. Gooner was a very tall child, precocious and a bit of a wiseass. His nerdy voice made him sound like he was sixteen. Gooner told Mrs. Spector that there were several theories about the origin of the universe, and that some were creationist.

Mrs. Spector glared at Mark.

That evening, Mark cornered his father.

"You taught me that God made me," he said.

Mark wanted to know what the truth was. It had to be one or the other: either God made us, or we evolved from the primordial slime. Mark's father said that different people believed different things.

Mark tuned him out. He didn't want his father to tell him what people believed. He wanted him to tell him the truth. Was God like Santa Claus? Mark wondered—something his father invented to get him to behave? The lesson for Mark was this: if God didn't make him, if we're all here by chance, then rules are to be followed only if people have the power to enforce them. Mark's father diminished in his eyes that day, and so did his authority. Breaking rules only mattered now if you got caught. By the end of sixth grade, Mark had started smoking, been suspended, and landed in juvenile court.

That recklessness continued until just before Mark's seventeenth birthday, when he found Jesus. At that point, he began reading deeply—not just about Scripture, but about how the truth embedded in that Scripture should govern the way human beings treat each other. Dr. John M. Perkins, a veteran of the civil rights movement whose beatings by police in Mississippi still caused him physical pain decades later, captured Mark's imagination. Perkins argued that Christians who wanted to help the poor needed to live among them.

It sounded radical, but in the mid-1980s when Mark was moving to the house on Hunter's Run Drive, his best friend Allan Tibbels—another white Christian under the spell of Dr. Perkins—was moving with his wife and two little girls from an affluent neighborhood in Howard County to a renovated shell of a rowhouse in Sandtown-Winchester, one of the most racially isolated, poor, and violent neighborhoods in West Baltimore.

More and more, Mark's frictionless existence in Bel Air riled him. Why was his lifestyle afforded to so many white Americans when so many people of color were denied it? Why, he kept asking himself, was he born white in America?

It had been a decade since Mark and Allan had moved to what may as well have been different worlds—Mark out to Bel Air, Allan to the inner city. In that time, Allan, his wife, Susan, and a pastor named Mark Gornik had helped start a multiracial congregation in Sandtown called New Song Community Church. During that same decade, Dr. Perkins had helped start the Christian Community Development Association.

The Christian Community Development Association (CCDA) asked its practitioners across the nation to have something personally at stake in efforts to bring economic development and social capital to struggling communities. Perkins's belief that anyone who wanted to help a poor black neighborhood ought to move there was rooted in what CCDA proponents call "incarnational ministry": the idea that God became flesh and shared in human suffering. The CCDA helps its member organizations to build relationships within a community that bridge racial and economic divides, hoping development will grow outward from that foundation.

What this meant to Mark Lange was that an infrastructure existed to help people like him move to places like Sandtown. New Song Community Church was a Christian Community Development Association member. Allan began bringing longtime residents of Sandtown up to Mark's house to watch movies. Mark started visiting Sandtown to help New Song set up their IT system.

As Mark felt himself pulled into New Song's orbit, an emptiness grew in him. Once again, he questioned the truth that he felt should direct his life. On top of that, he and Betty had been arguing. Part of it was about children—they'd had trouble conceiving, and Mark hadn't been willing to spend as much money on fertility treatments as Betty had been. But more generally, their worlds were drifting apart, and Mark was drifting toward Sandtown.

"Why don't you move in with Allan and Susan?" she would ask him.

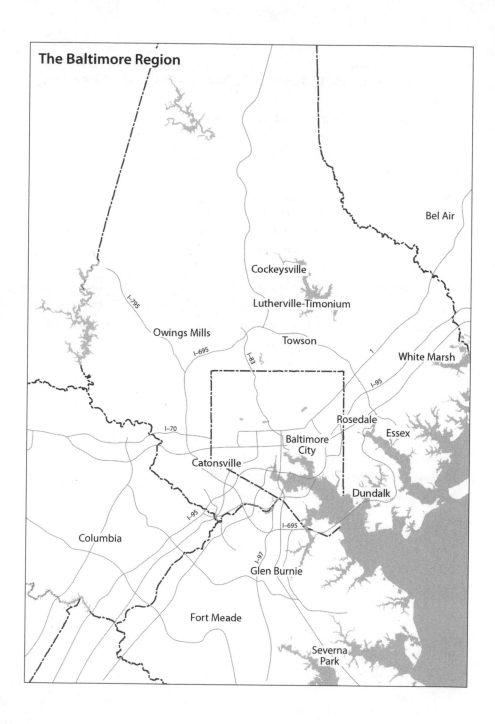

The Baltimore Region

Bel Air

Cockeysville

Lutherville-Timonium

I-795

Owings Mills

I-695

Towson

I-83

White Marsh

I-95

Rosedale

I-70

Essex

Baltimore
City

Catonsville

Dundalk

I-95

Columbia

I-695

I-97

Glen Burnie

Fort Meade

Severna
Park

Baltimore City

1. Barre Circle
2. Brooklyn
3. Canton
4. Hamilton
5. Hampden
6. Inner Harbor
7. Johnston Square
8. Lafayette Courts
9. Murphy Homes
10. Port Covington
11. Roland Park
12. Westport Homes

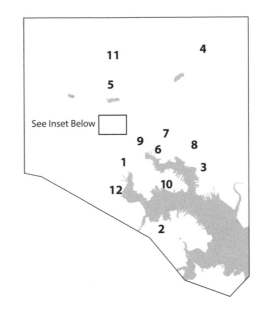

See Inset Below

West Baltimore

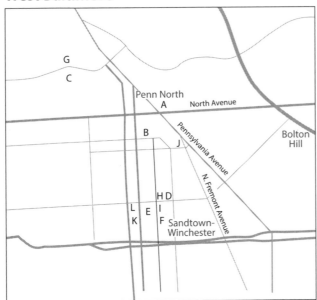

A. CVS
B. Freddie Gray's arrest
C. Frederick Douglass H.S.
D. Gerry's Goods
E. Gilmor Homes
F. Lange household

G. Mondawmin Mall
H. New Song Center
I. New Song original bldg.
J. Penn. Triangle Park
K. Sandtown ReStore
L. Strength to Love 2 Farm

ONE

One Region, Two Worlds

MARK LANGE AND NICOLE SMITH HAVE NEVER MET, BUT IF THEY WERE TO MAKE the moves they were contemplating—Mark, a white suburbanite, to West Baltimore, and Nicole, a black woman from a poor city neighborhood, to a prosperous suburb—it would contravene the way the Baltimore region had been programmed for a century. It is one region, but separate worlds. And it was designed to be that way.

An affluent "White L" runs down the middle of Baltimore City and along its waterfront. To the east and west are wide swaths of high poverty and racial isolation for African Americans. The segregation aggravates countless racial disparities that afflict every aspect of Baltimoreans' lives. For instance, the average life expectancy in Baltimore City varies from sixty-three years in a nearly all-black neighborhood to eighty-three years in a four-fifths white neighborhood. To understand how Baltimore's separate worlds came to be, one need look no further than Gilmor Homes, a low-rise public housing project in West Baltimore's Sandtown neighborhood.

The Housing Authority of Baltimore City (HABC) designed Gilmor Homes as a black-only project in the late 1930s. HABC originally picked a construction site on vacant land in a white part of Baltimore's southwest corner. When residents complained that the project would make it "dangerous for white school children and white persons going to and from work," HABC instead chose a four-block stretch of Sandtown.

By placing Gilmor Homes in a black neighborhood, Baltimore officials reinforced a deliberately created pattern of segregation. The message was clear: certain races belonged in certain places. But it hadn't always been that way. In the nineteenth century, the geographical separation of whites and African Americans that is typical in northern states today didn't yet exist in Baltimore. African Americans lived all over the city then in an arrangement that kept them residing close to whites, but in substandard alley houses that were disconnected from the water system.

Around the turn of the century, that changed as the black population rapidly grew. African Americans flooded in from out of town, and their demand for housing outpaced the supply available to them, leading to overcrowding in a so-called "Negro district" just west of midtown. Better-off black families moved northwest, and by 1910, the border of the district had reached West Baltimore's N. Gilmor Street, encompassing some of present-day Sandtown.

The next year, city officials passed an ordinance prohibiting African Americans from moving to all-white blocks, and whites from moving to all-black blocks. It was, in effect, a quarantine. Progressive reformers cited unhealthy conditions in black slums, but the quarantine was just as much about containing crime and depressed property values. As it is today, integration of housing was perceived by many white property owners as a financial risk.

In 1917, the Supreme Court struck down segregation ordinances. Baltimore's white power structure became craftier. The city demolished black neighborhoods in the name of "slum clearance" but failed to create enough replacement housing. When landlords rented to African Americans in white areas, the city came sniffing for code violations. The real-estate industry ostracized agents who sold white homes to black buyers. Some sales contracts contained covenants barring owners from selling or renting homes to African Americans. The federal government developed residential security maps to highlight areas where mortgage lending was risky—areas that correlated with high black populations—and went on to insure home loans disproportionately in the white suburbs.

City leaders segregated public housing by race and placed it in a way that some believed would protect home values and racial homogeneity in white neighborhoods. The city's housing authority placed Gilmor Homes along a four-block stretch between Gilmor Street and Fulton Avenue in the early 1940s. By that point, the border of the "Negro district" had pushed west precisely from Gilmor to Fulton. To build Gilmor Homes, the city demolished not just "slums" but the kind of solid rowhouses where one finds "self-respecting families," according to a *Baltimore Evening Sun* editor at the time.

Gilmor Homes was placed strategically, and it may have been *faced* strategically. On the Fulton Avenue side, the front doors faced inward toward the other units and away from white Baltimore. Some believed that the idea animating these placements—and the city's increasing demolition of dilapidated housing—was creation of a barrier to stave off "the encroachment of colored [people]"—or,

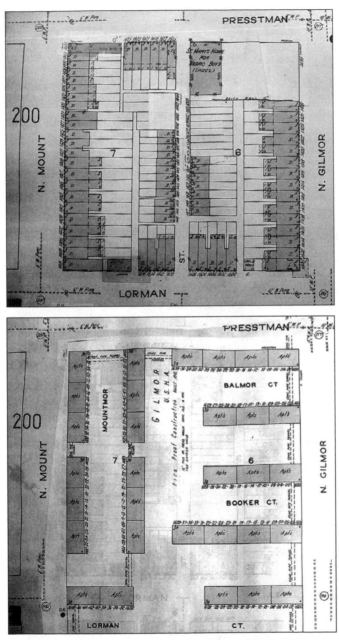

Insurance maps from 1933 and 1951 show the transformation of the 1300 block of N. Gilmor Street in West Baltimore from rowhouses into public housing. Mark and Betty Lange would eventually move into a rowhouse on the east side of the street. *Baltimore City Archives*

A storefront at 1336 N. Gilmor St. and a man using a rope to hoist a ladder at 1406 N. Gilmor St. Both structures were razed to make way for Gilmor Homes. (1939) *Baltimore City Archives*

as the federal Home Owners Loan Corporation termed it, "Negro infiltration." One scholar called the city's strategy "clearance and containment."

Gilmor Homes opened in June 1942. That same year in south Baltimore, the housing authority opened Brooklyn Homes. If Gilmor Homes constrained the black population, Brooklyn Homes created opportunity for the white population. Brooklyn Homes was built for defense workers on a southern sliver of Baltimore that is cut off from the rest of the city by a fork of the Patapsco River. There were several shipyards along the Patapsco, and Brooklyn Homes, so close to so many jobs, was a *de jure* white project. In 1943 there were already twenty thousand units of housing for white war workers, yet it was not until 1943 that the first "Negro" war housing—the temporary Banneker Homes—was built and occupied, partly because white residents objected wherever black public housing was proposed. "If something isn't done to relieve the plight of the colored people in this city," a black physician named Robert Jackson told the City Plan Commission in October 1941, "they will be sleeping on top of each other."

There were nearly twenty thousand black war workers in 1943, double that a year later. Black war workers needed low-income housing the most, since unions had relegated most of them to the lowest paying (and most dangerous) jobs by privileging "seniority," which overwhelmingly benefited white workers. The city's housing authority did make some provisions for black war workers, but the only permanent black war housing, Cherry Hill Homes, opened in December 1945, months after Nagasaki was leveled and Hitler's corpse had cooled.

One of the war workers who took a unit in the all-white Brooklyn Homes was Winfred Farrar. Farrar turned twenty-six the day Japan attacked Pearl Harbor. It brought him to tears, but flat feet kept him out of World War II. With employment scarce in his hometown of Lynchburg, Virginia, Farrar went to Baltimore in 1942 to take a job in Bethlehem Steel's Key Highway shipyard on the south shore of the Patapsco River, just beyond the downtown inner harbor. Farrar worked 3:00 p.m. to midnight and slept in a rooming house. His wife, Kitty, and his three daughters soon came north to join him, and they moved to 4120 Hyden Court in Brooklyn Homes. The three girls shared one bed.

The guys at the shipyard gave Winfred a nickname: "Big Bill the Burner." Burners used acetylene torches to cut steel. With his huge hands, Big Bill could cut the damaged section out of a hull faster than just about anyone else. Some days he'd come home with burns on his legs. Every day he came home with asbestos caked on his pants. In 1950, Winfred and Kitty bought a home on St. Margaret Street, a skinny strip of little brick rowhouses near Brooklyn Homes. In 1953, they bought a 1,900-square-foot house with tan pebbledash siding less than a mile away at the southeast corner of 5th and Jeffrey Streets.

The family began worshipping at St. John's Lutheran Church, just four blocks away. In the early 1950s, Winfred's oldest daughter, Mary Frances (known as Frances), got to know a fellow parishioner, Melvin Lange, who sang in the church choir with her. Mel had already spent two years at Gettysburg College and four years in the navy. On July 17, 1954, they were married at St. John's. Frances was eighteen and Mel was twenty-six. They moved in with Frances's family at 5th and Jeffrey, then took an apartment across the street. A little more than a year later, Frances and Mel had a son: Mark Stephen Lange.

Mark was born a year after *Brown v. Board of Education*, the U.S. Supreme Court case that ordered American public schools to desegregate, became the law of the land. Baltimore City tried to desegregate its schools by allowing families "free choice" on where to send their children. What little voluntary integration did take place didn't reach Brooklyn. When Mark was a little boy there, there were two kinds of people: not black and white, but Protestant and Catholic.

Brooklyn Homes was built as a white project, but Baltimore's housing authority ended segregation in public housing in 1954, opting, as the school board did, for a free-choice system. When the Langes left the area in 1962, however, Brooklyn Homes remained all-white.* By 1962, the Langes didn't need the kind of public assistance that Mark's grandfather had tapped to make his move into the middle class. They had, however, benefitted from the upward mobility of Winfred and Kitty Farrar. When Mark was one year old, Winfred and Kitty helped his parents buy a rowhouse just over the county line. A year later, Mark's parents sold that house to Winfred and Kitty and bought a small single-family house nearby. In 1962, when Mark was seven, the family made an even bigger move, ten miles northwest to Baltimore County.

In 1962, Baltimore's suburbs were in transition. Interstate 695, a "beltway" around the city, opened that year, as did Interstate 83, which offered Baltimore County an uninterrupted commute into downtown. Rapid economic development and widespread single-family home construction had come to the growing suburbs, thanks not just to highway expansion but also to federal housing policy. Veterans

---

*It stayed that way until 1966, when the U.S. Department of Housing and Urban Development intervened. Robert Weaver, HUD's first secretary, ordered the Housing Authority of Baltimore City to desegregate Brooklyn Homes and two other all-white public housing developments.

had the G.I. Bill, and the Federal Housing Administration was making loans with low down payments and repayment periods as long as thirty years.

The new opportunities in the suburbs were reserved mostly for white people. Jim Crow still operated. The Civil Rights Act of 1964, the Voting Rights Act of 1965, and, most importantly, the Fair Housing Act of 1968 had yet to come. In April 1962, the first black family to move into the Sun Valley community of Anne Arundel County—just a few miles south of the Langes' Brooklyn stomping grounds—endured three days of vandalism and violence. It was only in June 1962 that a fair housing group called Baltimore Neighborhoods, Inc. convinced the Real Estate Board of Greater Baltimore to discourage agents from using racial designations like "colored" in newspaper classifieds.

That November, President Kennedy signed an executive order banning discrimination in any housing receiving federal aid, including loans guaranteed by the Federal Housing Administration (FHA). For decades, the FHA's practices had favored lending in racially homogenous—read "white"—areas, keeping the growing suburbs out of reach for most black families. In addition, it favored lending for single-family homes at four to seven times the rate of multifamily developments like apartment buildings, compounding the exclusionary effect on lower-income black families, who were more likely to live in multifamily developments.

At the peak of its suburbanization, Baltimore County didn't just grow—it got whiter. Between 1950 and 1960, the overall population grew by 76 percent, from around 270,000 to nearly 475,000, while losing almost one thousand black residents.

This was the dynamic when seven-year-old Mark Lange and his family moved to Baltimore County.

On December 17, 1962, Mel Lange settled on a brand-new house in Chadwick Manor, a new development just off the Beltway, and Mark was enrolled in a public school named Johnnycake Elementary. In the early 1960s, Johnnycake was nearly all white, as was Chadwick Manor. Just down the road from the Langes' new house, however, was an island of integration.

The Social Security Administration (SSA) had helped pioneer the integration of the federal workforce. By the time President Franklin D. Roosevelt banned discrimination in the federal defense workforce in 1941, the agency had already hired significant numbers of African Americans for clerical positions. In 1960, the expanding agency moved from downtown Baltimore to Woodlawn, an area of Baltimore County just west of the city. By 1970, about 30 percent of the sixteen thousand employees at the headquarters were black. Many of them, however,

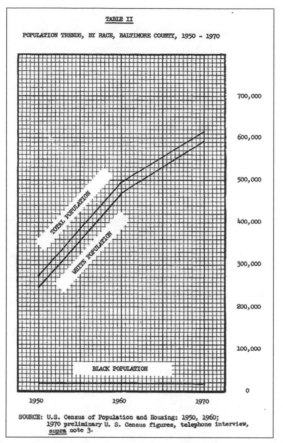

In a report prepared for a U.S. Commission on Civil Rights hearing, a graph shows the change in Baltimore County's white and black populations between 1950 and 1970. (1970) *Historical Publications of the U.S. Committee on Civil Rights collection at the University of Maryland's Thurgood Marshall Law Library*

commuted from the city because of a lack of affordable and open housing in the county. Between 1960 and 1970, the county had added another 128,000 residents, but the black population grew by only about 2,500.

The ten-story building at the center of the SSA campus held a one-thousand-seat auditorium. Around 9:30 a.m. on Monday, August 17, 1970, a man in a Roman collar announced, "This hearing of the United States Commission on Civil Rights will come to order."

The Reverend Theodore Hesburgh, a cigar-smoking Catholic priest and president of the University of Notre Dame, had linked arms with Dr. Martin Luther King Jr.

at a 1964 Chicago rally. Hesburgh, his wavy gray hair smashed back with pomade, and the other commissioners sat on a dais behind a long line of brown paneling in front of a black and white audience of about six hundred.

Hesburgh said that the hearing would focus on the "racial implications of suburban development," and that the commission would apply their findings across the country. "Situated as it is in Baltimore County, but with close ties to Baltimore City, this facility is symbolic of the suburban-urban relationship that we will be exploring in depth today," Hesburgh said.

Over three days, several dozen witnesses cycled through their turns at a table at the edge of the stage, an easel behind them displaying statistics and graphs. A planning consultant named Yale Rabin testified that most black residents lived in fifteen or twenty "enclaves" throughout the county that lacked the basic services—such as paved roads—found in adjacent white areas. Furthermore, the county had demolished many of these black areas in the name of "development," or changed their zoning from residential to commercial, which triggered more protracted expulsion of the county's black population.

Mary Cardillicchio, housing director at the Baltimore County Community Action Agency, complained that with no public housing in the county, she could not find housing for any families below the poverty level. The city—whose housing authority had a waiting list of 2,700—discouraged her from sending families there, she said. Baltimore City housing commissioner Robert C. Embry Jr. had publicly criticized what amounted to a "one-way street" for the poor from the county to the city, but the city's policies were partly to blame. "Someone who applies from Baltimore County or Anne Arundel County is treated in the same way and given the same priorities as someone who applies from the city," Embry testified.

While Baltimore County had an exploding white population and stagnant black population in 1970, Baltimore City was the opposite. Despite efforts by groups like Baltimore Neighborhoods, Inc., to fight blockbusting and white flight, the city had lost over 130,000 white residents since 1960, while gaining 94,000 black residents. Baltimore Neighborhoods, Inc., director George Laurent lamented a lack of support for integrating places like Baltimore County. "You can pour funds into the ghetto; the foundations are willing to do that," Laurent testified. "But if you want to come into suburbia where the taxpayers are and where the power structure is to change society at that level, you are not going to get much financing."

Baltimore County officials, including county executive Dale Anderson, defended the county's practices. Planning and zoning office director George Gavrelis questioned what the county could do when its housing solutions could only come through the private sector. "I have, as yet, not found out how to get a certain kind of housing or a certain kind of rental level from development with a zoning mechanism alone," Gavrelis said.

Commission chairman Hesburgh admitted that many factors shaped the lack of affordable housing in Baltimore County in 1970, including a scarcity of financing for multifamily developments. What continually frustrated the commission, he said, "is that things don't look as though they are going very well here or anywhere else in the country, but no one is ever doing anything wrong. I can't believe that."

Homer Favor, a local civil rights luminary and Morgan State University economics professor, explained why it was so difficult to isolate the causes of a regional racial division that itself was as clear as day. "If you go back in the '50's, it was overt," Favor said of housing discrimination. "It was blatant. It was flagrant. As you move into the '60's, it became less of this variety and more covert[,] and if you, in your investigation, expect to find the kind of nefarious practices which abounded in the city of Baltimore back in the '50's, you are not going to find them. But by the same token, you will still find the same proportions of black people participating in the mainstream of life as it exists in this metropolitan area."

After three days of testimony—and a bomb threat that prompted an evacuation and search of the building—the priest concluded the hearing. "During these three days, a picture has been drawn of a polarized society," Rev. Hesburgh said. "Inside the city, the population is about 50 percent black; outside in Baltimore County it is over 96 percent white. Clearly this means there are two separate worlds in existence and the gulf that widens them produces growing hostility and fear.

"It's obvious that things are not going well," he continued, "but yet if we are to rely on the testimony we have heard for three long days, no one is doing anything wrong."

The hearing ended in the early evening of Wednesday, August 19, 1970. By that point, the U.S. Department of Housing and Urban Development had written to the Baltimore County Office of Planning and Zoning to disapprove of the county's planning process, particularly when it came to ensuring fair housing choices for poor and minority residents. HUD also took the remarkable step of freezing funds for Baltimore County projects related to "water, sewer, and open space."

Two provisions of civil rights law undergirded the funding freeze. Title VI of the Civil Rights Act of 1964 outlawed racial discrimination "under any program or activity receiving Federal financial assistance." Title VIII of the Civil Rights Act

Homer Favor testifies in front of the U.S. Commission on Civil Rights at Social Security
Administration headquarters in Baltimore County, Maryland. George Collins reports on
the hearing for WMAR-TV. (1970) *Rob Brockmeyer; WMAR-TV Collection, University of
Baltimore Special Collections and Archives*

of 1968 (the Fair Housing Act) said that HUD-funded programs must be done in
a way "affirmatively to further" the act. HUD officials had interpreted that phrase
to mean working proactively to mitigate the harm caused by decades of explicit
segregation and discrimination. The Act's architects had hoped to achieve "truly
integrated and balanced living patterns."

HUD asked the county to submit an "Overall Program Design," a wide-
ranging document covering the county's approach to planning, including how
that approach would help low-income and minority groups find housing and participate in the planning process. The county had withdrawn an application for
some HUD funding just a year earlier rather than prepare one of these reports. To
"thaw" the freeze, they'd need to do one now.

Taking place just two years after the Fair Housing Act had passed, this action by HUD exemplified an important distinction in civil rights law—and in how racism now worked in America. To "affirmatively further" the Fair Housing Act, a place like Baltimore County had to do more than just figure out whether anyone was, in Hesburgh's words, "doing anything wrong." HUD didn't ask who the racists were or what they did. It simply required the county to document the damage that had been done and to figure out ways to undo it.

Over the next few years, HUD and Baltimore County battled, with HUD reinstating funding after promises from the county, then freezing funding again when the county submitted tardy or inadequate documents. County executive Dale Anderson directly accused HUD of "harassment." He downplayed the effects of discrimination, and he essentially told minorities who failed to find housing in the county to pull themselves up by their bootstraps.

In 1974, the U.S. Commission on Civil Rights published *Equal Opportunity in Suburbia*. The seventy-two-page report described a nationwide trend of affluent whites moving to the peripheries of metropolitan areas, creating "white nooses" of suburbs around decaying, majority-black central cities. "In Baltimore County restrictive zoning prevented the growth of housing for workers from keeping up with the growth of employment opportunities in the central part of the county," the commission concluded.

While Dale Anderson was defying HUD in the early 1970s, Mark Lange was defying just about everyone. The truth Mark needed to have in order to exist was getting blurrier every day. The youth revolution of the late 1960s emboldened his own tendency to question authority. The world had stopped making sense to Mark, and the death of thousands of Americans in Vietnam made him question the existence of God. He'd go to church retreats, but he'd sneak in liquor bottles and get drunk at night. At church with his parents, he heard, as he put it, "religion but not the gospel," and eventually he stopped attending. He now had two moods: anger and depression. During junior year at Woodlawn High School, he frequently cut school and sometimes fought when he was there. Mark's mother's sister, Patricia, gave Mark *The Cross and the Switchblade*, a book about a pastor whose inner-city ministry convinces a wayward teen to give up gangs and drugs. It didn't take.

Are we just machines, Mark began to wonder, the process of a million years of evolution? The strong eat the weak—is that it? If that's the truth, he thought, I can live that out. Or maybe the people who said there was *no* truth were right.

Just before he turned seventeen, Mark's mother, Frances, again turned to her sister Patricia. Just three years earlier, Frances had assured Mark's "Aunt Tish" that he was a good boy. That boy was gone, Frances said, and she asked her sister to intervene. Aunt Tish persuaded Mark to attend a retreat at St. James Lutheran Church on Liberty Road just outside the Beltway, a couple miles north of Woodlawn. The retreat was led by a youth pastor who had an evangelical background, and his take on Scripture spoke to Mark. On Saturday night at the retreat, Mark bowed his head and listened to the pastor talk. He was radically changed. He went home a Christian.

A couple of months earlier, this pastor had had the same effect on a teenager named Allan Tibbels. Mark and Allan met at the retreat after Allan led a Bible study on the Book of James. They remained friends thereafter.

They shouldn't have gotten along. Mark was a jock who liked to drink. Allan was a "head" who liked to get stoned. Mark was an angry young man. Allan was a pacifist. Mark lived in the moment. Allan had his life planned out. But they were the same age, both newly converted and living for Christ. Plus, Allan was a go-getter, and Mark considered himself a "right-hand man" kind of personality. They'd make a good team. After high school, Allan began running Youth for Christ "Campus Life" clubs, and Mark helped him out. They also worked together for a janitorial business, each running a franchise on opposite ends of Baltimore City.

When Allan left the janitorial business to do Campus Life full-time, he and Mark began losing touch. Allan and his wife, Susan, whom he'd married right out of high school in 1974, moved to Columbia, a planned community in Howard County. In 1977, Mark married his girlfriend, Betty, and moved out of his parents' house into an apartment complex in Middle River, a working- and middle-class community near the water in southeast Baltimore County. A year later, they bought a four-bedroom house just steps from the Bush River in Harford County's Long Bar Harbor, half an hour northeast of Baltimore.

In 1979, Allan asked Mark to help him run the Howard County Campus Life club. The money, around $11,000 a year, was nothing like Mark was then making in sales, and Harford County to Columbia was a long commute.

Mark chose to follow Allan anyway.

On May 27, 1981, Mark and Allan joined a pickup basketball game in the gym at Chapelgate Church, just outside Columbia, with some youth from the church. Allan went for a layup and tumbled over another player. The wall was too close to the basket. Allan hit his head and instantly broke his neck.

———

Allan Tibbels with Mark and Betty Lange at their wedding. (1977) *Mark and Betty Lange*

Melinda Smith stirred in the middle of the night. "I've gotta go home," she said.

No one was next to her to hear it. Her husband, Levi, had left her over three years before—left the very day her youngest daughter, Kelly, was born in January 1984. When Levi split, Melinda took Kelly and her two other daughters, Jessica and Nicole, and moved in with her mother. It was in her mother's rented house on W. Lanvale Street in West Baltimore that Melinda was sleeping this particular night.

Where was this "home" that shook Melinda from her sleep? In the course of just twenty-five years, Melinda had called many places home. Until the age of two, she lived with her great-grandmother "Ninny" and her grandmother in Lane, a tiny black farming town in South Carolina. In 1964, she moved north to live with her mother and father in an apartment on Bethune Road in Cherry Hill Homes, a south Baltimore public housing project, but returned to South Carolina every summer.

In December 1970, Melinda's parents bought a house on northwest Baltimore's Elderon Avenue. Melinda remembered that time fondly. Her father ran a record store near the intersection of Pennsylvania and North Avenues just outside West Baltimore's Sandtown-Winchester neighborhood. Every time a big hit song came out, he brought it home for Melinda and her siblings. The new house quickly filled with the sounds of The Jackson Five, who had placed four songs at the top of the charts the previous year. After about a year, Melinda's parents went into default and lost the house.*

Melinda loved the house and couldn't bear to leave it, but her mother moved the girls to Herbert Street in West Baltimore—but without their father. He refused to move out of the Elderon Avenue house. Melinda still attended Grove Park Elementary on Elderon Avenue, and sometimes after school she would walk the half-mile to the old house and sit on the steps, crestfallen. Even after her father had physically been put out of the house and boards had gone up on the windows, little Melinda continued her ritual.

In 1974, Melinda's mother moved Melinda and her sisters to Westport Homes. Westport, a neighborhood of brick rowhouses on Baltimore's south side, backs up to railroad tracks along a neglected strip of Patapsco River waterfront. Melinda was twelve when the family moved into the projects there, and she was still living there with her mother when she married Levi Smith six years later. Melinda and Levi rented a studio apartment across the street from Penn Station, a columned Beaux Arts landmark in central Baltimore. Every weekday morning, Melinda walked across the street, passing under the station's iron clock and canopy to catch an Amtrak train to her new job in Washington, DC. Now a clerk with the Federal Bureau of Investigation, Melinda helped restore archival documents. Every once in a while, she'd get a grotesque glimpse of American history courtesy of the FBI's photographs, such as those of the St. Valentine's Day mob massacre in Chicago and the naked, autopsied bodies of Jesse James and Al Capone.

By the time their first daughter, Nicole, was born in November 1980, Melinda and Levi had moved to an apartment complex on Sayer Avenue, in a quiet rowhouse neighborhood in the city's southwest corner. Then the young family moved across the Baltimore County line to an apartment in Arbutus, where their second

---

*The mortgage—$14,550 at 8 percent interest, with a monthly payment of $108—was handled by James W. Rouse and Company. At the time, the Rouse Company was one of very few Baltimore lenders participating in a U.S. Department of Housing and Urban Development program that allowed homeowners to pay one percent of the mortgage interest. (The government paid the rest.) Melinda's parents' mortgage was not part of the program—they paid the full 8 percent interest. After the default in 1971, the city's Circuit Court assigned ownership of the house to the Rouse Company, who sold it to HUD the next year.

daughter, Jessica, was born in January 1983. Levi had also landed a job at the FBI by this point, and the couple would drop the girls off at a daycare program and take a vanpool from West Baltimore to Washington.

When Melinda's youngest daughter was born in January 1984 and Levi left, Melinda put in an application with the city for public housing, took six months' maternity leave from work, and moved with the girls into her mother's town-house in Westport Homes. Melinda's mother had landed in the projects after the dissolution of a marriage; now Melinda was doing the same. There wasn't much wealth in the family to fall back on. Melinda's mother and uncles were the first generation in the family to leave rural South Carolina, where her grandmoth-er and great-grandmother grew up sharecropping and, according to Melinda's great-grandmother, where previous generations had been enslaved.

After a few months with her mother, Melinda found a townhouse to rent in Cherry Hill and moved there with her daughters, paying the rent with her savings and child support money. When her maternity leave was up a month later, she returned to the FBI. After a few months, things became unmanageable. Levi was still working there, which was stressful enough, and she had to catch a commuter van before the sun came up. On top of that, her child care had become unreliable.

Melinda put in two weeks' notice at the FBI, cashed in her retirement savings, bought a yellow and white AMC Hornet, and put aside the rest to help cover rent. She eventually found a temporary job with the U.S. Census Bureau and, after that, a gig providing home health care to elderly people. After about a year and a half in the Cherry Hill townhouse, Melinda received a letter from the Housing Authority of Baltimore City: an apartment had opened up in Murphy Homes, a sprawling public housing complex of four high-rises and twenty two-story buildings built in 1963. The city had put Melinda on a waiting list of more than 35,000 people when she had applied a couple of years earlier. Despite the length of that waiting list, high-rise apartments became available fairly frequently. Units remained vacant in the towers because applicants often turned them down, wary of the buildings' reputation for drugs and crime. The housing authority filled some of the vacant units with homeless people from an "emergency admissions" list.

Money was tight and Melinda didn't want to move back in with her mother, so she took the Murphy Homes apartment. It was on the second floor of a high-rise at 900 Argyle Avenue, near the corner of Martin Luther King Boulevard and Penn-sylvania Avenue. Murphy Homes was one of the most notorious projects in the city. Federal investigators pinned four murders in the Murphy high-rises on the legendary Timmirror Stanfield drug organization, and Stanfield was convicted of murder for an incident in 1985 during which, prosecutors said, he shot a man six times in the head at Murphy Homes for failing to show "appropriate respect." Another infamous drug lord, Nathan Barksdale, tortured three people on the eleventh floor of a Murphy Homes high-rise, according to court records cited in a January 1987 report by *Baltimore Sun* reporter David Simon.

Residents of Murphy Homes felt powerless to change their circumstances: the urine-soaked stairwells, the using and dealing in the hallways, the leaky pipes, the broken elevators, the lack of fire sprinklers, the cockroaches and mice. They felt ignored by the police and too afraid of retaliation to report crime. The Housing Authority was so slow to react to deteriorating physical conditions that tenants eventually organized to demand that the city renovate some of the vacant houses it owned across the city and move them in. When that didn't happen, some of the tenants started a rent strike.

You'd think all this might faze a skinny 5' 2" parent of three little girls, but Melinda was not only living in the projects, she had given up the home health care job to work as a security guard for the Housing Authority of Baltimore City. She worked at projects all across the city, full-time on the midnight to 7:00 a.m. shift, leaving her children with her mother and taking them to school in the morning. Melinda's job was to sit in a booth and decide who could enter a project and who

One of the high-rises at the Housing Authority of Baltimore City's Murphy Homes complex. (1989) *Baltimore City Archives*

Nicole Smith, age six, at Murphy Homes. (1987) *Melinda Smith*

couldn't. If someone was unfamiliar or had no identification, she refused them entry. She didn't call in every drug deal she saw from her booth, but if a dealer didn't live in the building, he wouldn't get past her booth in the first place.

Despite that temerity, Melinda spent as little time in Murphy Homes as possible. She considered it just a place to lay her head. When each work week was over, Melinda piled the girls into the Hornet and drove down to spend the weekend at her mother's place on W. Lanvale Street.

It was on one of these weekends that Melinda woke up on W. Lanvale saying "I've gotta go home." And when she said "home," she meant the second floor at Murphy Homes.

After she woke up, something told Melinda not to go back to Murphy Homes in the middle of the night and she went back to sleep. In the morning, she and the girls drove back and walked up a flight of stairs to their apartment. The door was already open. The TV, her girls' brand-new coats . . . everything was gone. The burglar had entered through the balcony. The next-door neighbor, Melinda thought—she just knew her next-door neighbor had done it. She went to the rental office, threatening to move out unless something was done. If she moved out, she was told, she would never live in public housing again.

"Okay," Melinda said. "Fine with me."

When Barbara Samuels wanted to learn her way around a new place, she just hopped in the car, got lost, and found her way home. It was a nice day for a drive: Sunday, low 60s, clear skies. She pulled her Honda Civic station wagon away from her sister's home in the suburb of Millersville and found her way to Maryland Route 3. She drove north through Anne Arundel County, took the Beltway high over a lush stretch of the Patapsco River, and then exited onto the Baltimore–Washington Parkway, which threaded its way between Cherry Hill and Westport and into downtown.

On 1590 AM, Joe Miller called Game 5 of the 1983 World Series. The Philadelphia Phillies, down three games to one, were hosting the Baltimore Orioles. Orioles star Eddie Murray had been struggling at the plate the whole series, but in the second inning he connected. Miller's shouting pierced the light squelch of the AM dial: "Murray has it off his back, his first home run of the 1983 World Series!"

Barbara rooted for the Red Sox while growing up in Wayland, Massachusetts, half an hour outside of Boston. But now she was in Baltimore, driving down, as it happened, Boston Street. Lining the street were the canneries and tin decorating plants that had kept the Polish American families of the waterfront Canton neighborhood working for decades. Lately, yuppies had started buying up the little brick and Formstone rowhouses where many of those families still lived, and as the plants along Boston Street began to shut down, developers were petitioning the city, hoping to renovate old industrial buildings into restaurants and apartments. As Barbara drove past the still-functioning American Can Company, she saw forty brand-new townhouses right across the street, some of which had already sold for $160,000, more than double the nation's median home price. Behind the townhouses, the outer harbor of the Patapsco River shimmered beneath the Port of Baltimore's cranes and the stupendous flag at Fort McHenry.

By the time Barbara got back to Millersville, the Orioles had won the World Series. The corner-bar city went crazycakes. At a dive near Memorial Stadium, the floor jounced, beer shot through the air over spontaneous embraces, and a man bared an ass cheek with a brand-new tattoo of the Orioles' cartoon bird mascot. Later that Sunday, word went out that the O's would parade through downtown Monday at noon.

On Monday morning, Barbara reported to her first day as an attorney at the Legal Aid Bureau—the job for which she'd moved to town. Her office was just three blocks from the parade route. Despite it being her first day on the job, Barbara hoped to get out and see the parade. That morning, Legal Aid's managing attorney introduced Barbara to her new colleagues. "I'm going out to O'Donnell Heights," she told Barbara. "Why don't you come with me?" There would be no parade-watching. Instead, Barbara found herself back on Boston Street.

This part of Boston Street was not the burgeoning "Gold Coast" of Canton. Two miles east of the American Can Company building, alleys fanned out from Boston Street like little inlets. Along these skinny blacktop "cuts," as residents called them, were long two-story barracks. The O'Donnell Heights landscape was much like that of Brooklyn Homes: the same cheap screen doors in the front facing grass courtyards, the same cracked sidewalks and dull gray clothesline posts along the cuts out back. And like Brooklyn Homes, O'Donnell Heights was a public housing project built in 1942 for whites that remained all-white twelve years after a 1954 desegregation order. The project was still more than three-quarters white in 1978 when O'Donnell Heights residents, angry with the housing authority about rodents, roaches, and exposed wires, launched a rent strike.

Barbara Samuels, accompanied by her new boss, entered the home of a black woman the city was trying to evict. The housing authority, the woman told them, had declared her middle-school-aged son to be a danger and wanted the family out. The boy had tampered with a gas line, trying—and, fortunately, failing—to set it on fire. The woman claimed that the boy had emotional problems and that she had attempted unsuccessfully to get him help.*

Barbara quickly lost track of the case. It was her boss's case, not hers, and her own plate was filling up. Eventually, she moved out of her sister's house into an apartment in the city's Charles Village neighborhood, just north of the geographical center of Baltimore. Here was city life, something very appealing to someone in her mid-twenties who had spent the last three years in coal country. Barbara's previous job had been with a Legal Aid office in southwestern Virginia, where she had lived in a carriage house in the tiny historic town of St. Paul. The house had no central heat, and Barbara had warmed it with a woodstove, which she'd occasionally fire up with chunks that had fallen off coal trucks.

---

*Barbara would remember this case for the rest of her career, because it taught her that poor parents in the city were unlikely to get any help for a child until that child was already in the system.

The caseload at her Virginia job, which she had taken right after finishing law school at George Washington University in 1980, pertained mostly to coal-mine health and safety and some land and water environmental issues, plus some housing work that came along when one of the counties in her region started a brand-new housing authority. In Baltimore, Barbara saw some parallels to her experience in Appalachia, like dirt basements and homes with no central heat that families used small, unvented gas stoves to keep warm. Mostly, though, Baltimore was another world. Someone at her last job had said, "Just wait till you get that big-city housing caseload," and that person had been right. When Barbara went out one night in Baltimore by herself after dark to gather evidence, her new coworkers chided her. "Don't do that!" they said. "Go out in pairs!"

Most of Barbara's caseload in Baltimore involved going to rent court to represent poor people against private landlords or the Housing Authority of Baltimore City. Some tenants, like the woman Barbara met in O'Donnell Heights on her first day of work, were fighting eviction. Others were trying to put their rent in escrow with the court until their landlords responded to maintenance requests.

The 1980s were a hell of a time for a legal services attorney who was trying to keep poor people under a roof. For one thing, the stock of affordable apartments was under pressure, thanks in part to low-income units that were turning back over to market rate. Public housing itself suffered under the administration of President Ronald Reagan. Six months into office, Reagan convened a commission on housing. Its 1982 report took as a given that "the genius of the market economy . . . can provide for housing far better than Federal programs." The commission claimed that the problem was no longer the quality of housing but affordability, and it advised against construction of housing for people who were poor in favor of "income supplements" to help them find existing housing. Under Reagan, the U.S. Housing and Urban Development Section 8 program ceased new construction, and those receiving assistance for housing in the private market saw their required contribution toward rent rise from 25 percent of their adjusted income to 30 percent. Cuts during the Reagan era meant tighter budgets for local housing authorities. Federal funding for subsidized housing through HUD dropped 82 percent between fiscal years 1981 and 1989.

Toward the end of the 1980s, Barbara started to notice the deterioration of public housing through her clients' experiences. The most tragic symbol of neglect in the projects came in June 1989, when a three-foot-long piece of concrete fell nine stories from a Murphy Homes balcony. Someone had thrown a heavy object at the balcony, shaking the chunk loose. A twelve-year-old boy named Raymond

Toulson was walking beneath the balcony. Five years earlier, in 1984, Raymond Toulson's father, a correctional officer, had been killed by an inmate at a state prison. Tragedy visited the family again when the falling concrete struck the boy's head and killed him.

Naomi and Ciera sat on the bottom step of the stoop. Nicole faced them with her hands behind her back.

"Okay," Nicole asked, "which hand?"

"That one," said Ciera, pointing.

"Uh-uh."

Nicole pulled her other hand out and opened it to reveal a rock. The game was called "School." The person with the rock was the teacher. Nicole loved being the teacher. A "student" who picked the correct hand got to go up one step—and one grade. With just three steps to a stoop, a student who made it to fourth grade had to start at the bottom step of the next house over. If they graduated high school, they'd be four doors down. For guessing wrong, Ciera was "held back" in first grade.

It was 1989, and Nicole was in third grade at her real school, Harriet Tubman Elementary, just around the corner on Harlem Avenue. In the afternoons, she'd come home, do her homework, and then go outside, where Naomi, Ciera, Duane, Paul, and the other kids on the 1800 block of Rayner Avenue would emerge one by one from their rowhouses to join Nicole and her two sisters in making up cheers, jumping rope, and playing games like "Hide and Go Seek."

As Nicole and her "students" went from stoop to stoop along the strip of row-houses on Rayner, grownups began to arrive at the house on the very end. Nicole's mother, Melinda, ran a daycare program called "Joy of Toddlers" out of the first floor of her home. As on most days, the parents picking up their children lingered in front of the house to chat, their laughter ricocheting between the two rows of houses.

Rayner Avenue is anything but an "avenue." The 1800 block is just three car-widths across and half a block long—an incision in a larger block bounded by Harlem Avenue, W. Lanvale Street, and the major north–south routes of Monroe Street and Fulton Avenue. From the vantage point of its terminus at Monroe Street, Rayner Avenue looks slightly unreal, like a diorama or a movie set: a dozen tiny rowhouses on each side enveloping a narrow slice of concrete that dead-ends at an alley. The houses on the Smiths' side of the street had Baltimore's famous marble stoops and measured 845 square feet inside. Houses across the street were a comparatively luxurious 872 square feet, with cinder block and concrete stoops. The block was almost entirely treeless.

In 1990, when the Smiths lived on Rayner Avenue, their neighborhood of Harlem Park was one of the most dangerous and down-and-out parts of Baltimore. That year, half of Harlem Park's residents lived in poverty, and the neighborhood's population had dropped by 19 percent since 1980. Ninety-nine percent of residents were black. The Smiths ended up in Harlem Park because Melinda's mother was living there when Melinda decided to leave Murphy Homes after the burglary in 1987. Melinda had moved Nicole and her sisters from Murphy Homes into the house her mother was renting on W. Lanvale Street. Melinda's brother and two sisters were living there, too, and after about a year Melinda had decided to find a place just for her herself and the girls.

Melinda didn't bother looking for apartments out in the county, or even outside West Baltimore. She knew what the rents were, and she couldn't afford them. Instead, she rented an apartment on Harlem Avenue, just a block south of W. Lanvale. Melinda didn't feel safe there, and after about one more year, she and her sister decided to rent a place together with all their kids. They found a house a couple of blocks away: the end unit on Rayner Avenue.

Harlem Park—indeed, much of West Baltimore—was full of vacant houses, but Rayner Avenue was not. It was a close-knit street. Little Nicole may have been annoyed at the nosy old couple across the street who watched children from their front window and reported bad behavior to their parents, but Melinda loved how everyone up and down the block took care of each other. Nonetheless, Melinda made sure the girls stayed on the block. The only places Nicole could go outside the block were the playground at Harriet Tubman Elementary, a friend's house around the corner on Monroe Street, and a convenience store where the alley at the end of Rayner spit out onto W. Lanvale.

Wherever she went, Nicole knew that she had better be inside the house when the streetlights buzzed to life. It was the things happening under those streetlights that earned such a bad reputation for Harlem Park and for a neighborhood just a block and a half north of Rayner Avenue that, with Harlem Park, formed the nucleus of a poor, nearly all-black swath of West Baltimore: Sandtown-Winchester.

Betty Lange woke up, longing to return to her own house. Once again, everyone had been up late talking. Once again, she faced another day of work and another forty-five-minute commute back to another sink full of everyone else's dishes.

Betty and Mark still had the four-bedroom house on Longley Road up in

Harford County. It was brand new, the first house they'd ever owned. They could go back to it anytime; most of their stuff was still there. But they'd moved into Allan and Susan Tibbelses' house in June 1981 when Mark took over the Campus Life club for Allan, and they'd brought only their clothes, a few personal items, and the stereo. (Mark had insisted on the stereo.)

When Mark and Betty moved in, Susan was rarely there, spending most of her time with Allan at the University of Maryland Hospital's shock-trauma unit in downtown Baltimore. Mark and Betty did not, however, have the house to themselves. Therese Khrenbrink was already living at the house, and Joe Goucher was spending a lot of time there. Mark and Allan were just two years out of high school when they met Therese and Joe, as the young men volunteered with a Campus Life club just outside the northeast section of Baltimore. Therese and Joe were high school students who'd joined the club. When Therese moved in with Allan and Susan in 1981, she was just establishing herself after nursing school, trying to figure out her faith and taking gigs where she could get them as a temporary nurse. Joe was helping Allan work with middle schoolers at Campus Life. Between Therese, Joe, and visits from neighbors and Campus Life teens, there were many conversations lasting late into the night.

The Tibbelses' house was a 1974 split-foyer ranch house with a finished basement, full of early American–style furniture. Mark and Betty slept in the master bedroom, and Therese slept in the basement. Weeks passed as Susan followed Allan to a critical care unit at the University of Maryland Hospital and then out to a rehabilitation facility in Elizabethtown, Pennsylvania. Occasionally Mark and Betty would make the two-hour drive to Elizabethtown, holding their breath as they drove past the rank chicken farms of Lancaster County. It broke their hearts to see Allan with a metal halo brace bolted to his skull, pausing between words to catch his breath, but they were encouraged by his slow progress.

Eventually Allan and Susan began coming home on the weekends. The Tibbelses realized that there was no way they could stay in the house long-term. A split-foyer was no place for a person who was a quadriplegic: there were steps as soon as you opened the front door. For the moment, they had plenty of help with their friends in the house. Allan had lost so much weight that Mark could easily carry him up the stairs. Mark learned how to transfer Allan from his wheelchair to a car and back, as well as onto a toilet.

As summer turned into fall, Allan and Susan made more frequent weekend trips home. Allan slept in a special bed and Susan slept on the sofa, leaving Mark and Betty in their room and Therese in the basement. The pressure of the crowded house drove Mark and Betty into arguments, and Betty eventually moved back to Longley Road without Mark.

The Tibbelses' house, for all its increasing upheaval, sat on a cul-de-sac named Deep Calm. Deep Calm was off of Windharp Way, which fanned out into several more cul-de-sacs, among them Sunset Light, Oaken Door, and Browsing Deer. A pathway at the end of Deep Calm wound behind the houses, connecting to more cul-de-sacs, like Scarlet Petal, Tawney Bloom, and Rising Moon. The street names were not thoughtlessly poached from a potpourri catalog. They were handpicked from John Greenleaf Whittier poems. The street names of two nearby neighborhoods were inspired by poets Paul Laurence Dunbar and Vachel Lindsay. The Whittier, Dunbar, and Lindsay neighborhoods made up the "village" of Owen Brown. Owen Brown was one of nine villages that made up the planned city—the meticulously planned city—of Columbia.

The city of Columbia was the vision of a meticulous man named James Rouse.

At the beginning of the Great Depression, a bank foreclosed on James Rouse's family's home; he was just sixteen. By twenty-one, he was working for the Federal Housing Administration and attending law school at night. By twenty-four, he was the president of a mortgage company that prospered as FHA-backed loans filled the suburbs with single-family houses.

Rouse had the kind of charm that allowed him to put his feet up on other people's desks. He was a problem-solver who liked big problems. His energy, geniality, and optimism sold people on an increasingly ambitious series of ideas.

In the late 1940s, he joined the Citizens Planning and Housing Association. CPHA was teaming with the city government on the "Baltimore Plan," which pushed landlords to improve dilapidated properties. Fixing houses wasn't enough, Rouse believed. He partnered with social workers, clergy, and educators to improve social conditions. And he solicited funds for a documentary about the Baltimore Plan that featured a gratuitous close-up of a bloated rat corpse in an alley and dramatizations of judges lecturing slumlords. (Rouse had a gift for publicity that kept his projects in the limelight.)

Rouse began conceiving of himself as an "idea man," and Washington bought in. In 1953, President Dwight D. Eisenhower put Rouse on a committee to figure out how the federal government could help America's crumbling cities. Rouse and his colleagues recommended that the government do anything it could do, whether it was building housing, razing or rehabbing buildings, insuring mortgages, or helping the private sector do redevelopment. They also recommended attaching

strings to federal funds. Congress included the committee's urban renewal recommendations in a 1954 housing law.

In his real estate development work during the early 1950s, Rouse had to find
his way in a region that was experiencing racial transition when there were fewer
legal tools for white communities to buttress segregation than had previously
been available. During the first half of the twentieth century, developers like the
Roland Park Company had used restrictive covenants and unwritten policies to
keep Jews and African Americans from living in its developments. A 1948 U.S.
Supreme Court decision, *Shelley v. Kraemer*, found that judicial enforcement of
racially restrictive covenants ran afoul of the Fourteenth Amendment's equal protection clause. Yet in 1951, the Baltimore Jewish Council accused Rouse of maintaining a quota for Jewish tenants at an apartment building that he co-managed
with the Roland Park Company.

Rouse soon challenged the status quo. In 1953, he started developing a northwest Baltimore shopping center called "Mondawmin" despite a consultant's warning about "encroachment from an advancing Negro settlement." Two years later,
Rouse became chairman of the board at the Greater Baltimore Committee, which
convened business and civic leaders around the task of improving the city, and
in 1959, Rouse helped that organization launch Baltimore Neighborhoods, Inc.,
which advocated for racial integration in the Baltimore region. Two years after
that, Rouse bought a golf course in north Baltimore and planned to build on that
land a mixed-use development called Cross Keys that he intended to keep open to
African Americans.

Rouse's plans at Cross Keys needed zoning approval from the city government, which was unlikely without the support of neighboring Roland Park. Rouse
downplayed race, touting Cross Keys as a place for "people of extremely high sen-
sibilities." He also scheduled multiple meetings with small groups of Roland Park
residents, rather than one large meeting in which outspoken residents could whip
up us-versus-them resentments. The neighborhood association backed his zoning
request, and the city signed off.

By the time Roland Park got behind Rouse's vision for a community of five
thousand people at Cross Keys, Rouse had already created shell companies to veil
purchases of farmland in Howard County for a much larger vision: Columbia.
Profit mattered to Rouse, but he wanted to show the world a new way for humans
to live together. To "respect the land," Rouse included lakes, green space, and an
84-mile network of trails. To create a "whole city, not just a residential suburb,"
Rouse and a fourteen-member "Non-Physical Planning" team—which included

an economist, a physician, two sociologists, and a psychologist—planned out schools, libraries, a hospital, and a downtown. To "encourage human growth," Rouse placed interfaith worship spaces and "village centers" with retail stores and groceries within walking distance.

Rouse directed builders and realtors in Columbia not to tell anyone the race of their potential neighbors. He sent out "testers" of different races to see how they would be treated at various homes on the market. When Rouse discovered that one cul-de-sac was about to become all black, he encouraged reverse steering to integrate it, and the last house on the cul-de-sac landed in the hands of a white buyer. Many of Columbia's first residents were attracted by Rouse's ambitious social ideals, and the first baby born in Columbia—on September 13, 1967—was the child of a white mother and a black father.

In 1970, the U.S. Commission on Civil Rights invited Rouse to the Social Security Administration office in Woodlawn to testify at its hearing on suburban housing discrimination. Rouse attributed segregated housing patterns not to bigotry but to a natural human fear of the unknown. A way around that fear, he argued, was to build a city from scratch and leave the race of renters and buyers unspoken. In a large enough community, he believed, there would be "absolutely no problem" with an open housing policy. "You have to believe that the same thing can happen anywhere in the Baltimore metropolitan area," he testified.

Rouse saw a role for the federal government in achieving an open housing market. Through its "insurance and mortgage insurance and rent supplement programs," he said, the government could help builders create "a really wide range of housing choices so that [no developer] thinks he will be an island." Rouse argued that the federal government could attach strings to road and sewer funds to compel local governments to create a fairer housing landscape. "If the government really took its whole construct of leverage and said, 'We are just going to have an open housing market in America,' then we would have it," Rouse told the commission.

By 1970, Rouse had fallen short of a goal to make one out of every ten homes affordable to low-income households. However, one out of eight Columbia residents was black, a proportion three times the average in American suburbs.

Mark and Betty Lange stepped out onto the shoulder of Interstate 95 near the Baltimore County/Harford County line nine miles northeast of the city. Mark opened the hood of their 1979 Plymouth Horizon TC3, a sporty, angular coupe. The wiring harness was blown. So much for the party they'd planned on attending.

Luckily, two Campus Life teens who'd been staying with them were back at home at Longley Road—and so was the Langes' van.

Mark and Betty hoofed it along the shoulder to the next exit. It was so cold and windy that they walked backwards at points to keep the chill off their faces. Eventually they found a bar with a pay phone out front. Thankfully, Rhonda answered. Sure, Rhonda told Mark—she and Eve could come down in the van and get them.

Mark and Betty waited . . . and waited . . . and waited. Finally, they spotted the two-tone burgundy and white van that Mark's grandmother had handed down to them recently. Rhonda stepped out of the driver's side. It looked like the wind could carry her away by her wispy blonde locks. Eve, who was short and muscular, with pudgy cheeks and a couple inches of natural hair, opened the passenger-side door.

Mark asked Rhonda and Eve what took them so long. They said they had trouble finding the keys. When the four of them got back to Longley Road, Eve and Rhonda laughed and said that they hadn't really lost the keys: they'd been baking Mark and Betty a cake when the call came. As Betty started cutting a slice, she felt the knife hit something hard. In their hurry, Eve and Rhonda had baked a spoon right into the cake. (Mark wondered if it was more than just the cake getting baked while he and Betty were gone.)

The two teenagers had been staying at the house on Longley Road ever since Mark and Betty had moved back from the Tibbelses' house a couple of months earlier. Eve and Rhonda were typical of the kids Allan and Mark had recruited into the Campus Life club in Columbia. While most Campus Life clubs went after the popular kids, Allan and Mark went after the heads and misfits—the ones who, like them, bristled at the status quo. Rhonda was a white girl from Columbia who was rebelling against her wealthy family and strict father. Eve, who was black, was trying to get out from under the police in Catonsville, a suburb in southwest Baltimore County. Eve and her mother were arguing too. The girls appreciated the break from their chaotic home lives and the guidance they found at Mark and Betty's house.

Whatever education Mark thought he could give Eve by getting her out of her environment, it was Eve—and her environment—that ended up educating Mark. Eve lived in Winters Lane, the black section of Catonsville. When Mark picked Eve up to take her to Campus Life meetings in Columbia, he noticed that her neighborhood was nothing like the rest of Catonsville. In fact, planner Yale Rabin's 1970 report to the U.S. Commission on Civil Rights had singled out Winters Lane. It still had some unpaved roads then, and only one of its roads connected to any white neighborhood; the others just ended or looped in on themselves. Mark got the sense that police treated people differently in this isolated, segregated community. There were a lot of tough kids in Winters Lane; Eve was tough, too. Mark worried that Eve would wind up behind bars if she stayed there long enough. Mark's experience with Eve was the first time he really grasped how different life was for a person of color in the region he called home.

Despite moving back to Harford County, Mark and Betty stayed in touch with Allan and Susan. Mark continued commuting to Columbia to run the Campus Life club, and the two couples talked about finding a big piece of land on which they could each have their own house. Allan turned Mark onto books and music. Mark bought LPs and dubbed them to cassettes for Allan, who was unable to move his arms enough to work a turntable. Allan was particularly engrossed in the work of Bruce Cockburn, a Canadian wordsmith and guitar whiz. Mark scoured record store after record store for Allan until he finally found a copy of Cockburn's September 1981 release, *Inner City Front*. On the album, Cockburn described the world as "pain and fire and steel," the galaxy a "broken wheel."

Mark's vision of the world was being shaped by the work of theologian and writer Francis Schaeffer. Mark and Allan both read a lot of Scripture, but Mark didn't read many books *about* Scripture. When he went to work at Campus Life, Mark told Allan that despite being a believer, he had no theology, no doctrinal position—no knowledge of who God even was. Allan recommended Schaeffer's works. Mark was struck by Schaeffer's discussion of a passage in the Book of James—the same book Allan spoke about at the retreat where Mark met him— that urged believers not to be "stained" or "polluted" by the world. The passage set Mark thinking about the time and place he felt God had placed him in the world, and what responsibilities he carried in that time and place.

Mark, who never made it past high school, appreciated the glossary Schaeffer included in his book *The God Who Is There*. He kept reading Schaeffer's so-called reformed theology, and when Allan told Mark about the Philadelphia Conference on Reformed Theology scheduled for late April 1982, Mark and Betty made plans to go.

By the spring of 1982, Allan and Susan had moved out of the house on Deep Calm onto thirteen acres in Clarksville, fifteen minutes west of Columbia. Mark and Betty had hoped to build their own house on that land, but when they found out that they couldn't subdivide the land, they rented a townhouse in Woodlawn to shorten Mark's commute. They gave their van to Allan, who had it converted so that he could drive it himself (and took Allan's car for themselves). A clasp on the van's steering wheel allowed Allan to steer with one hand, and where you'd normally find the stick shift there was a lever that he could push forward for gas, and down for brakes.

The conference was held at Tenth Presbyterian, a gorgeous church at 17th and Spruce Streets, around the corner from well-manicured Rittenhouse Square. The large brick church, which held one thousand people, was wide open inside, and had Byzantine flourishes throughout the sanctuary and faux-marble arches supporting a narrow balcony on each side.

Hundreds of people attended a lecture by John Gerstner, a church history professor at Pittsburgh Theological Seminary, who was, according to Mark, the "grandfather of orthodox Presbyterianism." Gerstner was an expert on Jonathan Edwards, one of the most important Protestant theologians in American history. Edwards had helped usher in the Great Awakening, a religious revival that swept the colonies in the early eighteenth century.*

Having been awakened themselves not that long before, Mark and Allan listened closely to Gerstner's lecture. About sixteen minutes in, Gerstner said, "You can't be a true Christian without being a member of an evangelical church." Allan and Mark glanced at each other. They had both fervently embraced Christianity, but they had done it on their own terms. Campus Life wasn't a church, it was a so-called parachurch activity—a Christian mission operated outside the oversight of a church. They hadn't subjected themselves to the authority of other believers.

When they got back from Philadelphia, Mark and Allan kept talking about Gerstner during Scripture studies held at the Tibbelses' new house on Trotter Road in Clarksville. Gerstner was probably right, they agreed. The Langes and the Tibbelses both started looking for a church to join. Mark and Betty joined the large congregation at Chapelgate Presbyterian Church, the same church where Allan had broken his neck in the gym. Mark liked that Chapelgate had all its theological i's dotted and t's crossed. Their truth was firmly established and easy to follow. Allan and Susan joined the small congregation at Grace Reformed Pres-

---

*In a 1740 letter, Edwards told a pastor in Boston that the young people in his home of Northampton, Massachusetts, had largely abandoned "fornication" and "tavern haunting," as well as "reveling, frolicking, profane, unclean conversation, and lewd songs." Edwards added, "There has also been an evident alteration with respect to a charitable spirit to the poor." Jonathan Edwards, "From a letter from Mr. Edwards, Minister at Northampton, to Mr. Prince, Minister at Boston, December 12, 1743," *Historical Collections Relating to Remarkable Periods of the Success of the Gospel*, The Rev. John Gillies, ed., (London: James Nisbet & Co., 1845), 359.

byterian. It was a cute little church with blue trim and cedar-shake siding in Relay, a historic railroad town on the border between Baltimore and Howard Counties.

Mark criticized Allan's choice. "I don't need to be a big fish in a small pond," he said. Mark and Allan began to fall out of touch. Allan was getting around easier, thanks to the customized van and to fellow worshippers at Grace who stepped in to provide the kind of help his friends had been giving him.

In the summer of 1983, Mark answered an ad in the newspaper for a job as an assistant manager for Edison Parking. He went to an interview in downtown Baltimore. Most of the employees were black. Almost all of the applicants were black. One of the men who interviewed him was black. Mark didn't think he had a chance of landing the job. He was wrong. And the job would serve as another awakening.

Edison Parking brought Mark on as an assistant manager at a downtown garage. Part of his job was to supervise the employees who cleaned the garage, which accumulated pulverized rubber dust from the constant stream of cars circling up and down the garage's eight floors. One day, Mark sent two young black men out to vacuum. They came back after just a couple of minutes.

"It died on us," one of them said.

Mark looked over the vacuum. The engine was burned up—the men had forgotten to check the oil. Mark was incensed. This wasn't an ordinary household vacuum. It was a $1,000 vacuum meant to clean a garage.

"Didn't your fathers ever show you how to check the oil in a lawn mower?" Mark asked.

One of the men said he didn't know who his father was. The other said his backyard was concrete.

Mark felt like shit. With tears in his eyes, he apologized. As it had when he visited Eve in Winters Lane, the one world he thought he knew broke into two, right in front of him: white Baltimore and black Baltimore.

In 1984, Edison Parking sent Mark to be the manager of a garage in Bethesda, just outside of Washington, DC, and that November he and Betty bought a three-bedroom Cape Cod for $60,000 in Owings Mills, a Baltimore County suburb about ten miles northwest of the city. Eventually the company offered him a general manager position in New York City. He turned it down, but shortly after he accepted an offer from Edison to work in Philadelphia. A week before he settled on a house in Delaware, however, Edison pulled out of Philadelphia altogether.

The company offered to pay closing costs if Mark and Betty bought a house back in Maryland. The Langes decided to have a house built in a new subdivision in Harford County, for $111,775. The subdivision, Hunter's Run, was in a rapidly developing part of Harford County between Interstate 95 and the small town of Bel Air. A brand-new four-lane highway running from the interstate to the town was nearing completion nearby, and a great deal of new development promised to follow in its wake.

In 1986, Mark and Betty moved into his parents' home while the builders worked on Hunter's Run Drive. Melvin and Frances still lived in Chadwick Manor. Frances was in her early fifties and suffering from cancer. Mark suspected the cancer was from the asbestos Frances had washed off of her father's clothes every day when he came home from the shipyard. While their house was under construction in Bel Air, Mark and Betty helped Melvin take care of Frances.

Frances died on March 18, 1987, which happened to be Allan Tibbels' thirty-second birthday. By the time Allan turned thirty-two, he and Susan had already put their Howard County property on the market and moved with their two young daughters to one of the poorest, most racially isolated and devastated neighborhoods in West Baltimore: Sandtown-Winchester.

When Mark and Allan were volunteering at the Loch Raven Campus Life club, they read "Mississippi Ambush," a *Campus Life Magazine* article from 1975 about Dr. John M. Perkins. Perkins grew up very poor in New Hebron, Mississippi. One summer evening in 1946, someone called out to sixteen-year-old John that his brother Clyde had been shot. Word was that a marshal had roughed up a line of black moviegoers outside a theater, and Clyde, who had begun walking more proudly after serving with the U.S. Army in Europe, had grabbed a nightstick before it landed on his head. The marshal shot Clyde twice in the stomach. John Perkins rode with his bleeding brother up Highway 49 to a hospital in Jackson. Clyde died before they arrived.

"A few days later I left Mississippi for California," Perkins told *Campus Life*. "I vowed never to come back."

Perkins arrived in California with a belief that the black church helped keep black Mississippians meek in the face of oppression, but after his son dragged him to Sunday school, he had an overnight conversion. In 1958 he was ordained as a Baptist minister. Shortly afterward, Perkins heard a call from God, one he wasn't eager to answer: God wanted him back in Mississippi. Perkins returned in 1960 with a theology that regarded social ministry as useless, but the civil rights movement convinced him otherwise. Perkins added hundreds of voters to the

Mississippi electoral rolls and helped launch several cooperative grocery stores. In the fall of 1969, Perkins stood before the courthouse of a small Mississippi town called Mendenhall and asked a crowd of black residents to boycott white businesses. "They treat us like niggers, but they love our nigger money," he said. "Let's bring this town to its knees. Then they'll listen to us."

In February 1970, someone called Perkins to alert him that police had pulled over a group of white and black boycotters and taken them to jail. Perkins and a friend decided to drive to the jail, hoping to post bail. They pulled onto Highway 49, the road where Perkins had comforted his dying brother. At the jail, a dozen police officers came out and arrested them.

Inside the jail, Perkins told *Campus Life*, police beat, kicked, and stomped him; made him read his group's civil rights demands aloud; taunted him as a "smart n—r"; poured moonshine on his wounds; stuck a fork up his nose and down his throat; put a gun with an empty chamber to his head and pulled the trigger; and made him mop up his own blood.

When Perkins recovered, he returned to civil rights organizing, but a slight heart attack and stomach surgery several months later landed him back in the hospital. Stuck in a sickbed, Perkins was beset by the specter of white hatred. He didn't see just pointy hoods or burning crosses. It was also the inaction of white Christians that bedeviled him.

Perkins saw two choices: hate or love. If he really believed what he preached, he thought, he must choose love. But in the late 1960s, Perkins was reading Eldridge Cleaver, Malcolm X, H. Rap Brown, and other emerging black leaders who looked beyond the church for more radical solutions.* Perkins ultimately decided that human beings—white, black, or any other color—were drawn to power and susceptible to cruelty.

"I can't hate the white man—it's a spiritual problem," Perkins told *Campus Life*. "God . . . washed my hatred away and replaced it with a love for the white man in rural Mississippi."

Perkins introduced racial reconciliation into his economic development ministries, moving in 1972 with his wife, Vera Mae, to Jackson, Mississippi, with a plan to attract middle-class blacks and whites to revive a declining neighborhood. Perkins's Voice of Calvary ministry left several transformed acres behind in the

---

*At the time, Brown was on trial for allegedly inciting a riot on Maryland's Eastern Shore. The trial was moved to Harford County, and then again to Howard County after two of Brown's associates died when dynamite blew their moving car to smithereens as they were driving just outside of Bel Air.

black section of Mendenhall, including a housing co-op, a youth center, a church, and a health center.

In 1982, Perkins outlined his community development approach in a book called *With Justice for All*. At the core were the "three R's": relocation, redistribution, and reconciliation. Perkins insisted that outsiders who wanted to help a neighborhood had to move into it. Communities had "felt needs" that outsiders fail to grasp, Perkins reasoned. The second "R," redistribution, meant using your wealth, education, and connections to empower your new neighbors. The third "R," reconciliation, required hard work across thorny lines of race and class. Perkins detested the "white savior complex." At Voice of Calvary, he kept a pamphlet around called *Submitting to Black Leadership*. In *With Justice for All*, he wrote, "After you have relocated and before you start any programs, listen."

The book helped Allan Tibbels and his friend Mark Gornik figure out how to engage with a troubled world. After graduating from college in 1984, Gornik enrolled at Westminster Theological Seminary in Philadelphia and interned for a year with Voice of Calvary in Jackson, Mississippi. When Gornik returned to Maryland, he and Allan researched Baltimore's neighborhoods. The Sandtown-Winchester neighborhood in West Baltimore had some of the most terrifying statistics in the city when it came to homicide, blight, addiction, and child health. It also had a rich history and residents whose families had lived there for generations. In late 1986, Gornik and Tibbels spoke with Ella Johnson, the leader of Sandtown's neighborhood association, about their desire to move there. Johnson approved. Gornik moved into a rental on N. Calhoun Street. Allan Tibbels moved with his wife and two young daughters to N. Gilmor Street.

Ella Johnson sent Clyde Harris to see what these white people were up to. Harris was born in 1950 on Stockton Street in Sandtown. He met his wife, Amelia— also a West Baltimore native—at thirteen. They married at twenty, and in the early 1980s, they started the Newborn Apostolic Faith Church of the Trinity.

Newborn was an all-black church in a virtually all-black neighborhood. "There's no way white folks would come in here to live with their babies," Harris thought. Tibbels and Gornik told Harris about John Perkins's vision of Christian community development. Harris loved it. A partnership was born.

In the five years after her husband, Levi, left, Melinda and her daughters lived in six different places, all in high-poverty areas with extremely high–percentage black populations: Westport Homes, Cherry Hill, Murphy Homes, two apartments in Harlem Park, and the house on Rayner Avenue. During that time, Nicole bounced around between four different elementary schools. In early 1990, Melinda's sister, who was living at the Rayner Avenue house with her son, bought a house and moved out. With the place to themselves, some long-lacking stability began to take root in the Smith household. Melinda's daycare program was running at full capacity, allowing her to fulfill her dream of serving parents with difficult schedules like the one she'd had when she worked at the FBI. She opened early for parents who worked in Washington. When a nurse took on an 11:00 a.m. to 11:00 p.m. shift, Melinda kept her program open till midnight. Her family was no longer living paycheck to paycheck, and they began traveling, mostly to the South. Nicole loved Virginia in particular. Melinda started a summer tradition of taking the girls to South Carolina to visit the extended family she had lived with every summer as a child.

Nicole settled in well at Harriet Tubman Elementary. Her teachers found her a bit hyperactive, but she was devoted to her academics. Melinda insisted that the girls do homework right after school, and Nicole always got passing grades. Melinda had high expectations of the girls, and they extended those expectations to their peers, which made Nicole feel more mature than her classmates. If that alienated some of the kids at school, well, Nicole was also getting tougher. Melinda modeled perseverance for the girls. They watched her overcome the few weeks she had spent in the dumps after Levi left, and Melinda told them over and over again, "We gonna make it." Levi himself stayed in the girls' lives. Melinda remained on good terms with him, and he reinforced the notion that the girls ought to develop some grit. "Don't be scared of nobody," he told them.

One day in fifth grade, Nicole's teacher passed papers back to the students, face down, to keep their grades private. Nicole peeled her paper back to reveal a rare failing grade. Disappointment welled up in her. Nothing draws a bully like a whiff of weakness, and Nicole noticed the class bully zeroing in on her long face. He was humongous and constantly intimidated his classmates. The boy grabbed her paper and waved it around while mocking her grade.

"Give me back my paper," Nicole said.

He refused.

"Give me back my paper!"

"What you gonna do?" he mocked.

Nicole punched him in the face.

The bully stood up and punched Nicole in the eye, knocking her to the ground. Nicole burst out of the classroom and ran down the hall. She went right out the door, crossed Harlem Avenue into the alley, ran around the first corner onto

Rayner Avenue, and stormed up the three marble steps into her little red brick home. Melinda and her daycare children looked up, stunned.

"What are you doing here?" her mother barked.

"I got in a fight," Nicole said.

As she recounted the situation to her mother, a school employee showed up to take Nicole back to school. Even though she had landed a blow, the school did not suspend her. As willing to fight as Nicole always was, in the end she would never be suspended. She did, however, develop an attitude the next year when she entered sixth grade at Calverton Middle School. Melinda got so tired of Nicole talking back that she sent her to stay with the pastor of their church for a weekend. Things got better at home after that. But school remained difficult. The Rayner Avenue house was a haven, but there was nothing to protect Nicole when she walked out the door.

Calverton Middle was one of the most dangerous schools in the city. The year before Nicole started at Calverton, school police arrested a sixteen-year-old who had walked through the doors with a sawed-off shotgun. During Nicole's first year, a custodial employee who stumbled upon a Friday afternoon burglary was stabbed to death in a classroom.

When Nicole was in eighth grade, an older man harassed her while she walked the half-mile from Calverton to her grandmother's house. "Come here!" he called from down the street. Nicole stopped. "What do you want?" she asked. The man ran up and pushed Nicole into an alley. Nicole shrieked "Get off of me!" and swung at him. The man sprinted off. Nicole, bawling, ran to her grandmother's house. Nicole's uncle and a friend then ran out of the house, hoping to find the man and beat him up. A police officer arrived and took them to see a suspect. "That's just an old crackhead!" Nicole thought. The handcuffed man was terrified. "You sure that's not him?" an officer asked. It wasn't. Nicole told the police to let him go.

Academically, Calverton was bad, and getting worse. It ranked 194th out of Maryland's 198 middle schools. The *Baltimore Sun* called Calverton a "dumping ground" for students suspended from other schools. When Nicole started in sixth grade, Calverton didn't even have a library. When students walked the hallways, loose insulation hung from the ceiling pipes above them. (The principal didn't bother putting up tiles, believing that the students would inevitably knock them out.) In February of Nicole's eighth-grade year, the state superintendent of schools ordered the city to reform Calverton or submit to a state takeover of the school.

Many of Nicole's classmates' families were in turmoil—addiction, unemployment, and instability caused by evictions were rampant—and you could see it in the school's enrollment numbers. Every year, one out of four students turned over. When Nicole was in eighth grade, a twelve-year-old girl transferred into Calverton three months into the fall semester, after having had problems at another school. The very next week, the girl got suspended for skipping class. No one ever saw her again. On the first night of her suspension, someone shot and killed the girl as she stepped out of an East Baltimore rowhouse.

Nicole didn't know too many of her classmates when she started at Calverton Middle, and she found some of the teachers to be downright mean. One day Melinda took Nicole out of school for an audition in Virginia—she indulged Nicole's dreams of becoming a famous actor or singer, taking her all over the place for auditions and talent shows—and when Nicole returned to school, someone told her that a teacher had called her a "black bitch" behind her back.

Nicole began daydreaming about South Carolina. She remembered her first trip down there when she was nine. The eight-hour drive blew her mind. Everything in South Carolina was so different. Williamsburg County, South Carolina, was eerily quiet and empty. People still farmed tobacco and cotton. Kingstree, the biggest town in the county, had a population of less than four thousand people.

Every summer after that, Melinda and the girls drove down and stayed for two weeks with Melinda's Aunt Candy and Uncle Kenny. Kenny was an electrician, and Candy was a substitute teacher. They lived in a long trailer that expanded from year to year as the family put on brick additions. Candy and Kenny had four children. Their son Dan had a Nintendo in his room; Nicole played her first game of Super Mario Bros. there with him. On Saturdays, Aunt Candy would wake the kids up early and assign each one a chore: washing clothes and hanging them on the line, doing the dishes, or cleaning the bathroom. After chores, they'd eat breakfast together. Later, she might take them shopping in Kingstree.

Nicole's extended family lived in different houses on the same large patch of land near Lane, the closest town—if you can call a post office, general store, and a couple of churches a town. The family kept pigs and chickens on the land. To visit her cousins, all Nicole needed to do was walk out of Aunt Candy's backyard, walk across a field, or walk through the grass along the road. Nicole loved walking down Marion Church Road, the isolated two-lane country route that passed by her family's land. It was one of the most relaxing things she'd ever done. All she could hear was herself talking and the wind in the trees. "Who wanna walk in the road with me?" she'd ask, too scared to walk on the road alone. Her cousins would join her, listening for noises through the tall pines as their sneakers went *pfff-pfff-pfff-pfff* on the pavement. "What's that?" Nicole would yell, hearing a dog howling but imagining a wolf, and her cousins would laugh.

Time passed slowly in Lane. Nicole would look at the clock expecting to see four o'clock, and it would only be one o'clock. But as she got older, the two weeks she spent in South Carolina each summer seemed shorter and shorter. She talked to her mother about spending more time there. One day, Nicole said to her mother, "I wanna live down south with my cousins."

As always, Melinda's reaction was cool and calm. "Wow, you do?" she asked.

Melinda was already thinking the same thing. Her parents had sent her to live down south, after all. She knew why Nicole loved it. It was slower, more serene. There was family everywhere you went. Melinda was also nervous about the school Nicole was zoned to attend the next year: Frederick Douglass High.

Melinda called her Aunt Candy and then returned to Nicole with some news. In the fall, Nicole would attend C.E. Murray High School in Greeleyville, South Carolina.

Melinda would soon make a move of her own. One day in 1994, she got a letter from her landlord, offering to sell her the Rayner Avenue house for $32,000. Melinda didn't know that the landlord had bought her house *and* seven others for just $73,000 a decade earlier. But she did think $32,000 was crazy for a little alley house in Harlem Park. She turned down the offer.

A few months later, Melinda got a call from a church friend who worked as a property manager. After the letter came from the landlord, she'd asked her friend to keep an eye out for homes she could buy. Her friend told her that one of the landlords he worked with wanted to get rid of a house. Melinda thought she'd have to be out of the Rayner house sooner or later since the landlord was making moves to sell it, so she went with her friend to take a look.

The house was in Penn North, a neighborhood named for the major intersection of Pennsylvania and North Avenues. There was a library, a stop on the region's one-line subway system, and a social club where African American men in the city had been convening for more than eight decades. The house was two blocks from the intersection, near the end of a stretch of twenty rowhouses that ran up a side street from North Avenue. The house's two stories were slathered in Formstone, and it had been vacant for months. It was considerably bigger than the Rayner Avenue house. There were three bedrooms, which meant one of Melinda's daughters could have her own room. There was a basement with a door to a small backyard: perfect, Melinda thought, for her daycare program. The price was right: $16,000.

The woman selling the house offered to lend Melinda the money herself. It would be a five-year mortgage at $219 per month. The interest rate was 16 percent, double the average at the time, and if Melinda didn't pay off the principal in five years, a balloon payment would come due. Melinda didn't understand the risk she was taking on; it was her first home purchase, and she didn't research mortgages. On February 10, 1995, Melinda bought the house with just a couple hundred bucks down.

Melinda quickly set to work establishing a daycare business in the house. In the basement, she painted a cartoon cityscape with cars, skyscrapers, and puffy clouds to make the children in her daycare program feel at home in their new space. Owning a home gave Melinda a good feeling. She remembered the house on Elderon Avenue. She and her family had been happy until they had had to leave that house, and she wondered how much different life would have been if they hadn't had to leave the house and move to Westport Homes. Here was a chance to redefine their lives on their own terms.

As Melinda built the daycare program back to its full capacity by spring of 1995, Nicole finished her eighth-grade year, making a two-mile, two-bus commute down to Calverton Middle School. In August, Nicole moved to South Carolina.

Mark and Betty Lange both thought Allan and Susan Tibbels were crazy for moving their family to Sandtown. Betty's brother-in-law, a cop, had worked Narcotics in the Western District in the 1970s. Western District's headquarters were on Riggs Avenue in Sandtown, so Betty had heard the worst. Mark and Betty understood the impulse, though. Mark and Allan had discussed Ronald Sider's 1978 book *Rich Christians in an Age of Hunger*, and Mark, like Allan, had never shaken the story of Dr. Perkins. Mark and Betty were already tithing, sending part of their earnings to Perkins's Voice of Calvary Ministries. When the Tibbelses moved to Sandtown, Mark and Betty began sending them money every month, too.

That didn't mean the Langes regretted their own move to Bel Air in June of 1987. Far from it: Mark and Betty loved their house. They still couldn't believe that they had been able to afford to move to Harford County. The home was the first home they'd had built, and the builder had won an award for its "Georgetown" design. Upstairs, an overlook along the front of the house led to a walk-in closet and a bathroom with a soaking tub. The master bedroom was huge, with French doors that opened onto a balcony overlooking the living room.

At the end of 1988, after a year and a half in the new house, Mark left Edison Parking. He took a managerial job with Broadway Services, a company that handled transportation and parking at the Johns Hopkins medical campus in the heart of East Baltimore. Mark spent his days with African Americans, just as he had at Edison Parking. He had black bosses. He trained and mentored black workers, trying to get them promotions. The managers and assistant managers were all black, and his frenetic work days were mostly spent with them, talking business. Over lunches, shooting hoops at a Johns Hopkins gym, and the occasional dinner in Hunter's Run, Mark got to know what life was like for his black coworkers in their city neighborhoods.

An uneasiness began to grow inside of Mark. He couldn't yet articulate the source of it, but he did recognize the exclusivity of his new neighborhood. Mark was making $45,000—good money in the late 1980s—and he knew that everyone else in Hunter's Run had to make good money in order to be able to live there, too. It was no different than any other American suburb. When housing is limited to those of higher economic standing, white communities often result. Spending every day at mostly black workplaces like Edison Parking and Broadway Services and going home to a new subdivision in a white suburb was agitating Mark, whether he knew the source of the agitation yet or not.

One day, just before the close of business, Jeff Missouri came into Mark's office. Jeff was over a decade younger than Mark, still in his early twenties. He had started at Broadway Services taking pictures for employees' work IDs. When a vacancy opened up in Mark's division, he became Mark's right-hand man. "Do you have time to meet with Don?" Jeff asked Mark.

Don Cleary was one of the shuttle drivers at Broadway Services. He had a handsome, round face and, like Jeff Missouri, he was a black man in his twenties. Jeff told Mark that Don had a problem he needed to discuss with him. Don appeared nervous and ashamed when he approached Mark. His grandmother had been strict raising him, and he always appeared polished. He had served in the Marine Corps, and here he was losing a battle—a battle with cocaine. The big scare had come recently. Behind the wheel of a shuttle, he thought he was having a heart attack. Don asked Mark for help. Mark told Don he couldn't let him drive anymore, but that he would find him a spot in the parking division. He also told Don that Broadway Services would cover outpatient treatment.

Don asked Mark for a favor. Would Mark come to his grandmother's house when he broke the news of his addiction? Mark agreed, and after work they hopped in Mark's Honda Accord and drove about five minutes into a nearly all-black neighborhood of Formstone rowhouses. Mark parked on Don's grandmother's street, N. Belnord Avenue, just south of where it dead-ended at E. Eager

Street. Above the dead end ran an elevated set of train tracks that afforded Amtrak passengers traveling between Washington and New York a grim and blurry view of East Baltimore's blight.

Mark and Don stepped into the well-kept living room of Don's elderly grandmother, Viola. There was a small fireplace in the living room. A picture of Don in his U.S. Marines uniform hung on the wall. Mark and Don sat together on a couch. Viola sat on a side chair across the coffee-table from them, her hair pulled back.

"Don has come to me with a problem he's got," Mark said. "He wanted me to come and talk to you. He's gotten involved in cocaine and he's pretty sure he's addicted. We're going to work on getting him clean." Viola Cleary shook her head, more sad than angry. She ate breakfast with Don every morning and had noticed he'd lost weight. Don always had an excuse, but now she knew for sure.

Don kept working at Broadway Services while he went through treatment. Mark talked to him in the office or out in the parking lot just about every day. Don told Mark that his grandmother really liked him.

"You're the first white man ever to be in her house," Don said.

After John Perkins published *With Justice for All* in 1982, he traveled the country speaking about his "three R's" community development philosophy, and a constant flow of visitors passed through Voice of Calvary Ministries in Jackson, Mississippi. Eventually, Perkins decided that his knack for cooperative organizing could serve as the foundation for a national group dedicated to supporting multiracial churches that pursue racial justice and economic development. Perkins and Voice of Calvary president Lem Tucker invited dozens of church and community leaders to a conference room at Chicago's O'Hare Airport for a daylong organizing meeting in February 1989. Over fifty people showed up. Eight months later, the first annual conference of the Christian Community Development Association drew two hundred people.

By that point, Perkins's approach was already being tested in a fifteen-block section of Sandtown. When Mark Gornik and the Tibbels family arrived in Sandtown in late 1986, they heeded Perkins's call to listen. Instead of pushing their own ideas about what their new community needed, they mostly hung out in the neighborhood and volunteered with existing community groups. To move in and be neighbors was enough.

Clearly, there was need. Drugs, prostitution, and violent crime drew police helicopters to the neighborhood practically every day. Four out of ten families—and two-thirds of children—lived below the poverty line. Nine out of ten adult males had no health insurance. The area including Sandtown and adjacent Harlem Park had the highest rate of vacant housing in the city. Sandtown's population was about one-third of what it had been just a few decades earlier.

When Gornik moved to Sandtown, many families remained from its heyday, when African Americans of all professions lived there and Pennsylvania Avenue was lined with music clubs and black owned businesses. A strong community spirit remained, and Gornik was overwhelmed by the way Sandtown residents accepted him. A core group of neighborhood men started shooting hoops with Gornik and joining Bible studies in his home.

Formal worship started with New Song Community Church's first official service in mid-May 1988 at Gornik's house. The church grew, and its members began discussing how to address the neighborhood's challenges. They started with housing. Allan Tibbels led an effort to buy a vacant house from the city. In 1989, New Song started a branch of Habitat for Humanity, and a passel of volunteers helped a Sandtown resident renovate the vacant building and move in.

As the members of the new church envisioned its community ministry, the model foremost in their minds was Voice of Calvary in Jackson, Mississippi, where Gornik had interned just a few years earlier. Baltimore was not Jackson, however, and they took small steps. The home renovation was New Song's first tangible achievement. Now New Song wanted a headquarters for their worship and community work. After trying unsuccessfully to buy a vacant three-story brick townhouse across the street from Gilmor Homes, New Song finally landed the building at an auction. Robert Embry, the former city housing commissioner who had lambasted Baltimore County twenty years earlier for not providing public housing, threw his support behind the renovation effort.*

The Abell Foundation, where Embry served as president, gave New Song Community Church its first grant. Volunteers from the neighborhood helped renovate the building, and it was ready for use by the fall of 1990. John Perkins, now sixty years old, agreed to be the keynote speaker at the dedication.

Before the dedication ceremony took place, Perkins joined Clyde Harris, Mark

---

*During his public service career, Embry had been a city councilman, commissioner of the Housing Authority of Baltimore City, an assistant secretary at the U.S. Department of Housing and Urban Development, and president of the city's school board. In 1986, Embry considered a mayoral run, but in 1987 he instead accepted a job that would give him considerable, if less conspicuous, influence: the presidency of the Abell Foundation. Arunah S. Abell had launched the *Baltimore Sun* in 1837. When a national chain bought the *Sun* from the A.S. Abell Company in 1986, the proceeds greatly expanded the coffers of the Abell Foundation.

Gornik, and Allan Tibbels for dinner at the Rusty Scupper, a glass-walled chain restaurant on the downtown waterfront. It was Harris's first time meeting Perkins. As the novel glitz of the redeveloped Inner Harbor flickered across the water, Perkins ate mahi-mahi and urged the trio to merge the congregations of Newborn and New Song.

On Sunday, November 11, 1990, Perkins found himself at the corner of N. Gilmor and Presstman Streets in Sandtown, standing beneath New Song's newly renovated building. Built in 1886 as a convent for the Sisters of Mercy, the three-story brick townhouse at 1385 N. Gilmor Street had a smooth concrete arch framing the front door, a marble foundation, and a long staircase spilling onto a wide sidewalk. The temperature struggled to get above 50 degrees, and strong winds made it feel even colder. Across the street, Gilmor Homes extended as far as Perkins could see under clear skies. A crowd grew in front of 1385 N. Gilmor, eventually numbering close to three hundred, including two U.S. senators and U.S. housing secretary Jack Kemp.

Perkins gave the crowd his pitch for relocation. "Jesus Christ did not commute to this earth," he told them. HUD secretary Jack Kemp said that from 1385 N. Gilmor, one could envision a "new chapter in civil rights." Kurt Schmoke, Baltimore's first elected black mayor, highlighted a partnership between local and federal officials that he claimed would "rebuild the walls of this community."

"Rebuild the walls" alluded to the Old Testament story of Nehemiah, who helped residents of Jerusalem rebuild its crumbled walls by rallying each family to construct the section of the wall in front of its home. Schmoke was partnering with the Enterprise Foundation and an advocacy organization called Baltimoreans United in Leadership Development (BUILD) on the federally funded Nehemiah program, which would build over two hundred modular homes in Sandtown and provide affordable mortgages and home-purchase counseling.

"We are witnessing the rebirth of a community," Schmoke told the crowd. The money was there to back up his claim. There was the Nehemiah funding, and, in 1990, HUD gave the Housing Authority of Baltimore City over $13 million to modernize Gilmor Homes. Schmoke believed that with enough resources from the private sector as well as from local, state, and federal governments, Sandtown could be revitalized in many aspects, including housing, education, crime, and health.

Schmoke and the Enterprise Foundation were embarking on an ambitious "neighborhood transformation" project. The coalition would not let the neighborhood be written off as an unredeemable slum. An internal Enterprise Foundation

document described their plan. They would "change all of a neighborhood's broken systems simultaneously: housing, education, employment, health care, human
services, public safety, and commercial real estate." If that sounds reminiscent of
the "Baltimore Plan" of the 1940s and 1950s, it's no coincidence. Schmoke's partner in Sandtown was none other than James Rouse, founder of the Enterprise
Foundation.

James Rouse was a decent-enough-looking guy, but he wasn't exactly magazine
cover material. Yet there was his sixty-seven-year-old pink pate on the cover of
the August 24, 1981, issue of *Time* magazine. Next to an illustration of Rouse in an
affable, open-mouthed grin, a headline shouted "CITIES ARE FUN!"

A decade after he launched Columbia, success came to Rouse once again when
he built Harborplace, a pair of waterfront restaurant and retail pavilions that symbolized downtown Baltimore's metamorphosis from a smelly wharf to a telegenic
destination.* To observers across America, Harborplace reflected the potential for
the rebirth of American cities. But despite the support of black Baltimore in the
1978 election—nearly three out of four African Americans voted for ballot measures to develop the waterfront parcel—Harborplace quickly became shorthand
inside the city for civic leaders' perceived willingness to favor shiny downtown
developments while ignoring the collapse of poor black neighborhoods in the
wake of deindustrialization.

The emerging portrait of two separate and unequal Baltimores came at a time
of transition for James Rouse. After retiring from the Rouse Company in 1979,
Rouse resolved to help house the poor. Ever eager to do good *and* do well, he
started a development company, plus a nonprofit organization called the Enterprise Foundation that would use the development company's profits to support
affordable-housing developments.

Rouse soon found himself once again in Washington, where he joined a Reagan
administration task force on "Private Sector Initiatives." In his quest to use private
sector techniques in the service of the public good, Rouse turned his attention to
"depreciation": the tax deduction that the Internal Revenue Service gave property owners to compensate for the deterioration that inevitably visits any aging
building. At Enterprise, Rouse packaged the depreciation write-offs of nonprofit-

---

*It was Robert Embry who had helped convince Rouse to build Harborplace. Several years
earlier, Rouse had recommended Embry to the Carter administration for a HUD post. Olsen,
271, 276; Robert Embry, personal communication.

owned buildings and sold them to for-profit investors. This was a handy source of income for nonprofits who were charging less than market rate to those who rented the nonprofits' apartments. When Congress revisited the tax code at the beginning of Reagan's second term and considered axing the depreciation benefit, Rouse lobbied Washington to preserve the depreciation write-off for nonprofits. When Congress passed the Tax Reform Bill of 1986, they gave Rouse more than he had asked for. The bill included the Low-Income Housing Tax Credit, which nonprofit developers could sell to investors, creating a revenue stream to make up for the income lost when they reduced rents to make their housing affordable.

In the mid-1980s, the Enterprise Foundation helped administrators in Chattanooga, Tennessee, write a ten-year plan for its affordable housing needs. The city chartered a private organization to enact the recommendations, giving it permission to enforce municipal codes to pressure landlords to fix up their properties. Enterprise told Chattanooga that the city of 200,000 needed about ten thousand more affordable housing units. Rouse moved on and the plan never fully got off the ground, but it rekindled his desire to take on an entire community at a time.

At age seventy-four, Rouse decided to solve all the problems of the poor in one neighborhood. Luckily for him, Baltimore's Mayor Schmoke was feeling aspirational about community development, too, after a trip to Israel. In the city of Jerusalem and the town of Kiryat Gat, Schmoke had been impressed by the "self-maintaining, self-sufficient community" that resulted from a national initiative called Project Renewal. When Rouse approached Schmoke with his dream of transforming all of the social and physical conditions of one neighborhood in five years, Schmoke agreed to partner with Rouse on one project only: his collaboration with BUILD to build new homes by securing federal money through the Nehemiah Program. Rouse kept badgering Schmoke. In late 1989, Schmoke agreed to join Rouse on his neighborhood transformation project, but only if it was in the neighborhood where the Nehemiah houses would be built: Sandtown-Winchester. (West Baltimore also happened to be Schmoke's political base.) Rouse preferred a section of East Baltimore close to Johns Hopkins Hospital and near where the city had piloted the Baltimore Plan four decades earlier, but he acquiesced to Schmoke's request to transform Sandtown.

To establish a "bottom-up" foundation for the Sandtown transformation project, the Rouse/Schmoke/BUILD alliance helped residents create an organization called Community Building in Partnership that would connect the residents to outsiders and get the "transformational" work up and running. Throughout 1990, the Enterprise Foundation convened private and public meetings to figure out what exactly needed transforming. The overall goals, as later enumerated by Enterprise, were astoundingly ambitious: knock unemployment from 22 percent to 9 percent; push the proportion of students meeting state education standards from 10 percent to 95 percent; eliminate "blatant drug dealing"; and reduce crime "to the level of that in typical middle-income neighborhoods."

The first sign of transformation in Sandtown was in its housing stock. The Nehemiah Program added 227 homes to the private market in Sandtown. Federal funding from a public housing modernization program brought new kitchens, bathrooms, plumbing, electrical work, roofs, floors, and more to Gilmor Homes. In 1992, former president Jimmy Carter came to the neighborhood to launch Sandtown Habitat for Humanity's campaign to renovate one hundred houses in five years.

The resident-driven Community Building in Partnership organization took formal shape in 1993 and worked outside of the housing realm. CBP launched a prenatal health program, organized a voter registration drive, opened an employment center at Gilmor Homes, and worked with the city's school system to write up a "compact" to reform practices and improve student achievement at three neighborhood elementary schools. The organization also helped neighbors start a newspaper, organize block captains, and spruce up parks. CBP even employed neighborhood residents, who made up over half of its thirty-five-person staff.

The early years of New Song Community Church coincided with the Rouse/Schmoke plan. New Song helped develop the overall scope of work for the public-private partnership, and the Enterprise Foundation provided support and interest-free construction loans for Sandtown Habitat for Humanity. A jobs program launched by the neighborhood transformation project eventually merged with New Song's existing EDEN Jobs ministry, and Enterprise gave New Song financial assistance to renovate a daycare center.

Rouse's ethos, as exemplified by his work in Sandtown, boiled down to a belief that opportunity could be brought to the inner city, no matter how poor the neighborhood. By the end of 1993, $60 million in private and public funds had been attracted to his unprecedented "place-based" campaign.

While Rouse's work there was still getting underway, a movement to get people who were poor out of neighborhoods like Sandtown was emerging. The "mobility" approach aimed to deconcentrate poverty by moving the poor to communities with better schools, safer streets, and more jobs. Rather than bring opportunity to poor places, this would transport the poor to opportunity. Any "transformation" would happen to poor *people*, not to poor neighborhoods. As Rouse and his partner Kurt Schmoke were working with the residents of Sandtown, Schmoke was also being drawn into the slipstream of Baltimore's growing mobility movement—whether he liked it or not.

Conditions had deteriorated to an unfathomable degree in Baltimore's public housing by the early 1990s. Even though there was a waiting list with over thirty thousand names on it, the number of vacant units in the city's public housing stock nearly doubled between 1988 and 1991. Many people on the waiting list refused to take high-rise units when the Housing Authority of Baltimore City offered them. With over $100 million in federal modernization funds becoming available over the next ten years, housing authority staff assembled a task force in early 1990 to figure out what to do with the towers. Given the towers' "many social problems and large operating costs," the housing authority specifically asked the tower task force to consider demolition as an option.

The task force convened community leaders and advocates for the poor. Representing the Legal Aid Bureau's Housing Law Center at a March 1990 meeting, Barbara Samuels said that with so many people on a waiting list for public housing, to "tear down structurally sound buildings has the ring of absurdity." Reporting back to the housing authority in November 1990, the task force stopped short of recommending demolition, but suggested emptying the towers of the more than 2,200 families who lived there. Only adults fifty-five and up, they said, should live in high-rise projects. Mayor Schmoke ordered the housing authority to figure out how to get families out of the high-rises.

Congress had amended existing housing law three years earlier to ensure one-for-one replacement of any decommissioned units. Emptying the towers would create even more work and expense for the housing authority. HUD had been stingy with funding for new construction over the past couple of decades, and the $100 million potentially coming down the pike from HUD was for modernization, not replacement. Task force members knew this and simply hoped that HUD would look favorably upon their plan to use modernization money for new construction.

In the wake of the task force's report on high-rise public housing, the Citizens Planning and Housing Association studied the replacement housing issue. As officials at the housing authority did, CPHA leaders sensed a crucial moment and desired "a new agenda for public housing for families in Baltimore City."

In January 1992, the city announced a plan to demolish five of the six high-rises at the Lafayette Courts public housing complex just east of downtown Baltimore and replace them with less dense two-story apartments. Citizens Planning and Housing Association executive director Hathaway Ferebee and housing director Jane Conover asked to collaborate with city housing officials on plans for the 252 units that required replacements. They queried whether the agency supported scattered site housing—a program in which the city purchased and renovated vacant homes for use as public housing—across the metropolitan area or not. A city official told them that some residents said they felt isolated after moving to scattered site units. Some Lafayette Courts residents, however, had told Conover that they wanted anything better than the towers. Conover told housing officials about promising research showing higher satisfaction among Chicago's public housing families who had relocated to subsidized units outside that city.

Chicago was moving public housing residents to the suburbs because of a pair of twenty-five-year-old lawsuits: *Gautreaux v. Chicago Housing Authority* and *Gautreaux v. U.S. Department of Housing and Urban Development*. Chicago had built most of its public housing in poor black neighborhoods, and its city council had blocked attempts to build public housing elsewhere. When the city proposed building even more projects in black neighborhoods, a group of public interest lawyers led by a thirty-nine-year-old named Alex Polikoff accused the city of violating equal protection and due process under the Fourteenth Amendment by maintaining segregation patterns. Polikoff also claimed a violation of Title VI of the new Civil Rights Act of 1964, which banned racial discrimination by programs using federal funds. With several Chicago public-housing residents as plaintiffs, Polikoff and his colleagues had filed a complaint in federal court in 1966.

After ten years and a U.S. Supreme Court decision, the *Gautreaux* cases had cleared a path for a metropolitan approach to desegregating inner-city public housing. The remedy found for the *Gautreaux* cases created special Section 8 certificates that could be used throughout the Chicago suburbs. By the end of the program in 1998, 7,100 families had relocated. Initial research from a ten-year study on *Gautreaux* families who chose to move to the suburbs showed educational gains for children and employment gains for mothers.

As Citizens Planning and Housing Association staff researched the *Gautreaux* mobility program in Chicago, it dawned on Baltimore's civil rights advocates that the potential demolition of public housing high-rises presented an opportunity at home. *Gautreaux*-style metropolitan housing vouchers held the potential to make a dent in the region's decades-long segregated living patterns.

Legal Aid attorney Barbara Samuels was skeptical of the city's ability to place scattered site housing outside of segregated areas. How would city officials replace 252 Lafayette Courts units anywhere off-site, much less in integrated or middle-class neighborhoods, when they had yet to replace the three hundred units they'd condemned at the Fairfield Homes public housing complex?

Fairfield Homes opened in 1942 as temporary war housing on a peninsula in South Baltimore, just across a set of railroad tracks from Brooklyn Homes. In 1987, the U.S. Department of Housing and Urban Development gave the Housing Authority of Baltimore City a $5 million grant to begin relocating one-third of the Fairfield Homes families because of extreme environmental hazards that had worsened in the industrial area over decades. In January 1988, city administrators decided to shut down Fairfield Homes entirely. It was three more years before the housing authority managed to relocate most Fairfield residents, and as of March 1992 officials had yet to provide the federally mandated replacement units.

Barbara Samuels wrote to the Baltimore City Council, noting that the housing authority had just twenty units under consideration as Fairfield replacements. Demolishing the Lafayette Courts high-rises, she wrote, would cause a "net loss of units available for families on the waiting list." She argued instead for addressing the towers' management and fixing the poor conditions that many of her Legal Aid clients were living with in the towers.

In the spring, the Citizens Planning and Housing Association applied to the Abell Foundation for a grant to fund their metropolitan housing campaign and continued to pressure the city. CPHA also forged connections with those who had led a similar charge in Chicago. At a June 1992 public forum in Baltimore, someone from the *Gautreaux* mobility program spoke about Moving to Opportunity, a *Gautreaux*-inspired mobility experiment HUD planned to launch in five cities. In August 1992, Alex Polikoff—who'd filed the *Gautreaux* suits and helped craft the legislative language for Moving to Opportunity—made a presentation to CPHA during which a Baltimore housing authority staffer committed to apply to HUD for Moving to Opportunity funds that were meant to spur mobility for families in public housing.

But that same week, an ugly episode in a white part of Baltimore City showed them the furor that could arise should the city try to create public housing outside of its poor black neighborhoods.

———

Four years after deciding to shut down Fairfield Homes, the Housing Authority of Baltimore City had yet to create any federally mandated replacement units.* However, the housing authority had gotten support from some HUD officials for its plans to convert a former public school in southeast Baltimore into low-income apartments. The school sat between two white neighborhoods—working-class Highlandtown and gentrifying Canton—meaning the site would partly satisfy a HUD requirement that the city place one-third of Fairfield replacement units in areas that were, in HUD-speak, "non-impacted"—in other words, had a smaller proportion of minority population and federally assisted housing than the city average.

Soon enough, fliers went up advertising a meeting about a "high rise housing project" coming to the neighborhood. "This will destroy your property value and fill Highlandtown with the drugs, crime, and violence," the flier read. At the August 1992 meeting, city housing officials told the hundreds in attendance that the building wouldn't be a high-rise. They couldn't get a word in over the shouting, and the meeting ended quickly.

Several weeks later, the city told HUD it was abandoning its plan to build Fairfield Homes replacement units in Canton. Housing commissioner Robert Hearn also asked HUD to waive the "non-impacted" requirement and let the city put *all* of the Fairfield replacement units in impacted—meaning, in Baltimore, black—neighborhoods:

> Whether we like it or not, the development of public housing locations in non-impacted neighborhoods and communities is perceived as an influx of the poor and a feared perception of devaluation of property by existing homeowners and landlords with an immediate reaction to sell and move.

HUD denied the waiver, but allowed the city to replace the Canton plans with a renovation of rowhouses in a black East Baltimore neighborhood.

The housing authority's failure to create units in a white neighborhood didn't

---

*Hearn told HUD in a September 1992 letter that he wanted to get construction started on Fairfield Homes replacement units by March 1993. "One of the more important reasons for requesting your assistance in expediting this project," Hearn wrote, "is the fact that we have received notice that the Legal Aid Bureau is about to bring suit against the Housing Authority of Baltimore City and the U.S. Department of Housing and Urban Development relative to the fact that construction has not started since the initial approval in 1987." Robert W. Hearn to Joseph G. Schiff, September 8, 1992, ACLU–Maryland Records, Plaintiff's Exhibit 310.

A flier inviting Highlandtown residents to protest the proposed conversion of a public school into low-income apartments. (1992) *ACLU-Maryland Records; University of Baltimore Special Collections and Archives*

bode well for housing mobility supporters, but the Citizens Planning and Housing Association continued its push for public housing outside the city. "Many cities have successfully sued their local Housing Authority and HUD to force them to build replacement housing," CPHA wrote to the Abell Foundation in November 1992.

In December 1992, CPHA housing director Jane Conover invited a group of public housing residents, aides to elected officials, and advocates for the poor to a meeting to discuss replacements for Lafayette Courts. Barbara Samuels represented Legal Aid at the meeting. Representing the Maryland branch of the American Civil Liberties Union was a lawyer named Susan Goering.

In the early 1980s, Goering had worked on *Missouri v. Jenkins*, a school desegregation case. Goering discovered in her research that decades of housing policy had helped create the residential segregation that made it so difficult to integrate

Kansas City schools. When Goering moved to Baltimore in the mid-1980s to start work as the legal director for ACLU–Maryland, she saw the same residential patterns. North Baltimore's York Road, she noticed, divided white from black, wealthy from poor, well-maintained mansions from deteriorating houses. It reminded her of Troost Avenue in Kansas City.

While conducting research for *Missouri v. Jenkins*, Goering found historical documents implicating policymakers in the patterns of residential segregation that had taken root in mid-twentieth century Kansas City. Surely, she thought, the same kinds of documents existed for Baltimore. She sent two law students to the National Archives, and they returned with what Goering considered smoking guns.

Susan Goering, Barbara Samuels, and others at the Citizens Planning and Housing Association meeting decided to write up proposals regarding high-rise conditions and replacement housing and possible ways to overcome opposition to public housing in the counties surrounding Baltimore City. Before they could get started, Housing Authority of Baltimore City commissioner Robert Hearn announced the closure of a tower at Lexington Terrace, a high-rise project on the west side of Baltimore. The next day, Jane Conover fired off a memo to the president of CPHA's board. "There is no plan for the vacated high-rise," Conover wrote. "This verifies our position and increases the urgency to find scattered site replacement public housing."

Barbara Samuels was livid. Here was another tower going empty—with the housing authority yet to replace the Fairfield Homes units, no less, and five towers possibly coming down at Lafayette Courts. At Legal Aid, Barbara had recently begun representing Lexington Terrace's tenant council. About one in four Lexington Terrace units was vacant despite the housing authority's long waiting list, and residents complained about abysmal conditions. Barbara was concerned that the housing authority might be ignoring maintenance requests in order to make demolition of Lexington Terrace a more attractive option. Complaints from Lexington Terrace residents prompted visits from Baltimore's city council president— who wound up stuck in an elevator—and mayor, who announced the tower would be renovated, not closed.

Schmoke replaced housing commissioner Robert Hearn with Daniel Henson III, a developer renowned for his political savvy, and in April 1993, Henson and Schmoke invited public housing residents and advocates—including Susan Goering, Barbara Samuels, and CPHA staff—to join a task force on the replacement of the Lafayette Courts units. At a task force meeting, Goering passed out an archival document from late 1945 that her interns had found: "Effects of the Post-War Program on Negro Housing," dated September 25, 1945. Baltimore faced a housing crisis at the end of World War II; there was no war, but there were still war workers. When temporary war housing came down, they would need real homes to live in, but the city had labeled 20 percent of private dwelling units "substandard." The city planned to demolish and replace much of what it called "slums" with dense public housing. It also anticipated "the arresting of blight in neighborhoods adjacent to public housing developments." By "removing" to new public housing those who couldn't afford market-rate housing, the city argued, "present buildings in the neighborhood will become desirable for tenants who can pay a profitable rent." Projects for the poor, and traditional neighborhoods for the rest: everyone, it seemed, would find their proper place.

The "Post-War Program" document said that developers almost never built new private housing for African Americans. Rather than challenge this, the city accepted it, arguing that developers were unlikely to bother when two-thirds of black households were too poor to buy a house or rent at market rate.

The authors saw another benefit to their public housing plan. "Racial and group movements within the City will thus be arrested," the document bragged, "removing one of the important causes of blight."

As Barbara Samuels read the document, she was stunned by the frankness of the language and increasingly appalled at what it added up to. A section on the difficulty of securing sites for black public housing included a passage that Barbara would be able to recite from memory years later. It said that tracts of land sufficiently large to develop housing for African Americans are "hard to find" and "almost invariably contiguous to white residential developments, usually individually owned, a cause for very violent neighborhood resistance to any in-migration of Negroes.

"This taxpayer resistance," the section continued, "is the major cause of the peculiarly difficult local problem of creating expansion areas for Negroes."

Barbara then read a related document, written by Baltimore housing authority chairman Cleveland Bealmear almost two years before the "Post-War Program" report was written. Bealmear saw slums not just as unhealthy places, but as concentrations of people who contributed little tax revenue to the city. "Rapidly depreciating housing means a rapidly increasing supply of low rents, and a more and more effective invitation for the incapable to migrate to the city," he wrote, and that meant "strangling the fewer and fewer persons able to earn enough to support themselves and their incompetent or unlucky neighbors.

"We *must* destroy slum houses," Bealmear continued. "They are being destroyed anyhow by the elements and by their occupants. Their expectancy of continued tax returns is almost nothing."

Bealmear was willing to destroy houses, but, bless his heart, he wasn't willing to destroy people. "Under the American idea, we can't shoot or poison the slum dweller," he wrote. "We are being forced to either rehouse him or pay the cost of keeping him where he is."

The report occasioned a "holy shit" moment for Barbara. The concentration of public housing in poor black parts of the city wasn't an unintended consequence of another policy goal. It was a concerted plan, she believed, to contain the black population. For a decade, she had been going in and out of public housing complexes, but she hadn't wondered why the projects were *where* they were. Now she knew: the powers that be had wanted it that way. She remembered a law article she'd read a few years back by Dallas fair-housing lawyers Elizabeth Julian and Michael Daniel that laid out the legal principles one could use to challenge segregation in public housing. Julian and Daniel had filed *Walker v. HUD* in the 1980s over the concentration of public housing and Section 8 tenants in minority-heavy sections of Dallas. The resulting consent decree ordered over $100 million to be spent on the redevelopment of public housing, new housing opportunities in white parts of metropolitan Dallas for public housing residents, and mobility counseling for public housing residents who had never lived in the suburbs before.

"The evidence of past and present purposeful racial segregation is painful to look at, but it is not hard to find," Julian and Daniel wrote.

Barbara wondered how she had missed this. Forget her mantra of "Don't lose units." Now it had to be "Where are the units?" Years before, Barbara hadn't been too sympathetic when people on the waiting list turned down apartments in the high-rises, what with so many of her clients desperate to get into public housing. Now, with all the talk of those high-rises being demolished, she sensed an opportunity to ensure that the segregation created when the towers went up didn't reassert itself when the towers came back down.

In the summer of 1993, Jane Conover and Hathaway Ferebee of the Citizens Planning and Housing Association declared, "Now is the time to begin to stem the tide of segregation of our city"; the city's task force on replacement housing sent Henson a proposal that leaned heavily on housing mobility; and ACLU–Maryland drafted an application to the Abell Foundation for a grant to "develop the legal basis for requiring that low-income housing opportunities for city public housing residents be made available in the suburbs."

That October, Mayor Schmoke, Maryland's Governor William Donald Schaefer, and HUD Secretary Henry Cisneros unveiled a plan to demolish every last public housing high-rise in the city.

The day after Cisneros, Schaefer, and Schmoke made their announcement, Barbara Samuels started a new job: working under Susan Goering as an attorney for the Maryland branch of the American Civil Liberties Union. Barbara would no longer be a housing lawyer. She would be a *fair*-housing lawyer.

In November 1993, Baltimore housing commissioner Daniel Henson sent a draft of an agency-wide replacement housing policy to his task force. It was full of qualifiers. "Efforts shall be made," it said, to put units in the counties. "To the greatest extent possible," the agency would avoid locating units in areas of concentrated poverty. Hathaway Ferebee and Jane Conover wrote back to Henson, saying that they recognized he was "confined by . . . political barriers" and that they would form a less constrained task force to develop new recommendations.

They called it the Citizens Task Force on Metropolitan Housing. Nineteen local organizations signed on, including Baltimore's NAACP chapter, and Citizens for Housing Action and New Grassroots Empowerment, a group formed by public housing residents. They got to work immediately, drafting a "statement of purpose" that called for a wide range of public housing choices in safe, prosperous communities, including outside of the city. The statement also demanded that the housing authority meet its obligation to affirmatively further fair housing and "dismantle the remnants of past segregation."

Before the task force even had its second meeting, HUD secretary Henry Cisneros announced a grant of nearly $50 million for the city's Lafayette Courts demolition and rebuilding plan. Housing commissioner Daniel Henson said he hoped to start demolition in the fall of 1994.

The Citizens Task Force on Metropolitan Housing met every few weeks to refine their vision of metropolitan public housing. They floated criteria for acceptable replacement locations, like access to jobs and high-quality schools, and they asked members to vote on acceptable levels of poverty and minority concentration for replacement sites. The group also pressured lawmakers.

In meetings with state and city housing officials, Barbara Samuels discovered that the city had less than two months in which to select Fairfield replacement sites before it would lose its HUD funding. Barbara acquired a list of the housing authority's proposed Fairfield replacement sites and passed it on to the Citizens Task Force, asking members to keep it confidential. Barbara visited some of the proposed Fairfield replacement sites with Citizens Task Force members and

Lafayette Courts residents. The forty-five "non-minority" sites on the list were in southwest Baltimore neighborhoods known for white poverty; many public housing projects and majority-black neighborhoods were close by. Perhaps the sites were "non-impacted" by racial concentration, Barbara allowed, but they certainly weren't offering much opportunity, let alone dismantling segregation. Some of the "impacted" sites—with high-poverty, large minority populations—were on Preston Street near Greenmount Avenue in East Baltimore's Johnston Square neighborhood. Upon hearing that news, one of the Lafayette Courts residents said, "They're going to throw us out of the frying pan and into the fire!"

In early March 1994, Mayor Schmoke and Housing Commissioner Henson met with the Citizens Task Force on Metropolitan Housing. The task force shared the replacement housing criteria they had recently put to a vote: less than 21 percent poverty, less than 26 percent minority population, low crime, high-quality schools, accessible to transportation and jobs, and located away from concentrations of subsidized housing. They also insisted that the housing be placed across the metropolitan area, not just in the city. Given the barriers to building and operating public housing developments outside the city, the city should focus on using Section 8 certificates to replace lost units, and anyone moving to whiter, more affluent communities should receive counseling. Notes from the meeting say that Schmoke and Henson indicated support for a metropolitan approach and asked the task force to "rattle some trees" to make it possible, but believed it was too challenging politically, and they still planned to limit replacement housing to sites within the city's borders. In a letter to Mayor Schmoke, the task force responded that Section 8 certificates could serve as "a 'quiet' approach to metropolitan housing because cooperation agreements [with surrounding counties] are not required."

Disappointed by the city's recalcitrance, the Citizens Task Force on Metropolitan Housing voted at a May 1994 meeting to put their support behind a lawsuit against the Housing Authority of Baltimore City, the U.S. Department of Housing and Urban Development, and the mayor and city council of Baltimore for perpetuating segregation in public housing.

By the end of June, the Citizens Task Force on Metropolitan Housing was ready to go public with their push for metropolitan-wide subsidized housing, and they focused their attention on building support in the suburbs and with public housing residents who might prefer to stay in the city. There would be "racist and classist beliefs" to contend with, but they believed that by listening to the concerns of suburbanites, they could engage "people of good faith . . . to reduce the NIMBY [not in my backyard] syndrome." The task force proposed bringing together community leaders and "representative tenants" with facilitators trained by Citizens Planning and Housing Association staff to help all sides air their concerns. Just as James Rouse had done in Roland Park while building support for Cross Keys thirty years earlier, the task force planned to conduct meetings in small groups—"to avoid the mob mentality," they wrote.

It was too late for that.

"HEAR US SHOUT," the flier read. "People living in drug and crime-infested Lafayette homes and Murphy homes could be moving to Essex. The Moving to Opportunity program could affect our neighborhoods, our schools, and the number of families receiving County social services."

The flier went up in June 1994 around Essex, a working-class community on the Back River in southeast Baltimore County. Economic and racial tensions were high in that deindustrializing part of the county. The unemployment rate in Essex was twice the rate of Baltimore County, and the minority population of Essex had doubled between 1980 and 1990. Residents of Rosedale, a town wedged between Essex and Baltimore City's eastern border, had battled the city over public housing since the construction of Hollander Ridge, a one-thousand-unit public housing complex that opened in 1976 on the city-county line.*

In the early 1990s, the city's talk of razing public housing towers caught the attention of southeast Baltimore County residents. When word of Baltimore's application for Moving to Opportunity (MTO) funds reached the county, residents started trying to connect the dots. The city applied for the program in November 1993, and in January 1994, a Democratic state legislator got his hands on correspondence between Baltimore County officials and a county nonprofit tapped to implement Moving to Opportunity, and he started passing the documents around.

In March 1994, HUD chose Baltimore as one of five Moving to Opportunity cities. Two hundred and eighty-five families from city public housing would get vouchers to use in parts of the city and surrounding counties with a poverty rate

---

*When construction on Hollander Ridge started, Rosedale homeowners who were concerned about crime formed a three-hundred-member community association. They initially wanted to see the project stopped. When that failed, they pleaded—in vain—for a twelve-foot brick wall to be built around the complex. Mike Martin, "Can Hollander Ridge Open Without Trouble?" *Essex Times*, August 12, 1976, 1; also, "Meeting Eases Tension at Hollander Ridge," *Suburban Times*, November 18, 1976; also, Antero Pietila, "Peering at Hollander Ridge: Project's Neighbors Torn Between Fear, Envy," *Baltimore Sun*, February 20, 1977, B1.

below 10 percent. Officials tried to keep the news quiet, but opposition quickly mounted in the county. The Citizens Task Force on Metropolitan Housing started working on their own flier about Moving to Opportunity in order to "avoid the spread of misinformation," but misinformation was already spreading at community meetings in the largely white communities of Essex and Dundalk where residents were rallying against MTO. One resident told an audience in Dundalk that eighteen thousand public housing families were on their way to the county. "What is the grand agenda?" he asked.

The flier in Essex and a looming primary election inflamed the rhetoric. "I've heard that the city is going to tear down the Lafayette and Murphy Homes highrise projects and move the people here to Essex," said a Republican running for a seat in the state legislature. A Democrat running for county council told his supporters that public housing residents "must be taught to bathe and how not to steal."

Officials behind Moving to Opportunity scheduled meetings to assuage residents' anxiety about the program. During a June 1994 meeting at a high school in Essex, they explained that most of the white working-class communities where opposition was loudest were too poor to qualify as destinations for Moving to Opportunity families. In other words, there wasn't enough opportunity in most of Dundalk or Essex to move *to*. According to a *Sun* report, that meeting devolved into "a noisy, racially tinged free-for-all," and officials held no more meetings.*

The Citizens Task Force pressed on through the summer of 1994 with its campaign for metropolitan public housing, which now included ambitious "longer term" strategies: a region-wide housing authority; and two pieces of state legislation, one of which would ban landlords from discriminating against applicants based on their "source of income" (e.g., a Section 8 certificate), and another which would mirror a law in Montgomery County, Maryland, that required new market-rate developments to reserve 15 percent of their units for public and subsidized housing.

The Citizens Task Force lobbied Democratic U.S. Senator Barbara Mikulski to fund an extension of Moving to Opportunity, but in September 1994, Mikulski helped cancel the program—and for all five cities, not just for Baltimore. The 285

---

*The Citizens Task Force found a silver lining in the brouhaha. "Baltimore Neighborhoods' Mike Bardoff single-handedly stood up to hecklers at one meeting and tried to give people the facts," a task force memo read. "This courageous effort changed the media coverage of that meeting from why people opposed the program to why won't the people of Dundalk listen to the facts. (*Yea Mike!*)"

families in Baltimore would still be offered certificates, but that would be the end of Moving to Opportunity. (Mikulski claimed there were no politics involved in the decision.)

On December 20, 1994, Housing Authority of Baltimore City commissioner Daniel Henson announced that his agency would start moving families out of Lafayette Courts in February 1995 and demolish the towers in April—all six towers. (The city had decided to construct a new 196-unit building for elderly people.)

Throughout 1994, ACLU–Maryland had been identifying plaintiffs for their lawsuit against city and federal housing officials for perpetuating segregation in public housing. Barbara Samuels proved to be an invaluable staff member, given her earlier work for Legal Aid, especially the stint representing the tenant council at Lexington Terrace. Toward the end of the year, Barbara Samuels and her colleagues finalized a class action complaint on behalf of "all African Americans who presently reside, or will in the future reside, in Baltimore City family public housing units." ACLU–Maryland hoped to stop the housing authority from demolishing the high-rises and developing Fairfield replacement units until there was a plan to further desegregation and give Baltimore public-housing residents more options for where to live.

On January 31, 1995, the ACLU filed a class action lawsuit against the U.S. Department of Housing and Urban Development. The complaint in *Carmen Thompson v. HUD* also named the Housing Authority of Baltimore City, the Baltimore City Council, and the mayor of Baltimore as defendants, alleging that they had failed to disestablish *de jure* segregation. The complaint drew upon the U.S. Constitution, as well as upon several passages of civil rights legislation, including Title VIII of the Civil Rights Act of 1968. In allowing segregation to perpetuate in public housing long after its so-called desegregation in 1954, the suit argued, HUD and Baltimore City had failed to uphold the Fair Housing Act's duty to "affirmatively further fair housing."

"If not halted by this Court," the complaint read, "the defendants will rebuild segregation for generations of public housing families to come. In complete disregard of their constitutional duty, defendants will squander a rare opportunity to right a wrong of historic dimension."

TWO

In Search of Home

WILLIAM SCIPIO HAD ALWAYS FELT A LITTLE DIFFERENT FROM THE OTHER KIDS IN Sandtown. He was sheltered in his grandmother's packed three-story, five-bedroom townhouse in the 1500 block of Presstman Street, where he slept head to toe with cousins on a California King mattress. On Saturdays, they scrubbed the stoop with Ajax, then swept the sidewalks and gutters. Sundays revolved around Sharon Baptist Church, just half a block away. Beyond William's one-block world was 1995 Baltimore, with open-air drug markets and an epidemic of heroin addiction, both of which had already sucked in some of his family. The previous year, Baltimore had logged 321 murders.

One day when William was on the stoop with his friends Vic and Steve, a van pulled up and a big man in overalls stepped out.

"Fellas, what are you doing?" the man asked.

"Nothin'," the boys replied.

"Want to come with me? I can give you some work," the man said.

It was Clyde Harris. Elder Harris, as most in the neighborhood called him, had large, welcoming dimples when he smiled. He possessed a tender love for Sandtown. He knew what its young people were capable of in deed and spirit, and he knew how deep the neighborhood's burdens cut. He had a term for the prevailing collective psyche in Sandtown: "costly joy."

Harris took the boys to his N. Fulton Avenue house, pointed at some wood, and said, "Put this shelf together." The boys' work wasn't perfect, but they were proud of it. Harris pointed out their errors and gave each of them a few bucks.

One day, William told Harris how badly he wanted to get out of Harlem Park Elementary/Middle School, one of nine schools the city had handed over to a private company to run. When teachers gave out assignments, William finished them in fifteen minutes and then twiddled his thumbs for the rest of class. He was jealous of Vic and Steve, who went to New Song Academy, which grew out of a before-school and after-school program that Susan Tibbels had started in 1991 in New Song Community Church's building on Gilmor.

New Song Academy had only about two dozen students. That was the size of one class at Harlem Park Elementary/Middle. William finished school at 2:30 p.m. Vic and Steve were at New Song Academy until 5:00 p.m. William was at loose ends all summer; his friends attended New Song Academy year-round in six-week sessions. Because the school was run by New Song Urban Ministries, students' families were closely connected to its many other opportunities, like health care at the clinic, job placement and counseling, and the potential for a Habitat house.

William pleaded to Elder Harris for help with getting into New Song Academy. One day in November 1996, Harris called William and told him he'd been accepted into New Song. "Tomorrow, I'm going to come by your house," he said.

During William's first morning at school, Susan Tibbels called William down to her office and asked him who he was. New Song Academy was a tiny school with a waiting list, and she didn't want to cause contentiousness in the community by letting someone skip to the top of the list.

"Elder Harris told me I was accepted," he said.

"No, I told him that you couldn't come in," she said.

Heartbroken, William pleaded with Susan. Susan dialed Harris on the speakerphone. Harris confidently recommended the boy. He hoped that with sufficient investment, William would become part of the next generation of leadership in Sandtown. "Susan," he said, "this is a young man you will never ever regret having as a part of your school."

"Please," said William, as he sat in a chair and cried.

"Go upstairs," Susan said. "Let's finish the school year out and see what we can do."

New Song Urban Ministries expanded quickly during the first half of the 1990s. In 1991, a health clinic began operating one day a week in the basement of the Gilmor Street building. In 1992, former president Jimmy Carter came to help build a house in Sandtown. In the wake of the publicity, Sandtown Habitat for Humanity set a goal of building one hundred houses in five years. The Enterprise Foundation offered technical support and no-interest construction loans, and after a year, Sandtown Habitat had built twenty houses, right on schedule. In keeping with New Song's dedication to empowering residents, lifelong Sandtown resident LaVerne Cooper joined Allan Tibbels as Sandtown Habitat's co-executive director. Its EDEN Jobs, an employment program, launched in 1994.

New Song's Community Learning Center expanded to serve a handful of middle-school students, with the hope that those students would get into college and return to Sandtown as community leaders. In 1996, the health center partnered with a downtown hospital, moved to a new building, and began operating full-time with Elder Harris's wife, Amelia, as the site director.

Throughout the 1990s, Elder Harris worked for Sandtown Habitat, running the program that supported families moving into Habitat rehabs. He tried to merge Newborn Apostolic Faith Church of the Trinity with New Song Community Church, as John Perkins had suggested, but it didn't last. Some members of Harris's small church left the congregation when he tried to merge with New Song. It already irritated some Sandtown residents that parking spots in their neighborhood disappeared every Sunday morning as black families who had left Sandtown for the suburbs double-parked in order to attend worship services. The growth of New Song Community Church meant that those black families were now competing for spots with white outsiders. Harris also felt slighted by New Song Community Church itself. The way he understood Perkins's "three R's," white relocators humbled themselves to a local religious leader and worked within an existing church. New Song Community Church was a member of the Presbyterian Church in America, and Harris looked askance at the denomination's focus on "church planting," comparing urban church planters to missionaries abroad. Also, Harris's wife was a preacher, and the Presbyterian Church in America didn't allow women to preach. Nonetheless, Harris believed that the two churches could overcome theological differences and worship together, despite his storefront Pentecostal background.

Harris didn't have a problem with Allan Tibbels. In fact, he had once told Allan that if white people were willing to work with them in the neighborhood, he welcomed them. Allan disagreed: he didn't want Sandtown flooded with white people. When Allan first moved to Sandtown, some members of Grace Reformed Presbyterian said they wanted to move with him, and Allan told them to stay back. After New Song Community Church was up and running, Allan discouraged any white people who approached him to talk about relocating, knowing that only the most serious believers would make the move. Harris remained dedicated to racial reconciliation, and he continued to sing and play tambourine at New Song services.

Harris's social mission remained the same as New Song's: empowering residents to lead Sandtown out of poverty. On that front, he was frustrated with the neighborhood transformation efforts being led by the city and the Enterprise Foundation. The efforts had started off well enough. The stated objective of Community

Building in Partnership sounded good on paper: a "viable, working community in which neighborhood residents are empowered to direct and sustain the physical, social, and economic development of their community." Harris attended the charettes and committee meetings that the Enterprise Foundation organized to help the neighborhood create a vision for itself, and he joined a work group on public safety issues.

Any outside group taking on a community development project of this scale faces a major source of tension, and Enterprise was aware of it. They had to help the community establish its own capacity to lead development, and that required a lot of time. But they also had to produce tangible results quickly enough to earn the kind of trust from the community that could sustain such an ambitious endeavor. Enterprise and city staff perceived diminishing interest from the community, and at the same time, they were under pressure from funders to demonstrate "outcomes." The city and Enterprise pushed onward, alienating some people in the community.

It wasn't until spring 1993 that the Enterprise Foundation, the city, and the residents of Sandtown agreed on a "blueprint." The blueprint set ambitious goals for health, education, public safety, housing, and economic development, and imagined Community Building in Partnership as a nonprofit managing it, with a majority of its board made up of residents.

The most visible part of the neighborhood transformation—housing construction and rehabilitation—started quickly and productively. By the end of 1993, Sandtown Habitat for Humanity had finished about thirty houses, and the 227 Nehemiah houses units were occupied. However, only one out of five of the Nehemiah houses went to Sandtown residents,* and the social aspects of the transformation project, such as community organizing, started to fall behind.

In November 1993, a *Baltimore Sun* article on the "urban lab" of Sandtown revealed tensions between the top-down part of the effort—the city and Enterprise Foundation's part—and the bottom-up part. The *Sun* reported from a community meeting where an Enterprise manager named Patrick Costigan was urging faster progress: "We have to do five hundred units a year," Mr. Costigan said, turning to Elder Harris, who represented Habitat at the gathering, "and we can't do it—with all due respect, with all our good efforts—by doing ten or twenty at a time."

---

*35 percent of the Nehemiah homes in Sandtown went to residents of "surrounding communities." Households with incomes as low as $11,000 were able to buy. Bock, "Hard Part Still Ahead"; also, Meyer, Blake, Caine, and Pryor, "Community Building in Partnership, Baltimore, MD."

Harris unloaded his frustration. "We've been meeting to death," he told the *Sun* reporter. "Gardens are nice, the newspaper is nice, but in three years, the folk just expect more. They're in the mode of, 'Show me or just keep on walking.'"

As all the parties tried to find a way to revitalize Sandtown without leaving its residents behind, money continued to flow into the neighborhood. About $60 million in public and private funding had arrived by the end of 1993. In 1994, the federal government chose Baltimore City for a $100 million "Empowerment Zone" program. Sandtown was in one of the zones chosen by the city, and most of the money went to economic and workforce development. By 1995, Community Building in Partnership had launched several youth programs and a community newspaper, reformed the curriculum at three elementary schools, and begun renovation of a public market on Pennsylvania Avenue.

That same year, Elder Harris read Elizabeth O'Connor's *Call to Commitment*, a book about the Church of the Saviour in Washington, DC's Adams Morgan neighborhood. The Reverend Gordon Cosby, a white preacher from Lynchburg, Virginia, founded the church in the 1940s. Like New Song Community Church, the Church of the Saviour was multiracial at its founding and housed itself in a historic city townhome. Community development was at the heart of Cosby's church. Harris made the connection between Gordon Cosby and John Perkins, and he started studying with Cosby in Washington. Before long, Harris had adapted his church's philosophy and theology to Cosby's teachings. The sky over Sandtown would be his steeple, and the people of Sandtown would be his church.

One day, Cosby asked Harris how the neighborhood transformation effort was going in Sandtown. "Not well," said Harris. "It's not working." He felt Enterprise was throwing money at the problem and rushing things. The missing link in Sandtown, Harris told Cosby, was the bottom-up approach Cosby took in the 1970s with his "Jubilee Housing" initiative. Harris felt that Jubilee Housing had "worked with people at their own level."

Harris didn't know it at the time, but James Rouse had been inspired by Jubilee Housing when he designed the Enterprise Foundation. Elder Harris had gotten to know Rouse through his work in Sandtown, but somehow their mutual connection to Gordon Cosby never came up. On April 9, 1996, not long after Harris had begun working with Cosby, Rouse died of Lou Gehrig's disease.

Harris had thought of Rouse as a dreamer with real dedication, but he didn't think Rouse had imparted his spirit to those leading the work in his absence. Those people, he felt, were not as invested in the kind of community leadership that Rouse and his mentor Gordon Cosby had treasured. They might have been building houses faster than Sandtown Habitat was, but they weren't taking the time to build relationships with the people in those houses.

A few months after Rouse's death, Patrick Costigan took a leave of absence from the Enterprise Foundation to attend graduate school. He was replaced by a bureaucrat from New York City's Bureau of Bridges. A *Baltimore Sun* article about Costigan's departure said that "progress has been slow," and that "residents grumble that home-grown leaders still are not in command of much of what happens in Sandtown."

Rouse's death and Costigan's departure were not the only transitions happening among Sandtown's big dreamers in the mid-1990s. In 1995, Mark Gornik announced his departure from Sandtown to write a book and replicate New Song's approach in New York City. In Gornik's wake, the Reverend Steve Smallman and the Reverend Wy Plummer took over as co-pastors. Smallman was white and Plummer was black.

Inspired by his studies with Cosby, Elder Harris bought a wide, vacant three-story house at 1928 Pennsylvania Avenue on the eastern edge of Sandtown in April 1995. The house stood on the corner of an unusual intersection where Pennsylvania Avenue, Presstman Street, and N. Fremont Avenue form a skinny triangle. The land in between the streets, which had an abandoned fountain, could have made for a nice park, but it was being used as an open-air drug market. Harris envisioned the intersection as a gateway to a thriving neighborhood.

In 1996, Harris left Sandtown Habitat for Humanity and started Newborn Holistic Ministries. He began renovating the house on Pennsylvania Avenue with hopes of starting a recovery home for addicted women from the neighborhood. Most weekends, William Scipio helped Harris renovate the house. William was thriving at New Song Academy. He loved the curriculum and the sense of community there. The students didn't fight him—they helped him when he needed help.

In fall 1997, William's eighth-grade year, New Song Academy joined the city's public school system. It would be run privately with public funding, but it wasn't exactly a charter school—Maryland hadn't approved those yet. The city let nonprofits propose experimental schools as a way to resolve a lawsuit over the school system's alleged failure to adequately serve disabled students. New Song Academy kept their full-day, year-round model and small classes.

When William finished at New Song, Susan Tibbels gave him an application to the Blue Ridge Boarding School, an expensive, preppy institution on a man-made lake just outside Shenandoah National Park in Virginia. William forged his grandmother's signature and brought it back. When Blue Ridge asked William for an interview, he called Harris.

"Do you mind taking me down there?" William asked.

"Are you sure you want to go all the way down there?" Harris replied.

William believed that the world as he knew it would make a statistic of him: done in by a needle or a bullet, or incarcerated, if he were lucky.

"I need this," he told Harris. "Baltimore is not where I need to be."

The school accepted William the day he interviewed, and he won a partial scholarship. Sharon Baptist Church and the family of a New Song Academy teacher ponied up, too, and William worked after school to fill in the gaps. Elder Harris stayed in touch with William, occasionally taking his mother to visit him in Virginia.

After leaving his job at Sandtown Habitat for Humanity, Harris remained on the board at New Song Urban Ministries. On December 11, 1999, he found himself at the corner of N. Gilmor and Presstman Streets for the groundbreaking of a $5.4 million building for New Song Urban Ministries on a vacant lot across the street from the Gilmor Street headquarters. Harris had lent his expertise during construction. As he looked over the scene, a swinging take on "Angels We Have Heard On High" burst from Sandtown Children of Praise, a New Song–sponsored choir.

As the mayor of Baltimore picked up a golden shovel, Harris said, "Let's dig!"

Nicole had always hated bugs. Flies buzzing near your ear, mosquitoes picking at your ankles—they were the nastiest. South Carolina, it turned out, was muggy and buggy. And it was a hot, humid day in the spring of 1996 when Nicole and her cousin Janet donned their Junior ROTC uniforms for a parade through the streets of Kingstree. Nicole's great-aunt dropped them off, and they joined up with the C.E. Murray High School JROTC battalion. Nicole and Janet marched in step, singing cadences back to their commander.

"Mama, mama, can't you see?!"

"Mama, mama, can't you see?!"

"What this Army's done to me!"

"What this Army's done to me!"

By the time Nicole and Janet finished marching, their uniforms stuck to their skin. They needed a rest. Nicole saw someone get up from a stone wall encircling a tree along the sidewalk, and she and Janet walked over to the wall and sat down.

After a moment, Nicole grimaced. "Why am I itching?" she wondered. She turned to her cousin. "Janet, what is on me???"

Ants were on her.

Nicole ran off, embarrassed, looking for a public bathroom. Janet trailed behind. When they found a bathroom, Nicole cried as she surveyed the bites all over her hands. When Aunt Candy picked them up two hours later, she tried to make a stop on the way home. "We gotta go!" Nicole yelled. When they got back to the house, Nicole ran straight to the shower.

Nicole later learned to laugh about the ant incident. It became one of her favorite stories, partly because it involved two of her favorite things about life in South Carolina: JROTC and her cousin Janet. It felt good to Nicole just to say she was in JROTC. She was learning discipline. She felt proud in the uniform, like she was somebody. Her weekends were full of drills and competitions, and sometimes she got to travel, which—now that she'd gotten a taste of it—she loved to do.

Janet was a year older, but a lot shorter. Nicole called her a "midget." Janet was fun and laid back, a little wilder and more boy-crazy than Nicole. At home, they would stay up "girl chatting" late into the night. At C.E. Murray, they ate lunch together. Nicole appreciated having an ally at her new school. It was tough being a northern city girl in a southern country school. She made a few friends, but other students antagonized her. She wondered if her tormentors were jealous. Nicole still felt she was mature for her age, and she got pretty good grades. Whatever their problem was, Nicole couldn't fight back the way she had in Baltimore City. Everyone in the South Carolina part of the family had gone to C.E. Murray, from her grandmother on down. There was a reputation at stake.

One breezy day that spring, Nicole and Janet boarded the bus to school. Janet found a seat immediately, but when Nicole tried to sit down, the boy next to the spot said, "This is my seat." Every empty seat Nicole tried to take was defended with an insult. The teasing continued throughout the spring, with one boy in particular mocking her loudly. Nicole had loved riding the yellow school bus through the country back roads when she first got to South Carolina. Baltimore City high school students rode city buses, not yellow buses. By the spring, though, the bus in the boonies had lost its charm. It was fourteen miles to school, and the bus arrived at 5:30 a.m. She had to wake up at 4:00 a.m. if she wanted to catch it in time.

Now that the students were making her life hell, she didn't want to ride the bus at all. Again and again, Nicole found herself trapped between an instinct to fight and the pressure to preserve her family's reputation. She would just shout back at the students. "You need to be quiet!" she'd yell. "Leave me alone!" Nicole eventually told her family what was going on, and her great-aunt talked to the principal. Her father, Levi, put in a call of his own, too, and the school gave her an assigned seat on the bus. The mocking continued, but the girl who sat next to Nicole defended her at the start. Or so she thought. "Don't be mean!" her seatmate said when the taunts came Nicole's way. But as soon as Nicole stood up, the girl mugged and wiped the seat, eliciting more laughs.

When Melinda heard about Nicole's troubles on the bus, she decided to bring her back to Baltimore for her sophomore year. Nicole had no problem with that. In the meantime, she kept up her studies at C.E. Murray. She had to. Her great-aunt, the teacher, was a stickler. When Nicole got back to Baltimore, she had Bs and Cs, an occasional A. She also had a lot of credits, thanks to JROTC and electives like a keyboard class and Black History. When Nicole finished ninth grade, she moved into her mother's new home in West Baltimore. In August 1996, she started the tenth grade at Frederick Douglass High School.

As a zoned school, Frederick Douglass reflected the neighborhoods it drew from: extremely poor and almost entirely black, a mockery of the U.S. Supreme Court's 1954 decision in *Brown v. Board of Education* to desegregate schools. Baltimore's school board had implemented a "free-choice" desegregation plan in 1954 following the decision, which led to more flight than integration. Eventually, the U.S. Supreme Court ruled that free-choice policies were only constitutional if they actually succeeded in desegregating a school district, but the city ignored the ruling. In February 1974, the federal government threatened to withhold funding unless the city further integrated its schools. The city would make plans to change school zones within the city, dial them back in reaction to outrage and protests in white neighborhoods, and send a diluted plan to the feds, only to see it rejected.

Despite the fact that metropolitan approaches to desegregating Baltimore schools had been floated several times—even by a mayoral candidate in the late 1960s—no such thing ever got traction. The U.S. Supreme Court's July 1974 ruling against metropolitan desegregation in *Milliken v. Bradley* put the nail in the coffin. When the federal government moved toward sanctions against the city, mayor William Schaefer filed for an injunction to stop them. An appeals court upheld the injunction in 1978, and that was that. Intensely segregated schools correlate with many factors that limit educational opportunity, like poorly achieving peers, unqualified teachers, and inferior materials and infrastructure. By the late 1990s, the Baltimore school system had the highest degree of racial isolation in the country.

Earlier on, Frederick Douglass High School had been nationally recognized for its academics. It graduated many African Americans who later came to prominence, like Supreme Court justice Thurgood Marshall, congressman Parren Mitchell, *Baltimore Afro-American* founder Carl Murphy, and jazz singer Ethel Ennis. By the 1990s, the students at Douglass were mostly poor, and the school had developed a reputation for unruliness and dropping out that pained its distinguished alumni. In 1993, the city's schools superintendent voiced disappointment in the school and closed it for two days to help teachers figure out how to regain control.

With nearly four out of ten students dropping out each year and a daily attendance rate of just 70 percent, Douglass became one of just two schools to earn an "academically bankrupt" designation from the state superintendent, and in January 1994 the state announced a possible takeover of the school. Six weeks later Douglass had a new principal, an alumnus from the class of 1966 who promised to personally work with the most troublesome students and transfer them if they kept up their nonsense. The city school system announced other changes, such as a curriculum reform that broke the school into several programs like music and JROTC. In response, the state backed off, waiting to see what kind of results the reforms produced.

A series of lawsuits soon inflamed tensions between the city and the state, and some state leaders worked toward gaining at least partial control over the city's school system. In January 1996, the state's schools superintendent added thirty-five city schools to an existing list of five—including Calverton Middle, where Nicole had just finished eighth grade, and Frederick Douglass High—threatened with a state takeover if the city failed to implement significant reforms. In April 1996, the state legislature passed a budget withholding $24 million in state aid for city schools unless the city partnered with the state on management of the system.

At the heart of the dispute was a difference in perspective. The state superintendent thought the students' problems were the fault of the schools' management. The city superintendent attributed the problems to a lack of resources. In essence, the argument was over how much money it took to help schools fix problems that poverty and inequality created.

The dispute came to a head on the campus of Frederick Douglass High School in September 1996—the beginning of Nicole's first semester there—when dozens of students, teachers-union members, and clergy rallied on the school's front lawn against the state's efforts to control city schools. "The state of Maryland has never funded our schools on an equal basis," said congressman and Douglass alumnus

Parren Mitchell. "The pattern as I see it is one in which we've continually become pawns, meaningless pawns, moved at the whim of the state of Maryland."

That October, a judge ruled partly for ACLU–Maryland in a suit against the state board of education. The state was responsible for providing an adequate education, the judge said, and Baltimore students weren't getting one. But he didn't say why, which left open the question of whether management or a paucity of resources was to blame. Finally in late November 1996, the city and state reached a settlement that included more resources *and* changes in management. The state would cough up an extra $230 million for city schools over five years. The city's school board, appointed by the mayor, would be dissolved. The state board of education would provide lists of candidates for future boards, which the mayor and governor would use to make appointments jointly.

Nicole Smith started her tenth grade year at Frederick Douglass High School in the fall of 1996, at the peak of the city-state battle. The chaos never reached Nicole inside the school's doors. Nicole liked Douglass's principal, Rose Backus-Davis, who had brought positive changes to the school climate during her first year on the job. Backus-Davis made news for hiring three former guards from the Nation of Islam Security Agency, who walked the halls in NOI's trademark dark suits and red bow ties, getting to know the most troubled students and connecting them with guidance counselors. Under Backus-Davis's tenure, outside organizations began to partner with the school, and seniors mentored freshmen.

The school wasn't perfect. In the spring of 1997, a gun fell out of a student's pants in the hallway, and the teenage rumor mill quickly spread word of an impending gunfight. Dozens of students tried to leave the building, but Backus-Davis talked them out of it. Despite the gun incident, Backus-Davis earned plaudits for restoring order in the school through a combination of discipline and caring.

With the school newly divided into "academies," Nicole had to choose between two of her passions: JROTC and music. She chose music, joining the Frederick Douglass choir. Choir rehearsals kept her busy, and the frequent performances indulged her growing yen for traveling. Other than choir, Nicole didn't care too much for Douglass. She rarely socialized, even "hooking" from the cafeteria during lunch to hang out in the bathroom with a couple of close friends.

By her junior year, Nicole was thinking about college. When she visited the school's guidance counselor to work out that year's schedule, the counselor was excited for Nicole and asked if she wanted to go away to college. She did. Nicole had never felt a part of the environment in West Baltimore. Her life revolved around her family and her singing. Her mother had instilled an appreciation of education and a love of travel in her. Nicole was still fond of Virginia, so that, she told the counselor, was where she wanted to go to college. The guidance counselor helped Nicole research scholarships.

Realizing that the courses she took at C.E. Murray in South Carolina had given her more credits than she needed at Douglass, Nicole asked the counselor if she could graduate after her junior year. The counselor asked her to stay through her senior year, but Nicole had the credits and she prevailed. She would graduate a year early.

One day Nicole got a letter in the mail from an older couple who had attended West Virginia State University. Every year the couple solicited letters from students and rewarded one with a scholarship to their alma mater; Nicole and her counselor had applied. The letter congratulated Nicole on being chosen. Nicole didn't know anything about West Virginia. She had thought plenty about *Virginia*. In fact, she had a little plan cooked up to go to school there, then stick around to live and work there too. *West* Virginia? Close enough. She accepted the scholarship. Frederick Douglass High School had been a blur—just two years, and not many classes. That was okay with Nicole. On a hot, sunny day at Frederick Douglass High School's football field in May 1998, Nicole crossed a stage in a white gown and collected her diploma.

It was a busy summer—shopping for dorm furniture, a going-away party at her mother's house. Nicole was excited to finally be out of that house, to be on her own, to make her own rules. But she was only seventeen. She was nervous about being away from her family and from the only place, apart from her year in Lane, that she'd ever lived.

In the second week of August, Nicole packed the car to the gills: clothes, TV, stereo . . . she was bringing everything. The Smith clan formed a caravan to watch the first person in their family head off to a four-year college. Nicole's mother, sisters, father, and stepmother drove six hours through the mountains to the West Virginia State University campus, which backed up to a set of railroad tracks overlooking the Kanawha River and two sylvan knobs that rose from its opposite shore.

The gaggle of Smiths parked, found their way to Sullivan Hall, and went upstairs to find Nicole's room. When they got there, Nicole got out her teddy bears. She didn't bring the entire collection; that would have filled two entire trash bags. She unpacked the six teddy bears she had brought and lined them up across her new dresser.

Nicole couldn't stop hugging her mother and her relatives as the time came for them to go back to Baltimore. And when the time came, Melinda wouldn't leave.

When all the freshmen were called to the auditorium, Melinda went right in with them and sat down.

"It's time to go," someone told her. "You're the only parent in here!"

Nicole loved dorm life at West Virginia State. Socially, she fell right in with the dorm residents, most of whom were black. West Virginia State was a historically black university, but after the state applied the 1954 *Brown v. Board* decision to postsecondary institutions, the student population swelled with white commuters. When Nicole and the other black students from the dorm went to class, they tended to sit together.

Nicole quickly fell behind academically. She slept in too much and had trouble focusing in her classes. She was put on academic probation, and when she didn't bring her grades up after a couple of semesters, the university suspended her. The school required academically suspended students to take a semester break, and nineteen-year-old Nicole moved back into her mother's Penn North house in the spring of 2000.

By the end of 1995, the workload at Broadway Services had overwhelmed Mark Lange, and he took a job with a wine distributor. Mark had sharpened his computer skills at Edison Parking and at Broadway Services by designing access-control systems that kept track of how much money and how many cars were coming in and out of a parking lot. He helped his new company build a system to take orders, send tickets to the warehouse crew, and get bottles into the trucks and on their way. He also brought in a subcontractor to install a new network, servers, and computer work stations. After two years, the company let Mark go.

While he was on unemployment, Mark started planning an information technology business called "Computing @home." When money got tight, he picked up work with an awning manufacturing and installation company and wrote his business plan at night. Eventually he got enough clients to go full-time. It didn't hurt that the turn of the millennium was approaching and small businesses were scrambling for help to patch the feared "Y2K" bug.

Mark's clients—some mortgage and medical billing companies, a couple of advertising and public relations firms—were overwhelmingly white. So was his neighborhood. So was his church, New Covenant, just down the road in Abingdon. Mark was no longer commuting to the city and interacting with people who lived there. The angst coursing through him rose closer to the surface, and he began to recognize its source.

One night in 1999 at the house on Hunter's Run Drive, Mark walked into the master bedroom, the great room downstairs visible through the French doors behind him, and saw a new message on the answering machine next to his side of the bed.

"Mark, it's Allan, returning your call."

Mark hadn't talked to Allan Tibbels in a couple of years, and they hadn't been in close contact for a long time. Allan and Susan had thrown themselves so deeply into their work in Sandtown that they rarely had time for socializing, especially not forty-five minutes up the road in Bel Air.

Mark called Allan back.

"What's up?" Allan asked.

"What's up with you?" Mark replied.

"You called?" Allan asked.

"No, I didn't," Mark said.

Allan said that someone had called while he was out and had told his assistant that he should call Mark Lange. When the assistant asked for a phone number, the person said, "Allan has my number." Mark told Allan again that it hadn't been him.

"Gorman!" said Allan. Jim Gorman was a buddy of Allan's from way back. Gorman wouldn't have known Mark's number, and he was a notorious prankster.

"How's the wine business?" Allan asked.

"I'm not in it anymore," Mark replied. "I own my own IT business now."

"You gotta come down here," said Allan. "Our systems are a mess!"

A week later, Mark drove down toward the offices of Sandtown Habitat for Humanity at 1300 N. Fulton Avenue. When he worked in the mailroom for ACME Supermarkets, where he met Betty in the mid-1970s, he had driven to ACME's distribution warehouse just a few blocks west of Fulton every day. As Mark remembered it, Fulton wasn't all that run-down in the 1970s, although his white colleagues from Towson and Woodlawn told him, "Don't get out of the car!" On this day in the late 1990s, however, there was trash everywhere—until he got close to the Habitat offices. The 1300 block was clean—thanks, Mark later learned, to a Habitat employee. Mark went inside and found Allan. They chewed the fat for a bit, and then Mark went around to check on the computer systems. They were a mess. They'd been built on a shoestring budget, and the guy who'd built them was gone. The computers were cheap. Mark cut his fingers up digging around inside of them because the metal edges were cut straight, not rolled like the ones inside the computers he was used to.

Mark visited the Sandtown Habitat for Humanity office every month or so after that to tend to problems with the computers and network. He charged $25 per hour, half his standard rate, and when he was flush, he did it for free. Mark's first impression among Sandtown residents at the office left much to be desired. He was abrasive with Allan. Allan would ask, "Can you fix it?" and Mark would spit back, "I don't know!" When Mark started tooling with the machines, employees would hear his salty interjections: "Son of a bitch!"; "Who did this shit?!"

Upstairs from Sandtown Habitat was New Song's employment placement program, EDEN Jobs. When Mark went to introduce himself to EDEN Jobs' co-founder Wy Plummer, Plummer was on the phone. Mark sat outside Plummer's office and overheard him say, "White people pluck my nerves." When Plummer hung up, Mark knocked and entered the office. Shaking Plummer's hand, he said, "I'm Mark. White people pluck my nerves, too!"

When Mark left Plummer's office to find a malfunctioning computer, he met Antoine Bennett and Gerry Palmer. Bennett and Palmer were both lifetime Sandtown residents. They'd known each other as kids. Bennett went to Harlem Park Elementary/Middle School, then spent a couple of years at Frederick Douglass High School before dropping out. Palmer was a little older, and he had let Bennett hang with his older crew. Bennett grew up on the 1400 block of School Street, an alley street near the corner of N. Stricker and Presstman Streets. Palmer had sold cocaine on that corner when he was younger. When Bennett was eighteen, he shot someone half a block up at School and Stricker Streets, and landed in prison for several years. Bennett and Palmer had since shaken the grip of the streets and had become employment counselors for EDEN Jobs. When Mark examined the computer, he quickly discovered the technical problem, one that has vexed IT workers since the advent of personal computers. "Come on, guys," he said to Bennett and Palmer. "You called me down here and the thing isn't even plugged in yet?"

New Song employees gradually warmed up to Mark. He was brusque, but he was himself; people in the neighborhood respected that. And they thought his heart was in the right place. Employees eventually let Mark in on the nickname they'd given him: "Dick Butkus," because he banged around the office like a foul-mouthed linebacker.

It had been a long time since Allan and Mark had spent this much time together, but they picked up right where they had left off. It turned out that Allan had gotten into some of the same musical artists, like U2, that Mark had without even knowing it. Their friendly battles resumed too. Mark was still more conservative than Allan was, and he told Allan that his approach to some of his more troubled Sandtown neighbors was paternalistic. But Allan was making Mark think. Mark loved that they weren't listening to each other just to be able to respond; they were listening to understand the other person and be challenged.

By 1999, Sandtown Habitat for Humanity had renovated one hundred houses. One day a construction manager took Mark on a tour. As Mark ambled down the streets of Sandtown, he realized that despite getting to know the residents who worked at the office, he hadn't really made a connection to the neighborhood. Coming from Bel Air, he was on interstates most of the way, then on the high-traffic boulevards of W. North Avenue and N. Fulton Avenue. Now he saw Gilmor Homes and the young men on the corner yelling, "Eight ball, eight ball here!" He didn't even know what an eight ball was.

In late June 2000, Mark volunteered at Sandtown Habitat for Humanity's "Build Week." Coming down every day to work on construction crews, he finally felt like he was starting to get to know the people of Sandtown. As Mark spent more and more time in the neighborhood and reconnected with Allan, he felt pulled. A white world still awaited him after every trip to Sandtown. When Mark found himself commiserating with the white neighbor about the nearby house that they believed was dragging down their property values, his angst came into focus. That tribal inclination to collude with his prosperous peers—how had that come so naturally after what he'd learned from John Perkins, from Eve, from his employees at Edison Parking, from Don Cleary and his grandmother? His conscience whirled. "Oh man, I bought it," Mark thought. "I'm everything I didn't want to be." Life wasn't about money or a house in the suburbs. Whatever he was doing, it wasn't what he believed God wanted him to do with his life. What exactly God *did* want him to do with his life is what he needed to figure out—and the need felt urgent.

Mark began to think about moving. Things were not going well in his current home. Now well into their forties, Mark and Betty had been unable to conceive a child. They tried in vitro fertilization once at the University of Maryland, but the first round, as it does for seven out of ten of couples, failed to take. It was expensive, too, and Mark refused to pay for more rounds. The in vitro failure intensified the anger with God that had been growing inside Betty. "You're not who you said you are anymore," she told God, shortly before she stopped praying altogether. "You're not the guy I read about. You don't listen. You don't do what you say you're gonna do."

Betty grew further and further away from God, and Mark became consumed with angst over his responsibility to God in this particular time and place in the world: the turn of the millennium in a Baltimore region that allowed suburban-ites like Mark to circle the wagons around their wealthy enclaves, while inner-city families watched their streets fill with blood and struggled to keep food on the table. Mark understood his angst well enough to feel a pull toward the city, but he didn't understand it well enough to articulate it to Betty. Mark and Betty withdrew from each other, their necessary interactions blurring into a years-long argument. Throughout much of 2000, Mark slept on the couch or in the spare bedroom.

In early 2001, Betty started seeing a counselor and asked Mark to join her. "We don't need a counselor," he said. "You just need to repent." After a few visits to the counselor on her own, it became clear to Betty that Mark would not be joining her. One night, she came home and said to Mark, "I think we need to separate."

Mark had already checked out. "Okay," he said.

After returning from West Virginia, Nicole found a job, commuting by bus to a cashier gig at a Giant supermarket on Edmondson Avenue in West Baltimore. She didn't get along with her coworkers or supervisors and quickly became miserable. Luckily, she found a new job at a Safeway supermarket in Southwest Baltimore. It was a much better fit.

Nicole got back involved with the family church, a Holiness congregation less than a mile down North Avenue from her mother's house. She started directing the choir there, and soon after her return from West Virginia, a young man in the congregation began talking to her. Nicole remembered him—they'd known each other at church when she was a little girl at Harriet Tubman Elementary. He told her he liked her, and she was shocked at his overture. Back in the day, boys in the congregation used to antagonize her. They thought she was mean and called her names, making fun of her for being thin and dark-skinned. She was thrilled by his attention and gave him a chance.

There was no magic moment, no violins played—but after a few months, they were still together. By December, however, the relationship was over. As Christmas approached, Nicole noticed her period was late. Her coworkers at Safeway had noticed her eating more than usual. "Girl, you pregnant!" one of them said. After work one day, she stopped by a pharmacy to pick up a pregnancy test. She went home and took the test. The telltale strip materialized.

Nicole called her friends from work. "Oh my God!" she said. "Guess what? It really says I'm pregnant!"

Nicole held off from telling her mother. All of her life, Melinda had told the girls she'd tear them up if they got pregnant. "I'll beat you with a brush like in that *Claudine* movie," she had told them, referencing a scene in which Diahann

Carroll, playing a single mother of six on welfare in Harlem, bawls and shrieks at the news of her young daughter's pregnancy while pinning her down on a bed and pounding her with a hairbrush.

When Nicole went to her first appointment at a clinic, she told her mother she was going to the store. Melinda was on the phone when Nicole returned.

"Ma, I gotta tell you something," she said.

"What?" Melinda asked, cradling the receiver.

"You might want to sit down for this."

"Let me call you back." Melinda hung up the phone.

"Ma, I'm pregnant."

Melinda wasn't going to beat her twenty-year-old. She didn't even get upset.

"I'm gonna have a grandbaby," she said.

Melinda got back on the phone and called everyone she knew.

Barbara Samuels wished she had a toothbrush.

It was 3 o'clock in the morning, and Barbara sat near the Amtrak gates at Union Station in Washington, DC. She'd been dropped off after midnight, and the last train to Baltimore had already departed. Had she brought a toothbrush, she would have just found a place to crash in DC and gone right back to HUD's headquarters in the morning for another interminable day of negotiating with lawyers from the U.S. Department of Justice. Alas, she had not brought a toothbrush, so she waited for a train to take her through the dawn to Baltimore, where she would change her clothes, brush her teeth, take a shower, and catch a train right back to Washington.

It was March 1996, over a year since ACLU–Maryland had filed *Thompson v. HUD*. Barbara and her colleagues were very close to offering hundreds of black Baltimore City public-housing residents a chance to move to the most prosperous parts of the surrounding counties. All that stood in the way were a few details to be worked out with the Justice Department.

It was remarkable that they'd come so far, considering the politics of the time. When ACLU–Maryland filed the original complaint in January 1995, it was just four months after U.S. senator Barbara Mikulski had ended HUD's Moving to Opportunity program. Republican and Democratic opponents of Moving to Opportunity had just been elected to local and national offices. One of them, a Republican state delegate from Baltimore County named Robert Ehrlich, had won a seat in the U.S. House of Representatives. In November 1994, the GOP turned over forty-nine seats in the House and eight in the Senate, taking control of both chambers of Congress. That December, Newt Gingrich, who would soon be elected Speaker of the House, said, "I would argue that you could abolish HUD tomorrow morning and improve life in most of America."

In March 1995, ACLU–Maryland filed a motion for a preliminary injunction to slow down replacement housing for Fairfield Homes and Lafayette Courts. The motion was long, with personal stories of plaintiffs' lives in public housing and a history of racial segregation in the region. In the motion, ACLU–Maryland asked U.S. District Court judge Marvin J. Garbis to ban replacement housing in any census tracts with more than a 25 percent minority population, a poverty rate above 10 percent, or more than 5 percent HUD-assisted housing—numbers straight from the Citizens Task Force on Metropolitan Housing. (Census tracts, which typically contain several thousand people, provide the U.S. Census Bureau with stable geographical units for statistical comparisons.) In June 1995, ACLU–Maryland filed a second motion for a preliminary injunction that added the other high-rise projects to the list: Lexington Terrace, Murphy Homes, and Flag House Courts.

On August 19, 1995, thousands of people gathered just east of downtown to witness the demolition of the high-rises at Lafayette Courts. Five years after the Housing Authority of Baltimore City had commissioned the task force on public housing towers, the agency was finally bringing some towers down. On a cloudy day, with temperatures in the mid-80s, Barbara stood on Central Avenue near Dunbar High School, surrounded by former residents of Lafayette Courts. There were conflicted feelings in the crowd. Too much suffering and young death had transpired in those towers, sure, but there had also been community. Barbara marveled at the six eleven-story buildings. Stripped to their bare bones and with their windows knocked out, the buildings appeared as a mosaic of colors and wallpaper prints: an imprint of lives lived.

Just after noon, tiny flashes crackled throughout the buildings. The ground rumbled, and a sound like a train on an elevated track followed as each building folded. Where six brick behemoths had loomed over East Baltimore since 1956, a line of trees huddled over a dust-enshrouded pile of rubble.

It saddened Barbara to see hundreds of homes, each of which had provided a roof for many different families, disappear in an instant. Not that she felt any better about where those residents would ultimately be moved. Barbara found the process of relocating Lafayette's residents to be rushed. Most residents of the Lafayette Courts towers had been relocated to other projects, including high-rises like Flag House Courts. Barbara heard that those moves were wreaking havoc by creating new battles over drug-dealing turf. Some former Lafayette Courts

Ella Nixon and her grandchildren, 11th floor, 130 N. Aisquith Street, one of the high-rises at the Housing Authority of Baltimore City's Lafayette Courts complex. (1994) *Courtesy of the Maryland Historical Society, Jones.234.19*

Residents of Lafayette Courts watch the implosion of a public housing tower. (1995) *Courtesy of the Maryland Historical Society, Jones.252.19*

residents were given Section 8 certificates to relocate, but it wasn't easy to find a landlord who would accept Section 8 outside of the city's poorest neighborhoods. Of those who had found housing on their own with Section 8 certificates, hardly any were leaving the city.

While the housing authority continued to place public housing residents in highly segregated neighborhoods, pressure built on the agency to stop the flow of Section 8 certificate-holders into city neighborhoods with growing black populations, like Patterson Park in the southeast—where over seven hundred families with Section 8 certificates moved into a one-square-mile area during the first half of the 1990s—and Hamilton in the northeast. Residents complained about crime spikes and deteriorating housing, and their neighborhood leaders blamed the Housing Authority of Baltimore City for lax oversight of negligent Section 8 landlords. One city councilman—a brash thirty-two-year-old named Martin O'Malley, from the tenuously middle-class Third District—sent a vituperative letter to housing commissioner Daniel Henson. "A great many residents of northeast Baltimore believe that you are actively using Section 8 vouchers as an aggressive blockbusting tool," O'Malley wrote. "Let me be as direct as the english [sic] language will allow. Are you flooding northeast Baltimore with disproportionate numbers of public housing residents?"

Barbara hoped Section 8 vouchers could help former high-rise residents move as part of a settlement, and some parts of O'Malley's district met the criteria for non-impacted census tracts that ACLU–Maryland considered acceptable for public housing residents. Now there were forces working against the desegregation of public housing not just in the suburbs but *inside* the city as well.

Nonetheless, by the time the Lafayette Courts towers went down, Barbara and her colleagues at ACLU–Maryland were nearing a deal with the city and HUD. By September, ACLU–Maryland, the city defendants, and HUD had mostly defined the terms of a settlement that would allow hundreds of families to move to census tracts throughout the region with low poverty rates and low proportions of minority residents. Just three years after Baltimore's housing advocacy community had seized on the notion of housing mobility, a plan was nearly in place that would echo the *Gautreaux* remedy developed in Chicago.*

---

*During negotiations, Barbara and her colleagues also pursued "equalization" provisions that they hoped would bring public housing up to par with other areas of the city regarding municipal services like policing, trash collection, and staffing at youth recreation centers. They suggested pursing equalization through the allocation of Community Development Block Grants from HUD.

After the *Baltimore Sun* published an article about the tentative settlement, Baltimore county executive C.A. "Dutch" Ruppersberger told the *Sun* that he would "do everything in [his] power" to upend any settlement, and the county hired a Washington, DC, law firm to help. Republican U.S. congressman Robert Ehrlich told the *Sun* that the agreement was "quota-driven, race-based, Section 8-style housing policy at its worst" and lobbied HUD chief Henry Cisneros to back off the agreement and talk to Baltimore County officials. Even Democratic congressman Ben Cardin, who represented a part of the county just northwest of the city, pleaded with Cisneros to reject the settlement plans. In response, Barbara Samuels raised the stakes, telling the *Sun* that if the settlement was scuttled, ACLU–Maryland might pursue litigation to force the construction of new public housing in the counties.

Just after finishing several days of nearly round-the-clock negotiations to forge a tentative settlement, ACLU–Maryland staff and officials from Baltimore City and HUD now had to present a unified front to suburban officials led by Baltimore County's officials and its lawyers. Barbara told the *Baltimore Afro-American* that Baltimore County had "an even more evasive history" than the city did of refusing to allow subsidized housing outside of poor black communities. Ruppersberger pointed out that Baltimore County had a faster growth rate of its black population than any other county in America. And it wasn't fair, he argued, to send poor residents out of the city on special Section 8 certificates when his own county had a Section 8 waiting list of ten thousand households.

In December 1995, Barbara Samuels met in the Maryland state capital of Annapolis with representatives from the city and the counties, as well as with Betsy Julian, HUD's acting assistant secretary for fair housing. It was Julian who had written the law journal article on public housing desegregation lawsuits that had influenced Barbara several years earlier. In a room with imposing dark wooden walls, Barbara listened as the counties tried to persuade Julian to modify the settlement. When someone requested limiting the ages of children in families who used certificates, Julian had a self-described "hissy fit." Her son went to a public high school back in Dallas, and his black friends hung out at her house all the time. Julian sternly insisted that the counties could not ban teenagers. ACLU–Maryland did, however, agree to a Baltimore County request to limit the number of certificates that could be used there.

A week later, HUD Secretary Cisneros made some concessions to the five surrounding counties and sent the proposed *Thompson* settlement to the

U.S. Department of Justice for review. The parties capped the number of families who could move to Baltimore County at sixty per year, about one-quarter of the 1,342 special certificates over the six-year term of the proposed settlement. HUD also helped the counties trim their own waiting lists by sending each an extra five hundred regular Section 8 certificates. The settlement sent more money to the Housing Authority of Baltimore City for relocating high-rise residents, and it pushed the deadline for demolishing the last of the high-rises from 1997 to 2001. Because the counties had complained about the cost of any problems that might accompany new families, the settlement added funding to a mobility counseling program meant to help families locate rentals and adjust to their new communities. Lastly, any apartment complexes with more than one in five tenants getting government housing assistance—e.g., Section 8 certificates—would be off limits for *Thompson* certificates. When the settlement finally came out of the Justice Department almost two months later, Barbara considered it watered down and less enforceable, so there was another round of all-day negotiations.

Which is how Barbara Samuels found herself, *sans* toothbrush, at Union Station in the middle of the night.

Finally, the Justice Department signed off, and on April 8, 1996, Barbara drove some of the plaintiffs to HUD headquarters in Washington for the unveiling of the settlement. ACLU–Maryland had benefited from the firepower of some DC law firms during negotiations, but Barbara was still exhausted, and she got misty-eyed when the plaintiffs shared their reactions with the press.

HUD promised $300 million for the plan—over $100 million more than they'd previously committed. The seventy-five-page "partial consent decree" laid out in excruciating detail how the sites at the four high-rise projects would be redeveloped and where the replacement units for the towers and Fairfield Homes would go. The decree kept 1,100 replacement units in the city—over one hundred in Sandtown, chosen for its promising revitalization plan. Two-thirds of the 1,100 city replacement units would stay on the former high-rise sites. The on-site units would reflect the low-rise "mixed-income" layout that HUD was beginning to embrace, with market-rate units to make up half of the new housing stock at the Flag House Courts and Murphy Homes sites. Some public housing residents in the Lexington Terrace redevelopment would even get a chance to purchase their units.

The decree created over 1,300 special Section 8 certificates for use in non-impacted areas: less than 26 percent minority population, a poverty rate of no more than 10 percent, and no more than 5 percent HUD-assisted housing. These certificates came with counseling and moving assistance, and the counties were promised $750 per certificate to provide services for each arriving household. Another eight hundred households would be part of a vaguely defined "home-ownership demonstration program" in non-impacted areas. The decree also demanded that the city develop forty "hard units"—essentially, scattered-site public housing—in non-impacted areas.

Over 90 percent of the non-impacted census tracts were outside of Baltimore City. The decree placed requirements upon the surrounding counties, including production of reports detailing "impediments to fair housing" and a certification by each county that it would affirmatively further fair housing. HUD reserved the right to take enforcement actions against the counties if they failed. Despite these prescriptions, leaders from the surrounding counties expressed acceptance of the settlement. A lawyer for Baltimore County said residents wouldn't even notice.

Congressman Ehrlich, however, said he'd keep trying to defund the partial consent decree, and he penned an op-ed in the *Baltimore Sun* two weeks after the settlement was announced. "Suggesting that the only way to improve the lives of black Americans is to ship them off to live in white neighborhoods," he wrote, "is an insult to blacks everywhere."

On June 25, 1996, Judge Garbis signed off on the settlement. A month later, Barbara Samuels stood on Martin Luther King Boulevard and listened while public officials and members of the clergy heaped praise on Mayor Schmoke before demolition of the five high-rises at Lexington Terrace began. U.S. housing secretary Henry Cisneros pointed out that Schmoke would be the first American mayor to see all of his city's high-rise housing disappear.

"Your leadership has made it clear to us what must come forth from this rubble," state housing secretary Patricia Payne said to Schmoke minutes before the towers crumbled: "Communities of opportunity and hope."

In January 1997, demolition began on Fairfield Homes, nine years after the housing authority had decided to relocate its residents. On July 3, 1999, Mayor Schmoke, who had declined to seek reelection and was six months from leaving office, presided over the demolition of Murphy Homes. Flag House Courts, the only property from the *Thompson* settlement still standing, was scheduled to come down early in the next mayor's administration. With the coming completion of mixed-income projects on the sites of the former high-rise projects, the physical landscape of Baltimore's public housing would be changed forever.

There was no such finality in sight for the public housing residents who had left the towers. For years, they had awaited full implementation of the partial consent decree. A full two years passed before the housing authority signed a contract with Baltimore Neighborhoods, Inc., to run the mobility voucher program.

In the meantime, demand for the mobility vouchers mounted. In 1998, Barbara went to Dunbar High School in East Baltimore for an information session with public housing residents about the special certificates, and Ike Neal, one of the *Thompson* plaintiffs, met her outside. "Ms. Samuels, Ms. Samuels," he said, "they're coming from all over. It's packed!" Neal had lived with his wife, Veronica, and three sons in Lafayette Courts, where he was a block captain and tenant organizer. He spoke at the meeting, as did housing commissioner Daniel Henson. Henson thought the mobility vouchers were useless, since regular Section 8 certificates were good anywhere a housing authority accepted them and many public housing residents wanted to stay in the city. But he made a good faith effort at marketing them.

At the end of 1998, after Henson had finished his outreach workshops, Baltimore Neighborhoods, Inc., had 1,233 applications for the special certificates. But by August 1999, only sixty-seven families had been awarded certificates, and fewer than half of those families had found a place to rent.

The city and the plaintiffs filed motion after motion in court. At the end of 1999, the plaintiffs and the defendants remained at an impasse. While ACLU–Maryland complained to the court about the housing authority's implementation of the decree, Henson complained that it was precisely the actions of the plaintiffs' counsel that was making implementation so difficult. That December, a new mayor took office: Martin O'Malley, who as a city councilman had excoriated Henson over Section 8 in northeast Baltimore four years earlier. O'Malley announced that he would not reappoint Henson, and Henson resigned.

In September 2000, *Thompson v. HUD* entangled O'Malley right in his own backyard.

Caroline Queale lived with her husband and two young children on Northway Drive, a skinny, tree-lined street near the county line. It was the quintessential northeast Baltimore house: a 1931 Craftsman bungalow with a big dormer, a wide porch, and a little stained-glass window on the side.

Next door, an identical bungalow had gone vacant. Caroline's parents thought about buying it, as did a local school teacher, but it wasn't listed for sale. Why, Caroline wondered, would it sit vacant for two years?

On Sunday, September 17, 2000, Caroline saw two men next door. "Do you guys know anything about this house?" she asked them. They handed her the agenda for the next weekly meeting of the city's Board of Estimates, which votes on major city expenditures. The agenda said the board would consider a loan to the housing authority for the purchase and renovation of fifteen houses for use as public housing. Eleven were in northeast Baltimore. One was the house next door, a foreclosure owned by the U.S. Department of Housing and Urban Development.

All Caroline knew about public housing was what she saw on the news and on her drive through East Baltimore to her job on the Johns Hopkins medical campus. It wasn't pretty. Caroline knew nothing about the *Thompson* partial consent decree, which required the city to put forty scattered site units in non-impacted areas.

Caroline and some of her neighbors attended the Board of Estimates meeting, and the board postponed their vote. Mayor O'Malley, whose northeast Baltimore home was just down the road from many of the proposed addresses, was out of the country, so City Council president Sheila Dixon pushed the housing authority to quickly explain the scattered site plan to residents, and a local community organization planned a meeting for October 2 at a local senior center.

Caroline made it inside the senior center, but the room quickly exceeded its capacity of two hundred. Outside, angry people stood on the lawn and sidewalk, some crowding at the front door and demanding entry. Police told the organizers to cancel. Inside, a man in glasses and a shirt and a tie walked to the front of the room. "The problem was we had a violent encounter out front here with a large group of people, and I'm not gonna endanger the safety of this type of meeting," he said.

Barbara Samuels was also inside when the news came. She saw the anger that night, yet when the meeting was rescheduled for the next night at the Hamilton Middle School auditorium, she decided to go. So did Caroline. The meeting was scheduled to start at 7:30 p.m.

Local television stations quickly latched onto the controversy, running footage of the previous night's debacle during their five o'clock and six o'clock news programs. The broadcasts interviewed white and black homeowners from Hamilton. "This neighborhood is already racially mixed," said a white man in a floppy fishing hat. "We've done it on our own."

"It's just that's what we moved away from before," said a black woman who lived next door to one of the proposed scattered site units.

The capacity of the school's auditorium had been overbilled. Outside, police officers held back several hundred people. At points, they pumped their fists and chanted, "Let! Us! In! Let! Us! In!" Inside the packed auditorium, some of the mostly white crowd fanned their faces with signs that read "NO SEC 8" and "HUD & CITY FAIL THE POOR, THE MIDDLE CLASS PAYS AGAIN."

Onstage, an electric fan blew toward a glum-looking group of representatives from the Housing Authority of Baltimore City, among them Dana Petersen, who had represented the city in *Thompson v. HUD*. Here and there, audience members stood and screamed at the officials, faces contorted in rage, and dozens took a turn at a podium with a microphone. "I would like to know why I do not see Roland Park, Mount Washington, Guilford, or Homeland as targeted areas," said a woman, as she waved documents related to the scattered site plan. The crowd roared. Barbara Samuels took a turn at the microphone too. Amid angry shouts, she placidly noted that anyone could call her.

The scene rattled Caroline Queale. She knew the city's plan meant to move just a dozen families to her corner of the city, but from the crowd's reaction, one might have thought it was thousands. People complained about crime and "drug families," and someone speculated that the Ku Klux Klan had come from rural Cecil County to stir the pot. Caroline wondered whether a race riot was going to start.

Mayor O'Malley arrived late to the meeting and approached the podium in a tie and with white shirt sleeves rolled to his elbows. "The fact that this even went to the Board of Estimates in the fashion it did was a mistake," O'Malley said.

The mayor promised to ask a federal judge to let the city amend the partial consent decree. "Don't put a noose around our neck and tie us to some reality when our neighborhoods have already changed," he told the crowd, grasping his own collar. By the time he finished, the boos had turned to cheers. And by the time a week had passed, housing commissioner Patricia Payne had announced her resignation. O'Malley named Paul Graziano, a New York City public housing official, to the post.

Shortly after the meeting, Caroline Queale got an invitation to an October 11 meeting at a community mediation center. In attendance were Barbara Samuels, Ike Neal, and a handful of residents of northeast Baltimore, some of whom were veteran social justice activists. Everyone—including Caroline—had been unnerved by the October 3 meeting.

Ike Neal impressed Caroline. The retired sixty-three-year-old and his wife had both worked while raising their three boys—Ike as a school custodian, Veronica in a cafeteria. As a block captain in East Baltimore, Ike had swept up trash and dirty needles every week. Caroline didn't even realize that the Neals lived in public housing. When she grasped that, it shook her perspective. Neal made the minimum wage and took the bus to work. In Lafayette Courts, he showed his children how to go flat on the floor at the sound of gunfire. Public housing wasn't always temporary, Caroline realized. Ike Neal lived in public housing because he couldn't afford to live anywhere else.

The Neals had managed to rent a house just north of Patterson Park on a Section 8 voucher, but that wasn't a whole lot safer. Neal dreamed of mowing his lawn at a house like the one next door to Caroline. Caroline thought the Neals would make ideal neighbors. But now that Mayor O'Malley was promising to fight the *Thompson* decree in court, the Neals wouldn't be going anywhere.

Thanks to Ike Neal, public housing was no longer a faceless institution to Caroline. And from Barbara Samuels, she learned the history of Baltimore's segregated landscape. Caroline resolved to find a way to make the forty units happen. The group from the meeting at the mediation center named itself Northeast Good Neighbors and started drafting a proposal to bring public housing units to northeast Baltimore in a way that would be palatable to the community.

By January 2001, Mayor O'Malley was still chafing at the partial consent decree. "I don't buy the argument that to live in a neighborhood more than 26 percent African-American is [to live in] a bad neighborhood," he told the *Sun*. "That's bullshit." Yet he had already begun backtracking on his promise to try to amend the decree.

Feeling guilty about setting the controversy in motion, Caroline Queale wanted to give O'Malley an out. As she and Northeast Good Neighbors worked on the proposal, they relied on advice from Barbara Samuels about keeping it in line with the partial consent decree. Caroline believed that with Barbara's legal expertise and real substance from the community, Northeast Good Neighbors could bring public housing residents to her corner of the city in a way that would please both the court and the people who had packed Hamilton Middle School's auditorium.

Caroline dragged her kids to church services, potluck dinners, and community meetings to help her Northeast Good Neighbors colleagues in drumming up support for a housing proposal. Caroline told people about Ike Neal, whom she was getting to know well. During these visits, Caroline saw a better side of the community than she had seen at the raucous October 3 meeting. They explained their worries: They didn't want to take on a "social experiment" amid a spike in shootings and foreclosures. Some had witnessed an increase in violence when Section 8 certificate-holders moved nearby. Black homeowners who had left poorer neighborhoods for northeast Baltimore resented the idea of the housing authority doing high-quality renovations of single-family homes for public housing residents when they themselves were getting by with old kitchen cabinets and window air conditioning units. Many residents felt resentful that rich north Baltimore neighborhoods like Roland Park, Guilford, and Mt. Washington seemed untouched by the partial consent decree.

One idea concerning implementation of the proposal seemed to persuade many of Caroline's neighbors: having a nonprofit—not the housing authority—buy, renovate, and rent out the homes. Vincent Quayle, who ran St. Ambrose Housing Aid Center, lived in northeast Baltimore and was well respected. What if the city got forty HUD foreclosures in Northeast for cheap, and Vinny fixed ten of them up for the decree and the rest for selling at market rate?

Caroline kept making the rounds collecting signatures for a petition to welcome ten public housing families, and Northeast Good Neighbors refined the proposal that Barbara Samuels had helped draft. In addition to the plan to rehab houses for public housing and market rate in Northeast, a nonprofit would rehab and rent ten homes in the north and northwest parts of the city, and the housing authority would help twenty families settle in apartment complexes across the city's non-impacted neighborhoods. In July 2001, Caroline met with housing commissioner Paul Graziano in person, handing him a petition with 450 signatures and a letter from a group of local religious leaders called the Northeast Ministerium promising to "undertake some form of mentoring and/or sponsorship" of public housing families moving to the area. A month later, Graziano wrote to Queale that the proposal "contains viable concepts" and that housing authority staff had already talked to nonprofits about implementing it.

Worried about a quickly approaching deadline in the partial consent decree, Graziano purchased homes with reserve funds in the summer of 2002, and shortly after, HUD signaled approval. That August, Graziano met with northeast Baltimore community representatives. The city had picked twelve addresses so far, seven in the northeast. All were HUD foreclosures, Graziano said, and two were already paid for.

This was a remarkable moment in the course of the partial consent decree. The city had finally engaged the community and gotten public housing into an area that had shown furious resistance. But it was too little, too late. The deadline to fulfill the obligations of the partial consent decree was just four months away: Christmas Day, 2002. In June 2000, Baltimore Neighborhoods, Inc. had told HABC that it couldn't meet the goals of the mobility counseling program, and HABC had terminated their contract. A "special master" appointed by Judge Garbis to work with communities and the parties to the lawsuit to implement the decree wrote in 2000 that "progress on the desegregative elements of the Decree has been extremely slow."

By October 2002, families had been chosen to occupy five of the hard units, but, in a letter to attorneys on both sides, Judge Garbis expressed disappointment:. "Not one of the families has been identified so that they can make their arrangements for the move," Garbis wrote. "In view of the 'history' of the matter and the fact that the City Defendants have let a five year period for compliance pass without fulfillment, there can be no further extensions or excuses."

Judge Garbis had assigned the case to a magistrate judge in May 2001, hopeful that the entire case could be settled. By January 2003, magistrate judge James Bredar was newly hopeful. "I have now concluded that it may be useful to re-engage in settlement discussions," he wrote to all parties. Bredar scheduled settlement conferences in his chambers at the U.S. District Courthouse downtown for March and May 2003.

November 2003 marked thirty months since Judge Garbis had sent the case to Magistrate Judge Bredar for settlement negotiations. There had been hours and hours of meetings and conference calls. "It was as substantial an effort as I have made to achieve a settlement of a case in the six years I have been a magistrate judge," Bredar told the *Baltimore Sun*, but he was giving up hope. The case would have to be heard in a courtroom.

In December 2003, it was.

THREE

Crossing the Lines

NICOLE SMITH ADORED "LOVE," A SONG BY R&B ARTIST MUSIQ SOULCHILD THAT came out on Christmas Day in 2000. "Love," the first verse went, "so many things I've got to tell you, but I'm afraid I don't know how." You couldn't tell whether he was singing to God, or a child, or a lover. It was a little like Stevie Wonder that way, as was the jazzy chord progression on a vintage electric piano.

Nicole pressed the Record button on her tape recorder and hummed the acrobatic melody to "Love." Then she played back the recording with a pair of earphones pressed into her belly.

Nicole felt like she was going to be a great mom, especially with the support at home of Melinda, who had raised three children of her own and had cared for many others. Nicole felt she had a second mother in Linda Smith (no relation) of DRU/Mondawmin Healthy Families, a nonprofit that guided young West Baltimore mothers from conception through a child's fifth year. "Miss Linda" was older than Nicole, with a loving demeanor. She taught Nicole to record songs, books, and nursery rhymes and play them into her belly. She visited every month to talk Nicole through what happens in each trimester. She accompanied Nicole to prenatal clinic appointments. And she came to the hospital for the birth of Nicole's son, Joseph, in August 2001. When Nicole brought Joe home, Miss Linda taught her anything she wanted to know about caring for a baby. Afterward, Miss Linda helped Nicole figure out her new life as a single mother, pointing her to social services and work leads.

Nicole gave baby Joe her bedroom at the back of the second-floor hallway in Melinda's house and moved in with her youngest sister in the room next door. The two windows in Joe's room overlooked the roof of an industrial building and framed a wide sky over West Baltimore. The southwestern exposure poured light over the walls that Nicole had painted the soft blue of a robin's egg.

It was a comfortable enough existence for Nicole, living with her mother, sister, and Joe, and having Miss Linda come around to show her the ropes. But Nicole had always wanted to live on her own. Where to live, though? The plan to finish college and work in Virginia wasn't going to happen, at least not yet, and her earnings as a Safeway cashier couldn't cover rent anywhere better than east or west Baltimore.

After two years, Nicole found out that the older one of her two sisters was coming home from college early—and pregnant. Her urge to move grew. The house that Melinda Smith had bought in Penn North may have seemed big to Nicole after leaving the little Rayner Avenue house in 1995, but when her sister moved in and had the baby, the house started to feel constricting.

In 2004, Miss Linda once again came through, helping Nicole apply for the city's public housing and Section 8 waiting lists. Technically, city Section 8 certificates were "portable" to other jurisdictions. However, Section 8 renters were disproportionately concentrated in the city. It was getting harder for Section 8 users to find a place in the city, too. In the early 2000s, there was massive demand for housing assistance in poverty-stricken Baltimore. The city's housing authority would never meet it even operating at full throttle—and it was nowhere near full throttle. About fifteen thousand families crowded the city's Section 8 waiting list, and a March 2001 audit by the U.S. Department of Housing and Urban Development had called the Housing Authority of Baltimore City's Section 8 program "barely functional." The program had fallen months behind in paying landlords when a panic over the Y2K bug forced the agency to temporarily shutter a mainframe computer and process payments using typewriters. The dysfunction at the housing authority had left over one thousand Section 8 vouchers sitting on the shelf.

Getting to the top of the waiting list did not guarantee getting a place to rent. The city's private rental market was tight, and when the housing authority demolished Hollander Ridge, a one-thousand-unit high-rise in East Baltimore, it offered Section 8 as a relocation option, sending even more vouchers into the market. Some of the more Section 8–friendly landlords maintained their houses poorly, having flipped multiple properties expressly to attract Section 8 renters. If you got a Section 8 certificate, you had to lease a unit in two to four months or you had to reapply. The 1996 partial consent decree in the *Thompson v. HUD* suit was supposed to relieve some of the pressure by authorizing 1,342 vouchers by 2002 that would be restricted to areas of low-minority and poverty concentrations—mostly outside the city. But by 2001, only a few dozen families had moved to these non-impacted areas. That number had only increased to around two hundred by 2004.

Nicole waited for good news from the housing authority. But it wasn't just Section 8 that had a long waiting list. The list for public housing units was 5,000 families long—even though half of the city's 2,800 scattered site houses sat vacant. When her mother had found herself waiting for public housing in the 1980s, at least the high-rise projects had offered a quick way off the waiting list. But the high-rises were gone. And her oldest sister and baby nephew now occupied the blue-walled room.

Nicole, now twenty-three, shared a bedroom with her youngest sister. Joe, now a toddler, slept in a bed with her.

In the fall of 2003, Barbara Samuels marked twenty years in Baltimore. In October 1983, she had left southwest Virginia to join Legal Aid in Baltimore. In the city's public housing complexes, her poor black clients had told her of the shoddy maintenance, ruthless drug dealers, hostile police, untreated illnesses, and inadequate schools. Poor white residents tended to live scattered around metropolitan regions and largely escaped that kind of concentrated misery.

By October 1993, thanks to her work with Susan Goering and other mobility advocates, Barbara had discovered the provenance of residential segregation: policymakers had deliberately created segregated spaces in which inequality could not help but flourish. She left Legal Aid for ACLU–Maryland, where she diagrammed the social structures that continued to bind the Baltimore region to its state of segregation. In *Carmen Thompson v. U.S. Department of Housing and Urban Development et al.*, she presented a sampling of policies and practices to the courts as unjust.

Now it was October 2003, and while the city and HUD had physically transformed the former high-rise projects, the 1996 partial consent decree was nearly a year past its original deadline but had produced few opportunities in white suburbs. As demanding as it was to monitor the partial consent decree, Barbara now had to prepare for the biggest housing discrimination trial of the decade: *Thompson v. HUD*, in which several Baltimore public housing residents were suing Baltimore City, the city's housing authority, and the U.S. Department of Housing and Urban Development.

Judge Marvin Garbis scheduled opening arguments for the first day of December 2003 and hoped to wrap up by Christmas. On the morning of December 1, Barbara and her colleagues arrived at the U.S. District Courthouse in downtown Baltimore. But it was another trial in the same building that held Baltimore's attention that day. Prosecutors accused two wannabe rap impresarios of running a heroin ring out of a recording studio. While the defendants sat in judge William D. Quarles's courtroom, perhaps wishing that they had named their studio something more discreet than "Stash House Records," Barbara watched Garbis ascend the bench in Courtroom 5C. Garbis had smooth silver hair and dark eyebrows that rose up and out in the manner of a great horned owl.

"It's quite obvious this is a significant case, and that it is a case that has a great deal of public interest," the judge said in a slightly gruff voice, sitting under a panel of dark wooden pilasters and an eagle-bedecked U.S. District Court seal. "The attorneys in this case have acted with the highest degree of civility and with professionalism."

Garbis could flatter and joke and turn on a dime from knotty legalese to colloquial banter. He could also be fierce and provocative when he wanted to yank a meandering lawyer back to a discernible point or to burn a coat of sophistry off an argument.

"This case involves two kinds of claims," the judge said. The simpler claim covered acts motivated by a clear intent to discriminate by race. "Let us be clear, this was the Schmoke administration," he said, invoking Baltimore's first elected black mayor.

The second type of claim drew on obligations triggered by earlier intentional discrimination (such as the *de jure* segregation that divided the projects until 1954). "Duties were established," Garbis said. "Duty to desegregate, to take affirmative steps toward eliminating the vestiges of the prior discrimination."

In his opening argument, plaintiffs' counsel Chris Brown said the defendants carried out a pattern and practice of discrimination for decades using "three interrelated tools." The first tool was siting: they placed most public housing in poor black neighborhoods and backed down from opposition to projects in white areas. Second, Brown said, the city turned the wrecking ball disproportionately upon places where African Americans lived, without creating sufficient replacement housing. Third, the housing authority "selectively applied" its protocol for assigning tenants to housing projects "so as to help basically white tenants and hurt basically black tenants."

Following Brown, federal defendants' counsel Diane Kelleher cast HUD as an agency reborn. "The plaintiffs want to go back and litigate the past," she said. "The evidence will show that many of the policies and problems that the plaintiffs complain about have already been fixed by HUD." The agency had made a "clean break." It was now "far from a do-nothing agency content to take a hands-off approach to Baltimore City." In fact, the city's housing agency "often chafed under

HUD's close supervision." Even HABC's improvements, she said, "are directly attributable to actions taken by HUD." Kelleher claimed that HUD in fact did affirmatively further fair housing, and that the city's public housing population was so disproportionately black as to preclude real integration. "Demographic changes and individual choices," she said, explained any lingering segregation.

Local defendants' counsel Thurman Zollicoffer gave his city an enthusiastic, chauvinistic defense. Right away, he asked the judge to "make sure the record reflects that HUD says [Baltimore's housing authority is] not the most troubled." He noted that "the plaintiffs are going to produce expert witnesses who are academics, who are not from Baltimore, and have an agenda. Local defendants will produce witnesses who we'd like to think are vested in this great city." Zollicoffer didn't mention it, but in the local defendants' reading of the law, every claim brought by the plaintiffs required proof of racially discriminatory intent, even the Fair Housing Act's mandate to affirmatively further fair housing—in other words, to proactively dismantle existing barriers to fair housing. Accordingly, he portrayed the city as innocent of bias even back to the 1950s. "While Baltimore, like the rest of this country, suffered through its own racial issues," he said, the city ditched its public-housing segregation policy voluntarily right after the U.S. Supreme Court's 1954 ruling against school segregation in *Brown v. Board of Education.*

Barbara Samuels entered the trial confident in the case she had laid out on paper in the plaintiffs' Statement of Facts. To tell the story in court, though, she needed social scientists and historians to make decades of institutional discrimination appear incontrovertible. HUD's counsel had their own academics to counter that narrative. They also planned to call the public housing director from HUD's Baltimore field office, Bill Tamburrino, to explain how he had coerced HABC into adjusting their bureaucratic policies and practices until they started generating less discriminatory outcomes. Samuels needed to make sure *her* story came out of *their* witnesses.

Mark and Betty Lange listed the Hunter's Run house in April 2001 and decided they would split the proceeds. After that, it would be "You go your way, I'll go mine."

Mark knew where he did *not* want to live: in the suburbs. He wasn't sure, however, where he *did* want to live. Both the city and the country beckoned. He pictured a shack on the Shenandoah River in Virginia.

Within a week, the Langes received several offers for the house, and they entered into a contract with a sales price of $168,201. They'd bought the house for $111,775 in June 1987. Buying a new home in a safe, white suburb had served them both well. The difference alone—$56,000—was much higher than the median sale price for a home in Sandtown. Because they had been paying down the mortgage for years, Mark and Betty would each walk away with about $50,000.

Betty moved quickly, putting in an offer on a 1,320-square-foot, ten-year-old townhouse in Foxborough Farms, a neighborhood much like Hunter's Run located just east of Bel Air. The sale price was $117,000. With "five figures" burning a hole in his pocket, Mark discovered that his dream of a shack on the Shenandoah was more realistic than he'd thought. During the month before the settlement on the Hunter's Run house, Mark searched online for properties in the Virginia boonies. He could get a lot of land for a little cash. He might not even need a mortgage.

The house search invigorated Mark. He felt like he was on a new adventure and that wherever he ended up would be where God wanted him to be. While Mark searched for properties in western Virginia, he hired a realtor to look for houses in Baltimore neighborhoods like Bolton Hill and Highlandtown. Mark considered Sandtown, too, but most of the listings required too much rehabilitation. He needed a home office ready immediately in the city to keep his computer business rolling.

Mark homed in on a listing for a century-old, three-story brick townhouse in Barre Circle, a pocket of historic homes just west of downtown. The house was on Scott Street, a block from Pigtown, an integrated, working-class neighborhood of small rowhouses. During a HUD "dollar house" program that Mayor Schaefer brought to town in the 1970s, homesteaders had rehabbed houses in Barre Circle. The house on Scott Street had a basement where Mark could set up a computer repair workshop and a nice office space on the third floor. The owner was a realtor who told Mark that he could rent the place until they worked out a contract.

Mark was still doing some work for Allan Tibbels at Habitat, and he concluded that God wanted him in the city. He gave up on his Shenandoah daydream. On Memorial Day weekend in 2001, a box truck and a moving van sat in front of the house on Hunter's Run. Betty took the dog and cat and most of the furnishings in the moving van and schlepped to Foxborough Farms. Mark took the living room set and an oak table from the breakfast nook to his rental home on Scott Street. Within forty-eight hours, Mark and Betty had settled on the sale of the Hunter's Run house in Bel Air.

The day after, Betty settled on the Foxborough Farms house. And Mark went to sleep in the city for the first time since he was a one-year-old.

Courtroom 5C on December 2 sounded like a graduate-level course on research methods. Independent variables were being controlled for. Maps of census tracts were being dissected. Statistical analyses like multiple regression were being debated. Someone actually stopped to spell the word "multicollinearity" out loud.

The lecturers—or, rather, witnesses—were Karl Taeuber, professor emeritus of sociology at the University of Wisconsin, and Rolf Pendall, associate professor of city and regional planning at Cornell University. Both had written research reports for the plaintiffs on public housing segregation in Baltimore. Taeuber explained that the Housing Authority of Baltimore City's abandonment of *de jure* segregation in 1954 had been ineffectual, and he showed the present-day effects of *de jure* segregation. Pendall analyzed the role of race in the housing authority's decisions about where to site public housing.

In the cross-examination, HUD counsel Alison Barkoff spotted mistakes in Pendall's data, some of which Pendall acknowledged. "In light of these errors, are you willing to withdraw your testimony?" Barkoff asked Pendall. He declined to.

City lawyers went after the plaintiffs' next academic witness. Arnold Hirsch's renown stemmed from his book *Making the Second Ghetto: Race and Housing in Chicago, 1940–1960*, which studied how policymakers and their white constituents had contrived to pen immigrating African Americans into racially isolated city neighborhoods. For the trial, Hirsch wrote a report called "Public Policy and Residential Segregation in Baltimore, 1900–1968." Hirsch took a confident and accusatory tone in the report:

> Slum clearance, public housing, and urban renewal, to cite the pre-eminent examples, permitted authorities to act on their segregative impulses in new and more effective ways. Local officials, with explicit state and federal support, eagerly seized the new tools placed at their disposal to uproot, consolidate, and contain Baltimore's exploding African American population in the central city. Not only was there no question that such programs reflected [the] white consensus from the 1930s through the mid-1950s, but there is no indication that they ever seriously considered any other course. If there were any shift in policy at all, it involved perceptions of white needs and desires.

At the end of his report, Hirsch wrote, "Baltimore's status as a 'hypersegregated' city was no historical 'accident,' nor were the hands involved in its creation merely the proverbial 'invisible' ones associated with an unfettered market. They are there to be seen if only we care to look."

Dwight Stone, an attorney for the city, read excerpts from a speech that HABC executive director Oliver Winston had given to his entire staff in June 1954, to Hirsch. Winston implied that he would fire subordinates who disregarded the new desegregation policy. "It marks a turning point where every American will be able to read the Declaration of Independence, the Constitution, and the Bill of Rights without ever a twinge of conscience or a moment's doubt," Winston said of the policy. "To be playing a role in bringing this to pass should be looked upon more as privilege than a problem by each of you."

Mustering his civic pride, Stone asked Hirsch, "Have you ever heard of the Sidney Hollander Foundation?"

Hirsch had not.

"Do you know who [Walter] Sondheim is?"

He did not.

"Do you know who Judge Watts is?"

He did not.

In 1955, Stone explained, the Hollander Foundation gave the Housing Authority of Baltimore City its annual award for "an outstanding contribution toward the achievement of equal rights and opportunities for Negroes in Maryland." Watts and Sondheim served on the award jury. Watts was one of Baltimore's first black judges, and Sondheim was one of Baltimore's most revered twentieth-century civic figures.

On redirect, plaintiffs' counsel Chris Brown asked Hirsch for "history's judgment" on the housing authority's 1954 desegregation plan. "There's consensus among some of the historians," Hirsch replied, ". . . that freedom of choice was not successful as a tool for dismantling the dual system."

Nicole's desire to leave the city intensified as she watched her neighborhood go downhill. More young men were hanging on the corners than when the Smiths had moved in. More fights spilled out of the bar across the street. Two recent shootings on her block had rattled her. One night in 2004, a man in a parked Lexus shot from his window, hitting a young man in the leg. The gunman got out to shoot again but missed. Nicole had Joe in her arms when she witnessed the other shooting. A commotion from the bar had drawn her, as it often did, to the window. A man and a woman took bullets in that incident. The man tried to walk away, and his friends and family surrounded him, screaming "No!!!" Nicole noticed that everyone went silent when the police showed up.

Nicole recognized one of the shooting victims as a former Frederick Douglass High School student, and one of the shootings took place just after her youngest sister had walked in the door. "Bullets don't have a name," her mother said. "They can hit anyone."

Gun violence wasn't new to Nicole. As a child in Murphy Homes, she once heard three loud cracks, ran to the window, and saw a man lying in the street. But it was her family's crowded house that finally drove Nicole to start apartment hunting. Her sister and nephew were still sleeping in Joe's old room.

Nicole started her search in Columbia, where the best friend of her aunt lived. On rent.com, Nicole took an interest in a neighborhood called Running Brook. Apartments there were affordable compared to other Columbia neighborhoods, but at $900 a month, they were too expensive for her. She made $14 per hour at Safeway, and despite being scheduled five to six days a week, she wasn't making full-time hours. Renting in Columbia would have taken nearly half of her income before taxes.

Penn North it was to be, at least until Nicole got to the top of the housing authority's waiting list. In the meantime, she restarted her postsecondary education. Baltimore City Community College's campus was just a couple of miles away, on the other side of Mondawmin Mall from Frederick Douglass High School. She chose the same major she had pursued at West Virginia State University: nursing.

Even if Barbara Samuels's expert witnesses established a convincing chain of discriminatory actions and intent stretching from the mid-twentieth century up until the early 1990s, she would still need to demonstrate how it impacted her clients and the class they represented, so she called several black public housing residents to the stand.

Only they could make the harm felt, the claustrophobia of neighborhoods like Sandtown and Johnston Square manifest, the accumulating disadvantage of residing there pellucid. A succession of public housing residents described their living environments, often with tears in their eyes: Dead bodies in Lafayette Courts. Armed robberies in Patterson Park. Racist slurs in Rosedale. On December 9, Barbara questioned Carolyn Sherry Bryant, a working mother who lived in a scattered site house on N. Monroe Street in Sandtown. Bryant wept as she described life in Sandtown. Barbara asked about the demographics where Bryant lived. "The racial makeup of my neighborhood is all black," Bryant replied.

"Do you know anyone who's moved from public housing to a mostly white neighborhood?" Barbara asked.

"Yes, I do," Bryant said. "She moved to Columbia."

Dana Petersen Moore cross-examined Carolyn Bryant for the city. Three years earlier, the hollering of the white crowd at the Hamilton Middle School auditorium had rattled Moore. She and several housing authority officials had gone there to make the case that public housing belonged in all neighborhoods, not just in poor black ones. In her cross of Bryant, Moore tried to make the case that public housing was good for places like Sandtown.

Moore told Bryant about her husband, Ralph, whom she'd married in early 2002. Ralph fondly remembered growing up on Mosher Street in Sandtown. Drawing to the surface a theme that emerged repeatedly throughout the trial, Moore challenged the idea that inner-city public-housing tenants needed an escape plan. She embraced the potential for a place like Sandtown to be transformed into a desirable neighborhood.

"Would you like to see the city or the Housing Authority or both or even HUD put money into that neighborhood, into the neighborhood that you're in, to fix the physical structure, to fix the houses, to fill the vacant land, to rebuild the community so that everyone enjoyed living there?" Moore asked Bryant. "To fix the community?"

"If you're saying like to fix the community as where it will not [have] people outside selling drugs, that the kids that you're moving into the neighborhood wouldn't have to see, or at least maybe put speed bumps down Monroe Street so we wouldn't have as many accidents, then, yes. I would like to see the Housing Authority do that, and then beautify the neighborhood and clean up the vacant houses and lots," Bryant said.

Mark Lange didn't bring much from Bel Air to his new home on Scott Street in Barre Circle. For a kitchen table, he used the oak table from Hunter's Run. He put a television with surround sound in the back room. He slept on the floor for the first couple of weeks, until he got a mattress and a frame. In July 2001, Mark finally purchased the house, putting $33,500 down and taking out a $52,000 mortgage.

He rarely left his neighborhood, much less the city. He could get whatever he needed on foot—even his bank was just half a block away. Most of his business clients were now in the city. Friends and family visited, sometimes parking on his street to attend Baltimore Ravens football games at the team's nearby stadium. Despite its historic charm, the neighborhood intimidated some visitors. When Mark's brother Jeff visited, Jeff's son asked, "Why are there bars on the windows? Can we go home now, Dad?"

Neither Mark nor Betty had ever lived on their own. The stillness of an empty house calmed Mark. Betty also enjoyed the peace and quiet after years of arguing, but she couldn't help wondering what Mark's new home looked like. One day at work, she told a colleague about the house. Together, they drove to Barre Circle. Mark was not home; an electrician who was working there offered to show them the house. The house was fourteen feet wide in the front and twelve feet wide in the back, and the top story only had one room. It looked tiny to Betty.

Sandtown, now just two miles up the road, exerted an even greater gravitational force on Mark. Susan Tibbels often invited Mark over to eat dinner with her family. Mark insisted to Susan that he wasn't lonely, but he kept going. Susan was a great cook, and Mark had been losing weight in reaction to his own meager efforts in the kitchen at Scott Street.

Every Sunday, Mark worshipped with the New Song congregation at "the Mansion" on N. Gilmor Street. The Reverend Thurman Williams had become the pastor in 2000. Like Mark, Williams grew up in the suburbs and started in parachurch work—in his case, a Young Life ministry in Towson. Like Mark, he had read Dr. Perkins's writings. Like Mark, that experience drew him to an urban church—in his case, Faith Christian Fellowship in Pen Lucy, a neighborhood near Memorial Stadium, and then to New Song. Williams's theology also lined up with Mark's. Both Faith Christian Fellowship and the seminary Williams had attended were part of the Presbyterian Church in America. Williams was black and Mark was white, but it seemed like everything else synched.

Williams blew Mark away. "This guy is like John Perkins and Francis Schaeffer rolled into one," he thought.

A lawsuit is often akin to a jigsaw puzzle. The plaintiffs place pieces of evidence until the picture they want the judge to see emerges. ACLU–Maryland's puzzle on behalf of public housing residents, with all its claims and theories, was too enormous to take in all at once. But one could visualize the individual pieces, the purported sins of Baltimore's housing authority and elected officials over the course of six decades: A school building in Canton that would have become public housing but for white opposition. A fence erected around the Hollander Ridge complex to appease racists across the city line in Rosedale. Poor white Baltimoreans filling out public housing applications, searching for "Brooklyn Homes," "O'Donnell Heights," and other project names that told them they'd be among their own kind.

But where was the U.S. Department of Housing and Urban Development in this puzzle? ACLU–Maryland had some clear shots at the city, but HUD was vulnerable primarily through its reaction to things the city did or failed to do. In the plaintiffs' telling, HUD's role was that of an enabler. Sometimes the city felt emboldened in an allegedly discriminatory practice because HUD did not disapprove. Sometimes HUD expressed disapproval and the city didn't listen.

At one point, plaintiffs' counsel Chris Brown neatly distilled this perception for Judge Garbis. "I guess the thumbnail sketch of our position is, whites were being protected in essence by the system as applied—not necessarily as understood by the mayor or the commissioner, but the system as applied," he said.

Another attorney for the plaintiffs, Susan Podolsky, reinforced HUD's role in this arrangement: "If the system in place is perpetuating segregation, then it's a constitutional violation whether it—"

Garbis interrupted. "Then it's HUD's violation, too."

"It's both," Podolsky said.

To portray what she saw as HUD's culpability within that system, Barbara wanted to use HUD officials' own admissions. If the city's deeds comprised most of the plaintiffs' puzzle, HUD's words filled in the rest: emails, speech transcripts, depositions, crude mimeographs from decades past.

On the first day of the trial, Susan Podolsky had called Elizabeth Julian, who had served at HUD under the Clinton administration, first as deputy general counsel for civil rights, then as assistant secretary for Fair Housing and Equal Opportunity. Julian testified that Henry Cisneros, HUD's Secretary at the time, admitted HUD's role in creating and perpetuating residential segregation. "That was the position of the department," Julian testified, "that we had been party to this, to the segregation that existed in public housing, and that we had a responsibility to do something about it." Secretary Cisneros and others in the department, Julian testified, wanted to resolve cases like *Thompson v. HUD* "in a manner that affirmatively reflected fair housing" and not "defend the indefensible."

Barbara's next chance to put HUD's admissions on the record would be when Bill Tamburrino, the director for public housing in HUD's Baltimore field office, took the stand. First, though, came direct examination from HUD's attorneys, eliciting a portrait of Tamburrino as a stern overseer pulling a chaotic, mismanaged, and recalcitrant city housing authority into line with its civil rights obligations. Tamburrino threatened to put the Housing Authority of Baltimore City's long-bollixed Section 8 program into receivership. Tamburrino and his colleagues with HUD's regional office hectored the city agency over its mismanaged waiting list, warning the housing authority that their process for assigning tenants to projects was inappropriate and could result in white applicants skipping ahead on the list for the whitest projects. He and his colleagues at Baltimore's HUD field office required the city to put one hundred of the three hundred Fairfield Homes replacement units in non-impacted areas, and when the city's housing commissioner asked HUD to waive that requirement, his office and HUD headquarters unequivocally rejected the request. Tamburrino even went to Anne Arundel and Baltimore Counties to request changes to policies that had hindered city holders of Section 8 certificates from finding apartments outside the city. Baltimore County, for instance, only held Section 8 briefing sessions once a month.

"I perceived that that practice was not appropriate, that the Baltimore County housing agency needed to make an adjustment, and I asked, perhaps threatened, that that be changed," Tamburrino testified. "And I understand now that those briefing sessions are much more frequent—I believe they're conducted weekly now."

Tamburrino came off as someone who knew the discriminatory potential of those practices and worked to quash them. Barbara intended to show that HUD didn't do *enough* to coerce Baltimore's housing authority and was, therefore, a participant in the denial of her clients' civil rights. When her turn came to cross-examine Tamburrino, she grilled him about HUD's oversight of the housing authority's tenant-assignment policy.

In 1954, the Housing Authority of Baltimore City had announced that it would desegregate its projects, but twelve years later Brooklyn Homes, O'Donnell Heights, and Claremont Homes remained 100 percent white. HUD pressured the city to take action, and the city broke its projects into geographical quadrants, allowing residents to indicate a preference for a particular quadrant rather than picking a particular project. The east quadrant contained just two projects, both white. In 1981, both of those projects remained more than two-thirds white, and Tamburrino's office sent the Housing Authority of Baltimore City a letter saying HUD had noticed a quirk in the housing authority's tenant-assignment policy that allowed applicants to "decline an unlimited number of units" without losing their places in line.

Barbara brought up the letter and asked Tamburrino if he recognized at the time that the city's tenant assignment system could have exacerbated segregation in Baltimore's public housing. Tamburrino referred Barbara to the letter itself.

"That's included in the first sentence of the third paragraph, yes," he said.

Barbara then listed further contacts between HUD and the Housing Authority of Baltimore City regarding tenant assignment in 1989, 1992, 1995, 1997, and 2003.

As Barbara built her case for ineffectual oversight on HUD's part, Tamburrino made one qualification along the way: the city's housing authority had handled the waiting list well in 1995 and 1996.

That left twenty years during which it might not have.

Strings hung from white and purple balloons all over the ballroom at a catering hall in northwest Baltimore. Joe, now almost four years old, got hold of some string and sprinted around the ballroom. His white shirt was buttoned up to the top, the gold tie he'd worn was who knows where. With Joe was his little cousin, who was just learning to walk. The string had gotten stuck under his cousin's arm, trapping the balloon behind his back. Like a dog chasing its tail, the toddler spun in circles trying to grasp it, then tumbled to the ground. Joe ran in larger circles, emitting one high-pitched squeal after another. Nicole sat at a nearby table in a pink blouse with a white collar and a puffy boutonniere.

"Joe," said Nicole, wincing. "Joe! JOE!"

Every summer, DRU/Mondawmin Healthy Families held a "graduation ceremony" for the parents in the program. Nicole was sad to leave: Miss Linda had stuck by her for years. The ceremony started with a parade of impressive women. A mom who'd just joined the program dazzled the audience with her powerful singing voice. Another young woman did a dance routine—she'd danced with gospel legends Cee Cee Winans and Kirk Franklin and had modeled on the cover of a teen magazine. Then the family support workers invited their families up to receive commemorative plaques. There were proud, supportive words for the mothers—and for one dad, the first father to come through the program. One woman had gotten engaged. Another now had a house. Nicole didn't have a boyfriend. She still lived at home.

Then Miss Linda walked up to the microphone to introduce Nicole. "She has a good family," Miss Linda said, Nicole at her side. "Her mother's back there." She spoke proudly of Nicole's studies at Baltimore City Community College and Joe's enrollment in a pre-kindergarten program. "In five years, she has accomplished so much," Miss Linda said. "She has her own car. She still stays with her mother, that's okay."

A few chuckles arose from the audience. Nicole felt hurt, and tears came to her eyes. So many accolades for the accomplishments of those other women—how far had she really come? But she knew Miss Linda meant well, and Miss Linda went on to show her love for Nicole.

"This is a celebration for me," she said. "I'm so proud of her, and I'm so glad to be in her life. We can give her another hand."

The audience applauded. Miss Linda walked back to the Smiths' table, one hand carrying a bouquet of flowers for Nicole, the other hand leading little Joe. Nicole followed, her arms full of gifts in purple wrapping paper.

Once Bill Tamburrino finished testifying, HUD attorneys called four experts in a row over the course of three days. Peter Phipps asked the first, University of Michigan historian Robert Fishman, what he thought of Arnold Hirsch's testimony and expert report.

"I think Professor Hirsch, I would say, is a better historian of Chicago than he is of Baltimore," Fishman replied.

HUD attorneys used Fishman to introduce doubts about what they considered to be the plaintiffs' selective rendering of Baltimore's housing history. While Fishman found white opposition to the original Gilmor Homes site to be tragic, he questioned what the Housing Authority of Baltimore City realistically could have done for black residents living in slum conditions. Under the "terrible weight of this squalid housing," Fishman said, the agency's choice was to "either build within these designated black areas or build nothing." Urban renewal, Fishman said, made sense at the time. Planners expected it not just to replace slums with "vastly superior" housing, but also, like James Rouse's Baltimore Plan, to pressure private landlords into modernizing their properties. Fishman also cited opportunities for black Baltimoreans in the private market: the lines of segregation moved outward over time.

"Baltimore is remarkable among American cities for the ability, especially the black middle class, to escape the older, the pre-1945 color lines, and to expand into middle class housing which was good housing," he testified.

The next day, December 10, demographer Shelley Lapkoff criticized the plaintiffs' focus on the presence of public housing in predominantly black neighborhoods. Sure, she pointed out, only 6 percent of public housing was in neighborhoods with a below-average black population *now*. But over a third were at the time their sites were chosen; the population of those neighborhoods had simply changed over time. In the expert report Lapkoff submitted, she argued that the presence of nine out of ten scattered site units in highly segregated neighborhoods did not necessarily reflect malevolence. The point of the scattered site program was to reduce vacancy, and that's where the vacant houses were. After Lapkoff left the stand that day, University of North Carolina urban and regional studies professor William Rohe testified for the federal defendants. Rohe's report pointed out that in 1961, nearly half of Baltimore's public housing units were in projects that had families of both races—nearly twice the rate nationally.

With their data, the three professors clouded the plaintiffs' portrayal of a constricting, hypersegregated public-housing landscape. On December 11, University of California at Los Angeles geography and statistics professor William Clark analyzed the motives of those who had created that landscape. Nothing the government did, he claimed, was responsible for the concentration of poor and black residents.

"I think the evidence points to the role of economics and preferences," said Clark, "and the models that we've run suggest that discrimination in general is a small proportion of the explanation for the patterns that we see."

Betty wasn't talking to God, but she was talking to a Christian counselor. The counselor tried to help her move past what she liked to call her "desert period," or "wandering period." He gave Betty instructions for getting back in touch with God: Tell Him exactly what's wrong. Pretend He's sitting at your kitchen table. See if He responds.

At her new townhouse, Betty took the counselor's advice. Afterward, she felt God gradually revealing Himself to her in various ways. A lunch group at work started talking more about God, and she became close with some of the members. Betty decided to go back to church for the first time in years. She cast around for a congregation to visit.

On a Sunday in October 2001, Betty went to worship at Harford Community Church, a nondenominational congregation in a crossroads town called Creswell. The pastor's name was Allan Gorman.

Allan Tibbels had a friend named Jim Gorman.

That was interesting.

Betty didn't want to feel alone, so she sat in the middle of a row, hoping other parishioners would settle near her.

No one did.

Pastor Allan preached about a West Baltimore neighborhood called Sandtown where another Allan was doing amazing work in God's name.

Really, now.

Betty sensed God speaking directly to her. All alone in her row, she felt like a spotlight shone on her. It was her first trip to church in about a decade. She had picked one church out of all the churches in Maryland, and it ended up being the one where they were talking about Allan Tibbels and Sandtown. Betty had kept in touch with Mark by phone. Mostly they talked about loose ends they needed to tie up, and other surface issues—Mark would tell her when Home Depot had something on sale, since they were both filling up their houses. But Mark did mention along the way that he'd been worshipping at New Song Community Church and dining with Allan and Susan Tibbels on Sunday nights. Now God was trying to tell her that she belonged at New Song too.

"No," Betty thought, "we always did what Mark wanted to do—I'm not going to New Song."

When former housing commissioner Daniel Henson and his old boss, former mayor Kurt Schmoke, took the stand, city attorneys played up their stars' homeboy credentials.

"Mr. Henson, good afternoon," said city solicitor Thurman Zollicoffer when Henson took the stand. "I'd like to start with you telling the court where you grew up."

Henson said he grew up in Poe Homes on the westside. Other than two years in Philadelphia, he'd lived his six decades in Baltimore City. He went to school in the city, and attending Morgan State College, he said, was the first time he'd left West Baltimore.

For Henson, the segregated westside had not been defined by the misery evoked throughout the trial. It was defined by role models who worked hard. "Living around me were people who had automobiles, who wore suits and ties," Henson said of his childhood. Seeing teachers and other role models on his street was the norm to Henson. Visiting Lafayette Courts and Lexington Terrace during his first days as housing commissioner, he quickly learned that that was no longer the case.

He resolved to bring the towers down and create in their place a community that welcomed all classes. "And I felt that in the mixed income environment," Henson testified, "at the very least they would have the opportunity to see people across the street from them who looked like them, who got up in the morning and went to work every day."

Zollicoffer noticed Henson made no mention of race in developing public housing. "Does race play any factor?" he asked.

"You can try to predict the income of people by the price that you put on the houses," Henson said. "But you cannot predict the race of somebody by the mere fact of building the house."

By the time of the trial, Henson had achieved his goal to some degree. HUD's HOPE VI program favored mixed income communities, and the replacements for Murphy Homes and Flag House Courts were mixed income.

"Was it possible to create a desegregative, or a non-segregated community in the HOPE VI environment?" Zollicoffer asked.

"Just in hindsight, probably not," Henson said. "Baltimore is a city of either black neighborhoods or white neighborhoods." Baltimore, he said, had a "segregated housing market" because the arrival of black families reliably triggered white flight. The best he could do, Henson said, was to design for economic diversity.

The day after Henson's testimony, Kurt Schmoke took the stand. Once again, counsel played up their witness's local roots. Schmoke had grown up on the segregated westside. He went to Public School 60, Garrison Junior High, and Baltimore City College High School. "And I understand that for a brief period of time you maybe even played football there with Mr. Thompson, our courtroom clerk?" asked city attorney William Ryan.

"For purposes of full disclosure, that's true," Schmoke said.

When Schmoke discussed the demolition of hundreds of vacant scattered-site units, William Ryan played with a bit of the cognitive dissonance that the trial had offered up: white lawyers accusing a black mayor of racial discrimination in a black city.

"Did you have any intent in making the decision to demolish those units, to make low-income housing unavailable to African-American families because of their race?" Ryan asked.

"No," Schmoke said.

"Okay. What was your intent?"

"The intent of knocking down vacant houses was to improve the neighborhood."

Rotting "vacants" helped no one, Schmoke argued. Why not put parks or even new housing in their place? Renovating vacants in poor neighborhoods was also a noble goal to Schmoke. "Having residents in those homes was viewed by the community as a plus," he said.

Once Schmoke defended his overall strategy of using scattered-site public-housing development to kindle revitalization in neighborhoods like Sandtown and Johnston Square, the questions turned to specific accusations of discrimination. The plaintiffs had criticized his decision to abandon the renovation of School 47 because of opposition in white Canton, but Schmoke said he heard no racial animus expressed. Rather, he said, neighborhood parents wanted a playground on the site.

In cross-examination, Chris Brown asked Schmoke, "Is it a fair summary of the School 47 situation that the white neighborhoods of the area got a playground, while 24 poor black families were denied housing in a non-impacted zone?" Schmoke disagreed, calling it a "net positive for the city." Yes, Canton got a playground, but in Johnston Square, he believed, those families got good houses with loads of jobs nearby at the Johns Hopkins medical campus and good bus lines to take them to other jobs.

City attorneys asked both Schmoke and Henson if they had perpetuated segregation. Both denied it. "Ridiculous," Henson said. "What I did was to attempt to rebuild our city in a way in which it would continue to grow." In fact, Henson was sore at ACLU–Maryland for keeping the city from building new housing for its poor residents. He brought up ACLU–Maryland's successful appeal of Judge Garbis's decision to allow senior housing at Hollander Ridge even though it was in an impacted zone, something *verboten* in the partial consent decree. The appeal ruling came days after the city had demolished the whole complex. "We thought doing a continuing care village was a significant benefit to the city and to the housing authority inventory," Henson said to the plaintiffs. "The ACLU stopped this process. I still think it's a good idea."

Henson said he'd wanted to listen to neighborhood residents when it came to public housing. He pointed to the Sandtown transformation effort, which incorporated the vision of neighborhood residents. As a result, the project went beyond housing to incorporate support institutions like health care, jobs, and education. It built "the human infrastructure of a community," Henson said. "Poor people aren't stupid. I mean, poor people just don't get asked a lot. If you open them up and begin to ask people what they want their community to be like, they will tell you."

So far in the trial, place-based revitalization and mobility programs had both emerged as laudable goals. In the city's telling, Baltimore was too broke to do both. Schmoke and Henson reinforced the perception of a city doing the best it could with what little it had, in a jurisdiction with far more than its share of poverty compared to the rest of the region.

"What we were looking for was decent, safe housing for people," Henson testified. "And at some point we were simply looking to be able to put a roof over people's heads[,] with the waiting list being what it was in the early and mid-'90s."

———

Melinda's younger half-sister lived around the corner from the house in Penn North and often came to visit. One summer day in 2006, Nicole and her aunt stood on the sidewalk outside the house. Nicole told her aunt how much she wanted to move out of her mother's house.

"I'm on the list for Section 8," Nicole said. She'd been on the list for almost three years.

"Have you ever heard of Quadel?" her aunt replied.

Quadel was Metropolitan Baltimore Quadel, the local branch of a consulting firm that handled the 1,342 special *Thompson* vouchers for the Housing Authority of Baltimore City. The city hoped Quadel could breathe new life into the court-mandated effort to move public housing tenants out of poor, segregated neighborhoods. The first firm to handle the vouchers, Baltimore Neighborhoods, Inc., had placed just thirty-two families between September 1998 and November 2000. Baltimore Neighborhoods, Inc. told the housing authority that it couldn't meet the program's goals, and the agency terminated their contract a month early for "failure to perform." Dissatisfied with the proposals that followed from other organizations, the housing authority solicited a proposal from Quadel, which had handled vouchers for Chicago's "Housing Opportunities Counseling Program." Quadel insisted that it be allowed to administer the vouchers, not just provide placement and mobility counseling. An audit in March 2001 had shown HABC's deficiencies in voucher management. By the summer of 2006, Metropolitan Baltimore Quadel had moved 586 families to non-impacted areas in the city and surrounding counties.

Nicole had not heard of Quadel. Her aunt had applied and been accepted, but said she had declined to participate in the program, deciding that she didn't want to move to the county. Nicole, of course, had already searched for apartments in Columbia, and she had left Safeway to work the floor and registers at Kohl's, a newly opened department store in Timonium, just a few miles north of the city line. County living was fine with her.

Nicole didn't jump on the Quadel lead right away. School and work were in flux. Nicole switched her focus at Baltimore City Community College from nursing to early childhood education, and then she left Kohl's for a job at a car title company in Baltimore County. Nicole no longer had a car of her own at that point, so she took a forty-minute ride on the region's light rail system each way.

It was 2007 when Nicole finally got Quadel's number from her aunt, made the call, and asked how she could move to the county. She filled out an application.

Quadel rejected it.

———

For their grand finale, the city's attorneys brought Walter Sondheim to the stand. At ninety-five years old, Sondheim was old enough to make trial observers feel like they were inside the room while civic leaders were making consequential decisions in the 1950s. Sondheim had occupied many of those rooms himself. He had helped James Rouse found the Greater Baltimore Committee in 1955, and he'd had the ear of every mayor. The *Baltimore Sun* once called Sondheim "the consummate public servant."

Sondheim served as the chairman of the housing authority's board of commissioners from 1951 to 1963, but it was his service on the city's school board, starting in 1948, that made his reputation. In 1952, a group of black Frederick Douglass High School students applied to the "A" engineering course at the city's well-regarded Polytechnic Institute, which was all white at the time. They were rejected, and the Urban League appealed the decision to the school board. *Plessy v. Ferguson*'s "separate but equal" was the standard then. Thurgood Marshall spoke to the board, saying that no matter the resources poured into Douglass, its students would never get opportunities equal to those available to graduates who carried Poly's prestigious reputation. Marshall knew this challenge would highlight the absurdity of the separate but equal doctrine, and put the school board on the spot.

On the stand, Sondheim reminisced about the episode and recalled the school board president under whom he was serving in 1952.

"The Urban League . . . appealed that decision to the Board of Education: Roszel Thomsen, later Judge Thomsen on this bench here," Sondheim said.

Sondheim's mention of former school board president Roszel Thomsen triggered one of the most memorable moments of the trial. Judge Garbis pointed to an oil painting in a corner of the courtroom. It was a portrait of a kindly looking older man with silver hair and spectacles, the knot of a red tie peeking out of his black robe, warm light reflecting off his ruddy cheeks, closed fists gently resting on the pages of an open law book. It was Judge Roszel Thomsen.

"There he is, Mr. Sondheim," Garbis said. "His picture's right there."

If the city's strategy was to paint over the plaintiffs' depiction of six decades of government discrimination with a rendering of benevolent civic leadership, they couldn't have been handed a more powerful image.

Sondheim continued his story. "Judge Thomsen was president of the Baltimore City School Board at the time, and I was a member," he said. "And we had a very tense and difficult hearing, and the board voted not unanimously to admit these young men to the Poly 'A' course, which caused considerable stir at the time."

Sondheim had voted to admit the boys to Poly, a courageous act in 1952. Two years later, Roszel Thomsen left his spot as school board president to become a judge in the U.S. District Court of Maryland. Sondheim took Thomsen's place as president of the school board the very same week that the U.S. Supreme Court ruled in *Brown v. Board*. Sondheim brought desegregation to a vote on June 3, 1954, less than three weeks after the Supreme Court ruling. The board voted unanimously to desegregate. Shortly afterward, someone burned a cross on Sondheim's lawn.

The vote was remarkable, one of the first in the nation. But as important as it had been, Sondheim testified, he wanted to draw a distinction between that decision and the housing authority's decision just weeks later to follow suit.

"One could say the school board did this in response to the Supreme Court," Sondheim said. "The housing authority did this on a more voluntary basis."

Betty liked the serenity that had come with her separation from Mark. She wanted to enjoy this time with just herself and God. But she did need to call Mark. He was still on her health insurance, and open enrollment season was approaching.

She spilled.

"I have some news for you," Betty said.

"What?" Mark replied.

"I've reconciled with God."

Mark was silent.

"You still there?"

"Yeah. What does that mean?"

"I'm talking to God now and I'm praying and we're okay now."

Betty explained everything: her visit to Harford Community Church, how the counselor was helping her work things out with God. Then she heard Mark weeping.

"You gonna say I told you so?" Betty said.

"No."

They talked for five hours, both of them apologizing for various offenses. Betty remembered a list of things she'd taken to a counseling session that she had wished Mark would apologize for. Mark covered nearly all of them during the phone conversation without Betty even bringing them up. Mark also agreed to see the counselor.

"You name the date and time, and I'll be there," he said.

Mark went to the counselor alone a couple of times. He told him that he felt he'd come home at New Song and couldn't live in the suburbs. When the couple went together, the counselor asked how they'd felt about living alone. They both said it had been wonderful.

In November 2001, Mark and Betty reunited. They prayed over where to live and where to go to church. Mark worshipped with Betty at Mountain Christian Church, another congregation she'd found in Harford County. In December, Betty worshipped at New Song for the first time.

Soon after that, Betty opened a letter from a realtor. Someone was interested in her Foxborough Farms townhouse. She hadn't put it on the market, so she called the realtor to ask if it was a random letter that went out in a mass mailing. It was not. Someone had seen her house and it was just what that person was looking for, right down to the fence. Betty made an appointment to show the house that Saturday, and the visitor put in an offer on the spot.

Betty fell for New Song and started attending every Sunday, beginning in January 2002. She grew closer to God than she'd ever been—praying an hour every morning, reading several Bible chapters a day. She felt like God had engineered everything that had happened in the past year: the Christian counselor, the sermon at Harford Community Church about Sandtown, the letter from the realtor.

"I guess I'm moving to Scott Street," Betty thought.

Closing arguments in a trial can seem tidy after all the directs, crosses, and redirects.

December 22, 2003, was not tidy.

In closing arguments that the *Baltimore Sun* called "unusual," judge Marvin Garbis told counsel that they had "essentially an unlimited time." He encouraged a "free-swinging barroom kind of conversation." And the parties closed down the bar, coming back to continue closing arguments through much of December 23. Garbis wanted as much as possible in the record because he assumed the case would be appealed. He didn't want the United States Court of Appeals for the Fourth Circuit to say he'd left any questions unanswered.

Before soliciting the plaintiffs' individual claims, Garbis threw a curveball. "There's been some, but relatively little attention devoted to the question of regionalization," he said.

The judge wanted to know why so much of the case focused on the city and so little on "the power and duty of HUD to do more than it has on a regionalization basis." He asked Barbara Samuels, "What's your shot at HUD to say that they should have done more and must be required to do more in the surrounding counties?"

"Your Honor, paragraph 362 through 365 of our statement of facts addresses the facts on that point," she said. "We alleged that HUD has historically and in the present concentrated its assisted housing within the Baltimore housing market within Baltimore City."

The statement of facts had 518 paragraphs. Would those four end up being the only relevant ones in the judge's mind? And could he even be convinced on those? After he raised the regionalization issue, the judge started a protracted battle with Barbara.

"Do you understand, Ms. Samuels," Garbis said, "your hypothesis is [that] HUD's going to take money from Baltimore City and is going to put it into the county?"

Barbara didn't see regionalization as a zero-sum game. "I'm saying that it should be used to serve the people of the city wherever it is they should choose to live," she said.

City solicitor Thurman Zollicoffer jumped in on Garbis's side. "Her solution is [to] take money from Baltimore City and disinvest from Baltimore City and send it out to the counties," he said. "And in about ten years they'll be suing us for that." In other words, for putting more resources into the county than into the city.

The idea, Barbara countered, was balance. She said they wouldn't have ended up in court in the first place if the defendants had just placed family projects and scattered site units "in a broad variety of neighborhoods all around the city, white and black, middle class, lower class, upper class."

"All right," Garbis replied. "We're going to move to the merits."

Susan Podolsky started with constitutional claims. "There are two ways of looking at it," she said. "One is a straight and what I would call a more pure intent claim, and the other is failure to disestablish." Podolsky requested to treat these alleged sins of commission and omission—of discriminating purposefully and of failing to repair earlier discrimination—separately, and Garbis acceded. He also went for her throat, demanding evidence that Kurt Schmoke had deliberately discriminated against African Americans.

"What's your clean shot?" he said.

Podolsky pointed out that their complaint didn't accuse Schmoke or Daniel Henson of racial animus.

"I think it's pretty well established that he . . . doesn't have to hate blacks," Garbis said.

Podolsky treaded more carefully, retreating to criticisms of "entities" rather than of individuals. "I think that the entities HABC and the city had to have taken actions that deliberately segregated African-Americans," she said.

"You can't hide behind that: Henson was in charge, Schmoke was in charge," the judge said. "It's their policies that are at issue here." Hate wasn't the issue, he explained. The plaintiffs simply needed to prove that Schmoke chose policies that deliberately treated African Americans less favorably.

This time, Podolsky appended the word "administration."

"The actions that are taken by the Schmoke . . . and Henson administration—I think we have to show that they are of the same pattern and practice that existed already," she said. "In other words—and I don't disagree they have to be shown to be deliberate acts, but I think what we're showing—"

Garbis interrupted. "Well, I think this: we've heard a lot of noise," he said.

The plaintiffs had argued that Schmoke caved to white opposition. "Let's not dance away from that," the judge continued. "Either you're contending it or you don't . . . You've made these people jump through hoops based upon these claims that Mr. Schmoke did things discriminatory against African-Americans, and he's had to defend that. And we're not here to give a history of Kurt Schmoke and what he may have done for or against racial relations. But you're accusing him, and he's the dean of the Howard Law School, and he's like anybody else, he's got to answer to it.

"But damn it," he continued, "if you're not making the accusation, say. But if you say it, let's get the evidence out so he can either be found to be a deliberate discriminator or cleared."

"All right," Podolsky said. "The policies and practices which we alleged that occurred under the Schmoke administration that are violations of the equal protection clause are as follows."

Podolsky ticked off her list: the fence at Hollander Ridge; the demolition of public housing units without replacements; a 1950 city council ordinance taking veto power over public-housing siting decisions; HABC's tenant assignment policy; and a broad claim of "pattern and practice of discrimination" that covered the housing authority's continued placement of public housing in predominantly black areas. For each claim, Podolsky summarized the plaintiffs' evidence, and the city and HUD responded separately. Throughout each party's presentation, Judge Garbis interrupted to sharpen their arguments.

Podolsky argued that the erection of the Hollander Ridge fence in response to "racially motivated" opposition was unconstitutional. The judge pointed out that

ACLU–Maryland and the racists wanted the same thing: for the city to demolish Hollander Ridge. "I mean if you and the Rosedale people were in the room, you'd vote with them, you'd vote for different reasons," Garbis said.

"I agree with that," Podolsky said.

"That's good. Are you a racist?" the judge asked.

"Of course not," Podolsky said.

"On the other hand," the judge said, "Mayor Schmoke was a racist, but he disagreed with the rednecks, and you are not a racist when you agree with the rednecks."

When it came to HABC's tenant assignment policy giving white applicants a special path to Brooklyn Homes, Claremont Homes, and O'Donnell Heights, HUD attorney Judry Subar pointed out that those three sites became less white over time. "The uncontroverted facts are by the 1970s, those projects were integrated," he said.

"The argument I think against you," Garbis told Subar, "is you saw that the city wasn't doing it right, and you didn't come down on them hard enough."

"By the early '90s," Subar said, "what HUD was doing was saying constantly to the housing authority, 'You're not doing it right.'" The housing authority eventually fixed the problems, he said, and "it got a considerable amount of help from HUD."

"I guess I can find that you didn't do it fast enough," the judge said.

"Well, the fact is—"

The judge talked over Subar: "[That] this lawsuit has caused you to finally wake up and do the right thing."

"Okay," Garbis said after hearing arguments about efforts to wipe out vestiges of *de jure* discrimination. "3608 is a lot more wide open."

The "3608" he referred to was the section of the 1968 Fair Housing Act that required HUD to "affirmatively further" fair housing. HUD counsel admitted that the statute applied to them. The city read the statute as requiring a demonstrable intent to discriminate. "We believe the Supreme Court, if it decided it was confronted with this issue, would rule that it's a completely intent-based statute," said William Ryan.

If that were to happen, fair housing advocates would lose one of the most powerful tools they had to fight covert housing discrimination at the local level. It was the ability to sue *without proof of intent* that made the "affirmatively further" provision such an effective way to challenge the institutional sins of commission and omission that perpetuated racial inequality.

Susan Podolsky cited a long list of those sins that the plaintiffs attributed to city and federal governments: siting in segregated neighborhoods; a fair housing plan that failed to address a list of barriers from the city's own analysis of impediments to fair housing; failing to replace demolished public housing units; and bollixing up tenant assignments. According to Podolsky, these all constituted failures to affirmatively further, as did HUD's ongoing failure to keep the city in line with fair housing obligations.

Subar argued that HUD had taken plenty of affirmative steps to help HABC comply with fair housing law. HUD had scrounged up money out of its own meager coffers for technical assistance to get HABC's computers up and running again, as well as to pay for a voluntary Section 8 mobility program HABC had launched outside of its partial consent decree obligations.

Subar also argued that HUD had successfully coerced the city into pulling its tenant assignment list into compliance. "Once upon a time there were issues, but those issues were addressed up through the mid-'90s, and HUD again got the Housing Authority to toe the line," he said. And HUD was still monitoring a voluntary compliance agreement it had forced the city into over the waiting list.

Plaintiffs' counsel Chris Brown questioned Subar's rosy portrait of the city's compliance. "The numbers," Brown said, "appear to indicate still in Brooklyn and O'Donnell Heights the number of whites moving in is unusually high in number compared to the very high 95 percent, 98 percent—whatever it happens to be— black waiting list. We think that suggests some sort of intentional scheme that is being carried out."

Brown called for tightening up enforcement of the waiting list. Subar implied that was wishful thinking. "O'Donnell Heights now is over 90 percent African-American," Subar said. "When you have numbers that high, you can't fix things by monkeying things the way the plaintiffs are suggesting."

In other words, how do you desegregate when there's hardly anyone left to be segregated *from*?

Nicole wondered if Metropolitan Baltimore Quadel rejected her voucher application for a technicality. The qualifications confused her. Did she need to be the head of her household? Did she need to be currently living in public housing, or was it enough that she had lived in Murphy Homes as a little girl? She filled out a new application and sent it off. Quadel rejected that one too. She called Quadel, and from the conversation she got the impression that her time in Murphy Homes qualified her for a voucher.

By the time Nicole sent a third application to Quadel—this time adding her stint in Murphy Homes—her search for new housing had become more urgent. Pressure came down on her from several sources. First was the continuing violence in the neighborhood. Then there was Joe's school, Westside Elementary. It had just escaped Maryland's list of "failing schools," but the place frustrated Nicole. Joe was hyperactive, and Nicole felt the school was treating him as nothing more than an academic failure. The other parents irked Nicole, too. She felt their kids controlled them. Sometimes when teachers informed parents of their children's misdeeds, the parents reacted by screaming at the teachers.

Nicole started looking at other options. The city had opened its first charter schools in August 2005. She had a car and was willing to drive Joe. Nicole wanted to raise her son like Melinda had raised her—apart from the streets—but that didn't seem possible at Westside. Even the first graders used the same language she heard on the corners, and while Joe was in first grade, some fourth and fifth graders jumped him, taking his hat during the school's aftercare program.

The aftercare was a saving grace, at least. Melinda had shut down her daycare program in 2006. An inspector from the state's child care office had told Melinda that a test revealed lead on her back porch. Melinda knew she couldn't afford remediation work. She argued to the inspector that the agency never licensed the porch as part of the daycare program. The inspector replied that it would look bad on Melinda's record later if the state had to shut her program down, suggesting Melinda shut it herself. Melinda's cousin had recently closed down a program at a house just a ten-minute walk away on N. Mount Street in Sandtown. Melinda decided to try to start over there, and she moved into the house. Her cousin helped her try to set up the new daycare.

When Melinda moved, she asked her daughters to take over the mortgage payments at her own house. It was a larger mortgage than she had started with. She had refinanced twice in the first few years to put in new windows and make other improvements. One of the "refi's" came with an adjustable rate that started at 11.625 percent in June 1998 and was pegged to switch to a variable rate three years later. She refinanced again in January 1999 with a fifteen-year mortgage that included a balloon payment. At that point she owed $37,600, more than twice what she'd paid for the house. Melinda would have owed less with better terms on her mortgages. American mortgage rates never went higher than 9 percent the whole time Melinda owned her house. The mortgage that she negotiated with the previous owner in 1995 had had a 16 percent interest rate.

One day, Melinda got a letter from the bank saying that they noticed she was having trouble paying her mortgage. Melinda got the impression that she had fallen behind on just one month's payment, and she tried to send the money to the bank. The bank refused the payment—it had started foreclosure proceedings. (The number of foreclosures in Maryland had jumped from fewer than one thousand in the last quarter of 2006 to nearly ten thousand in the last quarter of 2007.)

After deciding it was too much work to get the house on N. Mount Street ready for child-care licensing, Melinda moved back in with the girls in October 2007. After she moved in, the bank informed her that a huge payment was due. Melinda wasn't sure if that was the balloon payment or not, but she did know that she didn't have the money. In November 2007, as she scrambled to make things right with the bank, Levi, the father of her children, died.

On December 20, 2007, a court statement estimated Melinda's mortgage debt at $44,102.66.

On January 7, 2008, the bank sold Melinda's house for $45,400.

At the end of the last day of the trial, judge Marvin Garbis spoke briefly from the bench.

"All right," he said. "First of all, we came in under the wire. Have a happy holiday. Unfortunately, I have the job of writing this up."

Once again, Garbis then turned off the acerbity and turned on the charm.

"I'd like to really appreciate counsel," he said. "This is a very difficult case. It has a lot of importance, and a lot of issues, and a lot of emotions. I think it raises, presents a context, particularly in the nature of Baltimore City, and is extremely important. I'll do you my best, recognizing that whatever I do will be reviewed by at least one higher court, and who knows?

"I'd like to do what the Fourth Circuit does and come down and shake counsels' hand[s], because I really appreciate it," Garbis said. "Everybody contributed. Thank you."

A month later, the *Baltimore Sun* wrote that Garbis's decision was "expected in a few weeks."

It would be a little longer than that.

Betty settled on the sale of the Foxborough Farms house in May 2002 for $124,000, just $7,000 more than she had spent on it. Over Memorial Day weekend—one year after she and Mark had moved out of Hunter's Run—she moved in with him on Scott Street.

Betty's relationship with God continued to intensify. She couldn't help it—

providential things were happening, and after a decade, she had so much to catch up on with God. She had also picked up a book by Dr. John M. Perkins.

Dr. Perkins had published *Restoring At-Risk Communities: Doing It Together and Doing It Right* in 1995 as a manual for anyone embracing the "three R's." The fifteen contributors, all involved in Christian community development projects across America, laid out the theory behind the movement—and the hardships that awaited those who relocated to poor neighborhoods.

The book devoted a full chapter to each of the "three R's" (relocation, reconciliation, and redistribution). Chris Rice and Spencer Perkins wrote the reconciliation chapter. Rice and Perkins published a newsletter about racial healing called *The Reconciler* and they were members of the Antioch community, which was part of the Voice of Calvary Fellowship in Jackson, Mississippi.

Rice and Perkins's chapter described the elusiveness of racial reconciliation, even at ground zero of the Christian community development movement. "It is one thing to be 'integrated,'" they wrote, "but quite another to be 'reconciled.'" At Voice of Calvary, "ambitious whites" who joined the congregation had slipped right into leadership positions. In 1983, tensions had boiled over, and Rice was shocked to see himself and other white members accused of racism: "When Blacks had said, 'Step to the side,' I'd heard, 'Step back.' When they said 'mutual submission,' I'd heard 'Black domination.' When they mentioned the importance of Black leadership, I'd heard 'No room for White leadership.'"

It took twelve years, but Voice of Calvary developed enough black leadership that black parishioners decided that the 70 percent–black church needed to start reaching out to white Christians. From this experience, Rice and Perkins both learned that "good intentions can't rush a deep relationship into existence."

"Often, Whites think relationships are further along than they really are," Rice wrote. "Spencer once told me that trust really isn't developing between Whites and Blacks until racial and cultural differences can be safely discussed. I've found that to be a pretty reliable rule of thumb."

Betty liked worshipping at New Song, but she knew that the church embraced Perkins's insistence on relocation. Perkins's book made it quite plain that the spiritual rewards of relocating came with a cost.

"Sometimes visitors come to [Voice of Calvary] and see Blacks and Whites worshiping, singing in a gospel choir, and relating easily together and remark, 'What a wonderful place!'" Spencer Perkins wrote. "They don't know the many years of blood, sweat, and tears that are behind the joy.'"

———

It was the call that Barbara Samuels had been waiting for. Anne Perkins was the "special master" appointed to work with plaintiffs, defendants, and the court to implement the partial consent decree in *Thompson v. HUD*. Perkins had a momentous date to share with ACLU–Maryland: January 6, 2005. On that day, a year after closing arguments and ten years after the suit was first filed, Judge Garbis would announce his ruling in Courtroom 5C of the U.S. District Courthouse in downtown Baltimore.

However the judge ruled, "Thompson" had already earned a place alongside names like "Walker" and "Gautreaux" as ambitious regional cases in which fair housing advocates tried to force the dismantling of decades of public housing segregation by documenting—at great length—the exclusionary actions of American policymakers and bureaucrats throughout the twentieth century. The *Thompson* case had already generated some remedial action in the June 1996 partial consent decree.

Barbara Samuels hoped for more. The decree of 1996 only settled claims regarding high-rises and the low-rise Fairfield Homes. Baltimore's housing authority had thousands more units in its portfolio, and when the trial started in December 2003, ACLU–Maryland went after segregation in those units with what Garbis called "a plethora of claims based upon a broad range of legal theories." Under one theory, the defendants had a constitutional duty to disestablish segregation in public housing that the housing authority had created *de jure* decades earlier. The plaintiffs needed whatever theories they could get, with such short windows of time in which to pin the city or federal government to acts of discrimination, thanks to statutes of limitations: 1992 to 1995 for the city, and 1989 to 1995 for HUD.

An important distinction in the trial, and one that reflected the changing nature of American race relations, was the difference between discrimination with intent and discrimination without intent. The first kind of claim, which had so piqued Garbis regarding Kurt Schmoke, was about racism as most people understood it: Who were the racists? And what racist things did they do? But after the passage of the Fair Housing Act of 1968, more and more of the exclusionary policies and practices that disproportionately disadvantaged African Americans were racially neutral on their face.

The desegregation of Baltimore's public housing wasn't the only thing at stake in the ruling Judge Garbis was about to unveil. Just as ACLU–Maryland leaned on *Walker* and *Gautreaux* in making their case, future civil rights cases might lean on Garbis's ruling. If ACLU–Maryland lost on all counts, it would send a message to other regions whose bureaucracies were perpetuating racial inequality: perhaps there would not be any repercussion for failing to dismantle the practices that created the inequality.

With the ability to reorient bureaucracies toward racial equity at stake, Barbara and her ACLU–Maryland colleagues headed downtown on January 6. Courtroom 5C was full. Garbis took the bench. His ruling was a beefy 322 pages. Mercifully, he said he would read a summary, which he did in the focused, casual, and occasionally censorious manner he had shown during the trial.

"Plaintiffs have not proven intentional racial discrimination in public housing on the part of the local or federal defendants during the Schmoke administration," Garbis said. "And I just might comment on that as a sideline."

Once again, he zeroed in on the notion of a racist black mayor. He admitted that given the plaintiffs' choice of statutes, it would have been professionally negligent for them not to accuse Kurt Schmoke—the city's first elected black mayor, the dean of the law school at historically black Howard University—of discriminating against African Americans. "But I think this court has to say it," the judge continued. "Kurt Schmoke is far more worthy of being honored than being attacked by the ACLU."

Just like that, gone was any chance of winning the case on its most powerful charge: discriminatory intent by the city government during the open period.

ACLU–Maryland had argued intent claims for six episodes, including the housing authority's construction of a fence around Hollander Ridge to appease the residents across the city line in Rosedale; its cancelation of plans to renovate a school in a white city neighborhood for use as public housing after boisterous objections from neighbors; and a lax HABC tenant-location policy that allowed white public-housing applicants to reject assignments until they got a unit in a majority white project.

What saved HABC from liability was not anything the agency itself did, the judge ultimately ruled. It was demographic change. Garbis said the public housing population had become too overwhelmingly black for "meaningful desegregation" by the early 1990s.

What emerged from Garbis's review of ACLU–Maryland's intentional discrimination claims was a sympathetic portrait of a cash-strapped housing agency doing the best it could with a nearly all-black population of tenants, few "non-impacted" neighborhoods in which to place them, and a city that showed no desire to integrate. In his ruling, Garbis even quoted what could have been damaging testimony from Daniel Henson, Mayor Schmoke's housing commissioner:

Baltimore is a city of either Black neighborhoods or White neighborhoods. . . . [I]t's a segregated housing market. . . . So the likelihood
that we were going to be able to build . . . a community that would
be 50/50 White and Black simply because of the way that we did
anything that we would do, it just wasn't going to happen. So what I
decided to do was to accept things for what they are . . .

What could Baltimore do, the ruling seemed to imply, but make the best
of the way things were? Exclusive neighborhoods like Guilford and Mount
Washington—the kind of neighborhoods that were bashed at the 2000 meeting
in Hamilton for not taking their fair share of public housing—just didn't have
many rentals, the judge pointed out, and it was expensive to develop there. And
selling off city-owned plots in non-impacted neighborhoods for development
rather than for public housing wasn't so bad, the judge wrote. He cited the economic and quality-of-life improvements wrought by the "resurrection" of Canton,
which, in his eyes, benefited Baltimore's rich and poor alike. Garbis approvingly
quoted Schmoke's and Henson's argument that the demand for affordable housing
in the city was so high that it didn't matter where it went. In poor neighborhoods,
you just got more bang for your buck—certainly more than the city could get in
Roland Park. Specifically citing Henson's testimony about the Sandtown neighborhood transformation project, Garbis argued that public housing investments
could even contribute to revitalization and potentially draw higher earners and
role models back to poor, "vacant"-pocked neighborhoods.

Baltimore faced a "tension between the goals of equalizing racial distribution
in Baltimore and providing the maximum number of housing opportunities for
public housing tenants," Garbis wrote. Overall, he concluded, the city took "justified and acceptable measures to rectify the inequities inherited from the past."

At least Melinda's house had sold near the top of the market. A CNNMoney.com
headline just two weeks after the sale read "Housing Prices to Free Fall in 2008."
Melinda kept contacting the bank, trying to work something out. The bank sent
letter after letter saying the same thing: vacate or we'll lock the house up.

Before the bank could throw the Smiths out, Nicole got the letter she had been
waiting for. "Oh, look, Ma!" she yelled one day at the house. Quadel had finally
accepted her for the special voucher program. Another letter followed assigning
her a mobility counselor.

Nicole went downtown for an orientation on the fourth floor at 231 E. Baltimore

Street. After the orientation, she met with her counselor. The move wasn't going to happen right away. Nicole had to save $1,000 and raise her credit score above 550. She had to update her counselor once a month. She had to let someone from Quadel come and inspect her current living conditions. She had to keep a job (she had one at her community college's childcare center). If she didn't do these things, Quadel would drop her from the program.

After the orientation, Quadel staff took Nicole and some others on a van tour of the surrounding jurisdictions. When the van got to Columbia, Nicole knew she had found her new home. She had already searched for apartments there. Someone had told her that Howard County had the best schools.

In June 2008, the Smiths moved from Penn North to a rental in the 800 block of N. Monroe Street. The two-story brick bowfront rowhouse was a block south of Sandtown, and although some blocks of Monroe were rough, this one was well kept. When Quadel did a home visit, the Smiths had just moved in. There was little for the inspector to inspect beyond the freshly painted walls.

Nicole started saving her money and paying off her debts. One day, she opened the skinny black mailbox at Monroe Street and found a letter from the Housing Authority of Baltimore City. She had been accepted for public housing. The letter listed scattered site options and projects like McCulloh Homes.

Nicole threw the letter away.

The ruling wasn't all bad news for Barbara and her colleagues. As Judge Garbis moved through his summary, they discovered that they had prevailed on at least one claim against HUD.

"It is with respect to HUD, and its failure adequately to consider a regional approach to desegregation of public housing, that the Court finds liability," Garbis ruled. "Section 3608(e)(5) of the Fair Housing Act requires Federal Defendants to 'administer [housing] programs . . . in a manner affirmatively to further the policies of [the Act].'" Garbis used a 1973 Second Circuit Court of Appeals ruling to set the parameters of the "affirmatively further" duty that he said HUD had failed to follow: "Action must be taken to fulfill, as much as possible, the goal of open, integrated residential housing patterns and to prevent the increase of segregation."

The same portrait that got the city off the hook—limited resources, mostly black tenants, few white neighborhoods—Garbis now turned against HUD. Just as it was "impossible" for the Housing Authority of Baltimore City to desegregate within the city's boundaries, Garbis ruled, it was inappropriate for HUD to consider that to be the only option. "Baltimore City," he wrote in the ruling, "should not be viewed as an island reservation for use as a container for all of the poor of a contiguous region of Baltimore."

Whereas Garbis had expressed admiration for Schmoke to those gathered in the courtroom, he now expressed scorn for HUD. He told the crowded courtroom that the federal agency was "effectively wearing blinders that limited their vision" to Baltimore City during the open period, that they "at best . . . had abused their discretion," and that it was "high time" that HUD lived up to the affirmative duty prescribed by the Fair Housing Act.

"The statistical evidence demonstrates that HUD's various housing programs, as implemented, failed to achieve significant desegregation in Baltimore City," the ruling read. "This is true during the Open Period as it had been in the preceding decades." As a result, Garbis wrote, the city had become a "'regional magnet' for families unable to afford housing on the private market."

It wasn't just the continued segregation revealed in those statistics that ran afoul of Garbis's interpretation of the Fair Housing Act's duty to "affirmatively further." It was also HUD's failure, in his eyes, to "consider alternative sources of action" for dismantling it: specifically, regionalization. The judge believed HUD had left untapped "the provision of public housing opportunities beyond the boundaries of Baltimore City." The city didn't hold the regionalization card, but HUD did, and Garbis said the agency "presented virtually no evidence" that they considered playing that card.

Garbis also left open the question of whether that failure violated the plaintiffs' constitutional rights. The final score in the judge's ruling against HUD was one finding of liability and, potentially, one more. With that established, Garbis announced that the case would proceed to a "remedial phase" to determine what HUD would need to do to rectify their failure to consider regional strategies. He imposed two surprising conditions on the remedial stage. First, he would allow both sides to introduce evidence during the new trial over the lingering constitutional claim. Second, HUD could introduce evidence that they had, in fact, pursued regionalization during the open period. The court would consider all of the evidence in determining a remedy.

Garbis held out hope for a settlement and invited the counties to join the plaintiffs and defendants to hammer out a solution that would avoid the need for another trial. But it wouldn't be easy to get majority-white communities to welcome poor black families. The settlement negotiations in 1995 and 1996 had

amounted to major combat with Baltimore County. A tight and expensive housing market made it difficult to use Section 8 certificates in the counties. Robert
Ehrlich, who as a congressman had tried to undermine Moving to Opportunity
and the *Thompson* partial consent decree, was now the governor of Maryland.

Prospects for a settlement looked grim at the federal level, too. President
George W. Bush was about to begin his second term. Under his housing secretary,
Alphonso Jackson, HUD had vigorously denied all charges in *Thompson v. HUD*
and had filed lengthy motions for summary judgment, hoping Judge Garbis would
rule in their favor without holding a trial.

"Maybe we don't have to go through this remedial phase," Garbis told the
courtroom. "Maybe there is a way that people can recognize we're all together in
this region. But, if not, I'll do what I can to make sure that they do."

Living at Scott Street didn't make Betty like the house any more than she had the
first time she saw it. She and Mark began looking for someplace new to live. The
counselor had told her that Mark, as a matter of conscience, could not move back
to the suburbs. She knew they needed to find a place in the city. That was fine.

In fact, she knew exactly where they ought to live. The book by Dr. Perkins had
changed her more than Mark had realized.

"I think we need to move to Sandtown," Betty told Mark.

Five weeks after Judge Garbis's ruling, a group of fair housing lawyers sent a letter
to the Maryland Department of Housing and Community Development (DHCD).
The state was revising its protocol for distributing Low-Income Housing Tax
Credits (LIHTC), and it wanted comments from the public.

The lawyers had some comments.

The LIHTC program arrived in a 1986 tax-reform bill, targeting developments
for families earning less than a region's median income. By selling the credits,
developers could make up some of the income they lost from reducing rents.

These developments were not public housing, and LIHTC was a Treasury
Department program, not a HUD program. But the state housing agency that
doled out the credits received HUD funding every year; the lawyers believed that
the Fair Housing Act could be brought to bear. The lawyers' data analysis showed
that in the Baltimore region, poor and racially isolated black neighborhoods
contained a disproportionate share of family LIHTC developments. As in public
housing, so too in the private market.

In the letter, attorneys from the Lawyers' Committee for Civil Rights Under Law, the Poverty & Race Research Action Council, and the Maryland Legal Aid Bureau put DHCD on notice. And they used Judge Garbis's ruling to do it:

> As you are aware, the U.S. District Court in Baltimore ruled last month in *Thompson v. HUD* that the federal government has failed over several decades to promote regional housing opportunities for low income minority residents of Baltimore, a failure which has contributed to a racially and economically segregated region and deprived thousands of inner city residents of the opportunity to move to areas with lower poverty and segregation, more plentiful employment, and higher performing schools.
>
> Like the federal government, the State of Maryland and the Maryland Department of Housing and Community Development . . . have the authority to operate on a regional basis, and have the obligation, under the Fair Housing Act, to affirmatively further fair housing.

By the summer of 2009, Nicole had saved $1,000 and pulled her credit score up past 550. The voucher was hers. It worked just like a regular Section 8 voucher—she had to pay 30 percent of her monthly income toward monthly rent, and the government paid the rest—except that she could only use it in the non-impacted census tracts listed in the *Thompson* partial consent decree. Nicole went to one last orientation, then started apartment hunting in Columbia.

She needed more than an apartment in Columbia. She needed a job. For two years, she had worked in a childcare center that Baltimore City Community College ran for its students. That contract was about to run out. Fortunately for Nicole, Quadel's mobility program included job counseling. Unfortunately for Nicole, the economy had just collapsed. The unemployment rate had doubled in just two years.

Nicole visited a building all the way at the back of a sprawling garden-apartment complex in the north end of Columbia. She walked down a set of stairs, and entered an apartment. An open space seemed to suggest a small dining room on the left and a living room on the right. A narrow kitchen connected to the dining room. The sliding glass door in the living room opened right onto a grassy hill—a perfect place for Joe to play. There were two bedrooms, one on either side of the living room. Each had its own small bathroom. The apartment was just over

1,100 square feet—almost exactly the same amount as the house her mother had lost had contained.

This was the one.

Nicole signed a lease and lined up a cousin and some friends from church to help her move in August 2009 from N. Monroe Street to the new apartment in Columbia.

FOUR

One Region, New Worlds

IN 2002, THE REV. WY PLUMMER, WHO HAD RECENTLY STEPPED DOWN AS CO-pastor of New Song Community Church, heard that Mark and Betty Lange were considering moving to Sandtown. Plummer was looking for jobs outside of Baltimore, so he gave Mark and Betty a tour of his house—a Sandtown Habitat for Humanity rehab—in the 1300 block of N. Gilmor Street.

Betty loved the three-story rowhouse. On the outside, Sandtown Habitat had left the well-preserved Formstone, which capped each of the eight windows with a crown of vertically offset "bricks." The inside looked like any townhouse you'd see in the suburbs: an open first floor with a kitchen in the back, and carpet on the second and third floors. Betty and Mark told the Plummers that they were ready to buy if the Plummers were ever ready to sell, and they expected them to do so soon. Months passed, however, and New Song parishioners asked the Langes if they were really going to relocate.

In 2003, Allan and Susan Tibbels took Mark and Betty to brunch at The Gallery, a mall across the street from Harborplace. For two hours, the Tibbels told Mark and Betty all the bad parts about living in Sandtown. Burglars had ransacked their home while they slept. Someone had once put a knife to Allan's neck. The Tibbelses didn't say, "Don't move in," but they made a good case against doing so.

While Mark and Betty waited for the Plummers to move, they looked at other properties in the neighborhood. They liked one of the bigger Nehemiah houses, but the owner was asking too much. They put in an offer on a house on N. Carey Street, but the owner wouldn't accept it.

While Mark and Betty were hunting for houses, they finally got to meet John Perkins when he joined several potential relocators for a dinner party at the Tibbelses' house. Perkins left a big impression.

In May 2005, Wy Plummer got a job in Birmingham, Alabama. Mark and Betty got the Scott Street house where they were living under contract fairly quickly, but as they started packing up the house, the settlement fell through. The Plummers had already moved to Birmingham, so they let the Langes rent the N. Gilmor Street house. Luckily for the Langes, the housing market was hot, and their house on Scott Street sold again in less than a week. They scheduled a settlement for late October.

At the same time the Langes moved to Sandtown at the end of August 2005, hundreds of people were drowning in New Orleans. Americans watched, aghast, and started a fitful "conversation" about race and class. On N. Gilmor Street, Mark and Betty became self-conscious about their own race and class as they carried load after load of material possessions from two moving trucks—one with Betty's things, one with Mark's—into their new home, which faced Gilmor Homes.

The Langes' new block had all the contrasts of a "transforming" Sandtown. Drug dealers lived next door, and a vacant house rotted on the other side. But there was hope, too. At the corner of Presstman Street, the remodeled "Mansion" that Dr. Perkins had dedicated in 1990 sat directly across from New Song Center, the gleaming new building where Elder Harris had helped break ground in 1999.

The newsletters that New Song Urban Ministries published in 2005 told of countless services and activities, as well as partnerships that brought in resources from outside the neighborhood. Graduates of New Song's school had gone on to private high schools and colleges, including Tuskegee University and Allegheny College. New Song Academy alumnus William Scipio, one newsletter noted, studied at Coppin State, a historically black university in West Baltimore.

One newsletter listed all of the church's community work: the Habitat for Humanity branch, the school, the jobs program, a health program, an arts program, and a partnership with Elder Harris's Newborn Holistic Ministries. The calendar burst with activities: a Habitat house dedication; a graduation ceremony at Newborn's residential recovery program, Martha's Place; Habitat's summer building blitz; a "country-dancing night" at a suburban church to raise funds for New Song; and arts performances in New York, Virginia, and Maryland. Each fall, New Song sent a handful of representatives to the annual conference of the Christian Community Development Association in various cities throughout the country.

A newsletter entry detailed a visit from a member of the board of the Rouse Company Foundation in April 2005. The foundation had funded the construction of a preschool space in the original New Song building at 1385 N. Gilmor. Outside of New Song's sphere, the Enterprise Foundation continued working in

Sandtown, but it wasn't nearly the transformation so many had expected back in the 1990s.

Enterprise lost momentum in the neighborhood transformation effort during 1993 and 1994. And while Enterprise's partnership with BUILD and the city certainly got results in the 1990s, Patrick Costigan believed that outside partners needed to listen to what a community wants and build on the assets it already has. Even so, he wrote, it was naive to think a transformation could occur using only the resources that exist inside the geographical boundaries of a neighborhood. "If poor and distressed communities had all the resources needed to transform themselves, they would have done so under their own power decades ago," he wrote.

In the late 1990s, James Rouse died, Costigan left Enterprise, and Kurt Schmoke decided not to run for reelection as mayor. The pace of transformation slackened, and mistrust grew. Different factions inside the neighborhood battled over the comparatively small proportion of neighborhood transformation funding for community development. Rather than completely turn leadership over to the community, some on the city side of the partnership kept offering guidance, believing "community capacity" was lacking. This "babysitting" created more resentment. When Mayor Schmoke came to Gilmor Elementary School in the summer of 1997 to celebrate the progress in Sandtown, several hundred residents showed up to pour out grievances.

In the early 2000s, Enterprise Homes continued building in Sandtown, rehabbing thirty-six houses and building two hundred new ones in a partnership with BUILD. Neat brick rowhouses lined three blocks of N. Calhoun Street, making it look as if parts of Bel Air or Canton had been airlifted and dropped right in. The houses went to first-time buyers, and with a federal Nehemiah grant in play and the city willing to hold—and possibly forgive—a second mortgage, some buyers moved in with just a $40,000 mortgage. More than half of the homes were sold to people making 60 percent or less of the area median income of around $50,000.

Outside of homebuilding, comparatively little was happening at this point. Community Building in Partnership received less money every year. In 2001, Community Building in Partnership brought in over $1,800,000 in grants and other contributions, but that number dropped to under $1,000,000 by 2004.

Some attributed the transformation effort's dissipation to James Rouse's death. Elder Harris, who served on Community Building in Partnership's board, felt that community development efforts in Sandtown rarely built structures for new leadership to take over, which left organizations vulnerable when they lost strong leaders. Harris himself had brought Todd Marcus, a young white jazz musician who had relocated to Sandtown, into the organization. Marcus later became its executive director.

New Song Urban Ministries had an extremely dynamic leader in Allan Tibbels. Tibbels preferred to stay in the background, but some black and white members of the community believed him to be the glue that held the effort together. His charisma rallied people, and his connections outside the community kept resources raining down on New Song's ministries.

Mark and Betty made their own contribution to New Song when they finally became Sandtown homeowners in October 2005. The real estate bubble was fully inflated when they sold the Scott Street house. On October 27, 2005, the Langes bought the Plummers' house for $100,000. Four days later, they sold the Scott Street house for $239,900. They gave $21,000 to Sandtown Habitat for Humanity and $1,000 to New Song Community Church.

Mark loved his new home, and smoking cigarettes on the stoop introduced him to curious neighbors, including twenty-year-old Ahmad, who lived with his mother across the street in Gilmor Homes and hung out with a crew of teens next door to Mark's house. One of those teens, Arnold, spent about two hundred hours practicing in Mark's car before getting his license. Also part of the crew were brothers named Eddie and Freddie. One day, Eddie saw Mark suffering through a back spasm while trying to move a shed and said, "I got it. You're family." Freddie once told Mark, "I want to be sixty like you, sitting on the steps and feeding stray cats." (Mark was prolific in his provision of kitty victuals.)

Mark also befriended older women in the neighborhood. Miss Adelaide loved it when Mark brought her pepper-loaf lunch meat, and Mark and Betty gave Miss Adelaide rides to church when she felt strong enough to go. One Sunday, Miss Adelaide said she'd lost three grandchildren in less than two months, one from a heroin overdose. Miss Cathy, who lived in "the homes" across the street, dried her clothes on a clothesline, and so on rainy days Mark let her use his dryer. Miss Cathy needed dialysis twice a week, and Mark drove her when the driver from the state's transportation department failed to show up.

Betty mentored two girls, ages eight and nine, whom Susan Tibbels sent her way. The girls visited Betty three nights a week for dinner and help with homework. Betty was shocked at first by how tough the neighborhood kids were and the language they used. Over time, she realized they had to show how tough they were or they'd get beaten up. Betty also saw how children cycled in and out of foster care and relatives' homes. Those who lived with mom or dad would often leave one parent for another, thinking it might be better, only to find that things got worse.

A dark side of Sandtown revealed itself to Mark and Betty before long. For one, there were the health problems. Their new neighbors were dying younger than their neighbors back in the counties. And then there was the street drama. Their neighbors Flip and Little Billy got locked up soon after Mark and Betty moved in. The Langes had never seen policing like they saw in Sandtown. One night when Betty went to drive her two mentees home, she discovered that a police car had blocked her in. She got in her car, thinking an officer would see her and move the police car. After waiting a while, Betty asked, "Excuse me, are you going to move your car? I have to take these girls home."

"I'll move my car when I want to move my car," the officer replied. "I'm conducting business."

Betty couldn't imagine a police officer back in the suburbs speaking to her like that. Mark thought the Baltimore police behaved like an occupying army; he wondered if Sandtown had more in common with Palestine than neighborhoods just a mile away.

Mark's new friend Antoine Bennett knew the streets as well as anyone in Sandtown. Bennett was the fifth generation of his family to grow up in the neighborhood. His mother died just months after he was born. His grandmother, a secretary at a pharmacy, raised him while his father struggled with drug addiction. Bennett had lived in Sandtown his entire life, except for the stint in prison after the shooting at Stricker and School.

The Enterprise/BUILD/City Hall partnership was in full swing when Bennett returned to the neighborhood in 1993 after his three and a half years in prison. He could tell the difference. Neighbors used the language of homeownership in a way he'd never heard. People were buying houses in the 1500 block of Stricker where he'd hung out before prison, and family members talked about applying for Habitat houses.

Bennett came to know community development as well as he'd known the streets, joining a workforce development program called YouthBuild. Afterward, he worked for Amelia Harris as an intake person at New Song's health center, then moved on to EDEN Jobs. In the late 1990s, he got a house in the 1500 block of Leslie Street, a block that Habitat had knocked down *in toto* and rebuilt from scratch. It was the same block where his mother had grown up and met his father.

Having a foot in both worlds made Bennett especially valuable to New Song: he could help newcomers acculturate to Sandtown. New Song Community Church services had become whiter in the 2000s. Church leaders had abandoned "the talk," in which they approached visitors who had attended a few services and told them that they should not try to become members unless they intended to move into the community. The talk was New Song's way of remaining a church that served neighbors and kept neighbors in charge. Instead of the talk, Pastor Williams asked Bennett and Patty Prasada-Rao, an Indian American woman who had left Faith Christian Fellowship across town to join New Song, to explain what the church was about every Sunday morning. That was fine with Bennett; he had never liked the talk.

In April 2007, Allan Tibbels stepped down from New Song Urban Ministries and tapped Bennett and Prasada-Rao as co-leaders. The duo took on the responsibility of helping relocators adapt to the neighborhood. In essence, they became the conduit of Dr. Perkins's second "R": reconciliation.

Bennett believed deeply in Perkins's teachings, including submission to black leadership. White people often arrived in poor black neighborhoods with lots of ideas and assumed a role for themselves in leadership—or at least dominated conversation. White people under the spell of Perkins were more cognizant of the "white savior complex," but Bennett made sure that any ministries started by relocators included a co-leader from the neighborhood.

Bennett and Prasada-Rao also schooled relocators in everyday interactions. Neighbors, they explained, can be welcoming but suspicious. And they may not be as quick as a relocator to call the police. Bennett told relocators that if they saw a young black man in handcuffs, they should not ask neighbors, "What did he do?" That sent a message that a relocator believed black teenagers should be assumed to be guilty. Bennett suggested asking, "Is everything all right?"

Bennett worried not just about white relocators acting superior or paternalistic. He also worried about relocators falling victim to neighborhood violence. When Bennett and Prasada-Rao took over for Tibbels, homicides had jumped 14 percent in the previous twelve months and nonfatal shootings were up 24 percent—no small feat for Baltimore.

Bennett didn't want anyone to walk on eggshells, but he knew that any kind of conflict between newcomers and old-timers, whether violent or merely passive-aggressive, could unravel relationships across racial lines that had taken two decades to build. Prasada-Rao gave out her cell phone number, telling new relocators that if they sensed a conflict coming on, or even observed a conflict and didn't know whether or not to intervene, they should call her or Bennett first unless someone's life was in danger. Relocators called Bennett constantly as they adjusted to the neighborhood.

Bennett cared for the relocators personally, and he saw them as essential to the success of the neighborhood. He believed that any neighbors who intended to work for themselves and by themselves were destined to fail. Bennett felt personally responsible for relocators and grew close to many of them, including Mark Lange.

In 2008, Mark drew on his IT skills to help Bennett and his childhood pal Gerry Palmer open a café at the corner of Presstman and N. Stricker Streets. Mark approached the project the way he thought a relocator should: by asking what they needed him to do, and not asserting himself unless they asked him to. What they needed was a "point of sale" system for the front register. Mark set up the system. When Palmer and Bennett thought the space was finished, an inspector gave them a list of fixes they needed to make in order to qualify as a food establishment. Mark stepped in again, putting in a closet and installing some racks and a new toilet seat.

Gerry's Goods was one of New Song Urban Ministries' most exciting projects to date: the first real business project inspired by the Christian community development model. In fact, John Perkins had helped spark the idea. On a visit a few years earlier, Perkins had pointed out to someone that there was no place in the neighborhood to get a cup of coffee and a newspaper. Perkins believed places like Sandtown needed to move beyond giving a man a fish to eat for a day and even beyond teaching men to fish. He wanted residents to "own the pond the fish swam in."

Gerry Palmer had been thinking about opening his own business. One Thursday at the "Men's Luncheon," a weekly meeting at the New Song Worship and Arts Center, Palmer listened to men take turns sharing goals they hoped to achieve in the next five years. When his turn came, Palmer said he wanted to open a card and balloon store. Everyone has a birthday, he reasoned. Allan Tibbels asked Palmer if he'd consider opening a coffee shop or restaurant in a building New Song owned at 1500 Presstman Street. Palmer said he was willing to try. Tibbels told Palmer and Bennett that he'd send them to talk coffee with a pastor named Guy Pfanz, who ran a Christian coffee shop, trained baristas, and taught coffee roasting.

That church was in Muncie, Indiana.

Palmer and Bennett drove up to Indiana together and spent a week with him learning about the coffee business. Pfanz told them about Cornerstone, a Christian music festival in Bushnell, Illinois, where a crew from his church would go with coffee and smoothie equipment each summer.

When Palmer came back, Allan Tibbels and a couple from a Presbyterian church in Columbia had raised well over $50,000 for working capital. The couple, both of whom had backgrounds in finance, helped Allan and New Song Urban Ministries oversee the project. Allan sent Palmer to join Pfanz's crew of eighteen people at Cornerstone in late June 2007. At first, Palmer was intimidated. He hadn't even packed right. Under the hot sun, he cut the legs off his jeans, then tore up a shirt and tied a piece around his head. Palmer accustomed himself to the festival existence: pissing in the woods, running car headlights to see at night, shooing the raccoons that scratched at their tents. Unimpressed with the rice and beans his new friends ate every night, Palmer leaned on his Sandtown sensibilities, getting pizza from other vendors by trading for cappuccinos and smoothies. Palmer bonded with his colleagues as they set up their machines—latte, ice, smoothie—and worked in shifts from 6:00 a.m. until 2:00 a.m.

When Palmer returned, Allan and his team asked Palmer to get a part-time job at a coffee shop. Palmer landed a gig at a Starbucks that had recently opened inside a grocery store where he'd formerly worked. Seven months later, Palmer left Starbucks a certified barista, and the New Song crew asked him to interview potential employees for the Sandtown coffee shop. Palmer couldn't believe the autonomy he was given. He was in on all the decisions, right down to the color of the paint. He hired a childhood friend as an assistant manager.

Most corner stores in West Baltimore put thick plexiglass between their clerks and their customers. Gerry Palmer and Antoine Bennett did not want plexiglass. They believed an open counter would send a message to the community. The way Bennett saw it, the customers and the cashiers all came from the same streets.

When John Perkins came to town for New Song Community Church's twentieth anniversary in June 2008, the church held a ribbon-cutting at the space that was being renovated for Gerry's Goods. Blue and white balloons adorned the front of 1500 Presstman Street, and a yellow ribbon bound the door. The bright sun illuminated the crowd for the grand opening, which spilled across the street to the next corner.

"Good afternoon!" Palmer said, and the crowd greeted him back. "First of all I want to say—um, there's some of my friends that's not here right now, so I'm getting a little emotional."

"That's alright," said someone in the crowd.

"But I'ma keep it going," Palmer said as more tears came to his eyes. "A couple years ago, my mom was incarcerated and left me with my two younger sisters. And, um . . . they was teenagers, and I had no way to figure out how we was going to keep going. I was on this block right here serving—serving people. I was doing the bad thing serving."

Indeed, Palmer had sold drugs on the same corner as a young man.

"A couple guys I ran with, matter of fact, two generations of guys, all of them is gone now," Palmer said. "But I'm still here, and I thank God. I just thank God. God had a plan."

Palmer cut the ribbon, and the crowd filed in.

In 2008, Mark Lange got the opportunity to thank the person whose work had led him there. John Perkins was scheduled to give a sermon while he was in town for New Song Community Church's twentieth anniversary. Pastor Williams asked Mark to say a few words before the sermon about the impact Perkins had made on his life.

Mark prepared some remarks and when Sunday came around, he looked out at the rows and rows of people sitting in blue plastic chairs. There were a lot of white folks this particular week. Perkins, seventy-eight years old, with a long puff of gray curls on his chin, sat in the first row on the left.

It didn't take long for Mark's tears to come. He recalled reading interviews of Perkins in *Campus Life* as a teenager and learning of his jailing and torture by the Mississippi State Police. "I was a brand new Christian when I read those articles," Mark said. "So my heart was very tender and I was weeping for what they were doing to my brother."

That wasn't the only reason those articles made him weep, Mark said. "The second level of tears were tears of shame, because the people doing it to you were people of my color."

Thirty years later, Mark said, here he was, still trying to repent and reconcile with new neighbors whose history was the same as Perkins', a history of oppression and brutality.

"We're relocators trying to reconcile, hoping our neighbors will have us," Mark said. "Yeah, we brought a few resources, we had a little more money than our neighbors and stuff, but we're bringing no agenda, no messianic complex.

"I'm a neighbor," he continued, "and where it goes from here it's up to God. So far, my neighbors have welcomed me."

As fond as Mark had become of Sandtown, one of his neighbors had just moved away, hoping for a safer place to live. When Mark moved in, Marie had lived across the street in Gilmor Homes. Now she lived in a house about a half-mile to the northwest, near Coppin State University. Marie was the mother of Ahmad, the young man who hung with Arnold next door to the Langes' house.

Ahmad kept coming around, though, even though his family had moved, and in the summer of 2009, he told Mark that big changes were afoot. He and his girlfriend had just had a baby, and he had just interviewed for a job at a local hospital. The last step was a background check, and Ahmad was optimistic about the results—he had just worked with a lawyer to expunge his criminal record.

Late one Wednesday night when fall came around, Mark sat on his stoop smoking, and Ahmad walked out of Arnold's house next door. "I'm going home, Mr. Mark, see you later," he said.

"See you later, Ahmad," Mark said.

Ahmad crossed the street. A young man in a hoodie joined him in front of Gilmor Homes and they walked north toward Presstman. As they passed behind a parked car, Mark saw Ahmad put his hands up as if to ask, "What's the problem?" Mark felt a twinge of uneasiness. Even at 1:15 a.m., this night was too warm for a hoodie. But he shook it off, chiding himself for indulging a racist stereotype. Ahmad and the man kept walking. At Presstman, they turned left. After they disappeared around the corner, the still of the night vanished with a bang.

Two loud reports followed. Inside the Langes' house, Betty jolted awake. Downstairs, Mark felt for his phone and realized it was still in the house. He ran in, dialed 911, and started up the street. Before Mark got to the corner, two police vehicles had converged on the scene, one from Gilmor, one from Presstman. The officers parked and put up yellow tape. Standing at the corner, Mark saw Ahmad lying on the sidewalk, his feet pointing east, back toward N. Gilmor Street. The gunman had shot him in the chest and the middle of the forehead.

Mark hadn't recognized the gunman, but he told an officer the suspect's height and the color of his hoodie and hat. Another officer asked Mark to come to police headquarters for a witness interview. Mark got into the officer's car and they pulled away. An ambulance took Ahmad to Shock Trauma downtown.

Betty had come out to the street by this point and had no idea where Mark was. Miss Jolene, who lived in Gilmor Homes and had been Marie's and Ahmad's next-door neighbor, told her Mark left in a police car. Miss Jolene asked Betty for a ride to the hospital, and they pulled off in Betty's tan Mitsubishi Galant.

The idea of being seen with the police didn't faze Mark until a detective asked him if he wanted the police to put a car in front of his house.

"For what?" Mark asked.

"You just witnessed a murder," the detective said.

A couple of nights later, Mark sat on the stoop chatting with a friend of Arnold's named Scott, who was on the stoop next door. They both noticed a man walking up Gilmor with a jacket over his arm. As Mark exchanged pleasantries with the man, he saw out of the corner of his eye that Scott had backed into Arnold's doorway. When the man passed, Mark asked Scott, "What's up with you?"

"I didn't want to see nothing, Mr. Mark," Scott said.

Later, Miss Jolene and Marie told Mark he had nothing to worry about—everyone knew he was a retired policeman. When Mark met with Antoine Bennett and Patty Prasada-Rao a few days later, Bennett said, "You didn't tell them you weren't, did you?" Mark said he had.

Mark told Bennett that he was worried less about his personal safety than he was that he had ruined any chance of connecting with his neighbors. Bennett assured him that he had not. Bennett and Gerry Palmer knew that someone had spread a rumor that Mark was going to finger a particular person as the shooter, so they put the word out on the street that Mark had not been able to make out the shooter's identity.

That eased Mark's mind about retribution, but the trauma of witnessing a murder remained. He sought counsel from his friend Allan Tibbels. "I can't shake this," he said to Allan, about the despairing weight that hung on him. "I hear the gunshots every night in my sleep. I hear him crying out."

"It'll take about six months," Allan replied. After that, he said, Mark would be able to function, but he would never be the same.

Nicole jumped up and down in her new apartment, radiating happiness. There wasn't much for her church friends to help her carry in, but she did have a place—her very own place. Eight years to the day after Joe's birth and three years after the tearful DRU/Mondawmin Healthy Families ceremony, Nicole could finally say she was living on her own. She could hardly believe it.

Nicole knew it was just one step on a long road to independence. Her contract at the community college childcare center had just expired, so for the moment she lived off of unemployment checks. But Columbia seemed full of opportunity. In her apartment complex's parking lot, Nicole saw license plates from California, Ohio, Iowa, Florida. She knew that people moved to Howard County for jobs. In fact, her cousin had left South Carolina to take jobs in Detroit and Boston but ended up here, to work in Jessup, the next town over. The workplaces of Baltimore and DC were not too far away.

Metropolitan Baltimore Quadel's counseling continued, with visits to make sure Nicole was adjusting well to her new home. Quadel also helped her search for jobs. They asked her about her education, her work experience, her career goals. Sitting at a computer with her, a counselor helped Nicole search through employment listings.

Nicole was scared to take on a full-time job. Joe was only eight, and she didn't have a babysitter. She remained on unemployment for a year. Eventually, a Head Start program hired her as a substitute, and then she found a retail job at Victoria's Secret in Columbia's downtown mall that occasionally kept her working until midnight. Finally, Nicole found work in her field, doing before-school and after-school child care for the Columbia Association, which provided community services and preserved James Rouse's vision. By the time Nicole started working, Joe had turned nine. When family members weren't able to cover while she worked, she let Joe stay home alone.

Joe was enrolled in Running Brook Elementary. He had a year on his classmates because Westside had failed him once. The student body looked much different than the nearly all-black Westside Elementary student body looked. Running Brook Elementary provided free and reduced-price meals to 38 percent of its students. At Joe's old school, 94 percent of the students had qualified. One out of three students at Running Brook was white or Hispanic, and one out of ten reported more than one race. When Joe's birthday came around in Columbia, students of all colors attended his birthday party.

Nicole didn't care what color Joe's friends were. Like her mother did, she checked out *all* of her child's friends. And it wasn't the color of the students at Running Brook Elementary that struck Nicole, it was the education the school provided. Joe often forgot to turn in assignments, and he didn't like to write with a pen. His teachers let him email in his homework rather than write on worksheets, and they reminded Joe to turn in assignments, even if they were late. Teachers emailed throughout the day with Nicole when needed, and when Joe started falling behind in math, they reached out to Nicole, suggesting she hire a tutor. In short, they did not write Joe off like Nicole felt teachers had done at Westside. Nicole occasionally felt singled out as an African American; teachers sometimes said things to Nicole like "You're such a great parent. I wish other parents were like you." Nicole thought they meant "I wish other black parents were like you." But, overall, Nicole felt like the teachers saw her as a mother who wanted the best for her son, and she appreciated their devotion to Joe.

Nicole's education was another story. After four years at Baltimore City Community College, she had yet to get her associate's degree. Nicole landed in academic probation a couple of times, and she resented it when BCCC placed her in classes that did not count toward her degree, just to get her grade point average up. Her enrollment in BCCC dragged on for three semesters after she moved to Columbia. The whole time, Nicole chafed at the attitude she sensed from the teachers and financial aid staff.

Nicole wondered whether it was time to cut that tie to the city. In one sense, keeping a foot in Baltimore was comforting. Baltimore was what she knew. She had experienced everything in life with her family very close to her—with even extended family close by at the Rayner Avenue house and later on in South Carolina. The house in Penn North may have felt claustrophobic after Joe was born and her sister and nephew moved in, but Nicole loved her mother and sisters. They had supported each other emotionally and even financially, covering each other's bills when someone fell on hard times. Nicole's church and friends also bound her to West Baltimore. Leaving all that for Columbia had pained her.

But she had in fact finally moved, and she knew cutting some ties would be good for her. She had already stopped hanging out so much with friends back in West Baltimore. At first she had tried to stay close—she didn't want anyone to say that "Nicole acts different." But when Nicole celebrated her thirtieth birthday at a club in the city, her friends didn't come out. They didn't come to Columbia much, either—not least of all because many didn't have cars. Church kept Nicole coming back to the city, but in 2010 she joined a church in Columbia. Her social life began revolving around her spiritual life as she joined a singles ministry and went out with her new church friends during weekends.

Around the same time, Nicole stopped attending Baltimore City Community College. In fall 2011, she lined up some financial aid and enrolled in Howard Community College.

By the spring of 2006, the *Thompson* partial-consent decree had started generating results. The four former high-rise sites were almost completely redeveloped and occupied. All forty "hard" units (the scattered site dwellings purchased by the housing authority for use as public housing), ten of which had stoked so much controversy in Hamilton, were occupied. Metropolitan Baltimore Quadel had put nearly half of the 1,342 special vouchers from the original partial-consent decree into use around the region.

Judge Garbis's ruling against HUD had not yet generated a full settlement, however. As the remedy trial approached in March 2006, HUD and the plaintiffs were miles apart. The plaintiffs' proposed remedy demanded that nine thousand housing opportunities materialize in "communities of opportunity" throughout the region over the course of ten years, with one-third consisting of hard units. The other two-thirds could be created through special vouchers with counseling. (A "communities of opportunity" framework replaced HUD's race-based "non-impacted" standard, using an index developed by researcher john a. powell that scored each census tract on fourteen indicators related to jobs, transit, poverty, crime, and housing. New mapping techniques dramatically illustrated where opportunity was—and was not—in a given region. The index did not include race, but it did not matter. Wealth and opportunity still followed whiteness, and it showed in the maps.)

HUD still hoped to walk away from the *Thompson* case unscathed. In his January 2005 ruling, Judge Garbis had promised HUD an opportunity to introduce evidence that the agency had, in fact, pursued regionalization as a strategy. U.S. Department of Justice attorneys made a lengthy argument to Garbis that HUD was not liable under the "affirmatively further" Fair Housing Act provision. Furthermore, they argued, HUD was not liable under the Constitution, and even if liability were established, the plaintiffs would not be entitled to a remedy. During the remedy trial, HUD argued that it did operate regionally, for instance through portability of Section 8 vouchers from one jurisdiction to another.

While Barbara worked with her colleagues to monitor the partial consent decree and waited for a chance to negotiate with HUD, she partnered with local advocacy organizations to start the Baltimore Regional Housing Campaign (BRHC), an informal group that pushed for more affordable housing in "communities of high opportunity." In 2005, the group helped convene a focus group of developers to talk about Low-Income Housing Tax Credit (LIHTC) projects. Taking the lead for them was Trudy McFall, who had worked in affordable housing for decades in the state and federal governments and as a private developer. During the focus group, developers noted two main obstacles to LIHTC projects in communities of opportunity. One was the local approval provision in the Qualified Allocation Plan (which governs distribution of LIHTC credits); the provision stopped developers from applying unless a local government had signed off. Beyond that, noted Enterprise Homes' Chickie Grayson, local governments could stymie a project through zoning and permitting processes.

The Baltimore Regional Housing Campaign also lobbied for inclusionary housing laws across the region. Affordable housing advocates often lauded the "moderately priced dwelling unit" law in Montgomery County, Maryland, just outside Washington, DC. The 1973 law had generated over eleven thousand affordable homes by requiring large developments to reduce prices for renters and buyers in 12 to 15 percent of their units. In 1997, the Greater Baltimore Committee had recommended that the city and counties join forces to create a regional housing agency and implement an inclusionary housing policy. That never happened, but in 2007, the city council passed an inclusionary housing law that required developments with more than thirty units to reserve 20 percent of the units for lower-income households.

While Baltimore City figured out its path to inclusionary housing, researchers and policymakers across the country grappled with the future of regional housing mobility, occasionally incorporating *Thompson v. HUD* into their discussions. In 2006, an academic journal published a proposal by *Gautreaux* attorney Alex Polikoff to move fifty thousand black families out of America's "urban ghettos." The journal included a response from Case Western Reserve University historian Rhonda Williams, who wondered how the "migrating ghetto" would be received in the suburbs. Since the early twentieth century, Williams wrote, white America had viewed black bodies as "pathogens" and had found crafty ways to quarantine them. She quoted a white man who had testified at a "fairness hearing" in 1996 for the *Thompson* partial-consent decree, asking why he should bear the burden of living near public housing families when he didn't "urinate in the hallways" or "have illegitimate babies."

Williams also harnessed the mobility paradigm to the fate of neighborhoods left behind by families who opted to move. "I seriously wonder whether a national housing mobility program should have embedded within it a vision to provide those who remain behind with housing and other opportunities as well," Williams wrote.

The debate over whether to target government housing assistance toward the city or the suburbs also encompassed the federal Low-Income Housing Tax Credit. Derided at first by some as a tax shelter and "mediocre substitute" for the Reagan administration's cuts to direct housing provision, and criticized for sloughing off too much funding into the hands of middleman syndicators, the tax credit had produced over one million units of new and rehabilitated low-income housing by its twentieth anniversary in 2007. With new construction of public housing and project-based Section 8 both mostly abandoned by the 1980s, no other government program produced more low-income rental housing. A 2004 HUD report showed that Low-Income Housing Tax Credit units were disproportionately located in areas of minority and poverty concentration, particularly in cities.

Law professors like Florence Roisman and Myron Orfield argued for stricter application of civil rights law to the Low-Income Housing Tax Credit. Roisman wrote that the U.S. Treasury Department and state housing agencies were lackluster discrimination watchdogs. The only civil rights provision in the LIHTC statute, Roisman wrote, was one prohibiting landlords from denying a lease based on the use of a Section 8 voucher.

To make his case, Orfield laid out the damage that segregation causes. When enough minority families move in to a neighborhood, whites tend to leave, depressing home values. As lower-income minority households rent and purchase the newly affordable homes, racial isolation intensifies—further depressing values and depleting home equity, the main source of wealth for middle- and lower-income families. Orfield pointed out that while many middle-class African Americans live in poor neighborhoods, poor whites "live more dispersed throughout suburbia, live in middle-income neighborhoods and attend middle-class schools." Black children in poor neighborhoods are more likely to face educational and economic barriers, even if they're not poor themselves. Poor and segregated neighborhoods also have higher crime rates, more environmental hazards—and more of just about anything harmful. Integration, Orfield wrote, brought poor and minority households better health, higher earnings, and higher college graduation rates.

Orfield acknowledged the tension between regional housing mobility and place-based community development, the two solutions most often proposed for residential segregation and concentrated poverty. Proponents of place-based development criticized regional approaches for lacking "the support of minority communities, which fear losing political power and community control of services," Orfield wrote. "The Low-Income Housing Tax Credit is virtually the only capital available to neighborhoods that have been effectively redlined by the private market."

In 2007, Barbara Samuels joined the board of a Texas fair housing organization called Inclusive Communities Project, Inc. (ICP). Inclusive Communities helped Section 8 families in Dallas find suburban housing as part of the remedy in *Walker v. HUD*. Elizabeth Julian—who had helped file the *Walker* case, worked inside HUD to settle *Thompson*, and testified for plaintiffs in the *Thompson* liability trial—served as Inclusive Communities' president. In March 2008, Inclusive Communities and the law firm Daniel & Beshara filed a lawsuit against the Texas Department of Housing and Community Affairs over the perpetuation of racial segregation by disproportionately allocating Low-Income Housing Tax Credits to poor, racially isolated areas.

In the Inclusive Communities complaint against Texas, attorneys drew on the Constitution's Equal Protection Clause and two of the most seemingly straightforward sections of the Fair Housing Act, Sections 3604(a) and 3605(a). Mike Daniel of Daniel & Beshara had worked with Elizabeth Julian on *Walker v. HUD*. Neither Daniel nor Julian was afraid of pursuing a constitutional claim that defendants had acted with an *intent* to discriminate. A federal judge ruled in *Walker* that the city of Dallas and its housing authority had a "long, unbroken history of deliberate segregation and discrimination in public housing." But to be safe, they also pursued a strategy that didn't require proof of discriminatory intent. They filed a "disparate impact" claim.*

A disparate impact claim introduces evidence that a defendant's actions disproportionately harmed a protected class. The idea of disparate impact seems simple: a defendant says, "But I didn't mean to!" and a plaintiff says, "Well, but you did." It's trickier in practice. It's not enough to just present evidence of a disproportionate effect on African Americans, because that effect might stem from something a defendant does with a legitimate goal in mind. In administrating the Low-Income Housing Tax Credit program, for instance, a state housing agency might argue that affordable housing developments are most helpful in poor neighborhoods. Presenting *prima facie* evidence of a disparate impact is only the first step in pursuing a claim; a defendant can then argue a legitimate public or business interest. After that, it's a matter of determining whether or not an alternative course of action could have satisfied that legitimate interest without generating the disparate impact.

While Inclusive Communities went after Texas's state housing agency, Barbara Samuels kept pushing Maryland's housing agency to revise its plan for allocating LIHTC tax credits. She believed the provision requiring a jurisdiction's endorsement of any LIHTC development had a disparate impact on black renters and black communities. The plan that the state published on October 24, 2008, however, kept the local approval provision intact.

On November 4, 2008, Americans elected Barack Obama, a one-term

---

*The passage of the Fair Housing Act regarding the duty to "affirmatively . . . further fair housing" applies to the federal government, not state governments; in *ICP v. TDHCA*, the plaintiffs sued only a state agency. The Housing and Community Development Act of 1974 applied the "affirmatively further" duty to recipients of HUD funding—e.g., TDHCA—but gave the power of action only to HUD in the form of withholding funding. Even federal judge Marvin Garbis, in his 2005 opinion in *Thompson v. HUD*, ruled that the Housing and Community Development Act "neither confers a right of action nor a basis for suit." *Thompson v. HUD*, 348 F. Supp. 2d 398 (D. Md. 2005), 40.

Democratic U.S. senator from Illinois, to the presidency. *Fair* housing was not in the headlines when President Obama was inaugurated in January 2009. There was no room for it, thanks to the housing *market*, which was a ginormous shit-show train wreck that defied all hyperbole. Nonetheless, fair housing advocates hoped Obama's presence in the White House would lead to stronger civil rights enforcement at HUD. In September 2009—over three years after the *Thompson v. HUD* remedy trial began—Obama administration officials told Judge Garbis that HUD was willing to negotiate a remedy. Later that fall, city and county government officials started work on a new analysis of impediments to fair housing for the Baltimore region—the first since 1996. (HUD uses analyses of impediments from its grantees as a baseline to determine whether or not a jurisdiction is affirmatively furthering fair housing.) One of the group's stated goals in the analysis of impediments was to "balance revitalization with de-concentration and desegregation"—a recognition of the same tension noted by Myron Orfield, Elizabeth Julian, Rhonda Williams, and others.

In October 2009, the Baltimore Regional Housing Campaign and the Poverty and Race Research Action Council released a progress report on the *Thompson* mobility program. According to the report, over 1,500 families had participated in the mobility program, with about 90 percent of the families moving to the counties and just 20 percent moving back to the city after one year. Families reported high satisfaction with schools, safety, and health in their new communities. The report said the Baltimore Housing Mobility Program had "overcome some of the issues that bedeviled programs such as the federally sponsored Moving to Opportunity program, whose well-publicized shortcomings overshadowed its successes in the public eye." Critics had faulted Moving to Opportunity for the number of families who refused to move to the suburbs or quickly ended up back in the city, and the Baltimore Housing Mobility Program demonstrated better numbers on that front.

In 2010, Maryland's housing department announced that it would revise its policy for disbursing the LIHTC tax credits, and Barbara Samuels sent the agency nine pages of comments. She criticized the local "pocket veto," and, using HUD data on the location of LIHTC properties in Maryland, she accused DHCD of "perpetuating and reinforcing segregation in the market." Barbara also noted a distinction between elderly and family LIHTC projects. Nationwide, HUD data showed that elderly LIHTC projects were more likely to be found in census tracts with lower proportions of poor and minority households. In Maryland, Barbara found, a majority of suburban LIHTC projects created between 2007 and 2010

were for the elderly. Only eight family projects were created in the Maryland suburbs during that time.

In January 2011, the state released its final Qualified Allocation Plan. The local
approval provision remained, allowing local officials to block proposed LIHTC
developments. Barbara called Michael Allen, a lawyer with the civil rights firm
Relman Dane and Colfax, whom she had known for years. Allen served as co-
counsel for plaintiffs in a suit against Westchester County, New York, for falsely
claiming that it had affirmatively furthered fair housing, and he represented Baltimore City's law department in a disparate impact lawsuit against Wells Fargo over
foreclosed homes the bank owned throughout the city.

On August 30, 2011, Barbara Samuels and Michael Allen, serving as co-counsel
for the Baltimore Regional Housing Campaign, filed an administrative complaint with HUD against the State of Maryland and its Department of Housing
and Community Development over their administration of LIHTC tax credits.
The local approval provision established "an institutional mechanism for local
'NIMBY' opposition to LIHTC housing without regard to the worthiness of the
project," the complaint read. "The State's latest discriminatory housing practice
occurred on January 24, 2011, when DHCD adopted its 2011 Qualified Allocation
Plan."

As he had with Wells Fargo, Michael Allen pursued a disparate impact claim. He
and Barbara mustered data showing that Low-Income Housing Tax Credit rentals were "disproportionately unavailable" in Maryland's heavily white areas, and
that they were more segregated than the regular rental market: while half of all
rental units were in areas with a poverty rate below 10 percent, only one out of
three LIHTC units could be found in those low-poverty areas. With nearly half
of LIHTC-eligible households in Maryland being black or Latino, the complaint
read, "the relative scarcity of affordable units in predominantly White areas has a
disproportionately adverse impact on minorities who seek to reside in these areas
and who qualify for affordable housing."

Just thirty-one days later, Barbara signed off on another major housing discrimination complaint, this one against Baltimore County. Like the other complaint, this one drew on disparate impact theory and the duty to affirmatively
further fair housing. It also hung on this phrase in the Fair Housing Act: "otherwise deny or make housing unavailable." As in *Thompson v. HUD*, the attorneys
found several plaintiffs to illustrate what they saw as a disproportionate burden
that African Americans—especially those with disabilities—faced in finding subsidized housing outside of disproportionately black areas.

The complaint asked HUD to consider "the County's previous explicitly segre-
gationist policies, present de facto racial segregation, and the growing dearth of
affordable . . . rental housing for families in non-impacted areas." Barbara pulled
testimony from the 1970 U.S. Commission on Civil Rights hearing in Woodlawn,
including planning consultant Yale Rabin's report on exclusionary zoning. The
complaint also drew on the September 2010 draft analysis of impediments, which
stated that Baltimore County "has maintained a deliberate decision not to build
public housing in order to preserve its economic homogeneity."

The accusations continued to the present day. The county had let the supply of
affordable housing shrink by allowing private low-income housing to disappear
by demolition and attrition. The complaint pointedly criticized the county's hostility to Low-Income Housing Tax Credit developments for families. (New construction mostly benefited the elderly.) Baltimore County had "one of the most
onerous local approval requirements in the country," the complaint read, because
it went "one step further" than the state's restrictive policy: developers wishing
to build LIHTC units were required to "receive the approval of the individual
County Council member in whose district the project will be located before the
developer may meet with County staff."

The complaint argued that the county's conduct had created a disparate impact
for African Americans, families with children, and individuals with disabilities;
and that the county's certifications of "affirmatively furthering fair housing" were
invalid. The complaint asked HUD to deem those certifications "insufficient" to
receive HUD funding, force the county to redo its Consolidated Plan and other
planning documents, and declare the county's Housing Choice Voucher Program
to be afoul of its civil rights obligations.

The 2011 complaint against Baltimore County had the potential to either serve
as a bookend for a restrictive era or as an indicator of HUD's willingness to abide
segregation in metropolitan regions. It all depended on the reactions from HUD
and Baltimore County officials.

By the fall of 2011, *Thompson v. HUD* had twice been a shot in the arm: first
with the partial consent decree that mandated the placement of public and subsidized housing across the region, and then with Judge Garbis's 2005 finding of
liability against HUD for failing to handle public housing regionally. Through
the Baltimore Regional Housing Campaign and ACLU–Maryland, Barbara
Samuels had tried to use *Thompson* as a catalyst to further break down the lines
of exclusion across the region. There had been a few steps forward and a few
steps back. The judge had found HUD liable, but none of the plaintiffs' claims

against the city had succeeded. The Baltimore Regional Housing Mobility Program had finally started moving hundreds of families to parts of the region that had resisted subsidized housing—even acquiring some hard units—but a final deal to expand regional housing mobility remained elusive five years after the *Thompson* remedy trial. Baltimore City had adopted an inclusionary housing law in 2007, but it was full of loopholes. (Howard County had adopted a "moderate income housing unit" program in 1996 and a law banning discrimination based on one's source of income in 1992.) The city and counties had begun a new analysis of impediments, but there was no regional infrastructure to support bold reforms—certainly not enough to develop a regional housing authority—and collaborations between local governments over the previous decade had yielded little fair housing action.

In December 2011, the Baltimore Regional Fair Housing Group—a coalition of local governments—released draft analyses of impediments for Baltimore City, Anne Arundel County, Baltimore County, Harford County, and Howard County, as well as a separate draft for the region as a whole. The authors listed a dozen impediments to fair housing in the region. The local approval provision in the state's Qualified Allocation Plan received especially harsh criticism. The draft analysis of impediments asked the state to eliminate the local approval provision and pass legislation banning "source of income" discrimination.

The document repeatedly assailed the lack of regional fair housing infrastructure. "Thus far, fair housing efforts in the Baltimore region can be characterized only as loosely cooperative," the authors wrote. The authors hoped that the "heavily structured regional governance" they desired would come from the *Thompson v. HUD* lawsuit's elusive remedy.

The Maryland Department of Housing and Community Development sent back three detailed pages, almost all relating to criticism of its Qualified Action Plan. State housing official John Greiner pushed back on many assertions. He cited a federal preference for "Qualified Census Tracts"—areas with either a poverty rate of at least 25 percent or at least half of households earning no more than 60 percent of the area median income—and noted that Baltimore City had opposed giving more points to applications in communities of opportunity.

Eight years after the *Thompson* liability trial, here once again was a government housing official making the case that limited housing funds should be prioritized not for places where mobility advocates believed poor people ought to live, but for the under-resourced neighborhoods where poor people already did live. Greiner's comments indicated a belief, like that evinced by Kurt Schmoke and Daniel

Henson, that with government investment, neighborhoods like Sandtown could be transformed.

During the mid-2000s, Allan Tibbels had contracted multidrug resistant bacteria, and complications put him in and out of the hospital over the next several years. Mark Lange devoted himself to Allan during this period, and they became closer than they'd ever been. Mark felt Allan had stopped obsessing over helping other people and let himself be vulnerable. This, Mark believed, had finally allowed their relationship to become a two-way street.

One day, in a reflective mood, Allan ruminated about the past twenty years. What, he asked Mark, had they really accomplished? There were the Habitat houses and the school, but the brutality in the streets had not subsided. Maybe, he said, all they were in Sandtown to do was to come alongside people and suffer with them.

Mark had been there for big moments in Allan's life—handing out programs at his and Susan's wedding, riding in the ambulance after he broke his neck. All his life, Mark had fitfully pursued the truth, and the closer he had come into Allan's orbit, the closer he had come to finding it. When it came to living out the Christian faith, Allan was Mark's guiding star.

That star was going dark.

On May 28, 2010, Allan called his wife, Susan. He was at home with Mark, and he was so sick that he had decided to call an ambulance. Susan happened to be at Mercy Hospital in downtown Baltimore, visiting one of their adult children. After Allan arrived at Mercy's emergency room deathly ill, Susan went downstairs to check on him; he seemed relatively stable, so she went back upstairs.

Once Allan had stabilized further, Susan—thoroughly exhausted—left to rest and asked Mark to stay overnight with Allan.

Allan, Mark discovered, was still Allan. He was pissed off about an oxygen mask that pushed up into his eyes. If he pulled it off and broke the seal, it would automatically shut off and he'd go into respiratory arrest. Still, Allan wanted it off.

Mark refused to take it off. Allan looked Mark in the eye. "You are ruining our friendship," he said.

"It's alright," Mark said, "I'll be your friend again in the next life."

"Come here," Allan said weakly.

Mark leaned in, and Allan tried to grab him. "Take this fucking mask off my head!" he said.

"I know you're ready to go," Mark said, "but you're not going to go before Susan comes back. You need to say good-bye to your wife, and she needs to say good-bye to you."

"She's not coming back," he said. The morphine had messed with Allan's sense of time. "She's been gone two days!"

"She's been gone a couple hours," Mark said.

Allan improved, and when Susan returned, doctors were preparing to send him home with some IV drugs. As Susan and Allan discussed his care, Allan passed out, and Susan screamed for a doctor. She thought he had died. Doctors arrived and worked for about half an hour to resuscitate Allan. Then they moved him to a coronary care unit. When Allan came to in the morning, he said he did not want to be placed on a ventilator if he needed resuscitating again.

Allan's doctor at Mercy, Jeanette Nazarian, marveled at Allan. She had never spoken with a person like him. He seemed completely outside of himself, thinking of his community rather than of his own pain. Dr. Nazarian listened as he spoke with his visitors about the future of New Song's ministries. An infection had abscessed some of Allan's heart valves, and Nazarian spent hours fruitlessly trying to talk Allan into an open-heart procedure, even though his quadriplegia made him a high risk for dying on the operating table. Allan was certain of his relationship with God and seemed entirely unafraid of the torture that she knew lay ahead.

Eventually, Allan lost consciousness again. Doctors suggested taking Allan off of everything except the morphine, just as he had requested. Early in the morning of June 3, Allan flatlined, and Susan prayed aloud for God to receive him. After a minute or so, Mark and Susan said, "Amen."

As soon as they said that, the heart monitor produced a handful of beeps and went back to a flatline.

"He always had to have the last word," Susan said.

Jeanette Nazarian stood outside the room watching through a glass wall. She hadn't wanted to intrude. The young nurse in the room turned to her with a look that said "What?!?"

Death, Nazarian thought, could be just as mysterious as life.

Dr. Nazarian couldn't attend the funeral of everyone she saw pass in the ICU; if she did that, she wouldn't have time for anything else. But she made an exception for Allan Tibbels. She had been so impressed with Allan and his world. And when nurses had said things to Allan and his visitors like "Ah, it's so great that you do that," Nazarian had been struck by their response: it wasn't a "white savior" thing. Allan and Mark and Susan didn't want to be the white people who rolled in thinking they were going to save black people who couldn't help themselves. Nazarian had gone to city public schools, but after meeting Allan Tibbels, she realized that she had never been to Pigtown, much less Sandtown, and that growing up in a wealthy neighborhood had granted her choices that kids in other neighborhoods could never have imagined.

On June 14, 2010, Nazarian went to New Shiloh Baptist Church on N. Monroe Street, just above W. North Avenue. Around one thousand people had come to say good-bye to Allan Tibbels. A picture slideshow ran at the beginning, and, as Allan had requested, the sounds of Bruce Cockburn and U2 filled the church. Beneath a plain cross and a kaleidoscopic stained-glass window, many people paid tribute. "I can hear Allan saying, 'We are more John Perkins than John Perkins,'" said Dr. Perkins, who was two days shy of his eightieth birthday. "It was the best compliment I ever heard."

Antoine Bennett cried more over Allan's death than he had when his own father died. He worried what Allan's absence would mean for the New Song project. Bennett felt that the Sandtown Resident Action Committee—an organization that arose after the 2008 dissolution of Community Building in Partnership—had fallen apart after the death of its president, Charles Johnson, earlier in 2010. Johnson had taken on much of the Resident Action Committee's organizing, and Bennett felt it was dangerous for community development work to revolve too much around one person's charisma.

Allan had turned over the directorship of New Song Urban Ministries to Bennett and Patty Prasada-Rao three years earlier, but he had still possessed the most institutional knowledge. Allan had also served as a buffer to absorb tension in the organization, and Bennett felt Allan's aversion to burning bridges had encouraged cautiousness and even fakery within the ministries. What would happen to New Song without Allan Tibbels?

Thurman Williams knew Allan had done a lot of the work and refused to take credit for it. He knew it was Allan's magnetism that had attracted so much funding from outside the city. He knew people were already thinking, "It's over because Allan's not here." But Williams professed optimism to Allan's hundreds of admirers.

"We have come here to have a funeral for Allan," Williams said during his eulogy. "We have not come tonight to have a funeral for the mission that Allan gave his life to."

By the end of 2012, Nicole Smith was glad she had left Baltimore City Community College for Howard Community College. She had taken classes for years at BCCC without obtaining a degree; she found HCC's faculty and staff more professional and more concerned with her education. Her schedule was now filled with courses, like "Working with Infants and Toddlers" and "Child Health, Safety, and Nutrition," that built toward an associate's degree in early childhood development. She could see herself finishing at HCC in just a couple of years.

Nicole wondered what her life would have been like if she had remained in Baltimore. She thought she'd probably still be trying to fight her way out of BCCC with a degree. She'd probably have put Joe in a charter school. Nicole's sister's son attended Roots and Branches, which in 2011 had taken over the campus of Nicole's former school, Harriet Tubman Elementary, after the city closed it for underperforming. Maybe Joe would have ended up at Roots and Branches, too. Or not—charter schools accepted students through a random lottery. Nicole might have ended up driving all over town to get from home, to BCCC, to a job, to wherever Joe ended up being in school.

Not that it was easy in Howard County. She still had to drive. But Columbia Association, where she worked, and Howard Community College were both just a few miles away, and Joe took a school bus to nearby Running Brook Elementary. As Nicole racked up credits toward her degree, she began to picture her future: a home daycare program like her mother's, perhaps. Maybe one day she would run a daycare center or teach in an elementary school.

Kate Kenney, an assistant professor for early childhood education, knew that HCC's associate's degree in early childhood development was perfect for Nicole's goals. Under state regulations, the degree allowed graduates to direct a childcare center with as many as forty children. With several more classes on top of that degree, a student could earn an associate of arts in teaching and transfer to a four-year teaching program.

Kenney found Nicole to be an asset in the classroom. Humorous and humble, she got along well with the other students. Kenney also taught Nicole in two "practicum" courses, observing her occasionally in a child care setting. Nicole did well in the field. After all, she worked with children already and had grown up around a daycare program. (In fact, Nicole loved coming up with creative lesson plans and found the strict guidelines and supervision in the field to be stifling.) Nicole struggled with writing, however. Kenney found her to be apologetic about certain academic skills she thought she was lacking. This was common among

Kenney's students from disadvantaged backgrounds. Indeed, growing up, Nicole had attended two schools threatened with state takeover and one that the city later shut down.

Nicole worked very hard to incorporate feedback and improve what she'd written. Kenney believed that hard work and perseverance got people farther in life than any innate genius—she'd seen research that said as much—and Nicole had both characteristics in spades. When Nicole and her friends got the "math blues," for instance, they started study groups together. Other students from schools in poor neighborhoods struggled to get through noncredit remedial modules and spent years playing catch-up. Nicole was moving smoothly toward graduation despite holding down a job and raising a son on her own.

Nicole's progress impressed not just her professors, but also the staff at ACLU–Maryland. Every once in a while, they asked her and a few other mobility program participants to speak at various events. One time they took a van all the way to the headquarters of the U.S. Department of Housing and Urban Development.

In late 2012, Nicole agreed to join other *Thompson* voucher holders to speak at a court hearing in Baltimore. On the chilly morning of November 20, 2012, an ACLU–Maryland legal assistant picked Nicole up in front of her apartment in Columbia. Nicole stepped into the car, and under mostly clear skies they drove to downtown Baltimore.

The U.S. District Courthouse, a hulking white structure with long slender windows, stood back from W. Lombard Street behind an expanse of grass and a painted aluminum sculpture that seemed to depict a Cubist game of Twister. Nicole took the elevator to the fifth floor and walked into Courtroom 5C.

The courtroom quickly filled up with people. One of them was Barbara Samuels, whom Nicole had gotten to know a little bit since she started speaking publicly about her mobility experience. The ACLU–Maryland staff was trying to figure out what to do about the crowd. Some of the lawyers from the city's housing authority were stuck in a long line outside the building.

Nicole spied a young woman whom she recognized in the courtroom. Sandra lived in Gilmor Homes and had attended Nicole's mother's daycare program as a little girl. Sandra said the rumor in the projects was that you could show up at the courthouse and get a free voucher. Sandra wasn't the only one who wanted out of her neighborhood. Hundreds converged on the courthouse, and as the crowd grew, Judge Garbis asked for help escorting people out of the courtroom. A couple of paralegals went down to the lobby to collect contact information so they could mail out voucher applications.

Over the decades, the city had tried to modernize Gilmor Homes, and tried to "transform" Sandtown from top to bottom. People still wanted out.

Barbara Samuels had some idea why so many people had shown up to the courthouse. A mailer had gone out to members of the *Thompson* plaintiff class inviting them to submit comments on a final settlement by mail or attend the November 20 hearing at the courthouse. "If you are African-American and have lived in Baltimore City Family Public Housing at any time since January 31, 1995, or may live there at any time prior to January 1, 2027, you may be part of a Class Action civil rights lawsuit," it read.

Those criteria matched about forty thousand people.

Sixteen years after Garbis's approval of the partial consent decree, HUD and the plaintiffs had finally agreed upon a final settlement to the case. Barbara was grateful for all the help she'd had along the way. A local firm, Brown Goldstein and Levy, had stuck with her since the partial consent decree was issued in 1996. The NAACP Legal Defense and Education Fund had joined for the remedy phase, staffing their effort with native Baltimoreans. As part of the final settlement, HUD and Baltimore City planned to distribute 2,600 more mobility vouchers, on top of the 1,800 families who had been offered the vouchers and counseling in the 1996 partial settlement. Barbara had hoped for more like 6,700 new vouchers, plus equalization remedies to bring parity to communities with public housing, but helping 2,600 families move to "communities of opportunity" was still remarkable in the history of housing mobility.

Nearly three hundred people had mailed in comments or requested to speak at the hearing. Some of the stories moved Barbara deeply. People had seen family members shot. Some struggled to stay clean in neighborhoods full of drug dealing. Many shared their dreams of a better living environment. And now there was a line all the way down the block full of people who thought they could walk away with a voucher that very day.

In the courtroom, Judge Garbis addressed the crowd. "First of all, I am delighted to see as many people as are here," he said. "I understand there were a lot more, and we're trying to accommodate in terms of what they wish."

William Ryan, the attorney for Baltimore City who had sparred with plaintiffs throughout the liability trial, thanked the court for indulging his tardiness.

"Having practiced law in the city for 30 years, it was the first time I ever had to stand in line for 45 minutes outside our courthouse to enter it," he said. "And that shows how important what we're doing here today is." After saying how proud he was that the court refused to find the city liable, Ryan singled out Barbara Samuels—to thank her. They'd argued plenty, Ryan said, "but there's one thing that I learned along the way, and respect tremendously, and that is she had a singular devotion to her clients. And she helped get us to where we are today. And Barbara, I think your clients should know that."

Paul Graziano, now in his twelfth year as Baltimore's housing commissioner, praised Judge Garbis for his leadership. "Even the time," Graziano said, "when you threatened to put me in jail if I didn't finish a certain number of units by a certain point next year."

As laughter broke out, Garbis corrected him. "I might interrupt and say it wasn't jail. He was going to be forced to reside in one of his units."

"Where is Barbara?" Graziano asked. "And Barbara—yes—I sort of echo what Bill said, we've had some very interesting discussions over the years, and in the end, they've been very productive and fruitful."

Toward the end of the proceedings, Garbis called for testimony from Baltimoreans who had benefited from the mobility vouchers in the partial consent decree.

"Nicole Smith," Garbis said. "Is she here?"

"Yes," answered Barbara.

"Good morning, everyone," Nicole said. "My name is Nicole Smith."

Nicole breezed through her life story: a childhood spent partially in Murphy Homes and Westport Homes; a hardworking mom who bought a house in a struggling city neighborhood, only to lose it to foreclosure; applying for public housing, knowing that drugs, violence, and poor conditions awaited her and her son.

"I chose the Quadel program because it provided a way out for my then eight-year-old son," Nicole said. "He's now eleven."

In Columbia, Nicole said, the before- and aftercare center where she worked had promoted her to assistant director. "I also transferred from BCCC to Howard Community College, where I'm doing excellent," she said.

"Now, not only have I found opportunities and happiness here, but so has my son," she continued. "In the city, I did not want my son to play outside. He didn't have many friends, and he was struggling in school. Here he is doing very, very well at school."

Nicole described the diverse group of families that had come out to Joe's birthday party three months earlier. "I really enjoyed that, because we didn't have that in the city," she said.

"So yes, I support this," Nicole continued. "And not only for me but for other people who want to change their lives just like I have for me and my son."

"That's it," Nicole said to applause. "Thank you."

After attorneys for the plaintiffs, HUD, and the city formally declared their approval of the settlement, Judge Garbis jokingly cited the "rapid pace" of his written decisions and announced that this time he would render his decision right then and there in the courtroom.

First, though, he wanted to talk about how much things had changed since the partial consent decree was signed.

"I don't know how many were here in 1996 when we had the first fairness hearing. Was anybody here except Barbara Samuels?" Garbis asked, drawing chuckles.

Many spoke against that decree, he said, and there had been some "ugly remarks" from county residents. This time, the judge said, no one objected, despite twice as many vouchers becoming available for use in the counties. "You did it so well, 'you' being the people who have been moved, by the parties, that we don't have any adverse reaction, and I'm proudest of that, and that's the most significant part of this hearing, as I see it," Garbis said.

Garbis also highlighted the pickle HUD had been in ever since Barbara Samuels and her colleagues had filed the first complaint. "Most of this fight was not so much about what HUD wants to do, but what HUD can do, on two grounds," he said. First, HUD got caught up in local politics. County governments were not part of the suit, and they were not eager to participate. Second, he said, was "a fight over the power of the judiciary and the power of the executive and who has the power to tell which one to do whatever they want [it] to do." For one thing, he said, any remedy coming out of litigation rather than from a settlement would have been difficult to force onto HUD. "There's a real question as to how much can a court do to compel an agency to do things that they don't choose to do," Judge Garbis said.

"The other thing," he continued, "which is a little sensitive, and I really couldn't say this two weeks ago, but I can say this now, HUD is a political organization. It's under the president."

President Obama had been reelected on November 6. For all the years of contentious negotiating, one person forty miles away could pull the rug out from under all of them.

"It is the president's policy that's carried out. It is this administration—

President Obama who brought his administration to HUD that got HUD to take the positions that led to this settlement. And I think it's fair to say thanks to President Obama and his administration for having the policies," the judge said.

As applause filled the room, Judge Garbis added, "Two weeks ago, I could have been impeached for saying that." The applause turned to laughter.

Six thousand, five hundred and three days had passed since ACLU–Maryland had filed its complaint. Many buildings had gone down and come up. Three presidents had served, and in Baltimore, four mayors: Kurt Schmoke, Martin O'Malley, former city council president Sheila Dixon, and—after Dixon resigned following an embezzlement conviction—another city council president, Stephanie Rawlings-Blake. The region's population had changed, with many African Americans moving to Baltimore County. But the rate of residential segregation had changed little. Despite the potential for over four thousand families to move to communities of opportunity, many more thousands—both in public and private housing—would still be penned into highly segregated communities that offered little opportunity.

"I have no doubt, particularly in light of litigation uncertainties, that the settlement is fair. It is reasonable. It is adequate. It is approved, and I thank you," Judge Garbis said, and the hearing was adjourned.

Allan Tibbels left behind a large and busy organization in New Song Urban Ministries, thanks to his role in one of Dr. John M. Perkins's "three R's": redistribution. At one point, New Song Urban Ministries had over eighty employees on the payroll, due in large part to the school and Sandtown Habitat. And Gerry's Goods, the first business launched by New Song Urban Ministries, had become a community gathering place as envisioned, as well as the face that Baltimore's signature Christian community development organization showed to the world. Tour groups from across the country slept in the gym at the New Song Center and visited Gerry's Goods for soups, smoothies, and caramel macchiatos. Behind the counter was a welcoming presence: Gerry Palmer, tall, with a strong neck and a gold tooth, and Antoine Bennett, shorter and more rotund, with sympathetic eyes and a winsome grin. Despite the lack of plexiglass, no one had tried to rob the store.

New Song Community Church pastor Thurman Williams received invitations from all over the country to talk about New Song and Christian community development. He attended the Christian Community Development Association's annual conference in twelve out of seventeen years, and he landed grants to take members of New Song's staff with him. He hosted tours of New Song that included a "CCDA café." In the church's new-member class, Williams spoke about Perkins, and he asked Antoine Bennett and Patty Prasada-Rao to discuss the CCDA philosophy at welcome time each Sunday. Each January, Williams did a series of sermons on the CCDA core principles. The titles of some of his sermons—"Let Justice Roll Down," "The Ultimate Relocation," "Reconciliation: Making Room at the Table," "Redistribution: Blooming Where You've Been Planted"—reflected his dedication to Perkins.

Yet Williams was sensitive to criticism that "the tail was wagging the dog" at New Song—in other words, that social ministries had pushed discipleship to the back burner. New Song Community Church belonged to the evangelical Presbyterian Church in America. Discipleship—making disciples, bringing people to Christ—was a pastor's core responsibility. When Williams first joined the church in 2000, he'd noticed that despite all the ministries working on health care, homebuilding, jobs, and arts in the neighborhood, only thirty or so people showed up for worship on Sunday mornings at "the Mansion" on N. Gilmor Street.

The church's early days had featured "the talk" (where church leaders like co-pastor Steve Smallman would approach outsiders after a few services and remind them that New Song was a "community church"). If the church got overwhelmed by people from outside the neighborhood, the leaders worried, people from inside the neighborhood wouldn't come. Sometimes church leaders directed worshippers elsewhere, such as to Faith Christian Fellowship, a CCDA church across town.

But under Pastor Wy Plummer, New Song had eliminated the talk, and under Pastor Thurman Williams, New Song's Sunday services grew tremendously, moving from the townhouse on Gilmor, to a converted Boys & Girls Club building on N. Calhoun Street, and finally to the gym at the New Song Center. At one point, 150 to 200 people were showing up every Sunday. Williams was a presence: six feet tall, persuasive and energetic, as magnetic as a motivational speaker. He was practical-minded, and thoughtful of how Scripture could be applied in a neighborhood like Sandtown. Working from the original Greek and Hebrew texts, he explained Scripture in a way that resonated with people who had never finished high school and people with graduate degrees. His style appealed to white and black, rich and poor, urban and suburban.

In fact, Williams—who had lived in the suburbs for the first twenty-six years of his life—had felt self-conscious during his early days at New Song. At Faith Christian Fellowship, he had deliberately mixed styles, drawing from classical and traditional black church music. At New Song, he kept the music more traditionally

African American, and as he grew more comfortable as the pastor, he became more unapologetic about the service reflecting, as he put it, "the language of the neighborhood." If people had a problem with that, he believed, there were other places for them to go.

Yet he couldn't shake the feeling that the church was too white for black people and too black for white people. Longtime Sandtown residents kept worshipping at New Song even at peak attendance, but the congregation always had a large "commuter population." In the mid-2000s, New Song hired a consultant to help figure out what the church should be, what the ministries should be, and how the missions and values of the two should align. Along the way, New Song—long a self-described "community church"—began referring to itself as a "community-based" church.

The ministries weren't as healthy as they appeared to be from the outside. The Habitat houses were getting old, requiring maintenance that low-income families couldn't always afford. The nonprofit ministries had been dependent on foundations for two decades, and it was getting harder to raise money. The school, for instance, found itself competing against the city's growing network of charter schools for funding. Then the economy crashed just as Allan's health was declining. In a pinch, Allan had always been the one to find the money.

Allan's death in June 2010 shocked New Song's community and leadership. He'd had plenty of health scares and hospital visits, but even in the face of the most dire prognoses, he'd always come back. With Allan gone, some paralysis set in among staff and leadership. Also, Allan had served as a buffer, and now simmering conflicts between ministries boiled over.

In hopes of developing a strategic plan to move forward and shape its identity in Allan's absence, Thurman Williams and the leaders of New Song's ministries reached out to Mark Gornik in the fall of 2010. Gornik and his colleagues at City Seminary of New York solicited feedback from New Song Community Church's members and leadership, and in the spring of 2011, City Seminary delivered a report to the church. It was forcefully worded, and it focused heavily on the church itself. The report said commuters had grown to 75 percent of church attendance and that some community members had stopped attending, which was at odds with the vision of the church's founders. On top of that, the report said, communication among New Song's leadership team had broken down, the larger church community didn't fully understand decisions that were being made, and competing narratives were emerging about New Song's identity.

City Seminary suggested a new model for Sunday mornings: small gatherings at different homes, limited to residents of Sandtown. A larger afternoon service would encourage outsiders to think not about becoming church members but rather about a deeper involvement in the community. The report said little about community development; that would have to wait until the church had implemented the report's recommendations to a sufficient degree.

The report polarized New Song's leadership. A few people wanted to accept the recommendations in full. Others thought Gornik had lost touch with New Song's evolution after more than a decade in New York City. Moving forward, the church rejected many recommendations but embraced City Seminary's emphasis on redoubling its spiritual foundation and strengthening the church's connection to the community. Church leaders discussed tweaking the Sunday service to add more community flavor. Thurman Williams worked to bring the Harrises back to Sunday service. Eventually, New Song began detaching some of the ministries from the church, including Sandtown Habitat.

Toward the end of 2011, as the church began to move on from dealing with the report's recommendations, the umbrella that connected the church's various efforts in the community couldn't afford to keep Patty Prasada-Rao and Antoine Bennett on staff. Early in 2012, both resigned. Around the same time, Susan Tibbels took a sabbatical from her work at New Song. If Allan had worked himself to death—which wasn't much of a stretch as far as she was concerned—she wondered if she might not be right behind him. During the sabbatical, she continued to help New Song reconfigure itself. After a year of frustration and exhaustion, she withdrew from the church and its ministries.

One of Tibbels's last tasks, near the end of 2012, was to help deliver some bad news: New Song could no longer help keep Gerry's Goods afloat. The store had been spending about $8,000 per month and bringing in about half that. Palmer had already downsized. In a neighborhood with few job opportunities—on the very corner, in fact, where he had "slung coke"—Palmer had provided people close to him with a legitimate way to earn a living, and it had hurt to let them go. He worked long hours after the downsizing, but it couldn't keep the store open.

Palmer left with his head held high. At the peak of the country's worst recession in seventy-five years, he had opened a coffee shop in one of the country's most economically devastated neighborhoods. One-third of new small businesses in America failed within two years, and half went under within five years. Gerry's Goods had operated for four years.

Thurman Williams felt he'd been a good choice to lead the church in the aftermath of Allan Tibbels's death; he'd bucked up his faithful as best he could.

But he thought New Song might need a different kind of leader going forward, a more forceful leader with a clearer vision. In the spring of 2013, he told the New Song community that he and his family planned to move to St. Louis for a new job.

Williams's resignation hit Mark Lange hard. Mark had been in step with Williams on theology and a church's role in its community. Mark had uprooted his life—Betty's, too—to come to Sandtown and follow his truth. The friend who had led him here, Allan Tibbels, had died; the pastor he followed, Thurman Williams, was leaving. What did the future hold for New Song and Sandtown? Mark liked the church's growing rededication to discipleship, but what would happen to John Perkins's community development philosophy? Even under Pastor Williams, Mark felt the church hadn't attracted enough relocators for Perkins's model to succeed. Mark didn't want to see "the talk" return to New Song, but he was critical of church leaders for being too accepting of people getting involved with ministries while living outside the neighborhood. Mark considered relocators key to Christian community development in Sandtown. With Pastor Williams gone, would the fifteen or so who had relocated stick around? Mark knew it was easier for Betty and himself to stay because they didn't have children; what about those who had children or planned to? Even associate pastor Steve Smallman and his wife had moved to a safer West Baltimore neighborhood when their children approached their teenage years.

Mark wanted to see how other people were feeling about their own futures, not just in the church, but in the neighborhood too. He reached out to the core relocators and "remainers."

Bethany Lee agreed to host a pastoral search meeting at her house in the 1000 block of N. Fulton Avenue. Lee, who was white, had moved from St. Louis to Baltimore to become an assistant professor at the University of Maryland School of Social Work. Mark wanted to know who else among the relocators was truly committed to staying in Sandtown. This was the time to figure it out. Mark went around the room and asked people whether they planned to stay. Not everyone was as hardcore as Mark, who believed he'd live out the rest of his life in Sandtown. But one of the relocators, a young white woman named Bekah Yarian, offered encouragement. Yarian had arrived in Sandtown out of college in January 2009. She had bought a house on Presstman Street two doors down from the Gerry's Goods storefront just after the shop had closed down. Several relocators roomed with her there. Yarian planned to marry and have children in the neighborhood. She told Mark that she knew she would be in Sandtown until she heard very clearly from God that she was supposed to be somewhere else.

Nina Anderson offered the group some perspective. "Miss Nina" had lived in Sandtown most of her life. She owned a Habitat house. She had been with the church since the 1990s and once ran EDEN Jobs. Mark Gornik considered her to be a "saint."

New Song, she reminded everyone, had been through many transitions. People had worried the church would fall apart when Pastor Plummer left, but then Pastor Williams had come along. New Song, she believed, would carry on.

It was a gorgeous morning on August 24, 2012: calm, clear, 70 degrees. Barbara Samuels went to Crownsville in Anne Arundel County, where state housing officials were holding a "public listening session" about the guidelines they used to judge applications for LIHTC tax credits.

"This is the first time that the State of Maryland has been doing a comprehensive overhaul of its tax credit allocation plan," said one of several consultants the state had hired to help revise the guidelines.

Barbara had been trying for nearly two decades to weed out parts of the state's Qualified Allocation Plan that she felt contributed to segregation. During the public comment portion of the morning, Kevin Bell, senior vice president of for-profit developer The Woda Group, aggressively defended urban tax-credit developments. He called the Baltimore Regional Housing Campaign's 2011 administrative complaint to HUD over the local approval requirement an "attempt to strip these communities of tax credit funding."

"Saying that . . . they got no business living in their own neighborhoods is a proposal for social engineering that I find presumptuous, insulting, and potentially catastrophic," Bell said.

Bell launched a philippic against the ACLU, asking what their plan was for poor neighborhoods. "Take a flame thrower to them?" he asked. "Or just close your eyes and let them disintegrate?"

Bell brought up the federal preference for the poorest areas—the so-called Qualified Census Tracts—to discredit Barbara's argument for mobility. "You claim it's a violation of the fair housing laws to put any tax credit money into low-income neighborhoods," he said. "I say you're wrong. And anyway, that's for a judge to decide."

Bell plowed through interruptions from his hosts, calling Barbara "the lady from the ACLU" and threatening to take the ACLU to court.

"This is something, I think, that is not necessarily an either/or," said Baltimore City housing official Peter Engel, adding that he liked the idea of options outside the city. "That being said, we don't want to see that come at the expense of redeveloping communities in Baltimore. That's a tough trade-off."

"The obvious solution that nobody has mentioned yet," he continued, "is to actually increase the pie instead of just redividing the pie."

Toward the end of the two-and-a-half-hour session, Barbara spoke up again.

"Obviously, when you work at the ACLU, you have a thick skin about attacks," she said. "So I'm not going to respond on that level other than to say I think that this idea of either/or does a disservice to a reasonable and thoughtful discussion about policy."

Barbara acknowledged the need for affordable housing in all kinds of communities. "The issue is achieving a balance," she said. "And how advocacy of achieving of balance gets set up as a straw man to be knocked down is beyond me."

Near the end of the session, Kevin Bell spoke up again. "I would just like to say to Barbara from the ACLU that we'd love to see if we can expand the pie," he said.

However, he lamented, "there is a certain sized pie."

On February 15, 2013—less than a month into President Obama's second term—the U.S. Department of Housing and Urban Development released the final version of a rule about disparate impact. Federal appeals courts had uniformly upheld disparate impact as a legitimate civil rights theory. The new rule codified the process of establishing disparate impact liability under the Fair Housing Act. The first two steps remained the same: a plaintiff must make a *prima facie* case that a policy has a disparate impact on protected classes, and then the defendant can propose a legitimate interest served by that policy. The new rule established that the final burden rested upon plaintiffs: they would have to show that another practice could have achieved that interest without the disparate impact.

That settled disparate impact. If HUD were then to develop a strong rule on guiding local governments through the process of affirmatively furthering fair housing, it would fortify the two strongest federal tools for enforcing fair housing in the absence of provable discriminatory intent. In fact, advocates had criticized the Obama administration for dragging its heels on an "affirmatively furthering" rule, which many had expected during the first term.

In early 2013, the Poverty and Race Research Action Council (PPRAC) published a "report card" for the administration's first four years. The report card gave HUD credit for improving upon the reputation for timidity it had established in previous administrations. During Obama's first term, for instance, HUD settled *Thompson v. HUD* as well as two suits that claimed African Americans had faced discrimination in recovery programs following Hurricane Katrina. The report card also praised HUD for its increased scrutiny of analyses of impediments to fair housing. A 2010 U.S. Government Accountability Office report had shown that many local governments' analyses were outdated, and that some had pretty much been phoned in. In 2011, HUD froze $7 million in funding to Westchester County in New York after finding four separate analyses of impediments to be insufficient.

Despite the progress, the Poverty and Race Research Action Council and others criticized HUD's enforcement efforts, particularly in Westchester County. In November 2012, the investigative news outlet ProPublica called HUD "soft on segregation" for its failure to push back against the county's executive, Republican Rob Astorino. Astorino had inherited a settlement that called for the construction of 750 affordable units in mostly white areas. Under Astorino, the county placed eighteen units in a 90 percent white town called Rye—but in an area cut off from the rest of Rye by two interstates that lay right on the border of a heavily Hispanic town. Astorino continued to ignore HUD's entreaties after the agency cut funding, and ProPublica's Nikole Hannah-Jones wrote that HUD's response to Westchester County's defiance replicated a "long history" of watering down enforcement in the face of local controversy. The PRRAC report card specifically faulted HUD for accepting the Rye units and for failing to file motions to hold the county in contempt of court for defying the settlement's terms.

The report card also worried that any future rule on affirmatively furthering fair housing would be too heavy on data-driven guidance for local governments and too light on the kind of enforcement "necessary to force compliance among recalcitrant jurisdictions like Westchester." The lack of any rule at all, the report card said, constituted a "major piece of unfinished business."

By the time HUD released its final disparate-impact rule in February 2013, the Baltimore region and the state of Maryland were poised for their own advances in fair housing. Local governments throughout the Baltimore region had released final analyses of impediments that were stronger than their dusty predecessors. The *Thompson* final settlement had doubled down on a mobility program that the rest of the country was increasingly recognizing as a model. And not only had the state hired consultants for its first major overhaul of the Qualified Allocation Plan, the consultants had signaled the state's willingness to get rid of local approval.

In February 2013, the Maryland Department of Housing and Community

Development opened its doors to introduce a new draft of the plan. "You really do need to read it. It really is different," said Pat Sylvester, the agency's head of multifamily housing.

"The biggest change . . ." Sylvester started to say, then backtracked. "I shouldn't say the biggest change because they're all big changes. So we have changed the threshold for local support and contribution." She explained that applications no longer needed the explicit support of a local government. However, she said, local governments could quash an application by adopting a resolution of *disapproval*.

Barbara Samuels poked a hole in the local approval change. If a jurisdiction passed a resolution against a tax credit application, she wanted to know, did they have to give a reason?

"Barbara, I'd have to look at exactly what the words say," Pat Sylvester replied.

"It's not addressed in the draft," Barbara countered. "If you don't require them to state any legitimate reasons for the veto, you still have the local veto."

"Why didn't you make life clean and simple?" added Trudy McFall, speaking on behalf of the Maryland Affordable Housing Coalition. "The lawyers wouldn't let you?"

Two months later, Anthony Mohan, an assistant attorney general with the state's housing department, published a response to the "many written comments" regarding local approval. Mohan referred back to an opinion he'd co-authored in 2011 with Maryland's attorney general that cited a Maryland Court of Special Appeals decision that had interpreted a state statute as requiring local approval.

At the final listening session in April 2013, deputy housing secretary Clarence Snuggs announced a few more changes to the draft plan, including a concession to one of Barbara Samuels's criticisms. "The reason for any rejections would have to be provided with that rejection, very specific reason for that rejection," Snuggs said. Someone in the audience asked what the state would do if a county rejected a tax-credit development for a reason that appeared to violate fair housing laws. Would the agency reject the resolution of disapproval?

Anthony Mohan jumped in. "That would be difficult to do," he said, citing the Court of Special Appeals ruling. (The ruling interpreted a passage in state code requiring the state housing agency to "cooperate with local elected officials" to mean abiding local officials' refusals to accept developments.)

"Wouldn't fair housing—wouldn't federal law . . . in that regard override state law?" someone interjected.

"I think a court could decide that," Mohan said. "It would be difficult for the secretary of the department to decide that." Barbara Samuels, who had once again trekked to the listening session, heard gasps sound across the room.

"But if it's a clear violation of fair housing, it's a clear violation," the audience member responded. "And you guys are bound by law. Just like you are bound by the law that says cooperate, you are bound by a federal law that overrides that."

Mohan once again referred to the Court of Special Appeals ruling that said his agency could not just roll over the decision of a county. "It would be up to some party to bring an action to challenge the decision of the local jurisdiction," he said.

"It's obvious that the department is stretching to justify the local veto," said Barbara Samuels later in the session. "And that's in spite of unanimous feeling in the room, beyond the room, even among people who don't agree on other points, that the local veto provision is unwarranted, unlawful, a violation of the Fair Housing Act, an impediment to fair housing, an impediment to affordable housing, and it has been for a long time."

Barbara said she didn't think Mohan had persuaded anyone with his legal argument. Her concern wasn't the argument itself, however, but *why* he made it. "Is it just trying to put the onus on local governments to get sued if they reject a proposal?" she asked.

July 2013 brought new developments in fair housing at the federal and state levels. In a speech that month to the national NAACP, HUD secretary Shaun Donovan announced that the agency would finally release a draft rule to help HUD's funding recipients affirmatively further fair housing. Donovan said the rule would clearly define "affirmatively furthering," and create a "standard framework" for recipients of HUD funding to document their efforts and "offer targeted guidance and assistance" for them to do so. The rule specifically mentioned both place-based revitalization and "greater mobility" as legitimate strategies for localities wishing to affirmatively further fair housing. It replaced the "analysis of impediments" with something called an "Assessment of Fair Housing."

The draft rule also included digital tools, including data maps, for HUD grantees. This, Secretary Donovan said, was "perhaps [the] most important" aspect of the rule. Instead of spending time collecting and organizing data themselves, local governments could just use HUD's data tools and spend more time identifying impediments and figuring out what to do about them. Using HUD's powerful prototype map, administrators and leaders of regions where fair housing battles had played out could see the racial patterns behind those disputes vividly displayed.

Three days after Donovan's speech, the agency published the draft rule and opened a two-month comment period.

At the end of July, Maryland's housing department released the final version of its 2013 Qualified Allocation Plan. Local jurisdictions retained the power to disapprove Low-Income Housing Tax Credit applications, so long as they included the reason for the disapproval.

Three months later, the Baltimore County Council took up a resolution regarding "Homes at McCormick," a proposed low-income development in Rosedale. In September 2012, Trudy McFall's Homes for America had applied for LIHTC tax credits to help finance the development. Homes for America staff presented their plans to the Hazelwood-Park East Civic Association, and the community association responded with a letter. "Burglaries, shootings, stabbings, drugs, vandalism, and other crimes go hand-in-hand with 'Section 8' occupants," the letter read. "It does not matter if '[S]ection 8' occupancy is 5% or 100%, we will be inundated with crime."

Cathy Bevins, the Democratic councilperson representing Rosedale, introduced a resolution that said there was "little, if any, community support" for Homes at McCormick. The neighborhood lacked transportation and grocery shopping. The local school was overcrowded. The location did not fall within a "community of opportunity" on the state's official map. Given all that, the resolution read, the county council disapproved of the project.

On November 8, 2013, the Baltimore County Council supported Bevins's resolution in a 6 to 0 vote. Kenneth Oliver, the council's only African American, abstained.

Barbara Samuels considered the vote exactly the kind of "institutional mechanism" for NIMBY-ism that the Baltimore Regional Housing Campaign had complained to HUD about two years earlier. In a letter to Maryland housing secretary Raymond Skinner, she wrote, "BRHC and other stakeholders anticipated these problems, and urged the Department to exercise its authority to eliminate the local veto altogether. This particular decision, if sustained, will certainly have a disparate impact on low-income families of color."

It was one thing to try to persuade one county to accept a low-income housing development. Now, advocates wanted the state legislature to take away the counties' power to veto Low-Income Housing Tax Credit developments—for good.

Before the Maryland General Assembly kicked off its ninety-day session in January 2014, leaders of the Maryland Affordable Housing Coalition pressured

Maryland housing secretary Raymond Skinner. It pleased Trudy McFall, the coalition's president, when Skinner submitted a bill to the legislature that would spike the local veto. She knew that the quieter everyone kept a bill spiking the veto, the more likely it was to pass, and it certainly would not pass if it were seen as an "advocate bill."

McFall believed that the bill's success depended on the Maryland Association of Counties (MACo) declining to take a position on it. The powerful Annapolis advocacy association had a legislative committee that let one elected official from each of Maryland's twenty-four jurisdictions vote on bills the committee prioritized. That committee met on Wednesdays during the General Assembly session. With a Maryland House of Delegates hearing on House Bill 453 scheduled for Thursday, February 6, the Maryland Association of Counties scheduled its vote for Wednesday, February 5. That day, a storm covered central Maryland in a quarter-inch of ice, knocking out power to over 150,000 households. They held the vote anyway.

The committee voted to take no position. The vote left some rural counties sore. One Carroll County commissioner complained that the ice storm had kept representatives of rural counties from getting to Annapolis for the MaCO committee vote. At a Cecil County Council work session, council president Robert Hodge proposed a letter to the legislature opposing the bill. Council vice president Alan McCarthy threw his support behind Hodge. Building developments using LIHTC tax credits, McCarthy said at a late February work session, "attracts people to our county that we really don't want . . . They're not major contributors, they don't pay taxes to any great significant degree."

"You better watch it," councilwoman Diana Broomell said playfully, breaking into a laugh.

Hodge corrected McCarthy, saying that they were simply "lower to moderate income" people and did in fact pay taxes.

"I do not think this is the type of a clientele that we want to basically actively attract to come to Cecil County," McCarthy responded.

The council voted unanimously to support the letter.

At the February 6 House Environmental Matters committee hearing in Annapolis, Delegate Maggie McIntosh, a Baltimore City Democrat and the committee's chair, said, "I do want to mention that no one has signed up in opposition to this, and I also checked in with MACo . . . yesterday about local input and community input. And they said . . . that they were satisfied that all of those zoning and blah blah blah that you go through at the local level provides more than adequate input." After thirty minutes of testimony from Maryland housing secretary Raymond Skinner and other advocates, the hearing ended.

On February 18, the bill passed out of committee and came to the floor in the House of Delegates for a preliminary vote. As Speaker of the House Michael Busch, an Anne Arundel County Democrat, rushed through the approval of amendments at the speed of an auctioneer, a voice popped out to interrupt him.

"Mr. Speaker," said Republican delegate Pat McDonough.

Speaker Busch kept speaking.

"Mr. Speaker."

Speaker Busch broke his stride. "Are there any discussions on the bill?" he asked. "Gentleman from Harford County."

McDonough represented parts of Harford and Baltimore Counties. He had campaigned with signs that bore the phrase "Speak English!"

"Uh, Mr. Chairman," said McDonough, pausing. "What does this bill actually do?"

"This bill basically consolidates four different programs now in the Department of Housing and Community Development dealing with rental housing," said delegate Doyle Niemann, a Democrat from Prince George's County. Niemann was chair of the subcommittee and floor leader for the bill. "And," Niemann concluded, "it alters . . . the process of consultation with local communities."

"Does this bill in any way change the relationship of the state's authority to the county's authority, in the terms of the powers that the county had in relationship to these various programs? Does this provide the state with new authority?" McDonough asked.

"No," said Niemann. Jurisdictions still had control of local processes like zoning and planning, he explained. But, Niemann said, there was one part of the bill that made a change. "Currently there has to be a final resolution . . . on the part of the jurisdiction," he said. "It changes that requirement."

"I've had some calls on this legislation," said McDonough. "Would it be possible to special-order it until tomorrow?" Special orders effectively stalled Maryland legislation. The House approved this special order and another one McDonough requested the next day.

The two special orders made Trudy McFall anxious. On February 20, the bill came up again for a vote. McDonough said he had no further comment, but delegate Nicholaus Kipke, the Republican House minority leader, pushed Niemann again. "I'm just curious, Mr. Floor Leader," Kipke said. "With this bill, how does it affect local authority? Does it in any way reduce or limit local authority?"

"No, it's not intended to do that," Niemann said, again outlining the local processes any development would encounter. Local approval, he said, dated from the 1970s, before all the other processes were in place, and this bill was about streamlining. The local approval process was costly to both developers and the state, he said.

"So with this bill, local authority is not impacted?" Kipke asked.

"Local jurisdictions still have the authority to change a project, stop it, derail it, deny it, at many steps through the process," Niemann said.

The bill then passed a preliminary vote with amendments.

In late February, the bill passed a final reading by a 129 to 6 vote—delegates McDonough and Kipke voted against—and moved to the Senate.

At a state Senate committee hearing on the bill, no one testified in opposition. The hearing only lasted five minutes.

In April, the Senate passed the bill and governor Martin O'Malley signed it into law. There was little to no media coverage during the session, or even in the months after the bill became law.

Seventeen months after the final settlement of *Thompson v. HUD*, here was another victory for Barbara Samuels. However, she and co-counsel Michael Allen did not call off the complaint they'd filed on behalf of the Baltimore Regional Housing Campaign in 2011. Excising the local approval requirement, they believed, did not undo the damage it had caused for over a decade. The way Allen thought about it, local government should be the lubricant in the fair housing gears, not the sand in the gears. The absence of a local veto did not generate affordable housing units the way an inclusionary housing law could. A self-executing policy like that would grease the gears. Cutting the local veto had just gotten some of the sand out.

While advocates in Maryland were working toward a more suburb-friendly LIHTC allocation plan, the fate of Texas's tax credit protocol was bouncing around the courts. In an August 2012 remedial order, a federal judge had ordered changes to Texas's Qualified Allocation Plan, including the use of an "opportunity index" and extra credits for "high opportunity areas."* Texas appealed to the U.S. Court of Appeals for the Fifth Circuit, but before the appeals court could rule,

---

*The "extra credits" materialize through something called a "basis boost," a 30 percent increase in the costs used to calculate the amount of Low-Income Housing Tax Credits to disburse. Office of the Comptroller of the Currency, "Low-Income Housing Tax Credits: Affordable Housing Investment Opportunities for Banks," *Community Development Insights*, March 2014

HUD published its final disparate impact rule. The U.S. District Court had placed the burden on the defendants—the Texas Department of Housing and Community Affairs—to prove there was *not* a less discriminatory alternative. HUD's rule placed the burden on the plaintiff—Inclusive Communities—to prove that there *was* one. In a March 2014 ruling, the Fifth Circuit applied HUD's rule to the case and sent it back to the U.S. District Court to see what kind of alternative Inclusive Communities could come up with.

Technically, the state of Texas could have claimed a victory: the appeals court invalidated the burden-shifting methodology that had pushed the burden onto them. However, implicit in the appeals court ruling was the validity of disparate impact claims under the Fair Housing Act.

In May 2014, Texas attorney general Greg Abbott filed a petition for a writ of *certiorari* seeking to appeal the Fifth Circuit's decision to the U.S. Supreme Court. Abbott asked the justices to consider just two questions related to the case: "Are disparate-impact claims cognizable under the Fair Housing Act?" and "If disparate-impact claims are cognizable under the Fair Housing Act, what are the standards and burdens of proof that should apply?"

An answer of no to the first question—that such claims are not viable to be tried in a court—would devastate fair housing advocates. Many local- and state-level complaints—including the 2011 Baltimore Regional Housing Campaign complaint against the state of Maryland—relied on disparate impact. The U.S. Supreme Court "grants cert" to just 1 or 2 percent of the seven thousand or so petitions it receives each year, but the justices had granted cert to two petitions bearing the same question about disparate impact claims under the Fair Housing Act: once in 2011, and once in 2013. In both cases, the parties had settled less than a month before their scheduled oral arguments at the Supreme Court, meaning that the justices had never had an opportunity to answer the question.

Civil rights advocates had become wary of the Supreme Court. In a 2007 opinion, Chief Justice Roberts had written the following about a Seattle school desegregation plan that used race to assign students to schools: "The way to stop discrimination on the basis of race is to stop discriminating on the basis

(revised April 2014), www.occ.gov/topics/community-affairs/publications/insights/insights -low-income-housing-tax-credits.pdf. Betsy Julian noted that the basis for opportunity areas matched that used for high poverty areas, and that extra credits for either high poverty or high opportunity areas must not exceed "the amount the housing credit agency determines is necessary for the financial feasibility of the project and its viability as a qualified low-income housing project throughout the credit period." 26 U.S.C. 42(m)(2).

of race." In a June 25, 2013, ruling, the U.S. Supreme Court had voted 5 to 4 to scrap a section of the Voting Rights Act of 1965 that required nine states with a history of discrimination to obtain federal approval before changing voting laws.

In a 2013 public radio interview with Baltimore's WYPR, Columbia University law professor Ted Shaw noted the "great ironic age" he was living in: an age in which a "retrenchment on civil rights" could take place under the first black president.

"The Supreme Court is a tough place to be," Shaw said. "But it's only a one-vote margin. And everybody's looking at Justice [Anthony] Kennedy these days and seeing which way he's going to go."

In early 2014, law professor Olatunde Johnson—a colleague of Shaw's at Columbia—suggested a way to shore up disparate impact. Admitting that "rulings by the Supreme Court in recent years have shaken the disparate impact standard's footing," Johnson suggested a solution in the executive branch. The fate of disparate impact, she argued, was bound up with the "hybrid enforcement regime" of civil rights, "one that lodges implementation power not just in courts, but also in agencies." Congress made the laws, but the rules promulgated by agencies like HUD were the nitty-gritty of their enforcement. Disparate impact, she wrote, was a "reasonable construction and implementation of the ambiguity of the meaning of 'discrimination' that exists in all civil rights statutes." Johnson believed that a better understanding of the role of agencies could put disparate impact on firmer footing. In fact, she wrote, HUD had done as much with its new disparate impact rule. Furthermore, she argued, agencies had expertise that the courts didn't, and under the Supreme Court's *Chevron* doctrine, the judiciary deferred to certain agencies, including HUD, in the interpretation of congressional language.

Johnson later argued for "equality directives" across the executive branch that would "require states to take proactive, front-end, affirmative measures" to assure racial equity, "rather than relying on backward-looking individually driven complaints." If bureaucracies on autopilot tended to generate inequality, equality directives put someone behind the wheel. Equality directives were Michael Allen's lubricant in the gears—you didn't have to wait for someone to take inequality to court.

Olatunde Johnson saw a lot of untapped potential in equality directives. Her work documented examples of them throughout American law and regulation. The duty to affirmatively further fair housing ranked high, if underutilized, in Johnson's estimation. So did "disproportionate minority contact"—since 1992, the U.S. Department of Justice has had the right to withhold juvenile justice funds from states that fail to document racial disparities in contact with the juvenile justice system and outline specific strategies to reduce them.

HUD's revived attention to disparate impact and affirmatively furthering fair housing had given hope to civil rights advocates. If HUD ever issued a final rule on affirmatively furthering, it would make the agency's marquee "equality directive" even stronger. And thanks to the final rule on disparate impact, the precept upon which the affirmatively furthering directive was grounded had become even healthier.

At least until that pesky petition got the attention of the Supreme Court.

On Thursday, October 2, 2014, the U.S. Supreme Court granted *certiorari* to the Texas Department of Housing and Community Affairs. The justices agreed to consider just the petition's first question: "Are disparate-impact claims cognizable under the Fair Housing Act?"

Michael Allen worried about the future of disparate impact. Most of the people he talked to said the Supreme Court wouldn't have taken on such an important civil rights theory if they weren't prepared to do away with it. The same sentiment had dominated media coverage. It takes four votes on the Supreme Court to accept a case; Allen figured that four justices were eager to examine and maybe overturn disparate impact. When it came time for a decision, Allen considered the fifth vote to be a closely held secret.

In September 2014, Enterprise Homes applied to the State of Maryland for LIHTC tax credits to fund a development in Anne Arundel County's Severna Park community. It had been submitted as part of the first round of tax credit applications since the General Assembly struck down the local veto. By any measure, Severna Park was a community of opportunity. The schools ranked in the top 5 percent in the state.

Enterprise wanted eighty-four units; it had less than five acres to work with. The plot was zoned for just two units per acre, but the county had passed a "workforce housing" bill in 2011 that offered density bonuses. Democratic councilman Daryl Jones's bill allowed plots originally zoned for two to fifteen units per acre to be built at twenty-two units per acre as long as the developers reserved at least 40 percent of the rental units for households making no more than 60 percent of the median income for the region. The bill passed 6 to 1, garnering a vote even from John Grasso, a white Republican council member representing working-class Glen Burnie who had once said during a council discussion of affordable housing, "What kind of a quality person are you going to get who's paying $380?"

Grasso was incensed when he received a notification from the Maryland Department of Housing and Community Development in the fall of 2014 about Enterprise's tax-credit application. The letter offered the county forty-five days to comment. (This time, of course, they would not have a veto, thanks to the elimination of local approval in House Bill 453.) Local residents attended a series of meetings to complain about potential effects on traffic, school crowding, crime, infrastructure, and home values.

In early December 2014, Republican councilmen Michael Peroutka and Derek Fink co-sponsored a bill to roll back part of the workforce housing law. It was just a two-page bill, but it had enough words in it to put Enterprise's project on Ritchie Highway under if it passed. The county scheduled a public hearing and a vote for January 5, 2015.

Research analyst Pete Cimbolic, a colleague of Barbara Samuels, submitted testimony in opposition to Bill 82–14. "This proposal eliminates 92 percent of parcels that would potentially be available for Workforce Housing," Cimbolic wrote. "Thus, this bill is the functional equivalent of a ban on the construction of Workforce Housing in Anne Arundel County."

The January 5 hearing was scheduled to start at 7:00 p.m. That afternoon, staff at an Anne Arundel County homeless shelter first heard of Bill 82-14. Sarah's House provided its residents with financial counseling and help with résumé writing and job-interview preparation. There was even transitional apartment housing for working residents. The idea was to prepare clients for moving out on their own. The county's lack of affordable housing posed one of the shelter's biggest obstacles. A caseworker quickly reached out to several residents, asking if they would testify against the bill—in a few hours.

Derek Fink took up Bill 82-14 an hour into the council meeting. During the hearing, a Democratic councilman asked county attorney Nancy Duden, "Isn't it possible we could be open for litigation?"

"The Office of Law has taken a look at this bill, and we don't see the bill as a ban on workforce housing in Anne Arundel County," Duden answered.

The council then opened the floor to public comments. The president of a local riverkeeper association raised the potential environmental toll, alleging that the Magothy River was already making local pets sick. "Who really benefits from this?" he asked, citing the school overcrowding and extra traffic and taxes.

"Gentlemen: we live in the county because we like the suburban single family lifestyle."

Linda Schuett, who had served as Anne Arundel County's attorney in the early 2000s, testified that she believed Bill 82-14 violated the Fair Housing Act. "Under the Fair Housing Act," she said, "the county has received millions of dollars, and we have to certify that we used those funds for affirmatively furthering fair housing. What does that mean? It means that we create housing in areas of opportunity for folks and that we don't shove all the affordable housing into one area that doesn't have the same kind of opportunities."

"What's the violation?" Fink asked Schuett. "Does it say that we must have workforce housing in all zoning districts—"

"No."

"Or all residential districts?"

"No."

"Because we have it," Fink said. "If this bill passes, we'll still allow it in a majority of our current residential districts."

Fink and Schuett spoke over each other as they argued about what workforce housing was and what the bill would do.

"Rather than argue over the term," Schuett said, "I think there is a potential fair housing violation—"

Fink cut in again. "Potential," he said.

"Yes," said Schuett, "because the violation is, if you're going to create workforce housing, you need to be sure that you are allowing the folks who are going to live there to have the opportunity to choose to live in different locations. They may choose to live in Glen Burnie, they may choose to live in Severna Park."

Fink said the county could always rezone for denser housing later if the need arose. "We should never base our support for doing what's wrong or what's right based on a *potential* lawsuit because we know anybody can sue anyone over anything," he said.

"Yeah, and HUD has sued communities," Schuett said.

Chickie Grayson came to the microphone next. To a point that Fink had stated repeatedly—that no one had ever used the density bonus in Jones's 2011 bill—the Enterprise Homes CEO said, "Let's be clear about this. This is the first development that tried to use the workforce housing density bonus. And shortly after a proposal was submitted, a bill gets introduced into Anne Arundel County restricting the density bonus."

Soon after Chickie Grayson spoke, the contingent from Sarah's House made

their way to a long table with three microphones. Facing them on a raised plat-
form were all seven members of the Anne Arundel County Council. "The income
level requirement is way too high for anyone of modest means to live anywhere in
Anne Arundel County," said a black single mother named Keisha Scott, her voice
cracking. "I wish people would focus less on the zone and more on the need."
Scott, a former Sarah's House resident, now shared a rental with two other families. She told the council that she was raising her five-year-old son, working three
jobs, and going to school part-time. "I know plenty of hard working people that
are in the same predicament," Scott said. "You see them every day. You wouldn't
know. I don't have a place to live, you wouldn't know by looking at me. I'm going
to leave here and go to work, because that's what I do. That's all I have to say."

Councilman John Grasso was unimpressed. "When I came out of high school,
I had two full-time jobs and a part-time job," he said. "My heart doesn't go out to
any of yous [sic] with this problem."

"You get out of life what you put into it," Grasso lectured over the course of a
minute and a half. "You save your money, and if you can't afford it, you can't live
there."

A round of applause went up, and Keisha Scott walked out of the room mutter-
ing to herself, scowling back at Grasso as she neared the exit.

Like Derek Fink, John Grasso had voted for Daryl Jones's 2011 workforce housing bill. And like Fink, he now supported repealing the part of it that Enterprise
wanted to use on Ritchie Highway. Enterprise had already gotten some bad news
in December when the state of Maryland rejected their application to use LIHTC
tax credits for their development. But that hadn't shut the door permanently on
the project. Chickie Grayson considered the tax-credit rounds very competitive;
she knew projects often didn't win approval until the second or third try.

Even if Enterprise had been awarded the tax credits, House Bill 453's smiting
of the local veto would not have saved their development from Bill 82-14. Grayson
considered it financially impossible to build at two units per acre. A vote for Bill
82-14 would shut the door on the project.

Later that evening, the council voted 4 to 3 to pass the bill. Enterprise withdrew
their plans for the development.

If anyone was thinking about filing a disparate impact suit over Bill 82-14, they
surely had their eyes on the U.S. Supreme Court sixteen days later. A ruling for
Texas in *Texas Department of Housing and Community Affairs v. Inclusive Communities Project, Inc.* would mean one less tool for advocates who wanted to sue
over housing policy that they deemed exclusionary. Oral arguments, scheduled

for January 21, 2015, would provide the first clues about where the justices came down on disparate impact under the Fair Housing Act.

Barbara Samuels took a seat next to Betsy Julian in the visitors' section of the courtroom. All around her was marble from Europe and Africa, and Beaux-Arts friezes ran under the ceiling on every side. At the front of the courtroom, Texas solicitor general Scott Keller spoke to the justices. The Fair Housing Act contained twelve thousand words, but Keller immediately focused on words that *weren't* in it. "Its plain text doesn't use effects- or results-based language," Keller said. Before he'd spoken for a minute, the justices set in on him.

Associate justice Antonin Scalia said that the text itself didn't hang him up so much. What hung him up was that "Congress seemingly acknowledged the effects test in later legislation when it said that certain effects will not qualify," Scalia said. "You know what I'm referring to?"

Keller said he did.

"Well, why doesn't that kill your case?" Scalia asked.

Justice Scalia was referring to Fair Housing Act amendments that Congress passed in 1988 to permit certain actions, such as denying housing to convicted drug offenders. Three amendments in particular were widely recognized—including by Keller—as exempting certain kinds of conduct from disparate impact claims. For instance, if drug offenders were disproportionately black, denying them housing could create a disparate impact. The 1988 amendment essentially carved out a disparate-impact-liability-free zone for that particular practice.

Those amendments, Justice Scalia said, "make no sense unless there is such a thing as disparate impact. They are prohibiting something that doesn't exist, right? I mean, you're saying that they prohibit something that doesn't exist."

After the conservative justice pulled out the knives on Texas's argument, one of the most reliably liberal judges went after Inclusive Communities. "Don't you have a tension between two statutes here?" asked associate justice Ruth Bader Ginsburg. "I mean, you have the Fair Housing Act; and then there is the law that sets up this tax credit, right? And doesn't that law say that there should be a priority for revitalizing decaying communities?"

"Yes," said Inclusive Communities counsel Mike Daniel, but with a qualification: developments in qualified census tracts required a revitalization plan. The Texas remedy, he said, gave equal points for developments with a revitalization plan in qualified census tracts and those in communities of opportunity.

"Why shouldn't it get more if the tax law expresses that preference for the revitalization?" Ginsburg asked.

Before Scott Keller returned for a short rebuttal, the court called upon someone very familiar to Barbara Samuels: Donald Verrilli. Verrilli had worked *pro bono* for the *Thompson v. HUD* plaintiffs in the 1990s during litigation and settlement negotiations. Now the solicitor general of the United States, Verrilli came forth as an *amicus curiae*, or friend of the court.

Verrilli leaned most heavily on the 1988 amendments. Those, he said, "most clearly show that HUD's disparate impact regulations are a permissible interpretation of the Fair Housing Act." He also invoked one of the Supreme Court's most important principles: the "*Chevron* test." A 1984 ruling in *Chevron v. Natural Resources Defense Council* pushed courts to defer to agencies when ambiguous language made the interpretation of congressional statutes difficult. Justice Scalia was a big fan of *Chevron*, but the decision hadn't favored one political party or another. It helped the Environmental Protection Agency roll back regulations under President Reagan, and now Verrilli trotted it out to argue for the recognition of disparate impact claims under the Fair Housing Act.

"Remember, we're in *Chevron* territory here," Verrilli said. "So the question is whether the statutory text unambiguously forecloses HUD's interpretation." In other words, is the Fair Housing Act so clearly *opposed* to disparate impact claims that HUD couldn't use its interpretive latitude under the *Chevron* doctrine to argue that it *does* allow disparate impact claims?

Chief justice John Roberts asked Verrilli how one might distinguish between a good impact and a bad impact. He introduced two hypothetical situations: one in which new housing in a low-income area benefitted minorities, and another in which new housing in an affluent area promoted integration. "Which one gets credit?" Justice Roberts asked. "The one that is revitalizing a low-income area or the one that is integrating a high-income area?"

At this point, one voice had been noticeably silent: Justice Kennedy's, the justice whom Michael Allen had considered so key to the divided court's eventual decision in this case. If Justice Scalia had briefly sounded like he was in the tank for Inclusive Communities Project, Justice Kennedy's only foray into the conversation had indicated a deep skepticism of their argument.

Justice Kennedy took up Justice Roberts's proposition. He proposed a hypothetical to Verrilli. In one case, a jurisdiction wants to place an LIHTC development in the suburbs. In another case, a jurisdiction wants to place an LIHTC development in a poor neighborhood. The first step of a disparate impact claim is to prove that a policy has had a disproportionate effect on a particular class of people.

"Is it your position, it seems to me, and the position of the Respondents, that in either case, step one has been satisfied?" Justice Kennedy asked.

"That may be right, Justice Kennedy," Verrilli said, "but I think the point—"

Justice Kennedy interrupted Verrilli: "But that—that seems very odd to me."

Joe sat on the edge of the bed gripping an Xbox controller. He had programmed Madden NFL with the same matchup as the upcoming Super Bowl: the Seattle Seahawks versus the Denver Broncos. The digital field, like the parking lot outside Joe's window, emerged in small patches through trampled snow.

"Joe!" Nicole yelled from the living room. "You need to go and make your breakfast!"

It was 8:00 a.m., but with schools opening two hours late, Nicole was still in a T-shirt and pajama bottoms with her hair up in bobby pins. She walked over to the desktop computer in the corner of the living room. Giddy and on the verge of tears, she scrolled back to the top of the email she'd been revisiting all morning:

> Dear Nicole,
>
> Congratulations, you did it!
>
> Effective fall 2013, you are officially a graduate of Howard Community College. Your degree will now post on your transcript. You will receive your diploma in late February at the address you indicated on your graduation application.

Nicole had earned in just over two years what had eluded her for so long at Baltimore City Community College: an associate's degree in early childhood development. May 20, 2014, would be the big day: commencement at Merriweather Post Pavilion, a handsome outdoor amphitheater in Columbia commissioned by James Rouse and designed by Frank Gehry.

A grant that Nicole had received to pay for school required that she work in child care for two years after graduation. Howard Community College covered Nicole's tuition, fees, and books through the state's Child Care Career and Professional Development Fund. The fund's creators hoped to improve the level of education among Maryland childcare providers. HCC marketed the program aggressively, sending information about the grant to every childcare provider and daycare center in the county. So many HCC students used it that the grantees evolved into a helpful support and networking group. Nicole hoped to do her "service payback" with a daycare in her own apartment, offering care just as her mother had done.

In Maryland, nineteen community colleges and universities participated in the fund—but not Baltimore City Community College. At any given school, someone has to write a grant application to bring the funding in, and no one at BCCC had done so. Mimi Heimsoth, who coordinated the fund at Howard Community College, thought it was a shame that BCCC didn't participate. Heimsoth was glad Nicole had found her way to HCC, where her hard work and determination had been more richly rewarded.

On this particular morning, it was Joe's education that concerned Nicole. He would not come out of his room—not even for the pancakes and bacon she had set out on the dining room table.

"Joe!"

"Yeah?"

"Come on out!"

A roar issued from the digital crowd on Joe's Xbox.

"You screwed me up again!" he said.

At 8:30, Nicole called for Joe once more.

"Come on in and eat! Your food gettin' cold!"

"It might take another eight minutes," Joe lectured from his room. "We just went into overtime."

Nicole chuckled. "As long as you're out of here by 9:20," she said.

Joe emerged ten minutes later, smiling and leaning away as his mother embraced him. He was only twelve years old and still had the high-pitched voice of a boy, but he stood just one inch shorter than Nicole did.

Joe returned to his room after breakfast, and Nicole fretted about him missing the bus. Sometimes she had to drive him to school. "Joseph, your clothes on?" she yelled.

"Yeah!"

"Alright, it's 9:06; you have like ten minutes."

At 9:12, Joe donned his hooded black coat, hoisted a low-slung shoulder bag, and headed toward the door.

"Your gloves in your pocket?" Nicole asked. "Your hat . . . ? Hold up."

Finally, Joe got out the door. Their apartment was at the back of the complex, but with some long strides, he made it out to the road in time for the school bus.

In Columbia, Wilde Lake Middle School served as a good bellwether for the survival of James Rouse's vision. The school was diverse compared with Baltimore City's school system. Nearly half of Baltimore's schools had "apartheid" enrollment: at least 99 percent minority. When Joe started sixth grade in 2014, Wilde Lake Middle was 45 percent black, 30 percent white, 12 percent Hispanic, 8 percent two or more races, and 5 percent Asian. Just four out of ten students qualified for free or reduced-price lunch there, a common proxy for measuring poverty rates.

That diversity was hard-won and precarious. In 1998, the school had been 51 percent white and 40 percent black. The next year, the white population dipped to 45 percent. At that point, the county had an open-enrollment policy: families could enroll their children wherever they preferred as long as they could transport them there. But that didn't explain the dip at Wilde Lake Middle; county officials had frozen open enrollment at the school, claiming underenrollment.

In 1998, a group of Wilde Lake Middle parents from a mostly white neighborhood petitioned the school board to unfreeze enrollment. They cited rumors about gangs and fights, and some parents who had visited Wilde Lake classrooms said their children were too advanced to learn much there. Someone had even placed fliers on mailboxes that warned that Wilde Lake Middle was bringing down home values. When pressed, parents insisted it wasn't a race issue, but after the school board approved their request to unfreeze enrollment in April 1999, about fifty families enrolled their children at Lime Kiln Middle School, an 85-percent-white school seven miles away.

When the former Wilde Lake Middle families pooled $37,800 to charter a bus to take their children to Lime Kiln Middle every day, local newspapers jumped on the story. Readers wrote in, some understanding, some appalled. "The Columbia ideal is for people of all racial, ethnic, socioeconomic and religious backgrounds to live together," wrote one reader.

"If white Americans look honestly at our culture," wrote another, "we have to admit that ultimately we will run out of space to isolate ourselves from people of color."

Howard County officials called a meeting in October 1999 to discuss school equity, and about 250 people showed up. Later that month, officials created a citizen's committee on school equity. In December 1999, a *Baltimore Sun* article noted that black children were increasingly concentrated in a handful of Columbia's oldest schools. "It's unhealthy," Howard County executive James Robey, a Democrat, told the *Sun*. "I care about diversity in this county, and it is not healthy in this county in 1999 to have an all-white, all-black or all-Hispanic population in a school."

In March 2000, the citizen school equity committee called for county officials to redraw all school districts and place a three-year moratorium on open enrollment. The moratorium began a month later and lasted for more than five years. In the meantime, a new principal improved Wilde Lake Middle School, and almost three dozen new white students enrolled between 2000 and 2004. An article in the *Baltimore Sun* stated that Wilde Lake was an "exception" to a trend of declining white enrollment in Columbia's schools. When Joe enrolled ten years later, the percentage of black students remained essentially the same, and the percentage of white students had dropped from 45 to 30 percent.

Joe's behavior took a turn for the worse in sixth grade. Nicole felt Columbia was a safer place than Baltimore for her son to experience the tumultuousness of adolescence; she wondered if he might have taken up with a rough crowd back home. But she still wanted help, so, like her mother before her, she turned to the church. Some men from her church began mentoring Joe. Joe didn't care one way or another about the church, but he did calm down. By seventh grade, Joe had become obsessed with the military. He wrote an article on the F-35 fighter jet for school and claimed that his future lay in the U.S. Army.

As Nicole planned out her home daycare, she leaned on women from her church and other Howard Community College students for support and advice. In the summer of 2014, Nicole left her job at the Columbia Association and received her license from the Maryland Office of Child Care. That August, she gained her first client at Nicole's Fun and Learning Family Child Care.

Nicole kept pondering her future. Maybe she could buy a house so the daycare program wouldn't eat up all her living space. Maybe she could get a job directing a big childcare center. Maybe she could go back to Howard Community College for an associate of arts in teaching degree and move on to a bachelor's at a four-year college with a teaching program. Any of that was possible through Howard Community College and the Child Care Career and Professional Development Fund.

It was a Monday evening, and the first floor of the New Song Worship and Arts Center was deserted but for some foosball and air hockey tables and a group of nine men sitting in a circle. Most were middle-aged or older, and all were black except for one young white man: Matthew Loftus, a doctor in his late twenties who'd relocated to Sandtown from Harford County several years earlier with his wife, Maggie. Everyone listened to Elder Harris, who was leading his weekly

Men's Bible Study. Harris's cap sat backwards, the adjustable strap across his fore-head reading "I ♥ Jesus."

The group was discussing Exodus 3, in which Moses receives a call from God at the burning bush. It was a simple call: "Bring my people the Israelites out of Egypt." A call shouldn't be complex, Harris told the group. "God told me to do what you can to end poverty in Sandtown," he said, turning to Dr. Loftus. "What was your call to come to one of the poorest neighborhoods in Baltimore City?"

"It was to live in some community where you worship," Loftus said. "To be part of what was happening." Loftus felt conflicted about his service to Sandtown. "A lot of times, I think I'm not a good relocator, because I spend so much time at work," he said.

Loftus's way of redistributing his resources to Sandtown was to help residents access mental health resources. Loftus and his co-leader, Antoine Bennett, wanted to train residents to lead informal group conversations about everything from depression, to caring for sick loved ones, to keeping your finances in order. After Bible study, Loftus hung around to talk to Harris about finding some men to lead group sessions.

Harris brought up a "miracle" he'd just experienced. "I'm talking about the farming," he told Loftus. "We had a great festival over here with Reservoir Hill: sold out of our vegetables. Told 'em, 'No Ding-Dongs over here, no Snickers.'"

Harris was practically giddy about "Strength to Love 2 Farm," a Newborn Holistic Ministries project. A conversation between Gordon Cosby—who had been a spiritual mentor to both Elder Harris and James Rouse—and Rouse's son Ted had sparked the idea for an urban farm in Sandtown. Ted Rouse told Cosby about Big City Farms, a new venture of his that built "hoop houses" (similar to greenhouses, but made of plastic sheets pulled over steel tubes) around the city and supplied fresh vegetables to local high-end restaurants. Gordon Cosby told Ted Rouse that Harris had been thinking about starting an urban farm and suggested that Rouse go see him.

In 2011 and 2012, Rouse and Harris sketched out a vision for an urban farm that would hire formerly incarcerated people. Rouse knew farms. Harris knew the returning citizens, of which Sandtown had plenty. The city, whose leaders were trying to eradicate "food deserts"—neighborhoods lacking access to healthy groceries—was pushing for a network of half-acre farms across Baltimore. Sandtown had an acre and a half in the 1800 block of Lorman Street between N. Fulton Avenue and N. Monroe Street, where the city had knocked down a couple dozen rowhouses on both sides of the street in 2005. The city agreed to a cheap five-year lease, Rouse convinced his family foundation to pay for a few hoop houses, and the Abell Foundation paid for several more. Rouse and Harris made plans for a total of eighteen hoop houses. Big City Farms, which was already selling produce to local universities and restaurants, agreed to buy everything grown at Strength to Love 2 Farm.

In late November 2012, just weeks after Gerry's Goods closed its doors, workers broke ground on Lorman Street and put thousands of kale shoots in the ground. In June 2013, Harris, wearing a suit and a crisp "Sandtown" baseball cap, welcomed mayor Stephanie Rawlings-Blake for a ribbon cutting to celebrate the completion of hoop houses on the north side of Lorman Street. When Harris told Matthew Loftus at the May 2014 Bible study about Strength to Love 2's selling out of produce, he had just broken ground on ten new hoop houses on the south side of the street.

Like Gerry's Goods had done, Strength to Love 2 Farm employed Sandtown residents trying to break free of the criminal justice system. In fact, the farm started a "support system" for ex-offenders, referring them for services like transportation to appointments and help with legal documents. Like similar efforts at New Song, the farm operated from a racially inclusive philosophy. Harris took the farm's name from a collection of sermons by Dr. Martin Luther King Jr., and the farm's mission statement proclaimed a belief in "the unity of God's love across all divisions of race and creed."

In 2014, Elder Harris was formally back in the New Song fold. Harris and his wife, Amelia, had brought the Newborn Community of Faith congregation to worship with New Song shortly before Thurman Williams left New Song Community Church in the summer of 2013. As New Song's search for a pastor continued on for months, visiting pastors and elders from both New Song and Newborn gave sermons. Harris himself delivered four sermons in 2014.

After two and a half decades, the partnership between New Song Community Church and Newborn Community of Faith continued to benefit both churches. With the Newborn congregation in attendance and adding to the service—for instance, through their poetry ministry—New Song members felt more like they were a part of a community church. Being so close to a church with roots in the suburbs channeled some redistribution Newborn's way.

By July 2014, New Song Community Church had gone one year since Pastor Williams's departure. The church had managed to keep several of its ministries going. In November 2012, Antoine Bennett had received an eighteen-month, $60,000 "community fellowship" from Open Society Institute–Baltimore for his

Men of Valuable Action ministry, which supported neighborhood men who'd dropped out of high school or spent time in prison. M.O.V.A. incorporated part of the mission of the recently shuttered EDEN Jobs. The church also had a dedicated youth pastor and ran a college-and-career program. But at the end of July 2014, Habitat for Humanity of the Chesapeake announced it would merge with Sandtown Habitat for Humanity. The Chesapeake Habitat board boasted of "economies of scale," and even then-governor Martin O'Malley chimed in optimistically about "blending core competencies," but the loss disappointed some church members. Bethany Lee felt Sandtown Habitat had been one of the most visible ways the church had improved the lives of Sandtown residents. It was central to the vision of New Song and Sandtown that had greeted her six years earlier: Allan Tibbels maneuvering his wheelchair all over the neighborhood, people crowding in front of a rowhouse for a Saturday morning ribbon cutting. Those images had sustained the feeling in her that anything was possible in Sandtown.

Fortunately, Harris's Newborn Holistic Ministries was running strong, and, over the previous few years, another organization called No Boundaries Coalition had begun trying to strike the same balance New Song had: bringing people together across lines of race and class, while fighting to keep longtime residents in charge of community development. No Boundaries Coalition grew out of a series of annual block parties that drew together residents from neighborhoods across central West Baltimore. The 2011 "Boundary Block Party," for instance, had been held at the junction of mostly white Bolton Hill and mostly black Madison Park on Eutaw Place, the racial dividing line that had sparked Baltimore's segregation ordinance one hundred years earlier. The No Boundaries Coalition was made up of six neighborhoods, including Sandtown and Bolton Hill. Rebecca Nagle, a Native American graduate of the Maryland Institute College of Art who lived in Bolton Hill, helped found the group. Its president, Ray Kelly, was an African American and a Sandtown resident. The No Boundaries mission statement envisioned "a unified and empowered Central West Baltimore across the boundaries of race, class and neighborhood."

Ray Kelly made public safety a major focus of the organization and criticized the Baltimore Police Department. After the police put an early end to a May 2014 "Visibility Walk for Unity" that No Boundaries Coalition and other local groups had designed to celebrate central West Baltimore's culture, Kelly excoriated the department in a blog post. "If you want to change the CULTURE in Baltimore City, you must also change yours, as well as your TACTICS!" he wrote. "We are going to be just as intolerant of being placed in a POLICE STATE as we are of being held hostage in our Communities by the Drug Trade."

Kelly wrote an open letter to the Baltimore Police Department later that year that claimed "unequal allocation of resources to Baltimore communities from the police department." Frustrated by the department's response to his complaints about drug trafficking along Pennsylvania Avenue, he had attended a neighborhood association meeting in Bolton Hill to see how the police interacted with residents there. During that meeting, Kelly wrote, a Central District major promised to deploy four extra patrol officers as a response to some recent robberies.

"How can the same police district that can't even consider increasing patrols on Pennsylvania Avenue until March assign 4 patrols to Bolton Hill within days?" Kelly wrote. "We feel that the police department is much quicker to respond to the needs of affluent neighborhoods in Baltimore City, which has resulted in an inequitable distribution of our city's resources and a direct and negative impact on our residents' quality of life."

The election of November 2014 jolted Baltimore's criminal justice system. In the state's attorney race, Baltimore voters elected Marilyn Mosby, an African American who'd served the city as an assistant state's attorney and was married to Sandtown's city council representative, Nick Mosby. (She'd upset the incumbent, former federal prosecutor Gregg Bernstein, in the primary.) The 2014 election also put a Republican in the State House: Larry Hogan, a white businessman from Anne Arundel County.

Two weeks after the election, New Song Community Church's pastoral search committee finally voted on a senior pastor. The Reverend Louis Wilson had delivered two guest sermons at New Song in the past year, and he had helped the Presbyterian Church in America plant African American churches. Wilson, a self-described former drug abuser from Chicago, had amassed a liberal-arts bachelor's degree, and master's degrees in theology and sociology. He was at work on a PhD in religion and society. The pastoral search committee had chosen him because they wanted a pastor who could bolster the church's renewed focus on discipleship.

Wilson started preaching in January 2015. He met with the leadership of Newborn Community of Faith Church to discuss an arrangement for worshiping together. The churches couldn't see eye to eye on the details, so the merger didn't happen. But the churches remained close, as did their ministries. The program New Song ushers handed out each Sunday listed Martha's Place, Jubilee Arts, and other Newborn programs.

Both churches worked with a revitalized Sandtown Resident Action Committee. After a couple of mostly dormant years, the group had brought on a new president: William Scipio. Elder Harris had mentored Scipio. New Song Academy had educated him. A white family had taken him under its wing and helped fund his education at a Virginia boarding school. In Scipio, Sandtown could see two decades' worth of its hope, faith, self-determination, and willingness to reach across racial, class, and neighborhood lines.

One of West Baltimore's most vivid displays of inclusive community building was scheduled to take place in the spring of 2015. On April 9, Jubilee Arts announced that the 2015 Boundary Block Party would take place in Sandtown, with a fashion show, a dance performance, and produce from Strength to Love 2 Farm. (The farm's hoop houses, which now occupied both sides of Lorman Street, were themselves another symbol of what Sandtown could do for itself when afforded the resources and trust of outsiders.)

No Boundaries Coalition scheduled the party for May 9, 2015: nearly twenty-seven years to the day since New Song Community Church's first worship service on N. Gilmor Street. So many times over those two and a half decades, Sandtown's residents had joined together to conjure up beauty and goodwill and remind an indifferent world that neighbors in any given place could toil in hopes of creating a community where anyone would want to live.

But that indifferent world continued to visit suffering on Sandtown, and in greater measure.

In the spring of 2015, fair housing advocates watched Washington, DC, for two major clarifications of the Fair Housing Act. The U.S. Department of Housing and Urban Development worked on an "affirmatively furthering fair housing" rule while, fifteen blocks away, a U.S. Supreme Court justice wrote an opinion about disparate impact theory.

These were two of the most powerful tools fair housing advocates had to fight discrimination in the absence of a provable intent to discriminate. HUD's emphasis on affirmatively furthering, after decades of inaction, held the potential to integrate stubbornly segregated parts of America. A Supreme Court ruling against disparate impact, however, could embolden those whose policies perpetuated segregation.

The Baltimore region, which had endured decades of segregation and racial inequality, had a lot at stake in the looming decisions. White communities still offered scant low-income housing for families; such units remained concentrated in poorer, racially isolated areas of Baltimore City and its suburbs. An effort to compel development of affordable units within the city's few "communities of opportunity" had flopped. Baltimore's seven-year-old inclusionary housing law had generated just thirty-two affordable units despite over nine thousand total new housing units materializing since just 2010, according to a December 2014 report from the city's Inclusionary Housing Board.

The Baltimore Housing Mobility Program had moved over two thousand families to communities of opportunity throughout the region, but the neighborhoods they left behind remained devastated. In November 2013, the Abell Foundation singled out Sandtown for evaluation. According to analysis by sociologists Stefanie DeLuca and Peter Rosenblatt, public and private investment, including the Rouse/Schmoke transformation effort, had reached $130 million by 2000. The investment had moved the needle in Sandtown, according to the Abell report, but it had moved it both ways. Elementary-school student achievement improved, but Sandtown students' gains trailed those of comparable city neighborhoods. Crime had dipped—but it had dipped across the city. The poverty rate had dropped 8 percentage points, but it had dropped as much or more in Penn North and parts of East Baltimore. The homeownership rate in Sandtown rose from 24 percent in 1990 to 36 percent in 2009, but Sandtown had more foreclosures than any of the four comparison communities: over 350 between 2008 and 2010.

The law-enforcement and criminal-justice systems still battered Sandtown—literally. In September 2014, a *Baltimore Sun* series called "Undue Force" reported that police brutality settlements had cost the city $5.7 million since 2011. Two major settlements came from incidents in Sandtown: $170,000 for a man who alleged police broke his nose, fractured his face, and caused a hemorrhage in his eye while he was handcuffed; and $175,000 for a man who alleged an officer had smashed his face with a police radio. A February 2015 report by the Justice Policy Institute showed that more state prison inmates called Sandtown home than any other part of Baltimore: 458 in total, at a cost to the state of $17 million.

Justice Policy Institute also reported that elevated blood lead levels affected 7 percent of Sandtown's children, but no children at all in forty-seven out of fifty-five of Baltimore's community statistical areas. In early 2015, just about any social statistic in Sandtown reflected glaring inequality. The destitution and isolation of a place like Sandtown made it easy to police there in a way that one could not get away with elsewhere.

Meanwhile, the rest of the Baltimore region thrived. Few American regions could match its levels of income and wealth. Its economy—the nation's nineteenth largest—was diversified, with a reputation for talent in medicine, research, higher education, financial services, and information technology. Washington, DC's powerhouse economy lay just down the road; New York City wasn't far, either. Baltimore's port ranked eighth out of 171 nationally. Middle-skill industries were growing, and nearly all the jobs lost to the recent economic collapse had returned.

That portrait of the region's prosperity appeared in a series of reports that the Regional Fair Housing Group helped assemble in 2014 and 2015. The group, partnering with the Baltimore Metropolitan Council, adopted the name Opportunity Collaborative and mapped opportunity in the region in much the same way that john a. powell had during the remedy phase of *Thompson v. HUD*.

In March 2015, the Opportunity Collaborative released a workforce development plan that listed "Undermine Structural Racism" and "Help People with Criminal Records" as two of its main strategies. "Targeted law enforcement in lower-income and other communities of color ensure over-representation of African Americans in the criminal justice system, truncating their future employment opportunities," the authors wrote.

At the same time, sociologist Douglas Massey published an article on "hypersegregation" in the journal *Demography*. As co-author of *American Apartheid*, Massey had argued in 1993 that "segregation created a uniquely harsh and disadvantaged social environment for African Americans." In his 2015 article written with Jonathan Tannen, he cited more recent research by sociologists on the injury inherent to racially isolated places, such as Robert Sampson's 2012 book *Great American City: Chicago and the Enduring Neighborhood Effect*, which documented a great income disparity between white neighborhoods and black neighborhoods, and Patrick Sharkey's 2013 book *Stuck in Place*, which found that 70 percent of African Americans in poor, segregated neighborhoods were "from the same families that lived in the ghettos of the 1970s." Any "skills, resources, or abilities" that parents passed on to their children, Sharkey wrote, would be undermined if "parents pass on the place itself."

Segregation punished African Americans—and not only poor ones. "The most affluent African Americans routinely experience levels of neighborhood disadvantage that are rarely faced even by the poorest whites," Massey wrote. Inequality and segregation continued to inflame each other right up to the present day, according to Massey's portrait of American regions. He cited research showing that predatory lenders targeted previously redlined black neighborhoods and that the "strongest single predictor" of foreclosure rates during the housing collapse was "black-white segregation."

Of the twenty-one hypersegregated regions Massey found in 2010, Baltimore ranked tenth.

In the last paragraph of his article, Massey tied segregation to the racial conflict that was once again roiling America:

> It is perhaps no coincidence that as of this writing, Ferguson, MO, a predominantly black suburb in the hypersegregated St. Louis metropolitan area is under National Guard occupation to prevent rioting in the wake of a police shooting, putting it at the center of discussions about the meaning of race in the Age of Obama. Although the United States may have been able to elect a black President, it has not been able to eradicate hypersegregation from its urban areas, and we can continue to expect a disproportionate share of the nation's racial conflicts and disturbances to occur within these intensely segregated landscapes.

At 8:39 a.m. on the bright, cool morning of Sunday, April 12, 2015, Sandtown's church folk had already taken to the sidewalks. On N. Fremont Avenue at the eastern edge of Sandtown, the Catholics at St. Peter Claver were more than halfway through their first service. At N. Stricker and Presstman Streets, just around the corner from Mark and Betty Lange, Sharon Baptist Church was about to start Sunday School. The Langes hadn't left home yet: New Song's service didn't start till 11:00 a.m., and they often didn't make it there until 11:30.

About four blocks from the Langes' house, a young black man in a black T-shirt, open gray sweatshirt, and blue jeans saw a Baltimore police lieutenant looking his way. He bolted from the corner of N. Mount Street and W. North Avenue, and the lieutenant chased him on a bicycle. Police detained the man at the corner of Presbury and N. Mount Streets. As the young man lay handcuffed and prostrate against a short, crumbling stone wall that jutted out from the corner of a brick Gilmor Homes building, two police officers in bicycle gear knelt next to him.

"*Ahhhngh!*" yelled the young man. "*Ahhhngh!*"

His mucilaginous cries reverberated off the line of rowhouses across the street. The homes provided a disconcertingly beautiful backdrop for such a grotesque scene. In their sequential coloring—salmon, then slate blue, brick red, and light tan—the houses echoed beloved blocks in other Baltimore neighborhoods like Hampden and Charles Village. The mosaic effect communicated the presence of a functioning community, a common goal. In fact, ten successive houses in this row were Sandtown Habitat for Humanity rehabs; most had Sandtown Habitat's telltale diagonal house-number signs.

People stepped out of these homes to observe. The block remained quiet but for the murmuring of onlookers, the chirping of birds in a nearby tree, and the agitated voices of the young man and the growing group of people who swarmed around the police who were detaining him.

"Don't worry, Shorty, we recordin' it," said a man on Presbury Street who was filming the incident on his cell phone.

"Get off me, yo," the handcuffed man said to the police. Two officers picked him up, each grabbing a bicep. The man's legs hung loosely as police carried him to a van.

A woman filming on her phone from a cut in Gilmor Homes screamed at the police, "What you twisting his leg like that for?!"

"Shorty, it was after they tased the fuck outta him like that!" said the man filming from Presbury Street.

"Right . . . His leg look broke! Look at his fucking leg!" said the woman.

"Oh my God!" screamed her friend.

"His leg broken, y'all draggin' him like that!" said the woman.

"My wrist, yo, my wrist, *ahhhngh!*" cried the young man as police pushed him into the van, his legs still dangling. "*Ahhhngh!*"

"After they tased yo like that, they wonder why he can't use his legs," said the man filming, his voice restrained but swollen with contempt.

When police pulled Freddie Gray out of the van forty minutes later, he was not breathing.

Seven days later, he was dead.

FIVE

Spring 2015

Thursday, April 23, 2015

Two men stood in front of Terra Café, a black-owned restaurant five blocks above E. North Avenue, filming a video.

"Hi. This is Pastor Heber Brown."

"And I'm Dayvon Love."

Love, twenty-seven, was packed into a black sweater vest, dark blue shirt, and tie. Brown, thirty-five, went for Baltimore business casual: blue Oxford button-down, black O's cap.

"Certainly the two of us and so many of you watching this have been involved in the current struggle to secure justice in light of the murder of Freddie Gray and the larger issues of systemic violence that have a very long track record in Baltimore," said Reverend Brown, pastor of Baltimore's Pleasant Hope Baptist Church. "We would ask that for those who are not from Baltimore and those that do not have a track record of working here in the city on justice issues, that you would be so kind as to defer to those of us who have been in the community."

A full month before police took Freddie Gray on his fatal van ride, Brown and Love had helped lead a rally for police reform in the state capital of Annapolis. After the rally, state legislators listened to nine hours' worth of testimony on seventeen bills meant to increase police transparency and accountability. Love, the public policy director of an advocacy organization called Leaders of a Beautiful Struggle, testified in favor of a bill meant to modify Maryland's Law Enforcement Officers' Bill of Rights, which critics felt overprotected officers accused of brutality. When the legislative session ended on April 13, only three of the seventeen bills had passed.

Freddie Gray died six days later.

Local groups then began protesting in front of the Western District police station in Sandtown. As protests spread across the city, out-of-town activists and media descended upon Baltimore. Various local clergy tried to adopt leadership roles, as did Malik Shabazz, president of Washington, DC–based Black Lawyers for Justice and the former chair of the New Black Panther Party. Dayvon Love knew that not everyone who showed up at a protest was willing to, say, get themselves to Annapolis on a weekday for a 1:00 p.m. hearing. Love and Brown had seen white and black outsiders jockeying for influence on the streets in Ferguson; they wanted to preempt anything like that in Baltimore. The black-owned business in the background was not a coincidence. This was a video from black leaders inside black Baltimore communities to everyone else.

"If you'd be so kind to reach out to those—even if it's not Dayvon or myself—but reach out to people who are on the ground in the community to see how you can best help instead of assuming how you can help, it would really go a long way," Brown said.

On April 25, the video went up on the website for a group called Baltimore United for Change. The group had organized quickly after Freddie Gray's death to serve as a hub of sorts to help outsiders find grassroots social activists with long histories in the city.

In the video, Love and Brown said they were grateful for the attention and the energy manifesting in the city in response to Gray's death in police custody. Brown suggested that people rallying against police brutality and racial injustice look critically upon organizers. "Sometimes we can assume that just because people have bullhorns, that they should be credible and should be followed," he said. "Don't be afraid to do a background check."

Brown told viewers to ask so-called leaders for their track record in bringing resources to the black community. "One of my Muslim friends, Dayvon, has this saying," Brown said, turning to his friend. "He always says, 'You should give people a check-up . . .

". . . from the neck up," Love finished, chuckling.

"It's important that we organize not just for a moment, but we also look at the bigger picture and further out from just police violence as well," Brown said. "There's economic issues, educational issues, housing issues, planning and development issues. This is a moment when all of that should be discussed in addition to the murder of Freddie Gray."

Saturday, April 25, 2015

William Scipio ordered an Uber car for himself and his son. He had made reservations at Morton's, a downtown steakhouse, to celebrate his thirty-first birthday. His girlfriend planned to meet them there.

He knew downtown might be a little crazy. There had been protests around town since Freddie Gray's death, and Scipio had heard about what he called "some confusion" at city hall this particular afternoon, where hundreds had peacefully marched from Gilmor Homes. Apparently a contingent of them had marched away from city hall after Malik Shabazz shouted, "Shut it down!"

Scipio didn't think it would amount to anything. Morton's was on the west side of downtown, by Oriole Park at Camden Yards; city hall was north of downtown. He was wrong. A group of protesters from the city hall rally had massed across the street from the stadium in front of a row of sports bars where Orioles and Boston Red Sox fans stood outside drinking before the scheduled 7:05 p.m. game. Bottles began flying between the protestors and the sports fans, and eventually the metal security barriers separating them started flying too. Several times, protesters and drinkers ran toward each other and exchanged blows. The protesters then migrated a few blocks to W. Pratt and S. Howard Streets, where a young man put an orange cone through the windows of a police car. Then he smashed the windows of another car, climbed on the roof, and donned a police hat, eliciting a roar from the crowd. Police formed a line south of the crowd, but people had already started moving north, some of them smashing storefront windows along the way.

Scipio's Uber driver encountered massive traffic near downtown. There was no getting to Morton's, which was two blocks from the stadium. The closer Scipio got, the more people he saw on the street. Scipio called his girlfriend. Just a few blocks north was a landmark everyone knew: Lexington Market, a public marketplace where Baltimoreans had shopped for two hundred years. He told her to meet him there. He and his terrified son exited the Uber. A police officer approached them and asked, "Where are you going?"

"I'm trying to get to Lexington Market," Scipio said, stunned at sight of the officer's large gun and all-black outfit.

The officer led Scipio and his son through an alley to escape the chaos. When Scipio got to W. Redwood Street, a skinny mid-block thoroughfare, he activated his phone's video recorder and turned it on his son and himself as they walked past the brick arches and red awnings of the University of Maryland Medical Center. "I happened to come downtown and thought I was gonna have reservations over at the Morton's Grill," he said into the camera. "That ain't happening. There's a mob of people outside. It is crazy downtown. If you're down there, be careful: they're vandalizing, they're tearing up stuff, and it's definitely not safe to be down here."

Scipio sported a fresh haircut and beard trim, and he wore a pinstripe suit with a patterned purple tie. His son wore a dark suit with a purple bowtie and a red-and-white checkered shirt. Helicopters hummed above them. "You see William and I all dressed up," he said. "We all dressed up, we thought we was gonna have dinner—"

Two women walking by called to Scipio, interrupting his narration.

"We were going to Morton's Grill for my birthday," he replied.

"Oh, happy birthday!" one of the women said.

"But it's no way in the world we could have gotten down there," Scipio said.

"Oh, it's down near the protest?" the woman asked.

"Yes," he said.

"You look so adorable!" the woman said.

Later, at Camden Yards, as the Orioles and Red Sox headed toward extra innings, the stadium posted a message on the Jumbotron:

> Due to an ongoing public safety issue, the Mayor and Baltimore City & the BCPD have asked all fans to remain inside the ballpark until further notice. Thank You.

By the time the Orioles won with a walk-off home run in the bottom of the tenth inning, the stadium had reopened the gates.

According to the powers that be, Baltimore was safe.

Sunday, April 26, 2015

The Rev. Louis Wilson grasped the edges of a skinny wooden lectern. Wilson was tall; his suit jacket hung blocky from his shoulders, one button fastened. He eased into his sermon quietly; the lavaliere microphone clipped to his shirt captured little of what he said.

"I do want to let you know that the entire staff and elders have been praying," Wilson told the New Song Community Church congregation. "Some of us have been laboring daily about some kind of plan of action. One of my familiar phrases

On
Weste
the of
they'(
be to(
The le
Depa:
law er

At
were '

At
room
stay i1

Lee

Mark
Parkv
dump
the la

Th(
morn
lawle:
with :
schoc
tation
incluc
High
come

Pol
down
brick:

Th(
watch
Gilm(
teena;
and o

is, I like 'workable and sustainable solutions.' So we've been very cautious in what we do and what we support and where we take a stand."

After just four months on the job, the national spotlight was fixed on Wilson's new community. In fact, it had shone directly on him. A day earlier, the *Baltimore Sun* had run a front-page story about the response of the "black church" to Freddie Gray's death. The story quoted Wilson and ran a photo of him. Another pastor in the story called for the arrest of every officer who had come into contact with Gray in Sandtown on April 12. Wilson was more circumspect.

"I'm still the new kid on the block," he told the congregation. "And where I've spoken I've been asked to speak. I didn't assume I had authority to speak."

Wilson paused. "Y'all missed that," he said. This was one of his go-to tics when he wanted to drive a point home. "To get in my house you have to be invited, *heh, heh*. So I answered the call but I did not initiate the call. I allowed [Elder] Bennett and Elder Harris to take the lead. And then a few people asked me to make some comments and I did."

Wilson hadn't yet gotten a full grasp on Sandtown, but he knew what it was like to be black. He stepped out from the lectern and leaned against its side.

"Let me say this as an African American man, in particular one that's my age," he said. "Most of us—and even quite a few that are younger than I—have had to endure direct or indirect racism here in America."

Power corrupts everyone, he reminded his flock. White people just happened to be in power. "They exercise it unduly and wrongly," he said. "Some. Y'all missed that, too. Some."

Wilson walked through the white and black congregation. He picked up steam, his rangy body teetering and zigzagging. He walked backwards at points. More of his preaching tics came forth. His voice rose.

"All kinds of feelings and emotions get stirred up when you feel that you've been wronged unjustly by the other community that, at least in your experience, has always had the power to do something different," he said. "That, that, that—that'll make a brother get angry. And I wish in my blackness I could stay there. And just be upset with folk. Just because."

Wilson's arm shook, and he turned to Antoine Bennett, who sat in the front row in a bright yellow sweater. "In my blackness and my culture, that's what I would like to do, Brother Antoine," Wilson leaned in and barked. "But that won't help me towards developing a functional, workable solution."

Wilson froze, glowering at the congregation over the top of his glasses. They called back placidly.

Monday, April 27 and Tuesday, April 28, 2015

George Norfleet and his wife Phebe lived in a Sandtown Habitat rehab in the 1300 block of N. Fulton Avenue. Phebe knew how Sandtown looked and felt at night. She started her housekeeping shift at a suburban hospital at 6:00 a.m. She was often on the streets in the middle of the night, on her way to work. Both Phebe and George could feel something was off; George had started chronicling neighborhood events on Sunday, April 26, posting a picture to Facebook of himself on his stoop with this caption: "Sitting on my front [stoop] in the eye of the storm yet to come. All quiet on this western front for now. But we have a slow burning fuse. There are still blue lights and a uneasy feeling in the community. I just pray."

Early in the evening of Monday, April 27, Norfleet saw a line of law enforcement vehicles driving north up Fulton. Looting, destruction, and fires had already begun at the corner of North and Pennsylvania Avenues. Standing on his stoop, he pulled out his phone to take a video. From inside the house, someone called, "I got a prescription at CVS—can you go and get it?" Norfleet busted out laughing. "*Ha-ha-ha-HAAA!*" There were no city cruisers among the vehicles passing Norfleet's house—only unmarked trucks, SUVs, and vans, plus the occasional state trooper, all with colored lights flashing.

"Convoy, y'all, convoy!" he said.

"That's right, protect us!" said someone from inside the house.

"They ain't protecting us," Norfleet said.

Norfleet posted the video to Facebook with the caption, "The shit is hitting the fan." He followed up with short missives: "When it get dark. Its gonna get worse. Activate the guards now." "They coming down the street." "Its hitting this way." Then Norfleet shot video of his own living room television, which depicted dozens of people looting a corner store. Now he was watching Sandtown the way the rest of the world was. "This is up the street from my damn house," he said.

"Right where they doin' that shit at, I gotta get off the bus right there and then walk down," said his wife. Her eighty-minute, two-bus commute started at 4:45 a.m. (Despite its central location, Sandtown had the longest average commute of all city neighborhoods.)

"It's fucked up out here," Norfleet said. "When it get dark it's gonna get even fucked up more."

It did. In the middle of the night, Norfleet walked up N. Fulton Avenue and found chaos at W. North Avenue. A cordon of riot police marched past a car, engulfed in flames, to a soundtrack of screaming, strange alarms and ominous crackling. At one point, Norfleet stood in the middle of Fulton and filmed a line of riot police marching toward him. The line stretched all the way across the street; the car fire and an approaching fire engine lit them from behind. "Let 'em put it out!" someone behind Norfleet yelled. The police marched so slowly that the video captured the traffic light above them going through several cycles of red and green. Norfleet turned around and walked back toward home, the sound of smashing glass piercing the air every few seconds.

When Norfleet made it back to his house, he looked down Lorman Street and saw an orange flicker at the end of the block. Again, he shot video with his phone. "Car on fire down the street from my house," Norfleet shouted over the helicopters. "Ain't this some bullshit, man! Called the fire department so I can get somebody down in this motherfucker."

A crack rang out while Norfleet narrated.

"Boy, shit's getting real, shots has been fired already," he said.

He panned the camera, revealing a line of silver arches on each side of the street reflecting the firelight.

"Damn shame," he said. "Next to the organic garden and shit."

Elder Harris's son Duane lived next door to Norfleet on Fulton. He had been tracking his neighbors' Facebook feeds. When he got to Norfleet's feed, he couldn't believe what he was seeing on his screen.

"Man, that's the farm!" Harris said.

Tuesday, April 28, 2015

Elder Harris called it "Resurrection Intersection."

The corner of Presstman Street and Pennsylvania Avenue sparkled with renewal. On the northeast corner, a mural of sunlight bursting through trees tangled with the real trees of a meditative garden. On the southeast corner, a neatly renovated three-story brick townhouse guarded a long, grassy lot. The Harris-Marcus Center, named for Elder Harris, his wife, Amelia, and Todd Marcus, housed the offices of Newborn Holistic Ministries and Jubilee Arts.

Pennsylvania Triangle Park occupied the northwest corner. Once abandoned, Newborn Holistic Ministries had helped revive the park. Inside the intersection of Pennsylvania, Presstman, and N. Fremont Avenue, young trees enclosed a brick plaza. Day lilies and shrub roses lined a circular fountain along the park's southern border.

On the morning of April 28, 2015, William Scipio, now thirty-one years and three days old, stood in a prayer circle near the north end of the park. With a water bottle shoved into the back pocket of his jeans and an Oriole bird cap shielding the sun from his eyes, Scipio joined hands with a white woman and a white man. When he was a child, Sandtown had groomed him to become a leader. Now he was one.

There had been turbulence along the way. Scipio felt he had disappointed his mentors by becoming a father at the age of twenty. He tried to complete his bachelor's degree while working as a clinical assistant at the Kennedy Krieger Institute, a center for children with developmental disabilities, but even online courses at Coppin State University proved to be too much, and he dropped out. In 2011, he moved back to Sandtown.

The neighborhood seemed worse off than when he'd left it. Looking for a way to contribute, he reached out to the pastor at Sharon Baptist Church, his home congregation. As a young man he'd helped run a Boy Scout camp there. Now, the pastor occasionally sent Scipio to community meetings as a surrogate, and at one meeting he met an organizer for the Sandtown Resident Action Committee. Scipio began going to RAC meetings, too. One day in 2014, someone nominated Scipio to be the president of the organization. One year later, Sandtown erupted.

The vandalism, looting, and arson of April 27 had hit the neighborhood harder than any other community in Baltimore. Before sunup, someone had created a Facebook event called "Baltimore clean-up effort." The event page suggested that people take cleaning supplies to North and Pennsylvania Avenues, the heart of the chaos, where a CVS pharmacy was looted and burned. More than two thousand people—many of them white, some from outside the city—responded that they would attend. Contentiousness arose in the comment section of the online event page.

"It seems like the majority of these people are from outside the community, i.e., white students or people who have never seen this community," wrote one commenter, a young black college student from West Baltimore. "This event should be spearheaded by black people of the West Baltimore community and no one else. Know your place, white participants. This is not a trip to the museum."

Some white commenters reacted angrily. Why, they wondered, had she needed to "make it about race"? Some misinterpreted the comment as dissuading white volunteers from coming at all and said they would take their help elsewhere. One quoted Rodney King nearly verbatim: "Can't we all just get along?" If the lines between Baltimoreans had broken down the night before—indeed, even people in "safe" neighborhoods had felt anything but—the lines were already reasserting themselves, as some white commenters painted all black Baltimoreans with a broad brush. "Let them clean their own mess up!" one woman wrote. "You're literally the epitome of a racist," wrote another. It was an old Baltimore story in a new guise: poor and rich, white and black, indicating good intentions but talking past each other. This time it transpired in a crucible like the region hadn't seen since the riots after the 1968 assassination of Dr. Martin Luther King Jr.

The Facebook event page's organizers eventually got in contact with the No Boundaries Coalition and changed the listed meeting place to the same location that that organization had settled on: Pennsylvania Triangle Park.

Scipio was happy to have outside help; the volunteers could have just stayed home. But as dozens of people flooded into the park around 10:00 a.m., Scipio and other Sandtown leaders remained in control, greeting volunteers and directing them to areas that needed cleaning. The response reflected an attitude of self-determination and resilience: We're very grateful for the help. And we're going to remain in control of our own community.

When the prayer circle broke up, the crowd turned its attention to a trim man in an unassuming blue sweatshirt and an old-school pair of glasses.

"I wanna thank everybody for coming out," he said, his voice competing with a helicopter. "For those that don't know, I'm Ray Kelly of No Boundaries—I'm president, and a Sandtown resident." Kelly said he would take some volunteers to N. Monroe Street, where some residents had just requested a cleanup. "Then, we're gonna take half of this group and go over to the farm on Monroe and Lorman, because the farm got burned down—a community farm," he said.

Kelly set some ground rules for the dozens of faces before him, many of them white. "No negativity," he said. "We wanna try to keep any press or anything away from us because we're on a mission. We don't wanna bring any kind of publicity; we just wanna get in here and do the work."

Kelly led the crowd down Presstman Street. They passed Sharon Baptist Church. They passed the darkened Gerry's Goods storefront. They passed New Song Community Church's now dormant building at 1385 N. Gilmor Street and, across the street, New Song Center. They passed the spot where Ahmad had been shot to death in the middle of an autumn night in 2009. They passed a block of Gilmor Homes. They crossed N. Fulton Avenue, the city's former racial dividing line, now just another street in another apartheid neighborhood.

Along Presstman Street, Kelly came upon Corey Barnes. Barnes had worked for years as an educator at New Song Academy. When Kelly found him, Barnes was talking with some young men from the neighborhood, including Terrell Johnson. Johnson was deeply involved with New Song Community Church. He had attended New Song Academy and still played drums during Sunday worship.

"We got help, anything you guys need, volunteers to help you all clean up," Kelly said to the men. "We want to make sure through this whole process, we got resident leaders coming out and we are dictating what happens in our community."

Kelly turned to one of the young men. "This is Danny right here, he's gonna be our resident leader," he said. "If we could get five people with brooms and bags and shovels and gloves, help Danny out right here, and we're gonna keep going straight up to Jolly's."

Jolly's, a convenience store, had been looted overnight. Corey Barnes formed a prayer circle in the Jolly's parking lot and pulled in Terrell Johnson and his friends. "These are real leaders," he said. "They're from here. Let's surround them." The circle closed in around the men. Both Sandtown residents and first-time visitors laid hands on them as a chorus of individual prayers intertwined.

After the prayer, Ray Kelly told the group that some volunteers would remain at Jolly's to clean up, while others would keep walking to the community farm on Lorman Street.

"A thousand people maybe came out to support our community today, and we need to take all of these people to the polls so we can change this once and for all," he said before the group split up. "My goal when we said we were gonna do this effort, was to make sure that our residents are in every part of this restructuring, from picking up the first damn piece of paper off the ground to the day they sign that bill in Annapolis."

Despite the cleanup, news networks like CNN continued to broadcast footage of the previous night's burning and looting.

"A lot of people see what's on the news, they think we hopeless. Nah, that wasn't Sandtown acting fools, we know how to act," Kelly said. "This crowd is doing what a community is supposed to do."

Ray Kelly then led a group of volunteers carrying brooms and black garbage bags down N. Monroe Street. At Lorman Street, they discovered that most of the hoop houses had survived, the long rows of lettuce still sprouting from the rich brown soil. One hoop house, however, was mostly reduced to its steel tubing. Next to it sat the shell of a burned-out car.

"Okay, this is one of our Sandtown elder's sons," said Kelly, introducing the crowd to a man with a chin goatee and a plaid shirt buttoned to the neck. "So, Duane Harris here, he's gonna help with the cleanup effort around the farm, he's gonna be our resident leader around here."

The fire department had never responded to the 911 call that Harris and George Norfleet placed the night before. The two men had tried to drag a hose over to the car fire, but it hadn't been long enough. They and their neighbors tried to put the fire out with buckets but the car just burned itself out. In the morning, the entire range of city services was still stretched thin.

"I'm not saying that we don't need [city workers]," Harris said, as some volunteers climbed the scaffolding to tear off the burnt tarp, and others picked up the pieces that had scattered all over the farm. "But right now, I don't see them out here in their trucks coming to grab the debris. I'm just loving how the community says, 'We really don't need your help, government. We got it. We'll come in here. We'll fix it up. We don't need your National Guard. We don't need your state troopers. We got it.'

"That's what I'm loving," Harris continued. "That we got it."

Construction on the Mary Harvin Center, a Low-Income Housing Tax Credit development just below E. North Avenue in East Baltimore, was almost half completed by the last week of April 2015. On the morning of April 28, it was a heap of rubble and ash.

That morning, Kevin Bell called Reverend Donte Hickman, the pastor of Southern Baptist Church, which sat across N. Chester Street from the site of the previous night's three-alarm blaze. The Woda Group, where Bell worked, had partnered with the church to build the senior housing complex.

It had been one of the largest conflagrations of the previous night's rioting. It had been all over the news. It couldn't have been more disheartening. But Bell and his colleagues wanted to start over.

"Don't worry," Bell told Rev. Hickman. "We're not leaving. We're more determined than ever."

Thursday, April 30, 2015

Sandtown residents were used to outsiders treating their neighborhood more like a symbol than an actual neighborhood. The 1990s "transformation effort" had made it a symbol of renewal and, after the 2013 Abell Foundation evaluation, a symbol of expensive and fruitless "revitalization." The February 2015 Justice

Policy Institute report had reinforced the notion of Sandtown as ground zero for mass incarceration.

Now, in addition to being a symbol, Sandtown had become a stage. It was a stage for police brutality, for rallies and marches, for an outburst of arson, looting, and destruction. It had even become a stage for people to fight over how to symbolize the events that had just transpired. Was it "unrest"? A "riot"? An "uprising"?

For a lot of people who lived in Sandtown, it was a pain in the ass.

At a community meeting, No Boundaries Coalition members discussed writing a letter to the media to let the outside world know they'd had enough, that Sandtown was a real community where real people lived and worked and studied and worshipped. The letter, addressed to "anyone who is planning or organizing events in Sandtown from outside the community," went up at the No Boundaries Coalition's website on April 30. "Please do with and not for," the headline read. William Scipio and Ray Kelly authored the letter.

"For Sandtown residents, the past two weeks have been really hard. Living in Sandtown right now feels like living in a war zone," Scipio and Kelly wrote. Residents were stuck—bus lines were down. They couldn't get food and medicine—stores and pharmacies were burned and looted. Residents felt like the police had abandoned them to protect the downtown, with a few officers left behind to guard the gates.

"Residents on Mount Street near the police station have to pass through a police barricade to get in and out of their neighborhood," the letter continued.

It wasn't that the neighborhood didn't care about Freddie Gray. His death had outraged Sandtown residents, too. In fact, Scipio and Kelly wrote, police brutality had touched many of their own families. "As residents and leaders of this community we have been working on these issues before they were in the national spotlight and will continue to work on these issues after the cameras roll away," they wrote.

The letter made it clear to anyone planning an event in the neighborhood that residents should be in charge. As it stood, residents often found out about events only after they'd happened. Sandtown Resident Action Committee and No Boundaries Coalition had contacted two hundred residents since Freddie Gray's death. "We asked residents what feels urgent to them, what they wanted for the neighborhood and what their interactions are with the police," Scipio and Kelly wrote. "Among everything that is going on[,] the No. 1 thing we heard from residents is that they don't feel heard. They want to be recognized and respected."

Saturday, May 2, 2015

Lawrence Brown arrived at the corner of Pennsylvania and W. North Avenues just before 10:00 p.m. Two minutes remained until curfew, and several dozen people stood on the corners ready to break it. In front of the burned-out CVS, police had wound yellow tape around a subway entrance to create a "pen" for the press. A group called Food Not Bombs distributed water and food from a set of tables on the sidewalk. Sparse traffic flowed through the intersection.

Mayor Stephanie Rawlings-Blake had placed the city under a week-long emergency curfew starting on Tuesday, April 28. Three days later, Baltimore state's attorney Marilyn Mosby announced indictments of six officers in the case of Freddie Gray's death, including one for "second-degree depraved heart murder." By Saturday, May 2, a rumor had spread that the mayor would lift the curfew within twenty-four hours. Nonetheless, people around town planned to break the curfew as a show of defiance against the police and city government. Many believed the curfew amplified the repressive policing and policymaking that people had complained about for decades in poor black neighborhoods.

Brown, an assistant professor in community health and policy at Morgan State University, described himself as a "scholactivist." He had moved to Baltimore in 2010 for a postdoctoral fellowship at Morgan State. He knew nothing about the city. As part of the postdoc, he worked with the Men and Families Center near Baltimore's Middle East neighborhood. "What happened here?" Brown wondered, surveying entire blocks that were vacant. He answered the question for himself, delving into structural issues, such as displacement and segregation, that created such disparities between Baltimore's neighborhoods. He also worked with local coalitions that were fighting for residents affected by development and displacement, including those displaced by a massive redevelopment around Johns Hopkins Hospital.

Morgan State hired Brown in 2013. That year, he wrote a series of articles for a local publication called *Indypendent Reader* on displacement and the tax incentives the city gave to major developers. After a Missouri grand jury declined in late November 2014 to indict Darren Wilson, the police officer who had shot eighteen-year-old Michael Brown in Ferguson, Lawrence Brown began posting frequently on Twitter about police brutality, segregation, structural racism, and other forms of racial inequality.

In early April 2015, Brown published an essay online called "Until We Tackle Segregation, Cops Will Keep Shooting Black People." In the piece, Brown cited research that showed excessive force complaints correlating with levels of residential segregation. In Baltimore and other heavily segregated cities like Birmingham and Detroit, Brown wrote, fewer than one out of four police officers actually lived inside the city. The suburbs where they lived, he pointed out, were disproportionately white, thanks in part to their historic subsidization by the Federal Housing Administration.

"Racial segregation increases the odds that white, suburban police officers will see black people as a threat before they enter those communities," Brown wrote. "And it also increases the chances that a white officer will kill a black person before they leave."

Three days after Brown published the essay, police pulled an unconscious Freddie Gray out of a police van.

On the fourth night of the curfew, May 1, Brown tweeted, "If white folks are really serious about ending the curfew, then a bunch should show up at Pennsylvania & North tonight to protest it." But as Brown arrived at the corner of Pennsylvania and North the next night, a few dozen white protesters were crowding the southeast corner of Keswick Road and E. 33rd Street in the Hampden neighborhood.

The white racial justice allies in Hampden knew what was happening at Pennsylvania and North. They believed that by breaking the curfew in an 86 percent-white neighborhood, they could highlight the divergent policing styles of the "two Baltimores."

Richard Gibson, a white-shirted sergeant from the Baltimore Police Department's Neighborhood Services Unit, approached the Hampden protesters to announce the curfew. "We're here, we support you," he said. The sergeant told them they'd get another warning in five minutes.

An officer from the neighborhood services unit then spoke to the group. "We all want to go back to life as usual," he said. A protester expressed doubt that the officer's generalization—that everyone "wants things to go back to the way they were"—was true.

"I think that statement misses the point of this entirely," the protester said.

Sergeant Gibson returned after a few minutes, again adopting a more-in-sorrow-than-in-anger tone. "This is your second warning, okay?" he said. "I understand what you're doing and I respect it, but it's five minutes after ten."

Five minutes later, Sergeant Gibson made another announcement. With his hands clasped on his belly, he calmly said, "Do me a favor, guys. The last thing I want to do is put someone in handcuffs. Alright? And I'm actually gonna ask you right now to please leave. The last thing I want to do is put someone in handcuffs. Because you know why? Because we're the community, including myself, alright? And I want to work with you guys."

Sergeant Gibson raised his finger. "So this is going to be your last warning," he said.

A protester asked Sergeant Gibson about what was happening "at Penn and North now." Images and videos from West Baltimore were already up on Twitter.

"I can't answer that," Sergeant Gibson said.

In fact, by the time he had issued the white protestors their third warning, police at Pennsylvania and W. North Avenues had sent black protesters fleeing with a cloud of pepper spray.

It had started just after curfew when a black man walked through the middle of the intersection directly toward the police. A black "FUCK THE POLICE" T-shirt stretched across his beefy chest. His approach looked like something out of an action movie: calm stride, eyes fixed in a piercing stare, raspy and defiant voice.

"Arrest me! I *dare* you! Arrest me! I'm right here!" he said.

A white officer in a short-sleeved white uniform rushed forward with a large can in his hand. For two seconds, he released a thick blast of bright orange pepper spray directly in the man's face. The man reacted calmly, shuffling from his left to his right foot and puffing air.

Another white officer walked up to the man, grabbed his dreadlocks, yanked him to the ground, and flipped him onto his belly. Protesters and police rushed into the street from opposite corners like baseball players emptying their dugouts for a brawl. As police yelled, "Back off!" a woman in a white top threw something toward the police, spraying water in the air. A line of four officers rushed toward the crowd, each of them dispensing thick streams of pepper spray. The crowd retreated, and ten seconds later two glass bottles came flying toward police, one breaking in the road, the other shattering by the media pen. Officers picked up the prostrate man and carried him to the sidewalk.

The pepper spray glistened red over the man's entire face. It was easy to mistake it for blood, which reporter Darcy Spencer did on Twitter at 10:09 p.m. Above a close-up photo of the man's face, she wrote, "Man arrested by police bloodied #Baltimore #breaking." Twenty minutes later, Brown retweeted Spencer, adding, "This is the dude. Cop just grabbed his hoodie by the back & yanked him completely backwards, downwards to the ground."

Photos and video of the Hampden and Penn North curfew protests appeared on social media instantaneously. The protests drew sustained attention thanks to a widely circulated photograph taken by Robert Stolarik of Polaris Images. Stolarik's image shows three officers with the man in the "FUCK THE POLICE" T-shirt. The man's face touches the ground, and an officer holds his legs up. It looks like the officers are dragging him along the sidewalk by his face, especially given the red spray residue. It also looks like the officer in the middle, who holds the man's midsection up by his belt, is smiling. Part of Stolarik's caption read "One of the policeman [sic] appears to be smiling during the arrest." As much as it looked as if the police were posing with their detainee the way a hunter poses with his kill, the photo actually had caught them in motion as the "smiling" officer was straining to get the man off the ground. A moment later, the same officer poured water over the man's face to relieve his pain from the pepper spray.

But the picture bolstered the narrative that many took from the protests: that police reinforced the lines between the two Baltimores not just brutally, but gleefully.

Sunday, May 3, 2015

Sandtown had changed irrevocably since Pastor Wilson's last sermon. That Sunday, he had warned against the impulse to anger. Anger had come anyway.

The media were no longer just sniffing around the way they had been when Wilson spoke to the *Baltimore Sun* the previous weekend. The limelight now was blinding.

"We had a meeting Friday at church offices," he said, as a soft siren wound slowly down to silence outside the gymnasium. "Some people called up, and we specifically told them, 'This is not a news event. We don't need cameras. We don't need papers. It's about time to get something done.'"

Cameras sent people into performance mode, Wilson said. As he'd emphasized the previous Sunday, he said Sandtown didn't need posturing or emotional outbursts; it needed long-term solutions. "When the cameras are gone and the newspapers stop reporting and the next event takes place in the next town, we'll still be here in Sandtown."

Wilson led a short prayer, then pulled up a PowerPoint presentation on the projector. "Incarnational ministry: Coming alongside of Sandtown," it read at the top. New Song Community Church had long ago adopted Dr. Perkins's favored concept of incarnational ministry, which alluded to Jesus Christ's willingness to live among the troubled human race. Wilson wanted his congregation to understand something about connecting with the humans in this particular neighborhood.

"The black community is not monolithic," he said. "Let me just show you something here." The screen showed a bell curve; the left tail was labeled "other-centric," and the right tail was labeled "ethnocentric." People on the right, Wilson said, "think the world revolves around their ethnicity." On the other side, he said, "they're inclined to want to be like and act like the group they think has the status and the dollars."

Most people, he said, were somewhere in the middle. "Everybody in Sandtown don't wanna go out and jump on every white man they see—everybody walk with me now. Neither does everybody in Sandtown wanna *be* white," he said.

He said he was happy to have anyone from either extreme, but that each extreme had its faults. "When we have to interface and get our support, it's over here," he said, pointing to the "other-centric" tail. "If we want some of what they got, we gotta slide down the bell so we can get something. The problem is, for those of us especially in a church like this, if we slide down the bell, we're getting away from the bell, which is where most people in Sandtown are."

Wilson could be abstract and elliptical, but eventually he landed on an example: the way white churches turned a blind eye to the oppression of African Americans. "For a long time, folk ignored the fact that we were marginalized," he said. "Preachers ignored the fact that we were relegated to the back of the bus. Folk always tell me, 'This all happened when we took the Ten Commandments out of the courtroom wall and kicked prayer out of school.' I'm like, 'Y'all was lynching people with the Ten Commandments on the wall!'

"By the same token," he continued, "we need leaders in our community that take just as visceral a stand—oh Lord have mercy, start it up baby—when a black man kills a black man as they do when a white man kills a black man!"

This roused the congregation. "Right! Right!" someone shouted.

"There's still a man dead!" Wilson said. "I'd like to talk about just how many of us killed *us* since Freddie Gray!"

Wilson then turned to the story of Moses, who led the Israelites from bondage in Egypt, and ascended Mount Sinai to receive the Ten Commandments from God. Fearing that Moses would not return, the Israelites asked Moses's brother Aaron to make them a god. Aaron took their jewelry and made a golden calf for them to worship.

"They'd seen manna from heaven, they'd seen water from a rock, but because

Moses took a minute too long, folk back acting like they'd never left Egypt," Wilson said of the Israelites. "Watch what they do: when there's no leadership, they gather around Aaron. I think Aaron used the opportunity—oh watch it now—used the opportunity to get folks to follow him."

In Sandtown, he said, something similar was happening. "We need some leaders in our community," he said. "We got too many folks speaking for us! That don't live here! How you gonna speak for me when you never even been to my house?"

That leadership, Wilson argued, should be godly. He wanted no idols. "I want the police department to be fixed, too," he said, "but they're not my God, oh Lord have mercy."

The provision of material goods—even food in a neighborhood as poor as Sandtown—could also distract from godly leadership, Wilson argued. "I could go out here and give one thousand dollars to everybody in Sandtown," he said. "But that might not be the best thing to do. I will have pleased the most amount of people, but it might not be what they really, really need. We had food distribution centers all over Sandtown yesterday. And I guarantee you most of the folk gathering food did not need that food. Cause the folks that [need] it couldn't get there."

Wilson's sermon had gone from a bell curve depicting ethnic affinities to Freddie Gray, to lynching, to black-on-black violence, to Aaron's golden calf, to the Baltimore Police Department, to food pantries. But then he settled on a comparison that drew a distinction—if unspoken—between the way New Song had operated for twenty-seven years and the way he hoped to lead it.

"I think there are services that we need in Sandtown," he said. "I think we need better housing. But I can never forget all them things won't stop me from being a crazy sinner."

Pastor Wilson wasn't impressed with Dr. Perkins or his Christian community development approach. He'd done the research: black churches had been doing community development for one hundred years with the nickels and dimes of black people. He found the CCDA approach—even its implementation in Sandtown—paternalistic and pacifying. It all looked transactional to him: black people got resources, and white people salved their guilt. White people encouraged black leadership but managed to keep power, choosing residents that not everyone in the community recognized as leaders, or even as competent. White people were praised for moving to Sandtown; he himself hadn't gotten a badge for that. Wilson believed churches tended to adapt their messages to fit whoever was writing the checks, and he believed New Song's church had become just an addendum to its ministries.

Wilson had expressed his antipathy for CCDA as soon as he arrived at New Song and drilled the message home that the Gospel needed to come off the back burner. In early February 2015, he had given a sermon titled "Godly Principle & Precepts Before Projects."

"You can build a whole lotta homes for the wrong reason," Wilson said that day. "You can funnel a lot of people through all kinds of programs for the wrong reasons. If you're not doing it for the glory of God, then it's for the wrong reason."

Congregants conversed privately about the changes Wilson was bringing. Some appreciated the step back from programming and the rededication to discipleship. Others struggled. Some didn't like Wilson's confrontational style. Some resented the turn away from Perkins and CCDA, so core to New Song's identity.

The way Wilson saw it, New Song wanted a black leader, and they got one—just not the kind they had expected. And a week after the unrest that followed Freddie Gray's death, leadership was what concerned him. A whole lot of folks had been stepping up as leaders lately, and not all of them would be sticking around.

God, he reminded them, had not forgotten Sandtown. The newspapers? "A few months from now, they're gonna be gone," Wilson said. "And some of those big time preachers flying around the country? They gonna be gone, too. I'm glad I know a God who will tap me on the shoulder." Wilson leaned down and tapped a congregant in the front row, then looked up, smiled, and imitated God: "'I'm still here.'"

The congregation applauded, and some shouted, "Amen! Amen!"

"It's for his name's sake!" Wilson shouted. "Watch it now. Psalm 79, deliver us, Lord, for your *name's* sake!"

After he wound up the congregation, Wilson took his glasses off and spoke softly. "I know you've heard the newspapers say this is bigger than Baltimore, this has gone national," he said. "I got some news for you. This has always been eternal . . . Freddie Gray didn't slip up on God. Police brutality didn't catch God off guard. Oh, Lord have mercy. All I know is, when he does show up, I want to be standing right there with him. Cause he gonna show up!"

It was surreal for Nicole Smith to see the corner of Pennsylvania and W. North Avenues plastered all over the news networks. From age thirteen to twenty-six, she had lived just four blocks away. When Baltimore state's attorney Marilyn Mosby announced charges in Freddie Gray's death on May 1, the news networks ran photos of the six police officers she had indicted. Nicole thought she recognized some of them as cops who were always fussing with the dealers on her own street back when she lived there.

On the Sunday after the rioting, Nicole had to drive into east Baltimore. She decided to take W. North Avenue across town. She parked near her old house. It was a clear day, unseasonably warm. Nicole realized how hard it was to tell a regular West Baltimore neighborhood from one where rioting had just taken place. Trash in the streets? That wasn't new. The only thing that stuck out to her was the burned-out CVS, just blocks from where her grandfather had worked at a record shop a half-century before.

Monday, May 4, 2015

The conventional wisdom on HUD's Moving to Opportunity program was that the experiment improved participants' health but generated few economic or educational benefits. The *Washington Post* called the accumulated research "largely disappointing." On May 4, 2015, two headlines at "The Upshot," a *New York Times* data website, upended that narrative: "An Atlas of Upward Mobility Shows Paths Out of Poverty" and "Why the New Research on Mobility Matters: An Economist's View."

It had been twenty years since HUD handed out the first vouchers; some of those kids had reached adulthood. Three Harvard economists analyzed the Moving to Opportunity data and found no benefits for those who were teenagers when the vouchers arrived. However, younger children fared increasingly better with each year they spent in a low-poverty community. One stunning finding estimated that "moving a child out of public housing to a low-poverty area when young (at age 8 on average) using a subsidized voucher like the MTO experimental voucher will increase the child's total lifetime earnings by about $302,000."

The researchers reached a bold conclusion. "Efforts to integrate disadvantaged families into mixed-income communities are likely to reduce the persistence of poverty across generations," they wrote.

Over the past winter, Barbara Samuels had heard that some important research on Moving to Opportunity was in the pipeline. The Harvard report didn't disappoint. But there was more. Two of the economists behind the paper, Raj Chetty and Nathaniel Hendren, released additional data from following five million families over time and analyzing their tax records. The families had moved to new counties, so Chetty and Hendren were seeing the effect of a given place on a child's future earnings. They found that for each year spent in DuPage County, Illinois, for example, a child's adult household income grew by 0.76 percent compared to the national average.* DuPage County ranked first of the one hundred jurisdictions examined.

Baltimore City ranked last.

The Harvard economists noted that "the broader lesson of our analysis is that social mobility should be tackled at a local level by improving childhood environments." Their work acknowledged the same tension that had come up in the *Thompson v. HUD* trial, in Maryland's revision of its low-income tax credit rules, and in HUD's development of a rule for affirmatively furthering fair housing: whether to move people away from racial isolation and concentrated poverty or to improve the places they already called home. The authors did not suggest specific methods, but they did argue for "policies that reduce segregation and concentrated poverty in cities (e.g., affordable housing subsidies or changes in zoning laws)."

These two studies were boons for Barbara Samuels's work. What could be more relevant for the region she lived in, given the paroxysm just a week earlier, than a finding that Baltimore was the hardest place in America to escape poverty? *The Atlantic, New York Times,* and *Washington Post* all gave prominent coverage to the studies, but Barbara felt the research got lost at home, where it was needed most. The *Baltimore Sun* briefly mentioned the findings in an editorial two days later, and a week later it ran an op-ed on the studies by a senior editor of the conservative magazine *National Review.* Columnist Dan Rodricks, who for decades had followed the complex regional dynamics of racism and poverty, mentioned the research a few times over the next month. But it seemed like the newspaper hadn't seen fit to put a reporter on the story.

Barbara also looked to powerful civic leaders for a substantial reaction. How would mayor Stephanie Rawlings-Blake react? What about the Greater Baltimore Committee, which James Rouse had chaired sixty years earlier?

Barbara found mostly silence.

Monday, June 8, 2015

The Opportunity Collaborative published its marquee report just six weeks after Baltimore's unrest. Called the "Baltimore Regional Plan for Sustainable

---

*Chetty and Hendren write, "This implies that growing up in DuPage County from birth—i.e., having about 20 years of exposure to that environment—would raise a child's earnings by 15% relative to the national average."

Development," it offered some good news. The percentage of minorities in the region living in "extreme poverty" had dropped from 30 percent to 10 percent, and there had been much economic growth. However, that growth mostly benefited upper-middle class whites at the "outer suburban fringe and along the city's waterfront," while elsewhere—in the non-waterfront city and inner suburbs—poverty rose. Opportunity maps in the report clearly showed what had come to be known around Baltimore as the "White L": a contiguous trail of relative opportunity that started in the middle of the city's northern border, followed Interstate 83 to the harbor, then tracked east along the waterfront through communities like the newly developed Harbor East, historic Fells Point, and solidly gentrified Canton. Seven percent of African Americans in the region lived in "racially/ethnically concentrated areas of poverty," many of which marred east and west Baltimore, while it remained difficult to develop affordable housing in the parts of the region with "good schools and neighborhood amenities."*

In its suggestions for eliminating barriers in housing, transportation, and the workforce, the Opportunity Collaborative specifically mentioned structural racism, which it defined as "an array of societal dynamics—e.g. historic wealth disparities, disparate treatment by justice systems, disparate consideration in interviews—that routinely put job seekers of color at a disadvantage relative to white job seekers."

Between April 2015 and the publication of the report in June, the authors had connected the dots between the recent unrest and the disparities they hoped to help rectify.

> Reflecting on our application now, just a month removed from the civil unrest that drew national attention to the challenges we face in our region, it is clear how vital our original goal was. As pundits assessed the situation in Baltimore, they accurately articulated the region's challenges. We are not alone. A long list of American cities suffer from historically disinvested and segregated neighborhoods, the loss of manufacturing jobs, limited public transportation and a lack of safe affordable housing near employment centers.

---

*According to the report, "racially/ethnically concentrated areas of poverty" in the Baltimore region are census tracts with poverty rates of more than 35.1 percent "where minorities constitute the majority of the population."

The national discourse and punditry on Baltimore and similar cities often focuses on the right issues, but falls short in noting the scale of these challenges. Cities are not self-sufficient political entities; rather, they exist as part of metropolitan regions that share social and economic challenges and opportunities.

SIX

If Not Now, When?

THE SUPREME COURT PLANNED TO ISSUE OPINIONS ON AS MANY AS TWENTY-SIX cases in June 2015, including *Texas Department of Housing and Community Affairs v. Inclusive Communities Project, Inc.* Baltimore's April unrest loomed over the decision.

Plenty of people connected the dots: the rioting had started in one of America's most racially isolated neighborhoods. On April 29, Employment Policies Institute research associate Richard Rothstein published an article called "From Ferguson to Baltimore: The Fruits of Government-Sponsored Segregation." Rothstein mentioned Baltimore's 1910 segregation ordinance as the beginning of "a century of federal, state, and local policies to quarantine Baltimore's black population in isolated slums." Rothstein pointed out that inequality had increased since a report by the Kerner Commission—created by President Lyndon Johnson to investigate the causes of America's mid-1960s urban riots—blamed the existence of black "ghettos" on white society. Rothstein's article about Baltimore—and a similar one about Ferguson, Missouri—suggested that the new round of unrest was about more than just police brutality. "Without suburban integration, something barely on today's public policy agenda, ghetto conditions will persist, giving rise to aggressive policing and the riots that inevitably ensue," Rothstein wrote.

The Supreme Court's decision in *Texas Department of Housing and Community Affairs v. Inclusive Communities Project, Inc.* would play into this narrative one way or another: it would either make it easier or make it harder for poor African Americans to live outside of neighborhoods like Sandtown.

On June 25, the Supreme Court released its opinion, written by the enigmatic Anthony Kennedy.

Kennedy wrote that litigants could use the Fair Housing Act of 1968 to file complaints over housing policies that disproportionately harmed racial minorities or other protected groups, even if in the absence of discernible discriminatory intent. The language of the act, he said, referred to the "consequences of an action rather than the actor's intent." Texas had contended that the language in the Fair Housing Act supported claims based on discriminatory *intent* but not those based on disparate *impact*; the majority disagreed. Kennedy wrote that the law's language reflected language in other civil rights–era statutes that more explicitly authorized disparate impact claims.

Justice Kennedy did not settle *Inclusive Communities'* complaint, which had accused Texas's housing agency of distributing LIHTC tax credits in a way that furthered segregation. That went back to the lower courts for application of the Supreme Court's ruling. The decision settled only whether disparate impact claims could be brought under the Fair Housing Act and what standards and burden of proof applied.

Those standards were high. To prove disparate impact, Kennedy wrote, plaintiffs must demonstrate statistically that a policy has produced an unequal impact on a certain group of people and show a "causal connection" between the policy and the disparities in question. On top of that, they must establish that the policy is "artificial, arbitrary and unnecessary." Businesses could claim a "business necessity," and governments could claim "public interest." Challengers could win these cases only if they successfully identified an alternative policy achieving those interests without harming protected classes of people. Kennedy's standards closely matched HUD's guidance in the final 2013 disparate impact rule.

Kennedy discouraged the consideration of race in disparate impact remedies—but not entirely. The first remedy in the case of disparate impact, Kennedy wrote, should be to scrap the policy that caused it; beyond that, remedies should "strive to . . . eliminate racial disparities through race-neutral means." Yet, Kennedy wrote, "race may be considered in certain circumstances and in a proper fashion."

Oral arguments in the case had taken place only months after the unrest in Ferguson, and the decision followed the Baltimore unrest by a similarly short interstice. Justice Kennedy did not mention either town by name, but he might as well have. Congress passed the Fair Housing Act in response to the riots that followed the assassination of Dr. Martin Luther King Jr., he noted, insisting that the Act must help prevent the Kerner Commission's "grim prophecy" of "two societies, one black, one white—separate and unequal.'"

The news out of the nation's capital encouraged those who hoped to dismantle the lines of concentrated poverty and residential segregation in the Baltimore region. Locally, however, that news was tempered by an announcement the same day from the state capital. Maryland governor Larry Hogan said that the state would not build the much-anticipated Red Line, a light-rail route that would, if built, allow many of Baltimore's poorest residents better access to jobs across the region.

The Opportunity Collaborative had hung some of its hopes on a planned addition to the state's light rail network. But thirteen days after Hogan's announcement, fair housing advocates got more encouraging news from Washington when HUD released the final version of a rule clarifying the duty to affirmatively further fair housing (sometimes referred to by the acronym AFFH). The rule replaced the "analysis of impediments" with an "assessment of fair housing," a template HUD officials said would assure more consistency and uniformity. The rule also committed HUD to providing public data and mapping tools to help grantees find impediments and guide their decision-making.

The rule wasn't about enforcement, HUD officials said. Rather, they wanted to partner with communities to help them establish practices that affirmatively furthered fair housing. "The federal government should never plan *for* communities," HUD secretary Julian Castro told reporters when he announced the rule. "It should plan *with* them."

Castro cited Raj Chetty's research on the way poor, segregated areas constrict children's economic mobility, using Baltimore as an example. "We must give every young person access to a community of opportunity," Castro said. "We can do that by revitalizing struggling communities . . . *and* by giving people the chance to live in areas where they can thrive." In alluding to the ongoing tension between mobility and revitalization, Castro echoed a revealing section of the final rule, which contained revisions to clarify that HUD supported "a balanced approach to affirmatively furthering fair housing."

Conservatives balked at the new rule. Even before the rule came out, *National Review* writer Stanley Kurtz had accused the media and HUD officials of hiding the story of what some on the right eventually came to label "Obamazoning."

"AFFH will dramatically undercut the independence of local governments, will mean significant population transfers across metropolitan areas, and will force densified development on suburbs and cities alike," Kurtz wrote.

A month later, Ben Carson weighed in. The former Johns Hopkins neurosurgeon had recently declared as a Republican presidential candidate, and in a July 2015 *Washington Times* op-ed, Carson compared the rule to the "failed" experiment of busing children to achieve school integration. He admitted that there was more to white flight than busing. He specifically mentioned "redlining, restrictive covenants, discriminatory steering by real estate agents and restricted access to private capital." But this new "tortured reading" of the Fair Housing Act, Carson wrote, was a "mandated social-engineering scheme" sure to result in unintended consequences.

By November 2015, Carson led the polling for the GOP presidential primary.

During the month after Freddie Gray's death in April, homicides spiked, and local and national news outlets came to Sandtown to capture the mood. They found that residents were feeling less safe than ever. "Before it was over-policing," one Gilmor Homes resident told CBS News. "Now there's no police."

From April to May 2015, arrests across the city dropped 43 percent—and more than 60 percent in West Baltimore, the *Baltimore Sun* reported. Police complained about the charged atmosphere that officers were finding on the streets. "Any time they pull up to respond to a call, they have 30 to 50 people surrounding them," commissioner Anthony Batts told the *Baltimore Sun*. The department ordered Western District patrols to include two officers in each cruiser. Mayor Stephanie Rawlings-Blake fired Commissioner Batts in July, and two months later he stunned the region by saying that officers "took a knee" after the unrest.

By the end of September, the homicide count in the Western District stood at fifty, more than in any other district and over twice as many as the district had registered during all of 2014. September brought even more demoralizing news to Sandtown: that month, several residents of Gilmor Homes sued the Housing Authority of Baltimore City, alleging that some workers had demanded "sexual *quid pro quo*" for repairs and had denied maintenance to women who refused sexual advances.

By late November, Baltimore had recorded 310 murders, a 59 percent jump from the same time period the previous year, and a record per-capita murder rate. Yet the Sandtown community persevered. A new organization called Sandtown-Winchester United met several times throughout the fall of 2015. The group wanted a unified voice in the wake of the unrest, especially as the rest of the city was newly focused on providing resources to the neighborhood. Antoine Bennett and Elder Harris got involved, and some of the meetings took place at New Song Center and Jubilee Arts.

No Boundaries Coalition kept busy in 2015 as well, launching the "West Baltimore Commission on Police Misconduct" with a public hearing during which eight residents testified about their experiences with police brutality. No Boundaries Coalition collected police misconduct allegations with the intent of releasing a report that would argue for more civilian oversight of the police department.

Much was at stake for Baltimore City as 2016 approached. The first trial of a police officer charged in Freddie Gray's death was scheduled for December 1, 2015, and a primary election was scheduled for April 26, 2016. (Democrats so dominated Baltimore that the public treated primary elections as more consequential than general elections.) The incumbent mayor, Stephanie Rawlings-Blake, declined to run, and every city council seat was up for grabs.

With the unrest still fresh in everyone's mind, a sense of urgency gripped civically minded Baltimoreans. The moment was ripe for disrupting the city's long-standing patterns of racial inequality. The city had been building toward that moment even before Freddie Gray died. In 2010, retired *Baltimore Sun* veteran Antero Pietila published *Not in My Neighborhood: How Bigotry Shaped a Great American City*. The book, which starts off set in 1910, chronicles the passage of Baltimore's block-by-block segregation ordinance. It continues through racially restrictive covenants, blockbusting, and other exclusionary practices. Throughout Baltimore, the widely read book raised the baseline understanding of how the city's segregated landscape had come to be.

After April 2015, influential Baltimoreans grappled publicly with the root causes of the unrest. In September 2015, an advertisement appeared in the *Baltimore Sun* declaring "THE TIME IS NOW . . . for real, inclusive, and transformative change" and blaming Baltimore's biggest problems on structural racism. Over two dozen civic leaders' names ran down the side of the ad, including foundation directors, bank executives, religious leaders, and a hospital president. They were members of the "Racial Equity and the Future of the Baltimore Region" workgroup, convened by the Aspen Institute and several local foundations in 2011 to educate influential people throughout Baltimore's most powerful social institutions about structural racism.

One of the ad's signees, University of Baltimore provost Joseph Wood, created a for-credit course during the Fall 2015 semester called "Divided Baltimore: How Did We Get Here, Where Do We Go?" The university ran the weekly course in "town hall" style at an auditorium, and invited the public. Audience members interacted with people who had been trying for years, often out of the spotlight, to dismantle structural racism, such as A. Adar Ayira, a program director with Associated Black Charities who had done anti-racism training for years with a group called Baltimore Racial Justice Action. "I can tell you that twenty years ago, these types of conversations happened in pockets," said Ayira. "Now it is becoming more mainstream. Twenty years ago, very few people would say 'institutional' or 'structural' racism. Very few people would utter those words, and now you can even read those words in [the] media."

But Baltimore had a long way to go, Ayira warned. "We do not understand our history, we don't know it. And we are racially illiterate. We do not understand institutional and structural racism," she said.

In an editorial, the *Baltimore Sun* detected a "sea change in Baltimore's collective understanding of the urgent need to address such endemic social ills in distressed neighborhoods throughout the city." The *Sun* mentioned Leaders of a Beautiful Struggle—the five-year-old group of activists, organizers, policy advocates, and youth development leaders that came to prominence in the aftermath of Freddie Gray's death—as one of many groups that had "redefined the potential of 'people power' to achieve social justice."

Young black Baltimoreans didn't need to read a book, see an ad, or attend a lecture to learn about racial inequality and concentrated poverty, much less about the harm those conditions inflicted. Many of them had been living it. The outcry from young people at the bottom of the city's power hierarchy had clearly triggered a reckoning among the older establishment types. Perhaps now that the suits and the squares were more acutely aware of structural racism and the role of segregation in the region's gaping racial inequalities, city leaders would adjust their decision-making.

Perhaps. But as this historical moment lingered, it was the voices of young Baltimoreans that cut through the public conversation.

On a bright afternoon in October 2015, a high-school student named Makayla Gilliam-Price stood in front of Baltimore City Hall. A small public-address speaker sat on a park bench with a microphone and cable curled up next to it. Nearby were Adam Jackson and Lawrence Grandpre of Leaders of a Beautiful Struggle, Jackson with a "Black Excellence" T-shirt under his sweatshirt; Grandpre in a Baltimore United for Change T-shirt, an upraised fist sprouting from one side of the "U."

The city council had scheduled a final vote that evening on the nomination of interim commissioner Kevin Davis to become the official chief of police. During a hearing on Davis's appointment five nights earlier, Gilliam-Price and some of her classmates had occupied city hall's public balcony because they didn't trust Davis, particularly the way his officers had dealt with protesters over the so-called uprising of the previous few months. Shortly before dawn, police had led Gilliam-Price and about a dozen others out of city hall in handcuffs.

Yet here they were again. A crowd of young activists gathered around Gilliam-Price. Some of them belonged to City Bloc, a group from Baltimore City College. The young people had three demands. They wanted Commissioner Davis to agree to a "rules of conduct" memorandum regarding the policing of street protests. They wanted $20 million of the city's budget redirected toward community building. Lastly, they wanted Mayor Rawlings-Blake to fire housing commissioner Paul Graziano over what they called his negligence, particularly regarding accusations of maintenance workers demanding sex for repairs.

Gilliam-Price acknowledged the odds against seeing their demands met. "I am a seventeen-year-old girl and I don't have the right to vote," she told the small crowd in front of city hall. "Protesting is my voice."

Confrontation was nothing new to these young activists. Leaders of a Beautiful Struggle had taken an aggressive approach a few years earlier when fighting the proposed construction of a youth jail. After a U.S. Department of Justice report found that the Baltimore City Detention Center had failed to provide "sight and sound separation" between juveniles and adults, the State of Maryland proposed spending over $100 million to build a detention center solely for juveniles charged as adults. Advocates including Heber Brown and the Baltimore Algebra Project fought the jail proposal for several years, arguing that it would simply open more spots at the end of a racist school-to-prison pipeline.

Leaders of a Beautiful Struggle had formed a "strategic" alliance with whiter, more mainstream nonprofits that were also fighting to stop construction of the youth jail. However, members of Leaders of a Beautiful Struggle took umbrage at a November 2012 anti-jail rally downtown that, in their view, portrayed white-led nonprofits as leaders of the movement and failed to adequately acknowledge the importance of black grassroots advocacy. Adam Jackson from Leaders of a Beautiful Struggle took particular exception to Hathaway Ferebee, the former executive director of the Citizens Planning and Housing Association. Ferebee had gone on to lead the Safe and Sound Campaign, a youth-focused Baltimore nonprofit that had helped organize the rally. To Jackson, Ferebee symbolized white leadership of a policy agenda that affected black youth, and he posted a sharply critical op-ed on the Leaders of a Beautiful Struggle's website.

"The combination of her level of access to the Governor's office, her omission of Black grassroots organizations and her orientation to the nonprofit sector are clear indicators of her complicity and propagation of the Non-profit Industrial Complex," Jackson wrote.

For several years, Jackson and other advocates had criticized Baltimore's largely white-led world of foundations, charities, and advocacy organizations. In a 2011 *Indypendent Reader* article, Heber Brown wrote that they "professionally position themselves on the periphery of Black oppression for the purpose of financial gain and credibility." In a 2013 essay for Baltimore public radio station WYPR, Leaders of a Beautiful Struggle's public policy director Dayvon Love wrote that he'd noticed "a lot of black children and a lot of white adults" in the youth advocacy world. When white-led groups dominated the conversation and the grantmaking, he argued, black voices got marginalized, and white groups ended up directing movements that affected communities they didn't even live in.

"True commitment is working with and assisting black folks to speak for ourselves and lead the institutions that control our lives," Love wrote. "If that's not the primary thrust of people who want to do the work, they will be profiteering financially—and existentially—from our misery."

In January 2013, the state pulled the plug on construction of the youth jail, but the experience reinforced Jackson's and his colleagues' distrust of the "nonprofit industrial complex."

The October 2015 protest over Kevin Davis's nomination as police commissioner echoed the confrontational approach of the youth jail campaign. And it drew on a similar motivation: to counter the perception of the city's young people as threats rather than as assets. The morning of the protest, city officials announced the closing of the city hall balcony for "safety" reasons. The timing, just days after City Bloc had occupied the balcony and mere hours before another hearing about Kevin Davis would begin, sounded fishy. Adam Jackson told the crowd that the decision to close the balcony showed a "fundamental disrespect for youth of Baltimore City."

Around 5:00 p.m., the press conference ended and people filed into city hall. The city council voted 12 to 2 to confirm Davis's appointment. After the vote, the protestors interrupted the proceedings to voice their disapproval. Then they took to the streets, blocking downtown traffic during rush hour. Like most of the protests after Freddie Gray's death, their action was disruptive but ultimately peaceful.

The push for justice in the killing of Freddie Gray swelled the ranks of Baltimore's activist community. Social justice and antiracist activism was nothing new to Baltimore. In the 1930s, African Americans launched a "Buy Where You Can

Work" boycott in Baltimore, and black women began organizing in Baltimore public housing almost as soon as the first projects opened in the early 1940s. But by 2015, activism in Baltimore had established a decidedly twenty-first-century tenor.

The momentum that built toward Baltimore's uprising arguably started just after the turn of the millennium, when activists rallied behind East Baltimore residents who were displaced by the expansion of the Johns Hopkins medical campus. Then there was the Occupy Baltimore movement toward the end of 2011, followed by the killing of Trayvon Martin several months later, which drew hundreds of Baltimoreans to a rally outside of city hall. Over the next year, the deaths of two black Baltimoreans—Anthony Anderson and Tyrone West—in police custody fueled a movement around the issue of brutality in the Baltimore Police Department. West's sister Tawanda Jones began hosting "West Wednesdays," a weekly vigil at different spots around the city. When a grand jury declined to indict Ferguson police officer Darren Wilson in the killing of Michael Brown, a group of activists called Baltimore Bloc helped organize a march that blocked on-ramps to Interstates 83 and 395.

The movement in Baltimore extended beyond police brutality. From its inception, Baltimore Bloc had protested other inequality-related issues, such as homeless evictions and government subsidies to developers. And by the end of 2014, several groups were advocating for the development of affordable housing, including the Right to Housing Alliance, Housing Our Neighbors, and the Baltimore Housing Roundtable.

White people interested in racial justice had ways to find their role in the movement. Baltimore Racial Justice Action did racial equity and antiracism training and had a separate affinity group for white people. Leaders of a Beautiful Struggle ran a series of "white allyship" workshops. Several months after Freddie Gray's death, Betty Robinson, a white veteran of the civil rights movement who had helped launch Good Neighbors Northeast in 2000, helped organize a local chapter of a new national organization called Showing Up for Racial Justice. SURJ put the responsibility of dismantling white supremacy on white people and solicited "accountability partners" in the black community, including Baltimore Bloc and Leaders of a Beautiful Struggle.

If the movement sounded all over the place—police brutality, racial equity, homelessness, tax subsidies for developers—one person had become especially skilled at boiling it all down. Lawrence Brown (the professor at Morgan State University) had a knack for explaining the dynamics of white supremacy, structural racism, and regional inequality. In a post-"uprising" "Truth, Reconciliation, and Baltimore" issue of *Urbanite* magazine, a feature called "Fix the City" put Brown's fix first: "Make Black Neighborhoods Matter." His short, catchy headline played off of the familiar name of the "Black Lives Matter" movement, highlighted the role of place in shaping black lives, and found the common thread in the activism that had coalesced after April 2015. Brown described six decades of public policy that he believed had led to segregation and inequality, then offered a long list of proposed solutions. In less than five hundred words, Brown covered what had created two separate Baltimores, what maintained the great disparities between them, and what he expected policy makers to do to make black communities whole.

The vision of justice and reconciliation in a divided city that Brown described seemed particularly urgent at the end of 2015. On December 16, a Baltimore Circuit Court judge declared a mistrial in the case of William Porter, the first officer to be tried.

Two days before Thanksgiving 2015, Mark Lange emailed some dispiriting news to the New Song community.

"On behalf of Dr. Wilson and NSC staff, I regret to inform you that Elder Bennett suffered a minor stroke yesterday and is currently in the hospital recovering," he wrote. The stroke rocked Bennett. He seemed to sink into his bed as he waited for movement to return to his left side. He sought physical comfort in small things like a sip of ginger ale. He spoke softly and sparingly and felt discouraged by his inability to contribute to his community. By Christmastime, he'd recovered enough to be wheeled into a common room at his new rehabilitation center and celebrate with a couple dozen friends, family, and fellow New Song members who had come to fete him.

As Bennett recovered, Mark Lange entered a health crisis of his own. After several months with a persistent dry cough, Mark got an X-ray, which revealed a spot on his lung. Doctors performed a biopsy through Mark's back that felt like a root canal. The biopsy missed the tumor, which was nestled right up against Mark's rib. Mark's doctor told him he needed an exploratory operation that would require collapsing his lung. A successful lung collapse would be good news—if his lung stuck to the rib and wouldn't collapse, it would likely mean that the tumor had penetrated the bone. Mark's post-surgery recovery would depend on what the doctors found. With no cancer, he'd spend two days in the hospital and two weeks recuperating. If they found lung cancer, they'd need to take it out right away, putting Mark in the hospital for five days and home for a much longer recovery.

In January 2016, Mark went in for surgery. The doctors found cancer and removed the upper lobe of his right lung. After five days they sent him home with 25 percent less breathing capacity.

The sign—"NO PARKING MONDAY AND THURSDAY 8AM–12 NOON"—was useless. Hardly anyone ever parked in the 1000 block of N. Stricker Street. Even for Sandtown, the vacancy was astonishing: twenty three-story townhouses on each side of the street, and not one occupied. On January 5, 2016, Maryland governor Larry Hogan announced that they were all coming down.

That afternoon, Hogan and other elected officials surrounded a podium in the middle of the block, all braced in black overcoats against the below-freezing temperature. Hogan accentuated his coat with a blue tie and a gray scarf that hung over his shoulders like a pastor's stole. Baltimore mayor Stephanie Rawlings-Blake wore gloves and a cloche hat—both leopard print.

Sandtown was a stage once again. This time, state and city officials were announcing plans to eliminate blight across the city. Sandtown, of course, was the most potent symbol. Under Project C.O.R.E. (Creating Opportunities for Renewal and Enterprise), the state planned to spend $75 million to demolish vacant buildings, and the city promised to kick in close to $20 million. The state housing agency also announced $600 million in "financing opportunities" to revitalize blighted areas.

"Last year the streets here in Sandtown-Winchester were near ground zero for the riots," Hogan said. "As the world watched, homes and businesses were burned, looted, and ransacked while police officers and firefighters were attacked and injured. Fixing what is broken in Baltimore requires that we address the sea of abandoned, dilapidated buildings that are infecting entire neighborhoods."

After Hogan spoke, the crowd counted down from ten, and then a yellow hydraulic excavator clawed the facade of a three-story rowhouse onto the sidewalk.

On the evening of January 27, 2016, about 250 people crammed into Impact Hub Baltimore, a new co-working space in a gentrifying part of midtown. The crowd had slogged through the remnant of a record-setting twenty-six-inch blizzard to see the large pool of Democratic candidates who'd declared for the mayoral primary election. "I think everyone in this audience agrees that Baltimore is really at a critical inflection point and we really want to see the city go forward," said one of the moderators. "If you're elected mayor, what kind of difference do you want to see in the city in the next five years?"

The eleven candidates passed a microphone down the line. "A more inclusive city," said state senator Catherine Pugh, a sixty-five-year-old African American who'd served in the state legislature for eleven years and in the City Council for five years before that. "People working together, understanding that downtowns are important but neighborhoods are important, too. I want to see our city come together."

City councilman Carl Stokes unloaded on the Charm City Circulator, a free bus system that the city ran independent of the state-run transportation network. The Circulator mostly circulated through the city's "White L." "The people who live on East North Avenue and West North Avenue who are just trying to get to work and who are just trying to get to daycare, they don't have a free freakin' bus," Stokes said. "We just dismiss tens of thousands of mostly black folk, people who are below the poverty line."

The next question requested the candidates' plans for incorporating racial equity into the design and evaluation of their policies. The first few answers mostly described specific policies, like a $15 minimum wage, without any kind of plans to ensure racial equity. People noticed. On Twitter, where attendees and viewers of an online livestream were posting under the hashtag #mayoralforumIHB, one user wrote, "These candidates are literally circling the question of racial equity."

"There's a little thing called the Ten Questions for Racial Equity in Legislation and Policy," was the response of candidate Joshua Harris, a black twenty-nine-year-old community organizer. "Associated Black Charities released the study and they had a town hall about it about two months ago. So that's the first thing we need to look at when we're making new legislation and implementing new policies to make sure they're equitable."

Harris then criticized the city's use of Tax Increment Financing. So-called TIFs ostensibly attract development to the city that would otherwise be too expensive for developers to undertake. A TIF gambles on the potential of redevelopment to bring in more property tax revenue than a site had previously generated, thanks to an increase in the property's value. In the TIF process, a city sells bonds to help pay for roads and other public infrastructure at the development site. Any property tax revenue over and above that previously generated by the site must be used to pay down the debt on the bonds. Once the debt is fully paid, the city is able to keep all of the property tax revenue. City leaders promoted TIFs as a better way to attract development than raising taxes or spending out of the general fund.

Harris mentioned previous controversial TIF developments, such as a massive redevelopment around the Johns Hopkins East Baltimore campus and a mixed-use waterfront development called Harbor Point. Harris wanted to attach strings to TIFs in order to generate jobs and affordable housing for struggling neighborhoods. "What I've been working on is a community benefits agreement right now for a TIF of $17 million that an institution is asking for *without* a community benefits agreement," Harris said.

City councilman Nick Mosby claimed that three out of every four dollars spent on developer subsidies went downtown. "We have to invest more in our communities," he said. "What we need are community benefit agreements in every single TIF that we're doing."

Suddenly, someone loudly heckled Mosby. Audience members craned their heads, and Mosby stammered as he finished his point. A moderator called, "Time."

"Is there any way I can get ten more seconds?" Mosby asked.

"We'll give you five more seconds," the moderator said.

The heckler continued to talk.

"Let's let the candidates finish up their minutes," another moderator said.

In the back of the audience, a confrontation broke out between the heckler and a Mosby supporter. The room became tense with the potential for a physical fight in a crowded room. Some of the forum's organizers asked the heckler to leave.

When moderators asked the audience to submit their own questions on note cards, a community activist named J.C. Faulk walked to the front of the room and confronted the candidates. "I have a question," Faulk said. "How are you going to keep police from killing black people in this city?"

The morning after the Democratic mayoral candidates forum, the Baltimore Housing Roundtable released a report that began, "The history of development in Baltimore has been separate and unequal." One of the authors was Matt Hill, a lawyer who served as co-counsel with Barbara Samuels on the housing discrimination complaint against Baltimore County. The report, called "Community + Land + Trust: Tools for Development Without Displacement," criticized the city's "'trickle down' development policy." Over a quarter of the city's households earned less than 30 percent of the region's median income. Where, the authors wanted to know, was the plan to house them? The city's inclusionary housing law had been a bust, they wrote, and the Low-Income Housing Tax Credit program catered to families around 60 percent of the area's median income.

In just twenty-four hours, the candidates forum and the Baltimore Housing Roundtable's report had brought a great deal of attention to the role of housing and development in racial inequality. Two months later, March 9, 2016, made for another eventful twenty-four hours. In Baltimore County, the U.S. Department of Housing and Urban Development signed off on a settlement of the housing discrimination complaint filed five years earlier.

A U.S. Department of Housing and Urban Development official called its voluntary compliance agreement with Baltimore County and the plaintiffs "unprecedented." The county agreed to spend $30 million over ten years to encourage the development of one thousand "hard units" of affordable housing within a group of 116 census tracts in "opportunity" areas. The agreement also required the county to create a mobility counseling program and devote two thousand of its housing choice vouchers toward moving families into "communities of opportunity," and it eliminated the county's one-person "pocket veto." The county denied all the allegations in the original complaint, saying it had settled because of concerns about "the risks of litigation." The county specifically cited the Supreme Court's 2015 disparate impact ruling: "The Supreme Court case would have made it very difficult for the County to prevail in the courts."

One of the most remarkable parts of the agreement dealt with "source of income" discrimination. Housing advocates had pushed for laws banning this kind of discrimination since before ACLU–Maryland even filed the *Thompson* complaint, believing that segregation was intensified by the refusal of landlords in wealthier communities to consider applications from voucher holders. By 2016, Howard, Frederick, and Montgomery Counties had banned source-of-income discrimination, as had the cities of Annapolis, Baltimore (only for certain affordable housing developments), and Frederick. The Maryland General Assembly, however, had failed to pass a statewide ban.

The Baltimore County agreement did not ban source-of-income discrimination, but it did require the county executive—at the time, Democrat Kevin Kamenetz—to introduce legislation to the county council that would do so. The agreement could not, of course, mandate passage of such a bill.

All eyes would be on the Baltimore County Council once Kamenetz submitted the bill.

And in the city, all eyes would be on the Baltimore *City* Council. On the same day that Baltimore County settled its housing complaint, Sagamore Development, a privately held real estate group co-founded by Under Armour CEO Kevin Plank, applied for what could become the largest Tax Increment Financing package in Baltimore's history. The TIF would need the council's approval.

A Baltimore success story, Under Armour employed nearly two thousand people and sponsored athletes like basketball star Steph Curry and baseball slugger Bryce Harper. The company said it was outgrowing its headquarters in the Locust Point neighborhood on the city's southern peninsula. Under Armour founder Kevin Plank had purchased 160 acres in Port Covington, an industrial area adjacent to Locust Point. Sagamore Development planned to build a new four-million-square-foot headquarters there, alongside eleven million more square feet of development that would include office space, retail, manufacturing, a hotel, parkland, a connection to light rail, and over 7,500 housing units.

Mayor Stephanie Rawlings-Blake and Maryland governor Larry Hogan supported this "city within a city," hoping it would create thousands of new jobs. Critics saw it as more development for the whiter and wealthier part of the region and wondered whether residents in struggling city neighborhoods had a realistic chance of landing any of those new jobs or finding affordable housing in Sagamore's planned developments.

The Baltimore County settlement and the Port Covington development provided potential bookends to a five-decade-long fair housing struggle in the region. In 1970, the U.S. Commission on Civil Rights had called out Baltimore County for its history of exclusionary housing policy. In the ten years before that 1970 hearing, the expanding county's black population had grown by only 2,500 people. In the settlement that Barbara Samuels and her colleagues negotiated, the county agreed to create three thousand affordable housing opportunities in the county's most prosperous areas. That was on top of well over 1,000 created in Baltimore County through the *Thompson* partial consent decree and final remedy. If the county passed a law against source-of-income discrimination, even more poor black county residents would likely find housing in more prosperous communities.

In the city, Barbara's team had asked in the 1990s for an injunction to halt the demolition of public housing high-rises until the city replaced the lost units in more prosperous neighborhoods. Those towers came down, but now a developer wanted to put up luxury apartment towers in one of the city's whitest areas—93 percent white in a 30 percent white city—with no discernible plan for affordable units.

To make Port Covington more inclusive, Barbara and other advocates of fair housing and equitable development would have to sway the business and development community, a mayor who was leaving office at the end of her term, and a city council that, according to the *Baltimore Sun*, was "certain to prove substantially different" after an election that was just five weeks away.

It was, in short, a test of "people power."

———

Up on the roof of the Harris-Marcus Center, Elder Harris had a boom box. He had a tent. He had a bucket he could lower down to his staff when he needed something. He had a harness around his upper legs—just to be safe. He had a little stubble from being up there for over forty-eight hours. He had a fresh "Sandtown" cap on his head. He had on a loose black sweatshirt and sweatpants for comfort. He had two beach chairs: one was for his visitors, who had to wear a harness and climb a terrifying fire escape. He had a gorgeous view in every direction: St. Peter Claver Church, the fountain in Pennsylvania Triangle Park, miles of Baltimore's lovable rowhouses, downtown skyscrapers.

He also had a plan: to stay on the roof until five hundred Sandtown residents cast ballots during early voting in the primary election. No Boundaries Coalition members and members of Baltimoreans United in Leadership Development (BUILD) were out canvassing the neighborhood to see who had voted; they'd counted over 240 people so far.

Harris had hatched this plan just after the April 2015 unrest, when he had heard how low turnout had been in the neighborhood for the previous election. The day Harris climbed up on the roof, No Boundaries Coalition was running shuttles to early voting stations from the block party they were holding across the street.

Elder C.W. Harris camps out on the roof of Newborn Holistic Ministries headquarters in an effort to boost turnout in Baltimore City's 2016 primary election. (2016) *Lawrence Lanahan*

On this clear afternoon, Harris sat in his beach chair drinking a smoothie out of a coffee thermos. His cell phone rang and he answered. "How you doin', brother?" he asked. "Yeah—get one thousand people you want to take to the polls." A bit later, a *Washington Post* reporter came up over the ledge. After attracting several local television stations plus some radio and newspaper reporters, Harris was now going national.

That same day, the *Baltimore Sun* ran city council endorsements, keeping in mind "the importance of issues of social justice brought to light by the Freddie Gray protests—from police brutality and racial inequity in the prosecution of crime to broader issues of poverty, housing and education." Six incumbents had declined to run, and ninety-seven candidates had declared across the city's fourteen districts.

In the mayoral race, Catherine Pugh looked to be in the lead. Pugh was the Senate chair of a "Public Safety and Policing Work Group" that legislative leaders had formed in the wake of Baltimore's 2015 unrest. In January 2016, the task force had recommended placing citizens on police disciplinary hearing boards and letting the public observe the proceedings. The bill that had just passed in the recently ended General Assembly session didn't go that far. It made civilian presence *possible* on hearing boards for police facing internal disciplinary action, but it left the decision up to localities. Baltimore Police Department trial boards consisted of three officers. Under the new bill, the police commissioner could put two civilians on the board, but only after negotiations with the police union. That union, the Fraternal Order of Police, Lodge 3, had a contract expiring in just a couple of months and was sure to oppose civilians during negotiations.

Leaders of a Beautiful Struggle had pushed throughout the session for police reform, even holding a rally at city hall where people could board buses to attend another rally in Annapolis. It didn't take the group long to transition from Maryland's state house to the streets. One day after the session ended, Leaders of a Beautiful Struggle members joined other local groups for a press conference in Sandtown to announce a new project: Tubman House.

Over the winter, activists had discussed taking possession of a city-owned "vacant" near Gilmor Homes and turning it into a community center. Once the cold weather broke, the activists renovated 1618 Presbury Street, the house closest to the corner. They named the house after Harriet Tubman, who had escaped slavery in Maryland and led dozens of enslaved friends and family to freedom on the Underground Railroad. The coalition, which also included an American Friends Service Committee prison mentorship program called "Friend of a

Friend," envisioned a place where Gilmor Homes residents could take arts classes, learn how to become politically active, or even just read a book quietly.

On April 12, 2016, dozens of people and several local journalists showed up for the Tubman House "presser." Leaders of a Beautiful Struggle research director Lawrence Grandpre welcomed the visitors and introduced his organization's "cultural curator" for a poetry reading. Lady Brion—real name Brion Gill—attacked the conservative notion that the poor should "pull themselves up by their bootstraps." She pulled out a smartphone to read her poem.

"In Katrina-high water, what's a boot to a broken levee?" she read. "Like cowboy boots get us treated any less like a herd."

The poem blasted the corporate sector as well as African Americans with "special Negro syndrome" who, she suggested, did their bidding. "They'll have you believin' that the projects wasn't a project like rats in the lab experiment, an experiment like Tuskegee," she read, referring to a government study of syphilis in African American men during which researchers kept the subjects in the dark about their diagnoses and refused treatment to two hundred of them.

Grandpre took the mic again and claimed that his coalition had negotiated in good faith with the city to take legitimate possession of the house. The city had marked the entire block for demolition under its "Vacants to Value" program, and the coalition, he said, was frustrated with how long it would take to actually get possession of 1618 Presbury. Grandpre looked skeptically on Vacants to Value as well as on the state's Project C.O.R.E., which had recently demolished the 1000 block of N. Stricker Street, just a few blocks away. To Grandpre, the city saw vacants as a way to turn a profit, and the state saw them as something to be destroyed. "We don't think the folks in Annapolis understand the value inherent in building community where people are," he said. "We have a national narrative where we need saviors to come in and save Baltimore. And this entire effort is designed to challenge that narrative. Right across the street from where Freddie Gray was arrested, we are working as a community to say, 'We don't need these saviors to come in. We have the power to save ourselves.'

"I think that's exactly what this effort is trying to produce," Grandpre continued. "And the question is, will Baltimore City and whoever the mayor is be amenable to these types of grassroots efforts?"

Mayoral candidate and city councilman Carl Stokes was watching the presser. A reporter asked him, "Are you gonna get the city to sell this thing?"

"Why not?" Stokes asked. "You mean sell it—"

"Sell it to the coalition," the reporter said.

"Oh, sure," Stokes said. "Why wouldn't they? Give it to them. Why would you sell something that has such a good purpose to it?"

On April 19, Adam Jackson and Dayvon Love were back outside Tubman House, staffing a grill at a gathering to commemorate the one-year anniversary of Freddie Gray's death. In the lot next to the house, small green sprouts peeked out of raised dirt beds. Several women from a group called Mothers of Murdered Sons took turns at a microphone. At sunset, the crowd meandered across the street to the spot in Gilmor Homes where police had detained Freddie Gray. Some of Gray's family and friends held candles in front of a small memorial mural. A woman released three red, heart-shaped balloons, which rose over Gilmor Homes into the growing dusk. Tawanda Jones—sister of the late Tyrone West—began to speak. When she said, "I can't stop, I won't stop," the crowd finished for her: ". . . till killer cops are in cell blocks!"

As she finished, a man interjected with appreciation for Jones and her supporters: "They been out every Wednesday for three years!"

The next Tuesday, voters chose Catherine Pugh as the Democratic candidate for mayor. They flushed out two of the eight city council incumbents who had run. More than half of the fourteen Democratic primary winners were thirty-five years old or younger.

The general election on November 8 would usher in a new president. Polls showed reality-TV star Donald Trump surging toward the GOP nomination. Polls also overwhelmingly showed Hillary Clinton leading Trump in a hypothetical general-election matchup.

Nicole sat in her living room with a pile of sign-in sheets in her lap. In the background, Steve Harvey chattered away on the television. Nicole knew the state child care office could send an inspector by her apartment anytime, and she wanted her paperwork to be in order. The sliding glass door revealed a beautiful April afternoon.

Nicole now had five children in her daycare program, and she hoped to expand into a house somewhere. In the fall, she would begin her second associate's degree program at Howard Community College. She figured two degrees would make her more attractive to parents looking for child care. The second degree would also give her a second career option: an associate of arts in teaching degree in early childhood education would prepare her to transfer into a teaching program at a four-year college.

Nicole also wanted to get a van when she expanded her program. Transportation was getting to be a pain since she had offered to pick up some of her clients' children after school. On this afternoon, Nicole was about to drive out to a Head Start program in Harper's Choice, one of Columbia's nine "villages," to pick up some children for after-school care.

The Head Start program occupied space at a school complex next door to the Harper's Choice Village Center. A couple months earlier, Nicole had seen police responding to a fight near the middle school. She had noticed more fighting in certain parts of Columbia in recent years. So had Joe, who was two months away from finishing eighth grade. He didn't want to attend his zoned school, Wilde Lake High, because he felt the students brought too much drama and disruption into the classroom.

Joe had decided that he wanted to be an Army Ranger, and he had applied to Atholton High, another public school a few miles away, hoping to join its JROTC program. Joe interviewed with the JROTC lieutenant colonel there but was rejected. The guidance counseling staff at Wilde Lake Middle was trying to help Joe get a second look from Atholton.

While Joe was catching his bus home from Wilde Lake on this afternoon, Nicole drove out to the Head Start program to pick up two boys who attended her daycare program. Nicole greeted the two little boys, walked them out to the parking lot, and buckled them into car seats in the back of her gray subcompact. She drove away from the village center via Eliots Oak Road, a shady two-lane street. The further she drove, the less dense the housing became: garden apartments, then townhouses, then ranch houses, then split-levels, then colonials with garages.

Eliots Oak Road dead-ended into an older two-lane state route, Clarksville Pike, at a wide, lightly wooded expanse that Howard County had preserved under public and private conservation easements. It instantly felt like being in the country. Nicole turned right.

"I see the castle!" yelled one of the boys.

"I see the cow!" chirped the other boy.

Just past the conservation easements was Clark's Elioak, a petting farm that had relocated fairy-tale structures from The Enchanted Forest, a fantastical children's park that had shuttered two decades earlier. In addition to the castle and the cow, the farm had a giant Mother Goose, a "Three Bears' House," and an enormous purple shoe with a clapboard roof for the "Old Lady."

On past Clark's Elioak, the woods of Centennial Park closed in around the road. A fifty-acre lake with a looped trail lay at the center of the park. Nicole liked to jog along the path. (Joe insisted that she mostly walked and took selfies.)

A few minutes before Nicole reached her neighborhood, some typical preschool bickering arose in the backseat. Nicole wanted the children in her care to learn skills to resolve conflicts before they became fights. "Use your words, not your hands!" she scolded.

After a moment, one of the boys said, "I want to say sorry."

"Okay," said Nicole.

"Sorry," he said.

"It's okay," said the other boy.

Mark Lange had lost some of the focus in his life even before the surgery. He had put so much of himself into helping Allan Tibbels during the illnesses of Allan's last few years, and then Allan had died. Pastor Thurman Williams had anchored him theologically and in his dedication to Christian community development—Mark had even become a deacon at the church in 2009—and then Pastor Williams had left. And although Mark felt he had bullied the pastoral search committee

Dr. John M. Perkins in Jackson, Mississippi. (2016) *Lawrence Lanahan*

into bringing on Pastor Wilson, the new pastor lacked Mark's dedication to the philosophy of Dr. John M. Perkins.

Plus, Mark had given up his small business. While he was losing Allan, he was also losing business to the Great Recession. Clients were harder to find. Some of his existing clients wouldn't pay, and others went bankrupt. In May 2011, he'd started managing ReStore, the Sandtown Habitat for Humanity space on N. Fulton Avenue that sold used hardware, furniture, and building materials. After surgery, Mark's doctor insisted he take a few weeks off from ReStore and restrict his heavy lifting—no small part of his job—after he got back.

After the surgery, life felt different to Mark—a little surreal. He couldn't put his finger on it. Some of it, of course, was the confrontation with his own mortality. There was the physical pain and the oxycodone the doctors had prescribed. He had also lost stamina. The short walk to church the Sunday after he returned from the hospital had winded him, and the church itself had appeared darker than usual inside. And there were the changes to his routine: instead of working during the day, he was walking on a treadmill, and at night he began listening to music in bed—a playlist called "Chill," with the lighter songs of Bruce Cockburn, Joan Baez, Bob Dylan, and Neil Young.

Then the blizzard had come, less than two weeks after he returned from the hospital. His Sandtown neighbors—the people whom he had come to serve—served him. A New Song worshipper who lived on Presstman Street and a neighbor from Gilmor Homes shoveled Betty's car out so she could get to work. Ryan Diener, a white Baltimore City homicide detective and fellow relocator, also helped Mark. Diener and Mark were very close; like Mark, Diener was a New Song deacon, and they lived two doors away from each other. So much snow had fallen that Mark couldn't even open his back door. Diener knew that one of Mark's most important daily tasks was feeding the block's colony of stray cats, and that the food was out back.

The surgery had removed all the cancer from Mark's lung, but it had failed to cure his hard-headedness, and he insisted on joining Diener when he came to help. Getting to the back deck meant walking down the sidewalk and around the row of houses to Mark's alley gate. Thigh-high drifts of snow lay between the gate and the street. Mark reached the gate, but the trudge exhausted him so badly that he had to lie against the fence. Diener shoveled from the gate to the house, and several hours later, five cats filled a tall, snow-lined trench outside Mark's back door, faces deep in bowls of Friskies.

The weakness, the shock of surgery, the new routines—it all amplified the

Mark and Betty Lange inside their home on N. Gilmor Street in West Baltimore's Sandtown neighborhood. (2018) *Lawrence Lanahan*

unsettled feeling that was growing inside Mark. He grew detached, more intro-spective. He never felt distant from God; he just felt less sure about what God needed him to be doing. A Christian, Mark believed, needed an outlet, somewhere to dispense the grace constantly building up inside. Mark decided to focus on ReStore. Christian community development may have been slipping away from New Song Community Church, but Mark felt he could practice it on his own, and ReStore was a good place to do that.

Mark considered ReStore to be a ministry. He had relationships there, and it showed during his recovery. Customers texted him to see how he was doing, and when he returned to work in late February 2016, many came to see him. The store had become a kind of community. His customers joked that he should put in a checkerboard and a couple of barber chairs. Mark's personality wasn't built for the emotional labor of retail, and he'd often come home to Betty at the end of the day completely bushed. But he believed that the work he felt he was meant to do could be done there.

One day in early May 2016, an older white man came through the ReStore door. George Waite was a couple of inches shorter than Mark and ten years older. Mark's story of relocation intrigued Waite, and Waite lingered to chat with Mark and others who came in and out of the store.

The interaction was friendlier than the one they'd had the first time Waite had visited. That day, Waite told Mark he was volunteering in the neighborhood, and Mark gave him an earful. Freddie Gray had just died, and Mark had seen enough flash-in-the-pan white saviors come and go. He considered Waite just another white person with an agenda of coming to Sandtown to salve his white guilt, and he let Waite know it.

As it turned out, Waite had been coming to Sandtown before anyone outside the city knew who Freddie Gray was. Waite's wife was a Quaker, and in the fall of 2014, the couple had gotten to know some people who were involved with the prison mentorship program "Friend of a Friend." At a Friend of a Friend picnic at Gilmor Homes, someone pointed out to George Waite that the basketball court there had fallen into disrepair. Also at the picnic was Eddie Conway, an Army veteran and former Black Panther leader who was convicted in the 1970 murder of a Baltimore City police officer. (Conway maintained his innocence, and many considered him to have been a political prisoner—the FBI was infiltrating the Panthers at the time through its COINTELPRO program.) Conway worked with Friend of a Friend while he was incarcerated and after his parole in 2014.

Rather than wait for the housing authority to renovate the dilapidated basketball court, Waite, Conway, and another formerly incarcerated man working with Friend of a Friend decided to do it themselves. In the spring of 2015, Waite went to Gilmor Homes to work on the hoops just about every day, even climbing ladders to file down metal poles so that new backboards would attach smoothly. It took over a year to renovate the courts, and Waite got to know residents of Gilmor Homes. At first, he'd been intimidated by the projects, but he came to love the community there. No one ever vandalized the courts he was renovating—that was more than he could say about basketball courts in Bel Air—and over time, more and more Gilmor Homes residents joined him in the renovation work. And although someone had stolen tools out of his truck while it was parked in his Bel Air driveway, he worked every day with his back to the truck at Gilmor Homes, and no one ever took a thing. Waite felt a growing connection to the neighborhood, and in April 2016, he was there to see Friend of a Friend and Leaders of a Beautiful Struggle announce the opening of Tubman House.

Mark came to understand the extent of Waite's work in Sandtown and apologized for confronting him the way he had. Waite continued to marvel at Mark's story. Waite had never been very religious, but his work in Gilmor Homes—as well as some personal struggles—had led him to reevaluate his faith. He peppered Mark with questions about his theology, and Mark answered gladly. They also talked politics, and Waite discovered that he was considerably more liberal than Mark was.

During Waite's visit in May 2016, he told Mark that Mark's journey to Sandtown recalled an experience of his own. Waite had served in the Vietnam War with the U.S. Army, and he'd ignored his superiors when they said not to fraternize with the enemy. He enjoyed spending time in the villages and was appalled at the conditions people had to live in there. He saw some parallel in his and Mark's experiences. "I was staying, getting to know the villagers," he told Mark.

Waite lived in Bel Air, the very same suburb that Mark had fled for Sandtown. In forty-five minutes, Harford Road took you from an affluent white suburb to what Waite considered third-world conditions. And each time he visited Gilmor Homes, Waite made that forty-five-minute drive back to the affluent white suburb. Waite saw a parallel to his experience in Vietnam. As close as he got to the villagers, he'd always returned to the comfort of a safe American compound.

Sandtown was tugging at Waite—perhaps, he thought, the same way it had tugged at Mark. He couldn't get Mark and his fellow relocators out of his mind.

"When I go back home, I think about it," he said to Mark.

Mark needled Waite for his liberal outlook. The way Mark saw it, personal responsibility was a hallmark of true conservatism. His responsibility, he felt, was to live as a disciple of Christ. Mark believed that as a Christian, truly caring for a community didn't mean supporting government programs for people who lived forty-five minutes away. It meant making that community your home.

"My conservatism means you move to the 'hood," Mark said. "It means you can't live in Bel Air."

On the Wednesday of his last week of school in June, Joe arrived home from Wilde Lake Middle and found Nicole sitting on the living room floor with a toddler who was napping on a sleeping bag. A bright pink piece of art hung on the wall above her; Nicole had made it at a "paint and punch" event at her church. Next to the words FAITHFUL FIERCE AND FABULOUS NIKKI a stylish, skinny woman in a pink hat, white blouse, black skirt, and red high heels was depicted.

Joe's guidance counselor and assistant principal had finally persuaded the JROTC lieutenant colonel at Atholton High School to give Joe a second look. But he would only be interested, the lieutenant colonel had said, if Joe's attendance improved.

"The guidance counselor said they'll call today or next couple days," Joe told Nicole.

The last day of eighth grade was just two days away. There would be a dance and other social events after that, but Joe was finished with middle school.

"I don't feel like going to Activity Day," he said.

"When's that?" Nicole asked excitedly. "When is it?!?"

"It's not so you can come," Joe said.

"I'm not coming!" Nicole said.

Joe's fifteenth birthday was two months away. He was already taller than his mother, and he took many opportunities to assert his independence, often challenging and correcting her. He did it affectionately, however, and Nicole received it as such. Joe's independence extended to his social world. He avoided trouble just the way Nicole had, with his radar acutely tuned to drugs, fighting, and other activities among his peers that could hold him back.

Joe believed Atholton High School could help propel him forward.

Matt Hill, co-counsel on the original housing discrimination complaint against Baltimore County, thought he could count on at least three of the seven council members to vote for the HOME Act, which would ban source-of-income discrimination. He knew the essential fourth vote would be difficult to get, but he had hope.

In July 2016, the council peppered county planning director Andrea Van Arsdale and county housing office administrator Marsha Parham with questions about the bill for an hour. Along the way, council members voiced their own reservations about making someone's source of income the basis for civil rights protections. Democrat Tom Quirk said small-time landlords in his district worried that dealing with the federal government would be too onerous. Republican David Crandell, who represented Dundalk, Essex, and Rosedale, said, "My struggle is that I look at that conciliation agreement and I see Moving to Opportunity, which was a complete failure for my district."

Republican David Marks, who represented a nearly uninterrupted stretch of state-designated "communities of opportunity" from Towson to the Harford County line, brought up HUD's affirmatively furthering rule and the Supreme Court's decision on disparate impact. All three branches of the federal government, he said, had painted the county into a corner. "You have rulemaking from HUD which is under the executive branch, you had a Supreme Court decision from the judicial branch, and you had members of Congress who did nothing to help us," Marks said.

The bill, Van Arsdale said, simply outlawed any refusal to consider the application of a person with a Housing Choice voucher. "It does not force anyone to rent to anyone with a voucher," she said. Van Arsdale cited Raj Chetty's research on the effect of poor, segregated places on children's future economic mobility. "By discriminating against poor families, we may be denying their children the opportunity to better their lives and to break the intergenerational cycle of poverty," she said. Democrat Julian Jones, the only African American on the council, pleaded the case of equality, saying the bill would allow voucher holders "to show up and present themselves like anyone else."

Citizen testimonies followed. Members of a multifamily housing association complained about government inefficiency and incompetence. Fair housing advocates cited statistics showing that housing vouchers didn't affect crime and property values the way critics claimed. A resident who had worked her way out of poverty expressed her resentment at "free rent." Another resident with plenty of voucher holders in her neighborhood said she barely noticed any difference. One woman who used a voucher to help pay for rent cried, saying she was afraid to let her children play outside in the neighborhood where she had been able to find a rental. "We love God, we respect authority, we pay our rent, and we pay our bills," she said. "The HOME Act isn't demanding that you must accept us because of a voucher, it's stating that you shouldn't be able to reject me because I'm a voucher holder."

A large wooden inscription on the massive marble wall behind the council members loomed over the proceedings: EQUALITY AND LIBERTY UNDER LAW IS THE FOUNDATION OF A GOVERNMENT OF FREE PEOPLE. An observer of the session might have wondered whether the principles of equality and liberty were diametrically opposed. While supporters like Van Arsdale and councilman Julian Jones pleaded for equality, some opponents complained about assaults on their liberty. "I will not be forced by federal, state, or county government to rent to anyone," one landlord told the council.

"I'm a volunteer with the Baltimore County Campaign for Liberty," said a young man in a blue polo shirt, as the session entered its third hour. "We are opposed to [the bill] because it is a violation of civil liberties and property rights."

He blamed the county's expensive housing on excessive regulation. Cathy Bevins, the councilwoman representing parts of Rosedale and Middle River, broke in toward the end of the man's testimony. Bevins was familiar with Campaign for Liberty; they had already sparred on Facebook. She had a message for the man from one of the neighborhoods in her district. "The fliers you left there, the two thousand fliers that you delivered through the neighborhood, they're now in their storm drains and going out to the Dark Head Creek, so you might want to send the same volunteers back to that community to clean it up. Thank you," Bevins said.

The room erupted in applause.

The man left behind a box of 1,400 petitions opposing the bill.

Matt Hill had never even heard of the Campaign for Liberty.

On July 25, Joe and Nicole shared the good news with a visitor. The colonel had given Joe a second chance. He would attend Atholton High School in the fall.

"I was in school for this Wilde Lake High School leadership program or something," Joe said. "I was next to my guidance counselor, and my mom texted me 'you made Atholton'—well, she attempted to spell Atholton—and I said, 'No.' She said, 'No, the colonel just called and said that you made the program.' So me and my guidance counselor, you know, we were happy. The assistant principal found out, all my teachers were happy. It was on a school day—it was on the U.S. Army's birthday, so the fourteenth of June?"

"It was after graduation and all that," Nicole said. "He was excited. I had to run up to the school."

"All my teachers, especially my friends, were excited," Joe said.

"They came and hugged him, he hugged me," Nicole said. "[Then] they sent the letter. He goes to boot camp next week."

Joe and Nicole talked about the different paths he could have ended up on. Back in the city, the school's solutions to Joe's behavioral and learning issues had been to send him out of the system for therapy. At Wilde Lake Middle, his teachers and administrators had rallied around him inside the school. And now Joe would attend a stellar school in one of the most vaunted school systems in the state. Atholton's graduation rate was over 95 percent, and three out of four students went on to four-year colleges.

Joe and Nicole talked about the disparities one could find throughout Columbia: in education, in crime, in income. They both had come to understand which parts of the county were rougher than others. Having grown up in the city, Nicole didn't consider the disparities as drastic as Joe did.

"There's lots of crime over here," Joe said. "Robberies. At the 7-Eleven where the kids hang out, they're trying to keep cops around there."

"I know not every area is like that," Nicole said. "I hear Oakland Mills is a low-income area."

"My friends said that's one of the most ghetto schools in Howard County," Joe said.

"Howard County have their own idea of what a ghetto school is! They don't know ghettoes, honey, *ha-ha-ha!*" said Nicole.

A chalkboard advertised a "Trans Happy Hour" outside of Red Emma's, a café and bookstore at the centrally located corner of Maryland and North Avenues that had become a nerve center for Baltimore's activists and radicals. But the big draw this evening promised to be the event at which Barbara Samuels and Lawrence Brown were booked to speak: "Pushing Back Against the Proposed Port Covington TIF."

The Baltimore City Council had scheduled a hearing the very next evening on Sagamore Development's request for a $535 million Tax Increment Financing package to support their construction of new corporate headquarters for Under Armour and an upscale neighborhood along 260 acres of coveted city waterfront. In just four months, the TIF application had jumped through most of the bureaucratic hoops: unanimous approval from the board of the quasi-governmental Baltimore Development Corporation and the city's Board of Finance, and unanimous approval by the city's planning commission for a master plan for Port Covington that created four new zoning categories. The city had given Sagamore a waiver from its inclusionary housing law, and Sagamore had agreed to a memorandum of understanding setting a goal of 10 percent affordable housing for households

Nicole Smith in the Columbia apartment she rented with a special housing voucher created as a remedy in *Thompson v. HUD.* (2018) *Lawrence Lanahan*

The house in West Baltimore's Penn North neighborhood that Melinda Smith bought in 1995, as it stood in 2018. *Lawrence Lanahan*

Nicole's mother, Melinda Smith, in 2018. *Lawrence Lanahan*

earning less than 80 percent of the area's median income. A caveat would allow Sagamore to simply pay into the Inclusionary Housing Offset Fund if it found that affordable units could not be constructed "on a financially reasonable basis."

Less than two weeks before the scheduled city council hearing, Sagamore announced a community benefits agreement with a group of six South Baltimore neighborhoods promising $10 million to their communities over five years, with the potential for another $30 million in the following three decades. Nonetheless, advocates and community groups like Baltimoreans United in Leadership Development (BUILD) hammered Sagamore on housing and hiring in the months leading up to the city council hearing. Community coalitions—People Organized for Responsible Transformation, Tax Subsidies, and TIFs (PORT3), and Build Up Baltimore—negotiated alongside BUILD for a citywide community benefits agreement from Sagamore.

Barbara arrived at Red Emma's as dusk was settling on North Avenue. Through the café's large windows she could see a standing-room-only crowd of about one hundred. She opened the door and a wall of white noise from all the conversation in the room washed over her. Barbara, in a pair of photochromic glasses and a floral-print, short-sleeved shirt, took a chair behind a microphone.

ACLU–Maryland had generated thirty-three pages of detailed comments for the city's planning director and the city council president. But when Barbara's turn came, she revealed that at one point she had been somewhat sanguine about the potential of a brand-new neighborhood and corporate headquarters.

"My first reaction was, 'Oh, wow. This could be transformative for Baltimore . . . if it's done right,'" she told the overflowing crowd.

The closer she looked at the Sagamore TIF application, though, the more problems she foresaw. The wealth that the development potentially created for the city, at least on paper, could eventually lead to cuts in state aid to city schools. An analysis of Sagamore's plans showed only one-third of jobs at Port Covington would go to city residents. Sagamore's estimates of the number of residential units had crept up from 5,329, to 7,500, to 14,000, and its master plan requested new zoning categories that she believed would allow dense development at unlimited heights. And, of course, she connected the dots between the city's decision to exempt Sagamore from its inclusionary housing law and Sagamore's description of a "new waterfront destination for the highly educated, millennials and Baby Boom residents seeking a high quality live-work-play environment."

"Having worked for twenty-some years on trying to produce integrated housing opportunities in the city and in the region and to combat our long and sordid history of segregation," she said, "the question was inescapable: 'We're not going to build a whole, brand new segregated community, are we?'"

Speaking next, Lawrence Brown pointed out the lengths Sagamore Development had gone to woo the so-called creative class. A market analysis Sagamore commissioned touted Port Covington's potential to "reinforce the attractiveness of the city for young, skilled, educated Creative Class workers." Brown noted a recent finding from pop urbanist Richard Florida, who'd coined the term "creative class": African Americans made up just 8.5 percent of that class.

"So if they're recruiting 8.5 percent African-American," he said, "that means that that community will be 8.5 percent African-American in a city that's 63 percent black." The area around Port Covington was already lopsided: 88 percent white, 2 percent black.

That, Brown said, would intensify racial segregation in a city with a long history of racial segregation. Poor black Baltimoreans, he said, were largely consigned to communities with lead poisoning, violence, and poor schools. "It's not just that black and white people aren't living together," he said. "Racial segregation is an economic structure that penalizes people who live in black communities that are disinvested and redlined. So as we say Black Lives Matter, we also have to say Black Neighborhoods Matter."

———

Barbara Samuels speaks about a proposed Tax Increment Financing deal for Sagamore Development at Red Emma's in central Baltimore. (2016) *Lawrence Lanahan*

The next morning brought a bombshell development in the Freddie Gray case. So far, three officers involved in Gray's arrest had gone to trial. A judge had found two of them not guilty on all charges and had declared a mistrial for the third. In a bizarre press conference the morning of July 27, 2016, Baltimore state's attorney Marilyn Mosby stood at a podium at the same corner where Freddie Gray was arrested in Sandtown and announced that she would drop charges against the remaining officers.

The hearing on Port Covington was sure to be contentious; Mosby's announcement promised to make it even more so. Ratcheting up the tension even further was the heat. By 2:00 p.m., the temperature had risen above 90 degrees for the twelfth time in fourteen days.

Expecting a crowd, the Baltimore city council had decided to move the hearing from their own chambers to a larger venue. At the opposite end of a plaza from city hall was the War Memorial Building, a hulking 1920s neoclassical limestone box flanked by two seventeen-ton seahorse sculptures. Over a thousand people could fit in the high-ceilinged memorial hall that occupied the entire second floor. The first-floor assembly hall held 250. City Council went with the smaller hall.

Activists had already set up on the steps of the War Memorial Building by 2:00 p.m. Their signs reflected the complex nature of the issue at hand. One read, "Why don't we use TIFs to invest in poor black communities?" One of their chants played off of Under Armour's jock-y "Protect This House" slogan:

"We don't need no . . .

"Separation!"

"Protect this house from . . .

"Segregation!"

Passing cars honked in support, and as the scorching afternoon wore on, more people arrived—with more signs. One sign bore Lawrence Brown's coinage: "Black Neighborhoods Matter."

By 4:00 p.m., a line stretched around the block. Supporters wore yellow "Port Covington" T-shirts. Others wore blue T-shirts supporting BUILD. Lawrence Brown arrived in a crisp white shirt and dark skinny tie. When he was about twenty feet from getting inside the doors, the line stopped moving, and the crowd got antsy.

"You want to get in?" someone shouted.

"Yeah!" the crowd replied.

"You want to get in?"

"Yeah!"

Protestors demonstrate against a proposed community benefits agreement between
Baltimore City and Sagamore Development. (2016) *Lawrence Lanahan*

Word spread that the first floor assembly hall was full, and about ten minutes
after the hearing was scheduled to begin, a city employee came outside to speak to
the crowd. "We're full to capacity," she shouted. "We can try to open the upstairs,
but there's no air [conditioning] up there."

Voices barked back at her from the line, which still stretched around the block.
As a helicopter sputtered overhead, the crowd chanted, "Bring the hearing out
here! Bring the hearing out here!" The omnipresent activist Duane "Shorty"
Davis—sunglasses on, scarf and crucifix pendant around his neck, locs down to
the small of his back—led the crowd in a new chant. "Let us in! Let us in! Let
us in!"

It was the same chant heard sixteen years earlier for another packed meeting.
But the crowd chanting "Let us in!" at Hamilton Middle School had been overwhelmingly white and determined to shut public housing out of their neighborhood. This time, the crowd was of all colors, and many were there to pressure
powerful developers and elected officials into providing affordable housing.

Eventually, a burly man emerged from the building. He had a shaved head, and
an orange laminated card hung from a lanyard around his neck.

"Quiet!" the man barked, making a throat-slitting motion with his hand. He turned to a protester and poked a finger in his face. "You don't yell at me," he said. The protester pulled out a camera and began recording.

"We are trying to make accommodations to move the hearing upstairs, whether—Can you please get that camera out of my face?"

The man stuck his hand up to block the camera. As the protester moved the camera around to get a clear shot, the man waved his palm around like Pat Morita in *The Karate Kid*. Amid his "wax on, wax off" routine, he continued talking: "They are making accommodations to move the hearing upstairs. You need to be patient."

Two minutes later, Lawrence Brown yelled, "There's Stokes!" Councilman Carl Stokes, who chaired the committee that was holding the meeting, appeared in the doorway.

"Thank you for coming!" Stokes told the crowd. "They're gonna open up upstairs."

The crowd cheered.

Inside, the memorial hall looked majestic: the giant flag and eternal flame in the front, the classical mural in the back, the shiny metal shields from different military divisions all over the walls. It looked like someplace that might host the signing of a peace treaty—or a declaration of war.

Stokes and several of his colleagues sat behind a long table draped in black. They looked puny from the back of the grand hall. At least five hundred people filled the folding chairs that had been hurriedly set up.

Speaking through the piercing feedback generated by his microphone, Stokes started the proceedings. It was over an hour later than the hearing had been scheduled to commence. Stokes's words landed almost inaudibly in the back of the reverberant room. "We will stay as long as there are folk who wish to come forward and testify tonight," he said. Those people would have to wait through testimony from the Baltimore Development Corporation, Sagamore Development, a city finance department official, various fiscal analysts, members of BUILD, and several panels of advocates—including a housing panel featuring Barbara Samuels and Lawrence Brown.

Baltimore Development Corporation president Bill Cole and Sagamore vice president Caroline Paff put the prettiest face they could on the Port Covington development and its potential economic impact on the city. Paff bragged about Under Armour's projected growth and showed a graph depicting the company's number of employees quadrupling to ten thousand in just over two decades.

"This is Under Armour's growth chart," Paff said. "This is what they're talking about: space to grow. It's grow here, or grow somewhere else."

The crowd murmured. "Oh, that's a threat," Lawrence Brown said to himself.

Housing commissioner Paul Graziano explained that it would cost the city at least $184 million to help Sagamore create the affordable units under the city's inclusionary housing law. "We have less than $400,000 in the inclusionary housing fund," Graziano said. "So what we were required to do under the ordinance is to waive the requirement because the city could not meet that making the developer whole."

Several boos met that assertion.

Eventually Carl Stokes stepped back from the details of the 545-page TIF application and asked Jon Laria, an attorney representing Sagamore, "Are you philosophically saying you are going to exclude low and moderate income folk?"

"For the record, of course not," Laria said, and members of the audience hooted at him.

"Of course not," Laria continued, stone-faced but clearly annoyed. "It's a critically important question. It's come up in all the public hearings. I don't know how anybody can conclude from any of the presentations, any of the materials, any of the MOUs, that there's any intent to create any sort of segregated white gated enclave, which is the phrase that's been thrown around."

Some in the audience laughed, and a woman shouted, "Snow white!"

"We have commitments to affordable housing in the MOUs, we've described what they are, they are unprecedented," Laria continued. "There is absolutely no intention whatsoever to exclude anybody from participating in any aspect of Port Covington."

Another ninety minutes went by before the proceedings even arrived at the panel including Barbara Samuels and Lawrence Brown.

"I've been told that we must leave the building at 10:00 p.m.," Stokes said, as he waved around the sign-up sheets. "You already signed in. We will continue the testimony in another week and then we will have the work session on the following week. So, could the housing advocates please come forward?"

Barbara approached the podium at the front of the hall. She looked up at the council members. They were seated up on a stage beneath four marble columns, five enormous decorative metal grates, and an American flag so big you could wrap half the City Council up in it.

Such were the optics: before her, the power; behind her, the people.

Barbara lectured the council on what she considered the poor economics of

Sagamore's proposal, then turned to affordable housing. "We've also heard that because there was no money in a city inclusionary housing fund, that this project should be exempt," she said. "That's not what the city inclusionary housing law says.

"Yes, it's a weak law," she said with a big smile, "but it's not that weak!"

Barbara argued that the tax increment financing package should be conditional upon the creation of affordable housing. "Once you have authorized the TIF, you have given away the city's bargaining position," she said. "What we're asking for is twenty-five percent affordable," she said, "and that twenty percent of the TIF be reserved and set aside for the affordable housing."

Lawrence Brown kept his remarks short. He reminded the council that the Fair Housing Act was put into law seven days after Dr. Martin Luther King was assassinated, and called for them to affirmatively further fair housing. He cited the dearth of African Americans in the so-called creative class and said Port Covington would be the "fifth least black community in the entire city" if it were just 8.5 percent African American.

"We cannot allow that to happen," he said, and the audience began to applaud. "We cannot allow that to happen. We must have racial integration to help desegregate Baltimore City."

The applause continued, and Brown called upon an image of the divided city, of the white central and waterfront districts, of the two swaths of poor black neighborhoods that spread east and west from downtown.

"The two Baltimores that we have are the 'White L,'" Brown said, slashing his hand down and over, "and the Black Butterfly. And we have to deconstruct that if we want this city to be whole and one Baltimore."

Forty-five minutes later—almost four hours since the proceedings had started, and five hours past the expected starting time—Carl Stokes wrapped up the proceedings.

"With apologies to those we have not called as yet, we are going to recess the hearing—"

One man in the audience still had a live microphone, and he yelled into it.

"WHEN YOU GOING TO LET THE PU—"

Someone cut the mic, and the "*puh*" reverberated for a couple of seconds.

"And we will bring the hearing back together, we will reconvene the hearing next week, same time, probably in this building," Stokes said.

The man continued yelling off mic. One hundred and thirty members of the public had signed up to speak.

None had gotten to the microphone that day.

Fifty years earlier, a similarly long and contentious hearing in the very same building had addressed housing for poor African Americans. That evening, James Rouse had introduced supporters of an open housing ordinance, including Cardinal Lawrence Shehan. As revered as Shehan was in heavily Catholic Baltimore, his support for open housing drew loud boos from a significant portion of the two thousand people in attendance.

In post-uprising Baltimore, the boos at the War Memorial Building went not to those who called for affordable, integrated housing, but to those who seemed to resist it.

The Baltimore County Council started its August 1, 2016, meeting with a prayer from councilman Tom Quirk, who represented the southwestern part of the county. His district bordered the Patapsco River, which had gone over its banks the night before. On the Howard County side of the river, the flood had killed two people and devastated the historic downtown of Ellicott City.

Also hanging over the 6:00 p.m. meeting was the death just hours earlier of Korryn Gaines in an armed standoff with police in Baltimore County's Randallstown community. A police tactical team killed Gaines, an African American woman, and wounded her five-year-old son. No one on the council mentioned her death.

Council members went down the line expressing their alleged reservations about banning source-of-income discrimination: Why should a county pass such a bill if the state and U.S. Congress hadn't? Shouldn't the county concentrate on reducing poverty rather than spreading it around? Couldn't some landlords be exempted? What about a task force—shouldn't the "best and brightest" take a look?

Councilman Julian Jones defended the bill. "If you read the bill, what we're talking about here is plain and simple, and I can summarize it in two words. It's called discrimination and prejudice," he said.

After nineteen minutes of discussion, council president Vicki Almond asked the council secretary to call roll on the bill.

"Mrs. Almond?"

"No."

"Mr. Quirk?"

"No."

"Mr. Kach?"

"No."

"Mr. Jones?"

"Yes."

"Mr. Marks?"

"No."

"Mrs. Bevins?"

"No."

"Mr. Crandall?"

"No."

"Thank you," Almond said unceremoniously. "Bill 46-16 fails."

According to the terms of the county's conciliation agreement, if fewer than three council members voted in favor of a failing bill, the County Executive would not be required to resubmit it until after the beginning of the next term of office. With just one vote in favor, that meant the legislation might not go before the council again until 2019.

At 101 W. Dickman Street, one could get a glimpse of Sagamore Development's vision for South Baltimore. For years, the city had used this 140,000-square-foot building in Port Covington to repair its buses. In 2015, Sagamore got its hands on the property and announced the creation of a "maker space" for start-up companies.

On September 8, 2016, sports rock played from a PA system inside the fully renovated building at 101 W. Dickman, which Sagamore had christened "City Garage." Several people in clergy collars—and many more in suits—schmoozed by a catering table full of sandwiches. The walls of the long lobby featured the stenciled words of "The Star-Spangled Banner." At the end of the lobby was a mural of the words "MADE IN AMERICA" affixed to a United States flag. Next to the mural, a glass wall revealed robotic arms moving around inside a workspace that was completely devoid of humans.

Eventually, some VIPs filled the seats of a small stage in front of the mural, including mayor Stephanie Rawlings-Blake, city council president Jack Young, and three clergy members from BUILD. Carl Stokes was notably absent.

CEO Tom Geddes of Plank Industries, an investment group that serves as Kevin Plank's "family office," told the room that Sagamore Development had finished negotiating with community members on a citywide benefits agreement.

"We have been challenged by them to produce something big," he said. "The one we are announcing is not big. It is huge, it is transformational . . . the most generous and inclusive community benefits agreement by far in the history of this city."

The agreement was worth $100 million dollars.

"Let me say it one more time," Geddes said. "One hundred million dollars."

The jubilation continued as speaker after speaker came to the microphone. "Today Baltimore residents can rise to celebrate a brand new day," said the Reverend Glenna Huber of BUILD, who had given a scorching criticism of the previous agreement at the War Memorial Building in July. "This is a historic agreement that will change the paradigm of Baltimore."

Huber's BUILD colleague Bishop Douglas Miles said he had watched decades of downtown development since the construction of Harborplace in the late 1970s. "Nothing ever made it uptown," he said. "This agreement guarantees that never again will uptown be left out of the equation."

As he spoke, Huber and the Reverend Andrew Foster Connors, another BUILD partner, held up yellow T-shirts that displayed the Under Armour logo and the words "WE WILL BUILD ONE BALTIMORE TOGETHER." Bishop Miles led the room in chanting the phrase.

For all the jubilation, there were few details. Geddes mentioned "unprecedented commitments to local hiring, inclusionary housing, workforce development, and minority business participation." The mayor mentioned "prevailing wage guarantees." City comptroller Joan Pratt said Sagamore would fund an auditor in her office to track the developer's performance. But numbers were nowhere to be found.

After the presser, Sagamore released a summary of the agreement. There was a lot of dough: $25,000,000 for workforce development; $1,500,000 for youth jobs; $10,000,000 for a "venture loan or equity fund investing in minority and women-owned companies"; $7,000,000 for scholarships and a recreation center. Sagamore also increased its local hiring mandate.

The summary left questions on affordable housing. It mentioned a "doubling of commitment" to 20 percent affordable housing. But 40 percent of those units could be developed off-site, and Sagamore left itself plenty of wiggle room in a clause promising to "avoid off-site development which would result in a further concentration of poverty." Furthermore, if Sagamore found it was not "financially reasonable" to build affordable units, it could just pay between $30,000 to $60,000 per mandated affordable unit into the city's Inclusionary Housing Offset Fund. Even if Sagamore did construct affordable units, the developer was only required to make them affordable to households earning 80 percent of the area median income. Any units targeted to those below 60 percent of the area median income would depend on the state accepting a Low-Income Housing Tax Credit application, and units for households below 30 percent of the area median income would depend on the provision of "housing vouchers or similar assistance" to Sagamore.

It looked entirely possible that Sagamore wouldn't have to build *any* affordable units, and any units affordable to low-income Baltimoreans would depend on someone outside of the negotiating process deciding to provide vouchers or tax credits. The PORT3 community coalition and Build Up Baltimore had walked away from Sagamore's "final offer," partly because of these terms.

When the Baltimore City Council's Taxation, Finance, and Economic Development Committee convened hours later at the War Memorial Building, the public had yet to see the full memorandum of understanding. Committee chairman Carl Stokes asked Plank Industries CEO Tom Geddes to walk the audience and council members through the elusive document.

"With as much detail and attention as possible," Stokes said. "I don't want just a summary."

Several minutes into Geddes's response, members of the audience tried to shout him down.

"We don't want charity! We want justice!"

"Justice, you sellouts!"

Geddes paused.

"Where is our security?" Stokes mumbled.

"That's not the reaction I expected for a $100 million commitment to Baltimore City," Geddes said.

"Fuck your reaction!"

"Keep speaking," Stokes said to Geddes.

"Scab deal!"

Stokes stopped Geddes again and turned to the crowd. "Listen to me—"

"You listen to us!" someone yelled.

Outbursts continued throughout the evening, and people wore out their arms holding up signs that said "Baltimore deserves BETTER" and "WHO BENEFITS?"

The TIF consisted of three bills, all in Stokes's committee: two to create special taxing and development districts, and one to issue the bonds whose sale would fund the infrastructure requested in the TIF application. After nearly two hours, Stokes brought the first of the three bills to a committee vote, despite shouts from the audience to hold off on the vote until the community could see a copy of the memorandum of understanding.

Before he pulled up the first bill, Stokes registered a cryptic objection. "I very much dislike being put in this place again," he said. "It is unfair, it's unethical, and it's immoral to continue to act in this way for a public body."

As council members began to vote, parts of the audience chanted, "Baltimore deserves better! Baltimore deserves better!"

Councilman Bill Henry prefaced his vote with a statement. Many of his concerns about the TIF, he said, had been addressed. But not all of them. "One of the things that is a new concern right now—I received a copy of the MOU a little over twenty-four hours ago," Henry said. "I would like to have time to get further clarification, and I believe that time could be used to share the MOU with more people. In my preferred way of dealing with this, we would not vote this out of committee this night, but that does not seem to be an option." Henry voted to "pass."

Stokes voted yes. So did two other council members. With three "yeas" and two abstentions, the bill moved out of committee.

The next bill also passed with three yes votes, including Stokes.

That made two out of three. If the third bill made it out of committee, the full city council would get to take the first of two votes necessary to send it to the mayor.

That didn't happen. "The Chair asks for a motion to recess," Stokes said, after the vote on the second bill.

Some of his colleagues objected, but Stokes persisted.

"We move to recess," he said. "I'd like to talk to my president."

"Fucking cowards!" someone yelled from the audience.

Confusion seeped through the crowd, and many lingered in the hall as Stokes spoke to council president Jack Young, took a tongue-lashing from Bishop Miles of BUILD, and disappeared through a back door.

Barbara Samuels stood near the front of the room. "Pathetic display of self-governance," she said, grimacing. Barbara pestered passing council members. "This is not about Under Armour's expansion," she said to councilwoman Rochelle "Rikki" Spector. "This is about Kevin Plank's risky personal real estate venture."

She also caught the ear of councilwoman Helen Holton, who had just voted both bills out of committee. "I'm disappointed in your vote, councilwoman," Barbara said.

Holton gave her a long stare.

"Okay," Holton finally said, and walked away.

Four days later, eleven members of the fifteen-member Baltimore City Council used a parliamentary maneuver to yank the bill out of Carl Stokes's committee for a preliminary vote. By a count of 12 to 0, the body moved it to a final vote. Two days later, the city's Board of Estimates unanimously approved the memorandum of understanding. Finally, that afternoon, the public got to see it.

Five days after that, the Baltimore City Council took a final vote on the TIF package. They approved it 12 to 1.

The mayor signed the bills on September 28, 2016.

Mark and Betty stepped out onto N. Gilmor Street. The projects across the street were quiet. It was warm—Baltimore rarely hit 55 degrees before noon on the second Sunday of November. In the New Song Center gym, the church had set out about seventy-five of its signature blue chairs. Even though Mark and Betty usually arrived late, half of the chairs remained empty.

Pastor Wilson, in a suit and white button-down shirt, shared two items of news from the past week. The previous Monday, someone had been shot in front of the house that he and his wife Ella lived in on N. Stricker Street, near the corner of Presstman Street.

The other piece of news was from the day after the shooting. Everyone already knew what had happened on Tuesday, November 8: the United States had elected Donald J. Trump to be its next president.

"Let me just preface this with—let's be honest: this election left many folk in a daze," Wilson said before starting his sermon. "Some people are aggressively— even violently in some instances—declaring, 'This is not my president.'"

Wilson admitted to staying up late to see the results come in. "I think I went to bed at 1:30," he said. "At first, I'm like, 'What?!' But when it was pretty much over, I had to stop and think, 'Is God still in control? And how would God have me respond?' There is a verse. We don't like it. There is a verse in the Bible that says, 'Submit to the ruling authorities over you.' I know y'all ain't read that one lately—"

Here the lanky pastor paused. His congregation laughed.

"—but it is in the book."

Maryland, a reliably blue state, had gone for Hillary Clinton by a 26-point margin. But it wasn't just the rural counties that had voted for Trump. In the swath of southeastern Baltimore County covering Rosedale, Essex, and Dundalk, most precincts went for Trump by margins of 25 to 55 percent. Clinton took just three precincts in that swath, all in majority-black parts of Essex and Turner's Station.

Clinton won those precincts by even larger margins. It figured. During the campaign, Trump supporters openly made racist comments, and at one Trump rally, an elderly white man sucker-punched a black protester and told a news crew, "Yes, he deserved it—the next time we see'm, we might have to kill'm." During the campaign, white nationalists came out from the fringes and, having groomed themselves nicely, charmed their way into mainstream news publications. Trump himself directly pitched African American voters with the question "What the hell do you have to lose?" On the Sunday after the election, the Southern Poverty Law Center reported a spike in incidents of harassment against minorities: 250 in just a few days.

Pastor Wilson began his sermon, which was part of a series he'd begun on "restoration." America, he said, could use some. This Sunday, he focused on Psalm 126, which captured the Jews' elation at returning from captivity in Babylon to rebuild their temple. "When the Lord restored the fortunes of Zion, we were like those who dream," the Psalm began. "Then our mouth was filled with laughter, and our tongue with shouts of joy."

"Restoration is a journey, it's not a destination," Wilson said. "See, they thought that temple was the end of the story. God was *starting* the journey of the restoration."

Wilson put the psalm in a context the small congregation could understand. "There's nobody who would have thought that Allan Tibbels could have come here in a wheelchair and did what he did. Don't make sense! But God used him to do it. But that wasn't the destination, that's part of the journey. Our job is to keep going on because God ain't through with Sandtown. God's not through with New Song," he said.

The pastor had building plans of his own. He had begun working with architects and developers on plans for a complex down the street from Newborn Holistic Ministries' headquarters. Wilson envisioned a two-story building with a grocery store, kiosks for aspiring entrepreneurs, a plaza for socializing, a daycare center and playground, spaces for art and music programming, and a greenhouse and gardens on the roof. He pictured the church using space on the second floor. There, a church could do what he felt a church was best at: establish relationships.

That was the difference between his vision and how he perceived New Song's history with Christian community development. Church social ministries got bogged down, he believed; let the nonprofits do what they're good at, and let the church be a church. In his opinion, CCDA practitioners felt like they were finished when construction ended. He wanted to be in the building, developing relationships, and changing people's mindsets. And in Sandtown, he saw a lot of mindsets that needed changing.

"I'm sorry, what happened the other night in front of our home? That wouldn't have made a difference if Trump or Hillary had got elected," Wilson said. Beefs led to more beefs and an endless cycle of retaliation. "That ain't about Republican or Democrat," he said, "that's about somebody needs Jesus! We need to restore our community, restore our hearts, restore our values, restore our character. And the only thing I know that can do that in somebody who has forgot about what makes moral sense is the Gospel of Jesus Christ. That's all."

"That's all," someone called from the congregation.

"I'm not saying we ought not do the things that might be phase one," he said, alluding to economic development, "but that can't be phase two and three and four and five. Sometimes we gotta start working on people. Buildings don't tear communities down. Buildings are inanimate. People tear down communities. We gotta get that!"

The pastor then veered off into a description of the time someone attacked a Rembrandt painting with a bread knife at a museum in Amsterdam, and another time someone took a hammer to Michelangelo's *Pietá* at St. Peter's Basilica in Vatican City.

"Some people say, 'They just gone, lost, what we gonna do now? Throw 'em out'," Wilson said. "But when they brought in the experts, they said, 'No, we can restore those treasures.'

"See, God's the expert," he continued, pointing out that people sometimes consider their neighbors beyond repair. "It's just, 'Let's throw them guys on the corner of Presstman out. They ain't no good no more.' We forget that from the Gospel perspective, we all live on Presstman and Stricker. Aw, Lord have mercy. We're no better than the folk on Presstman and Stricker.

"But God took us, said, 'You know what? I'm gonna work with that'," Wilson continued, dialing himself down to a slow whisper. "'I'm a restorer. Don't look good. But I'm God. And I can do it. I know how to do it.'"

The shooting at Presstman and Stricker wasn't the first time the neighborhood's violence had hit that close to home for Wilson or New Song. In June 2016, gunshots rang out inside the New Song Worship and Arts Center on N. Calhoun Street during a memorial ceremony for a young man who'd been murdered in the neighborhood. The murdered man's brother allegedly shot his own father at the repast over a dispute about the obituary.

As Wilson wound down his sermon, he continued whispering his impression of a God who can restore the lost souls of Sandtown: "'I know how to do it. I know what it's gonna take to do it. Cause I got a plan that I ain't told you about.' Aw God, Lord God, you're good. In Christ's name. Amen."

A little after 1:00 p.m. the next Sunday, someone shot a twenty-seven-year-old man just blocks from New Song Center. Wilson and his wife had tried to build a relationship with the young man. He liked to help Ella Wilson take in her groceries, and she had accompanied him to court several times.

At the funeral, the man's father whispered in Ella Wilson's ear: "He loved you so much."

It was the second son that man had lost to murder in Sandtown in four months.

In the Obama administration's last few months, federal agencies released several guidance documents intended to strengthen fair housing oversight. These seemingly arcane adjustments addressed issues that fair housing advocates like Barbara Samuels had complained about for decades.

Just two days after the 2016 election, HUD and the Justice Department issued a joint statement regarding the application of the Fair Housing Act to land use and zoning laws at the state and local levels. Citing Justice Kennedy's 2015 opinion, the statement said that *intentional* discrimination need not be found in a state or local law to constitute a fair housing violation: disparate impact counted, too. (Justice Kennedy's opinion had mentioned "zoning laws and other housing restrictions that function unfairly to exclude minorities from certain neighborhoods without any sufficient justification.") This arguably cast a shadow over the Anne Arundel County Council's January 2015 vote to claw back density bonuses for "workforce housing" and thus undermine Enterprise Housing's planned development in Severna Park.

On December 27, 2016—just three weeks after president-elect Donald Trump selected Ben Carson to be Secretary of Housing and Urban Development—the Internal Revenue Service issued two important guidance documents. The first document addressed "local vetoes" in the protocols that states used to distribute LIHTC tax credits. (Maryland's legislature had dropped its local veto provision in 2014.) Citing HUD's final rule on affirmatively furthering fair housing, the IRS statement dismissed the notion that Section 42 of the Internal Revenue Code (the portion of federal law that guides federal and state administration of the Low-Income Housing Tax Credit program) could be used to justify local approval requirements.

The second piece of IRS guidance released that day addressed the federal preference for building LIHTC developments in poor communities. "Placing LIHTC projects in qualified census tracts risks exacerbating concentrations of poverty," the IRS noted. Federal law bestows a preference on those areas "only when there is an added benefit to the neighborhood in the form of the project's contribution to a concerted community revitalization plan." The IRS notice chastised state agencies for having allocated credits "without regard" to the presence of such a plan. Concentration of LIHTC housing among racial isolation and concentrated poverty had provoked Barbara Samuels to file a complaint against Maryland's housing department five years earlier, and Maryland's state housing department had already started giving applications in "communities of opportunity" the same number of points as those in poor areas.

The politics of housing mobility had shifted enough by 2016 that local governments around Baltimore had started collaborating on a regional voucher program—something unthinkable before *Thompson v. HUD*. The program, a partnership with the Baltimore Metropolitan Council and the nonprofit that administered *Thompson* vouchers for the city's housing authority, attached Housing Choice Vouchers to the rehabilitation or construction of multifamily housing developments. Of the one hundred vouchers in the pilot, the program reserved two-thirds for developments in opportunity areas. No complex would be allowed to accept vouchers for more than 25 percent of its units.

However pleased civil rights advocates might have been with the progress in dismantling the structural roots of racial inequality in the Baltimore region, they now had to confront the continued rise of bald-faced bigotry. Hate incidents continued to spike as Donald Trump's inauguration crept nearer. A Black Lives Matter sign hung by Towson Unitarian Universalist Church in October 2016, for example, was stolen or defaced four times in five weeks.

In the course of one week in November 2016, racist incidents took place both at one of Nicole's former schools and at her son's high school. Someone publicly posted a screenshot of a white Atholton student's Snapchat that showed the girl covered in a dark facial cream. The caption read, "I'm finally a n—r." The girl was a cadet in Atholton's JROTC program. At Harlem Park Elementary/Middle School, where Nicole had attended first and second grades, someone caught a white teacher on video shouting the N word during a tirade at a classroom full of black middle-school students.

In neighborhoods like Harlem Park it was clear, as 2017 approached, that Baltimore could no longer refer to its high rate of violent crime as a "spike." On December 19, a double homicide in Harlem Park took the lives of a twenty-two-year-old man and a sixty-eight-year-old man. They were killed in the 1800 block of Rayner

Avenue, where Nicole had lived so happily as a girl. The next day, the city's 310th homicide took Baltimore to its second highest per capita homicide rate ever. (The highest had come in 2015.)

And the city was losing confidence in its police, to say the least. In August 2016, the U.S. Department of Justice released a stunning 163-page report criticizing the Baltimore Police Department (BPD) for unconstitutional searches and arrests, excessive force, and "severe and unjustified disparities in the rates of stops, searches and arrests of African Americans." The report listed many of Baltimore's indicators of racial inequality and linked them to a century-long chain of policies in the region, including the city's 1910 segregation ordinance, the federal government's 1937 redlining map, and the alleged "reverse redlining" that led the city to sue Wells Fargo in 2008. "BPD made roughly 44 percent of its stops in two small, predominantly African-American districts that contain only 11 percent of the City's population," the report said. Hundreds of black Baltimoreans had been stopped at least ten times between 2010 and 2015—seven of them more than thirty times.

The Justice Department claimed that these disparate impacts violated Title VI of the Civil Rights Act of 1964. The agency also uncovered evidence of intentional discrimination. "This racial discrimination undermines community trust in BPD," the report concluded.

On January 12, 2017, the city and the U.S. Department of Justice agreed to a consent decree under which the Baltimore Police Department would reform its practices toward more constitutional policing. Before a federal judge even picked up a pen to approve it, another policing scandal—a scandal shocking even for Baltimore—gripped the city.

On March 1, 2017, U.S. Attorney for Maryland Rod J. Rosenstein announced the indictment of seven Baltimore police officers in a federal racketeering conspiracy. The indictment alleged a wide conspiracy among the officers, who were on the department's elite Gun Trace Task Force. According to the U.S. attorney, they used fraudulently obtained search warrants to steal money, guns, and drugs from people's houses; declined to arrest people they stole drugs from, in order to buy their silence; and conspired with high-level drug dealers to sell the dope they'd stolen. The U.S. attorney alleged that between fraudulently filing overtime and straight-up stealing stacks of cash, the officers had accumulated over $200,000.

Five of the indicted officers were black, and two were white.

All lived in the counties surrounding Baltimore City.

One of the white officers was the brother of a man who had organized opposition to HUD's Moving to Opportunity during the 1990s in southeast Baltimore County.

A sign in a woman's hands said, "END WHITE SUPREMACY."

Who could argue with that?

The popular image of white supremacy in America often took the form of a villain. The latest villain, a white man who had massacred nine black people in June 2015, had come right out of central casting. He had an exotic name: Dylann Storm Roof. He loved the Confederate flag. He wrote a manifesto. He crashed with a friend in a trailer park. Like the bigots in Birmingham, he did his killing at a black church.

It was easy, especially outside of the South, for white people to distance themselves from such treachery—to think, "Not one of us."

But to activists fighting for racial justice in Baltimore, "white supremacy" described not just villains, but a system—a system that absolved well-intentioned white people as they perpetuated a society and an economy that disproportionately rewarded them and pushed African Americans further behind. Like the phrase literally implied, white supremacy kept white people on top.

When Under Armour founder Kevin Plank joined the Manufacturing Jobs Initiative, a council convened by President Trump in February 2017, newly elected Baltimore city councilman Ryan Dorsey posted this comment on the "Baltimore City Voters" Facebook page: "White supremacy cozying up to white supremacy? Shocker."

Plenty of people argued with that.

Dorsey knew that Plank didn't walk around in a Klan robe. He just felt that the memorandum of understanding that Sagamore had negotiated with the city would widen the gap between white Baltimore and black Baltimore. "In issues of public policy, it is the actual impact on people, not the intended impact, that ultimately matters," Dorsey wrote after his comment blew up in the press. "Port Covington—at least this round—is a done deal, but we must learn from it going forward if we are to truly undo the structural racism holding our City back."

On March 20, 2017, America confronted another white supremacist villain. That day, a twenty-eight-year old white man stabbed Timothy Caughman, a sixty-six-year-old black man, with an eighteen-inch blade near Manhattan's Times Square. Like Roof, this villain had a racist manifesto. But it was a little harder for northerners to distance themselves this time—or Baltimoreans, for that matter. According to a *Baltimore Sun* profile, the man had taken a bus to

Manhattan from Baltimore. He grew up in Towson, the Baltimore County seat. He had gone to the Friends School, a private high school located between the elite city neighborhoods of Roland Park and Homeland. He lived in Hampden, one of the whitest neighborhoods in Baltimore.

A few days later, some Hampden residents held a vigil for Timothy Caughman. It was, they wrote, an opportunity for "white (and all) residents and friends of Hampden to show that we love and welcome our neighbors and visitors of color and that we stand against hate." Betty Robinson of Standing Up for Racial Justice attended, as did Ralph Moore—who had worked with Robinson to desegregate the Baltimore region through Good Neighbors Northeast—and Moore's wife, Dana, who had represented the city in *Thompson v. HUD.*

The Moores brought their ten-year-old granddaughter to the vigil. The girl attended the Friends School and worried that everyone hated her school because of what the white supremacist alumnus had done. Her grandparents brought her because they wanted her to know that there was lots of love in the universe, and the girl carried a sign with a red heart that said "Only LOVE." Very few other African Americans attended the vigil, and a local television news reporter approached Ralph Moore for his thoughts.

"It seems at this moment in our time in our history that hate seems to have a new lease on life," he said. "And people who are hate-filled seem to feel freer to express that."

Ralph Moore remembered Hampden from his childhood as a place that wasn't safe for African Americans to go to. Indeed, Hampden had a history of overt racism. In the 1920s, the Ku Klux Klan held ceremonies and paraded there. (At one ceremony, local clergy christened a baby "Katherine Karlotta Knickman" underneath a two-story-tall iron cross.) In 1979, a Hampden resident told oral historians that the Klan at one point had "over 870 members" in the neighborhood. In 1988, a black family vacated a house in Hampden just after they'd moved in because neighbors had screamed racial slurs, thrown rocks through their windows, and threatened to bomb the house. In the early 1990s, white supremacist skinheads openly recruited in the neighborhood, and the local middle school saw all kinds of trouble. An alleged Klansman ate lunch with his son in the cafeteria; a twenty-one-year-old member of a racist skinhead group was arrested for beating up a black student—and about a dozen students declared their allegiance to his group; and a black teacher found a sticker in his classroom that read "You are being watched by the knights of the Ku Klux Klan."

In 1998, the median sale price for a Hampden home was $50,000, but the neighborhood gentrified immensely in the 2000s, reaching a median price of $225,000 in 2016. From the vigil, one could see an ice cream parlor, a brand-new oyster restaurant, a "teaching kitchen" for aspiring chefs, and more antique stores and boutiques than you could shake a mid-century-Modern serving platter at.

The vigil in Hampden began serenely enough, filling the air with prayer, song, and pleas for inclusion. There were "Black Lives Matter" placards and other signs that ranged from the anodyne "HATE-FREE HAMPDEN" to the more challenging "White Apathy Is VIOLENCE."

Before long, a driver in a passing sedan yelled, "Fuckin' idiots! Wake up!" The "libtards" on the corner, he claimed, were on the payroll of philanthropist George Soros, perceived by the far right as a major bogeyman. Some at the vigil yelled back at the driver.

Megan Kenny, a forty-year-old white activist who had participated in Baltimore Bloc actions, found the crowd's response to the man nettlesome. The sentiment she heard as people yelled back at him—and that she had sensed during the whole vigil—was one of denial. To Kenny, the heckler was no less a part of Hampden than the people at the vigil. Hampden wasn't "hate-free"; Kenny knew plenty of black people who still felt uncomfortable even visiting the neighborhood.

Kenny had been active in protesting racism and police brutality in Baltimore since she showed up by herself to a march in Sandtown two days after Freddie Gray's death. The activist community had come to feel like family to her. During the curfew-breaking after Freddie Gray's death, she had chosen not Hampden but Penn North, where she felt her white privilege would be of more service.

At the Hampden vigil for Timothy Caughman, it was Kenny who held the sign that read "END WHITE SUPREMACY."

She knew the history of Hampden. It seemed to her that the crowd was in denial about what hate remained there. As she stood on the sidewalk, she faced the vigil and reminded everyone that Hampden was a "white community." A few feet away, Dana Moore started filming Kenny with her phone.

"We cannot 'other' them!" Kenny said, pointing to the street where the heckler had just driven. "They are a part of us. We cannot say, 'Oh, he was from Towson. Oh, he only lived here for two months.'

"He felt safe enough to live here!" Kenny continued, physically crouching to emphasize her point. "What about this place makes it feel safe for violent, racist people? What is it about this neighborhood?!?"

"That's a good question," Moore said to herself.

"We have to acknowledge as a white community that there is something about Hampden that makes racist people feel comfortable here!" Kenny shouted.

A woman responded to Kenny. "That's white privilege, that he felt that he could just go out there and kill someone in cold blood and no one would come after him," she said.

Kenny walked forward to confront the woman. "He felt he could live here!" she shouted.

"Yes, and that he could live here and that he could go to New York—"

Kenny interrupted the woman: "And what?"

"That's white privilege," the woman said. "That's white privilege."

"It's white supremacy," Kenny said. "What I'm saying is the neighborhood of Hampden was designed intentionally for working-class white people decades and decades ago. That system and structural racism continues, and we as white people benefit from it."

Kenny's voice then rose to a volume and intensity nearly impossible to describe, except to say that it seemed as if it aspired to reach every white ear in all parts of America, all at once.

"Where the fuck is everybody's anger?!!!! Where is everybody's anger?!!!!"

A few people clapped.

Dana Moore narrated into her phone: "She's absolutely right."

Now hoarse, Kenny shrieked, "This is not angry!"

"She's so right," Dana Moore whispered. "She's so right. I'm not saying anything, because this is for white people to figure out."

EPILOGUE

By late morning on September 17, 2017, the temperature in the Baltimore region had already inched up to near 80 degrees. Downtown, Ravens fans tailgated outside M&T Bank Stadium under a bright sky with high, fluffy clouds. In Baltimore County, Maryland governor Larry Hogan posed for photos with constituents at the 42nd annual Essex Day Festival. Harford Countians watched the Silver Eagle Cloggers pounce across a bandshell at the Bel Air Festival for the Arts. In Columbia, so many families turned out for an open house at the Robinson Nature Center that they ran out of parking.

On N. Gilmor Street in Sandtown, a gold Acura honked at Mark and Betty Lange as they walked out their door on the way to church. The driver of the Acura waved.

"Hey, Leroy!" Mark shouted.

As Mark and Betty crossed Presstman Street, an SUV passed, blaring a trap beat and a muffled "motherfucker."

"Nice music for a Sunday," Betty said.

"They should use that music in church," Mark said.

"I don't think you heard the words," Betty said.

Mark shrugged and said, "I was listening to the beat."

Mark and Betty opened the door of the New Song Center's gym, and music rushed into the lobby. "Rejoice in the Lord always, and again I say, again I say, rejoice!" sang associate pastor Steve Smallman. Patty Prasada-Rao and Ella Wilson—Pastor Wilson's wife and head of the "New Song Cares" ministry—added powerful harmonies.

"Summer's over," Mark said. "There should be more people in here."

There were only sixty of the church's signature blue plastic chairs out: four rows for a left tier, four rows for a right tier, and two rows in back.

In the service's program, Luke 5:1–11 described stunned fishermen watching Jesus summon scores of fish into nets that had hung empty all night. New Song's own nets needed a little filling. Another one hundred blue chairs in short piles lined the gym's wall.

In the back of the gym, a greeter at the door beat a tambourine. The sound of the tambourine, which found very little to absorb it on the way to the band, made the room feel even emptier.

When the band stopped playing, Pastor Smallman made some announcements and invited a congregant to the microphone.

"We're gonna have potlucks next Sunday," said a young white woman. People could sign up to host lunches at their homes, she said. The potlucks would be right after Sunday worship. That way, she said, "You can invite people to church, but then they don't go home for five hours and then maybe change their mind."

Smallman took the microphone again. "If you're here for the first time, we would love to have you introduced," he said.

"Anybody here?" Mark wondered aloud.

"We'd love to reach out to you and connect with you," Smallman continued, "so we'll have the mic come around, and if you'll stand, that'd be awesome. No? Okay."

After another song, Smallman said, "Let's take a moment to greet each other in the Lord."

As the congregants gathered into groups to chat, Mark ticked through the members who had recently left the church. Youth pastor Joel Brown and his wife, Latifahia, who had taught middle-school science at New Song Academy, had moved to Charlotte. Terrell Johnson had moved to Georgia—indeed, the rhythm from the band was coming not from Terrell's drums but from a drum machine. The core of New Song's dozen or so relocators remained, but worshippers from inside and outside the neighborhood had been disappearing from services. Even Antoine Bennett—who'd helped run New Song Urban Ministries, who felt CCDA had saved his life, who had felt the love of New Song members as he worked his way back to walking with a cane after his stroke—was now worshipping with the Harrises at Newborn Community of Faith.

Patty Prasada-Rao walked over with a smile. "You're still here," she said to Mark.

"I'm not going anywhere," Mark said. "They're gonna bury me here."

Smallman called the congregants back to their seats, and the band picked up again with a slow, piano-driven take on Donnie McClurkin's "Draw Me Close." Whatever the band lacked in drums, the vocal harmonies more than made up for. The song almost felt like a sedative after the unhurried, ten-minute-long greeting session. New Song Community Church services had a comforting ebb and flow.

In his sermon, Wilson considered the story of the fishing nets, and he shared a quote frequently attributed to radio commentator Paul Harvey: "Too many Christians are no longer fishers of men, but the keepers of the aquarium."

"That's why," Wilson said, "one of the things we're trying to do with potlucks is invite somebody that's either unchurched or doesn't know the Lord. Look for people. Y'know, fish don't just jump in the boat. Amen, somebody!"

Wilson knew that his early antagonism toward New Song's history had chased people away. In boxing terms, he felt you should just "sting" someone to get your message across. If you knocked people out, they couldn't hear what you had to say. In retrospect, he realized he'd done neither—he'd come on more like a machine gun! Nonetheless, he appreciated those who remained with New Song as a small but strong core to build upon.

In his sermon, Wilson addressed that future, saying that although he knew he had a reputation as a cynic, he had hope for the church. "Do you know the average church lasts three to five years?" he said. "God has sustained this church for thirty years! Trust God! I don't care what I said, *ha-ha*. Oh, help me, Holy Ghost, he can shut me up. I don't care what my critique is! 'Cause He said, 'I'll build my church, and the gates of hell will not prevail against it!'

"I think God is maintaining this church," Wilson continued. "Some of you don't know 'cause our numbers look small. Do you know our income has actually grown? I have no idea how that happens. I'm like, 'Lord, I see all this blue out here on Sunday,' *ha-ha*. God is blessing the church because he wants to. You know we're the only multiethnic church in Sandtown? Who would do that? That don't even make sense. There's a reason people plant monolithic churches. They're easier to do!"

After forty-five minutes—a typical length—Wilson closed out his sermon. Ever the master of dynamics, he drew his voice down and left gentle pauses between his sentences.

"Did you know we are exactly who we are supposed to be today?" he said. "I mean that. Everybody that's here is supposed to be here. Now I'm gonna get y'all to really start working on loving and caring so that when people look at New Song, they'll say, 'Man, couldn't nobody have done that but God.' Nobody. Only God can take a ragtag group of people like that and use them like he's done. Only God can sustain a church for twenty-seven years through the ups and downs and rounds and abouts and ins and outs."

In the New Song liturgy, the sermon was followed by the doxology—a short, four-century-old hymn of praise sung directly to God. The band began with a soaring piano and organ accompaniment.

Praise God from whom all blessings flow . . .

Mark and Betty stood up from their seats in the back and walked forward. Congregants from the left and right tiers shuffled into the aisle, singing along.

Praise him, all creatures here below . . .

There were white people, black people, Asian people. Not clustered in groups, but distributed seemingly at random, although it was assuredly not random; that was the whole idea.

Praise him above, ye heavenly host . . .

Everyone joined hands.

Praise Father, Son, and Holy Ghost . . .

They swayed.

Amen . . .

To hold hands and sway with the people was to feel like part of a light load of fish bobbing in a net.

Amen . . .

The room began to look less like a church empty of people and more like a community making space for people.

Amen.

Joe rose before dawn on Veterans Day and put on his Class B uniform—gray shirt, blue pants, gold belt, black shoes—and his black JROTC windbreaker. He also grabbed his exhibition uniform and the gloves Nicole had bought him when the cold snap arrived. It was 23 degrees as Joe walked out to Nicole's car—about fifteen degrees colder than average.

Nicole dropped Joe off at Atholton High School at 5:45 a.m. The sun breathed light from below a sharply defined horizon and slowly illuminated the clear sky. Joe joined the rest of his JROTC battalion for a sunrise bus ride to T.C. Williams High School in Arlington, Virginia, just outside of Washington, DC. The 2017 "Best of the Best" drill competition was starting at 7:30 a.m. sharp.

Joe saw his future in the U.S. Army. It had started when his grandmother gave him a DVD of a World War II movie during his childhood days in Baltimore. In sixth grade, he had become drawn to JROTC. A month before the start of his freshman year, Joe had spent three days marching, rappelling, and drilling at Fort A.P. Hill near Fredericksburg, Virginia, during New Cadet Orientation.

Atholton JROTC fell under the 4th Brigade, which covered battalions from Maryland to South Carolina, including C.E. Murray High School, where his mother had participated in JROTC freshman year. When Joe joined JROTC at Atholton, his battalion had more cadets than there were students in Nicole's entire class at tiny C.E. Murray.

Joe made Atholton JROTC's drill team freshman year and got a practice rifle for home. It weighed six pounds. Joe spun it a lot. The rifles at school weighed over nine pounds. Those things hurt if they hit you. That November, in 2016, the battalion went to "HoCo," the Howard County drill competition. Joe was just a backup for the exhibition team; its members were the ones who spun the rifles and got to do original routines. At HoCo, he took part in the regulation competition, during which he and his teammates reacted to standard Army commands from their cadet commander, and in the inspection competition, during which they answered questions from judges. HoCo was stressful; the cadets got upset with each other over mistakes. But Atholton JROTC came in first. Joe also joined the drill team for the 2016 "Best of the Best" at T.C. Williams High School—one of eight regional competitions held in the 4th Brigade. T.C. Williams impressed Joe. Its gym was enormous; the cafeteria looked like a mall's food court. The team placed third in that competition.

In December 2016, Atholton's JROTC instructors told Joe that his grades had gotten too low. He could remain part of JROTC, but he would need to step down from the drill team. At the end of freshman year, Joe attended a JROTC "change in command" ceremony in the Atholton High School auditorium. He wore his full Class A uniform: black oxford shoes, blue slacks, gray army shirt, black tie, blue four-button "Army Service Uniform" coat, and a varicolored ribbon rack placed one-eighth of an inch above the left pocket flap. From his right shoulder lapel hung the red cord he'd earned by competing earlier in the year with the drill team. Even though Joe wouldn't be going on stage, Nicole attended. She hoped the ceremony would encourage Joe to put more effort into his schoolwork.

The beginning of sophomore year brought a clean slate for Joe. He rejoined the drill team. The second week of school, his JROTC instructors designated him a staff sergeant, a role that came with leadership responsibilities. Sergeant Marian Johnson felt that Joe had blossomed over the past year. He'd been quiet and diffident at first, but had since developed more confidence and courage. Squad leaders oversaw at least five cadets. Joe taught his cadets how to march and called them with reminders about which uniforms to wear on which days.

Joe envisioned his future. He knew all his options, army-wise. With a GPA of

2.5, he could qualify for a U.S. Army scholarship to a college with an ROTC program. That meant an eight-year commitment to the army as an officer. But college
meant math, and math had long been a thorn in Joe's side. A math-less option
existed: enlisting in the U.S. Army right out of high school. He was old enough
to take the Armed Services Vocational Aptitude Battery, and he planned to take
it soon. The test told you which specialties suited you. Joe wanted to be infantry.

In October 2017, Joe got his first chance to perform in exhibition, during the
HoCo competition. Nicole recalled her JROTC days, doing unarmed drills. She
wished she'd stuck with it through graduation. In hindsight, she appreciated all
the practicing and the mental dedication and focus that went into it.

At the November 2017 T.C. Williams competition, Nicole sat with other parents, several rows up. Across the gym floor, thirty rows of blue bleachers had been
collapsed flush against the wall, standing two stories tall. Atholton's exhibition
platoon marched to the center of the basketball court in four rows of three, led
by their cadet commander, and began their synchronized maneuvers. They had
changed into their exhibition uniforms—all black with a gray beret. The cadets
spun their rifles twice to the left and once to the right. Joe, in the back, effort-
lessly arrested his spinning rifle perfectly perpendicular to the floor. The cadets
marched in place, slamming their rifle butts to the floor one row at a time.

After several more minutes of rifle-flipping, the cadets surrounded their commander at mid-court and began to circle him. The commander tapped his rifle
butt on the ground twice. The cadets placed their rifle butts on the ground and
kept walking. Each cadet picked up the rifle that the cadet in front had left teetering. One cadet lunged and missed. The rifle clattered against the ground, and
several people in the bleachers gasped.

After a few minutes, the platoon approached the exhibition judge, kneeled,
slammed their rifles, saluted, and shouted, "Sir!"

"Request permission to leave, sir!" the commander shouted. "Thank you, sir!"

The platoon stood and marched off the court in a straight line, the commander
at their side, Joe at the very front leading the platoon.

Joe led the platoon into the bleachers. Once they were a few steps in, some cadets
relaxed their bearing and let their rifles hang by their sides. Joe remained stiff,
clutching the rifle against his chest diagonally in the "port arms" position. Nicole,
bursting with pride, hooted and laughed gleefully as Joe approached. "Look at me
all in tears!" she said to the parents around her. Up the stairs Joe ascended, past
his mother, looking straight ahead, breaking into a jog as he neared the top of the
bleachers.

AFTERWORD

Nicole Smith pulled out of Howard Community College before she finished her second associate's degree. She still runs a daycare program out of her apartment. Nicole got engaged to "a sweetheart" in South Carolina and plans to move there once Joe graduates from high school. Nicole's mother, Melinda, works as a Baltimore City Public Schools substitute teacher. Nicole's son, Joe, enrolled in Wilde Lake High School for his junior year. He had struggled with his grades and attendance sophomore year, so he no longer qualified for JROTC at Atholton High School. Joe sees the military or law enforcement in his future: maybe volunteering with the Civil Air Patrol, an auxiliary of the U.S. Air Force; maybe enlisted as an MP in the U.S. Army.

Mark and Betty Lange still live on N. Gilmor Street and attend New Song Community Church. Mark still works at Sandtown ReStore and feeds the kittens on his block.

In October 2017, Maryland settled the disparate impact housing complaint Barbara Samuels and Michael Allen had filed six years earlier. Without admitting wrongdoing, the state agreed to finance 1,500 low-income housing units in "communities of opportunity" in and around Baltimore. The agreement also banned the state housing agency from reinstating a local veto for Low-Income Housing Tax Credit applications "unless required by law."

In August 2018, Maryland governor Larry Hogan's administration released a list of Low-Income Housing Tax Credit awards that included developments in white Baltimore suburbs like Bel Air, Towson, and Eldersburg. That round of awards financed 809 units in Baltimore-area communities of opportunity, compared to only 679 in the previous four years combined. Each unit that materializes will count toward the 1,500 required in the conciliation agreement.

By November 2018, 2,600 families had leased housing using vouchers from the final *Thompson v. HUD* settlement. That's on top of the 1,788 families who had leased housing using mobility vouchers from the partial consent decree. Baltimore Regional Housing Partnership data shows that 70 percent of these families have remained in opportunity areas. Many more families are seeking a way out of Baltimore's poor, segregated neighborhoods. The waiting list for *Thompson* vouchers closed on March 31, 2017, with nearly 12,000 applicants on the list. Over 20,000 city households remain on the list for regular Housing Choice Vouchers.

The central lesson Barbara Samuels has taken away from her decades of pressing for housing mobility is "Just do it." The fearful NIMBY reactions *precede* the construction of low-income housing, she says, and she sees little reaction once tenants move in.

Housing mobility emerged as a point of contention in 2018 local elections. The Republican candidate in Baltimore's county executive race said he would go to court to challenge the 2016 HUD agreement that promised to bring one thousand affordable hard units and two thousand mobility vouchers to communities of opportunity. In the state delegate race for the district that includes the Baltimore County seat of Towson, the Republican candidate ran primarily on opposition to the agreement. In a video about the "largest HUD relocation experiment in the USA," he included a picture of Barbara Samuels as the "unaccountable, unelected regional quasi-governor" who was plotting to bring "weaponized" Section 8 vouchers to the county.

When the state signed its conciliation agreement in 2017, Lawrence Brown hailed it as "a great victory for fair housing," but warned that housing mobility programs would "[divest] resources in Black schools and neighborhoods" if they weren't accompanied by measures to make black communities whole and integrate white city enclaves like Roland Park. "Housing mobility is often touted as an anti-racist strategy," he wrote, "but without making Black neighborhoods matter and maintaining funding for Black public schools, housing mobility is destabilizing Black Baltimore."

The city council that took office after the election in 2016 passed several bills to strengthen Baltimore's neighborhoods. City voters approved a ballot measure that directed the council to create an affordable housing trust fund, and in 2018 the council raised the tax on property sales in order to generate $20 million per year for the fund. The city believes the fund will generate 4,100 affordable units over a decade. City hall also approved racial equity bills that would put an "Equity Assistance Fund" on the 2018 ballot and require city agencies to monitor disparities in race, gender, and income. A "Children and Youth Fund" created by a 2016 ballot initiative awarded $10.8 million across the city in 2018. Adam Jackson, CEO of Leaders of a Beautiful Struggle, who co-chaired the fund's task force, told the

Baltimore Sun that he wanted to ensure that "grassroots, black-led organizations are positioned to get the funding."

Despite the attention to West Baltimore after Freddie Gray's death, Sandtown still lacks effective neighborhood-wide advocacy. Antoine Bennett and Elder Harris became frustrated with the leadership of Sandtown-Winchester United and pulled out.

According to *Baltimore Sun* crime reporter Justin Fenton, between 2015 and 2018 there were twenty months in which Baltimore City registered at least thirty killings. That had happened just eight times in the previous fifteen years. Sandtown alone registered more than forty homicides between Freddie Gray's death in 2015 and October 2018. And the police department remains in crisis. Eight officers from the city's Gun Trace Task Force pled guilty to or were convicted in federal court of several charges. The shocking details of the group's alleged crimes that emerged at the trial—drug sales, robberies, even a home invasion—were so outlandish, they would not have seemed believable on even the most salacious television drama. Mayor Pugh fired police commissioner Kevin Davis in January 2018. Davis's successor resigned in May 2018 after federal prosecutors charged him with failing to pay his taxes.

Public housing in Baltimore is primed for another transformation. In 2018, the Housing Authority of Baltimore City revealed plans to tear down six buildings at Gilmor Homes, and HUD awarded the housing authority $30 million in Choice Neighborhoods Initiative funding to demolish Perkins Homes—a sprawling low-rise project adjacent to long-gentrified Fells Point and the posh new neighborhood of Harbor East—and replace it with mixed-income housing.

At the national level, HUD secretary Ben Carson has tried to unravel some of the fair housing tools described in this book, tools that resulted from decades of organizing and advocacy. In January 2018, HUD neutered the Obama administration's 2015 "affirmatively furthering fair housing" rule by telling jurisdictions that they could wait until at least November 2020 to submit fair housing assessments. A coalition of legal organizations sued over this move, but a federal judge—an Obama appointee—threw it out. HUD then proposed new rules to revamp its approach to affirmatively furthering fair housing and interpreting disparate impact. Justice Anthony Kennedy, who wrote the opinion upholding disparate impact under the Fair Housing Act, retired at the end of July 2018.

When I started planning this book over five years ago, I wanted to address what HUD called "facially neutral" practices: policies, like exclusionary zoning, that lacked sufficient proof of discriminatory intent, yet still put African Americans and other protected classes at a disadvantage. Outright white supremacy seemed marginalized enough that I could concentrate on structural racism, on the kind of discrimination that took place behind desks, not under hoods. As I reported and wrote, it struck me how little purchase was achieved by epic efforts to dismantle segregation and inequality. What would happen, I wondered, if government took more aggressive action to make American communities more racially and economically inclusive? After the 2015 massacre of African Americans at a church in Charleston, South Carolina, I shuddered to answer that question. Violence had met attempts to desegregate schools just four decades ago in Boston. Structural racism seemed like a placeholder for—or maybe an accomplice to—something more sinister, more dangerous.

A menacing rise in hate crimes and explicit white nationalism reached a sickening crescendo at an August 2017 rally in Charlottesville, Virginia. A year later, a Ku Klux Klan leader who had called a black protester "n—r" and shot in his direction at the rally was sentenced to several years in prison. The man's Klan chapter was located in Rosedale, Maryland. He owned a house near Bel Air that he had used for Klan convocations. He lived in northeast Baltimore City.

I am writing this afterword five days before the 2018 midterm election. Just in the past week, authorities arrested a white man for mailing over a dozen pipe bombs to prominent Democrats, a white man for slaughtering eleven people at a Pittsburgh synagogue, and a white man for fatally shooting two randomly chosen African Americans at a Kentucky grocery store after the shooter failed to get inside a black church. That same week, President Trump proposed an executive order that would take away citizenship from babies born on U.S. soil to noncitizen parents. Also that same week, the chairman of the National Republican Congressional Committee publicly condemned displays of white nationalism made by Steve King, a Republican congressman from Iowa.

Trump and King may be trying to transform the GOP into a kamikaze white nationalist cult, but well-meaning white people cannot consider themselves above the fray. White supremacy never stops acting on—or benefitting—white people. Only white people can stop it. As a white man, rather than yearn for the day I am no longer racist, I must beware of the day I *think* I am no longer racist.

America has always had this sickness. This is just what the symptoms look like right now.

We must not abide it.

Lawrence Lanahan
November 1, 2018

ACKNOWLEDGMENTS

Let me first acknowledge you, reader. Thank you for reading.

This book grew out of a series at WYPR 88.1 FM in Baltimore. Thank you to the funders of the series, including Associated Black Charities, Baltimore Community Foundation, Cohen Opportunity Fund, Ethics and Excellence in Journalism Foundation, Open Society Institute–Baltimore, and other donors. Thanks also to the WYPR board, general manager Tony Brandon, and program director Andy Bienstock. Thanks to WYPR's staff, especially the talented *Maryland Morning* team: Sheilah Kast, Tom Hall, Stephanie Hughes, Matt Purdy, Jamyla Krempel, and Katherine Gorman. Thanks to the series' many contributors, both those we commissioned—for example, the Baltimore Neighborhood Indicators Alliance, which provided data maps, and Lionel Foster, who brainstormed with me about the series and wrote a sharp essay for it—and the listeners who shared their stories. Thanks to Baltimore writer and teacher Michael Corbin, whose work inspired me as I planned the series. WYPR's community advisory board and an advisory committee assembled by the series staff helped foster a sense of accountability in the producers and bind the series to the community. Love to WYPR's members, to all who discussed the series, and to everyone who listened.

My work and study in sociology has shaped all of my journalistic pursuits. Thank you to the sociology departments at St. Mary's College of Maryland and American University. Thanks to my good friend Shawn Bingham, who kept me engaged with academic sociology after I went into journalism. Thank you to American Institutes for Research, which paid for my graduate degree at American University while I worked as a research analyst, and to my colleagues at AIR, who pushed me intellectually and were a joy to work and hang out with.

Thank you to Ellie Mitchell, David Crandall, Jack Livingston, Dave Park, Brandon Wall, and others who were willing to edit and publish my earliest writing. Thanks to Lynn Anderson Davy for encouraging me to pursue journalism and Eric Siegel for helping me get my head around Baltimore. Thanks to Mike Hoyt and Brent Cunningham, who expertly edited my first major reporting on

Baltimore in *Columbia Journalism Review*. Thanks also to the teachers and staff at the Columbia School of Journalism.

I found the Aspen Institute's Roundtable on Community Change helpful along the way. Gretchen Susi put a lot of energy into Aspen's work in Baltimore; thanks, Gretchen. In 2011, Diane Bell-McKoy of Associated Black Charities invited me to attend Aspen's three-day seminar on structural racism and to join the "Racial Equity & the Future of the Baltimore Region Working Group," convened by Aspen, Associated Black Charities, and Baltimore Community Foundation. Thank you for that and more, Diane. In December 2014, Aspen invited me to another three-day seminar: the Forum on Journalism, Race, and Society. Thanks to ProPublica's Jennifer LaFleur and Investigative Reporters and Editors, Inc., for inviting me to present about "Investigating Racial Inequality" at a 2014 IRE conference. Thanks to Emily Steinmetz for inviting me to talk at American University, and to Seema Iyer for inviting me to talk at Data Day.

Columbia University's Alfred I. DuPont Awards recognized WYPR's series in 2014. Heartfelt thanks to the staff and jury, especially A'Lelia Bundles.

And here is an appreciation for the people in Baltimore's neighborhoods, especially black Baltimoreans, who have been talking about the topics in this book for decades. They feel these issues most urgently and work hardest to make things right. Appreciation is also due to media organizations—some of which are no longer around—who cover their communities deeply, like WEAA, the *Baltimore Afro-American*, the *Marc Steiner Show*, Baltimore *City Paper*, *The Real News*, and *Baltimore Beat*.

Several publications and universities kept my mind active and my cupboard full after I left WYPR. Thanks to *Al Jazeera America* (particularly editor Caroline Preston), *ColorLines*, *Slate*, *Baltimore City Paper*, *Baltimore Fishbowl*, *CityLab*, *Columbia Journalism Review*, NPR's *Morning Edition*, and . . . WYPR, for whom I freelanced occasionally. Thank you to my inspiring students at the University of Baltimore, Goucher College, and the Maryland Correctional Institute for Women. Thanks to Phaye Poliakoff-Chen at Goucher College and Amy Roza at the Goucher Prison Education Partnership. Thank you to Joe Wood, Stephen Percy, and others at the University of Baltimore who believed in my work on the WYPR series and gave me a wide berth to teach it. Joe Wood read an early draft of this book and provided helpful comments.

I want to give special recognition to A. Adar Ayira for her anti-racism work in Baltimore. I listen to Adar very closely. She is uncompromising in her advocacy for black people, and she is to be emulated in her respectfulness in dealing with all people. Adar actively advised the WYPR series. She also read a very long draft of this book—twice—and returned a slew of helpful comments and concerns.

When I had a "book idea" (ha!) and little in the way of structure, several people pulled me over the hump into actual authoring. I owe Emily Brady (*Humboldt*), Alia Malek (*The Home That Was Our Country*), and George Thompson (of the eponymous publishing house) for their advice. Steve Luxenberg (*Annie's Ghosts*, *Separate*) spent a few lunches at Belvedere Square lavishing wisdom on me. (I offered little in return; I hope the sandwiches were good, Steve.) I cold-called Steve's agent, Gail Ross, and she spent months guiding me through the proposal process, then took me on as a client. Thank you Gail, Dara Kaye, and the crew at Ross Yoon Agency. Thank you also to Larry Weissman for advice on my book proposal.

I am lucky to be publishing with The New Press. I admire their mission, and they publish Studs Terkel, whose book *Working* nudged me into journalism. I was deeply honored (and a little weepy) to receive The New Press's Studs and Ida Terkel Prize for this book. I am grateful to the entire staff, including Ellen Adler, Sarah Swong, Emily Albarillo, and especially my editor, Tara Grove. Tara is a terrific editor, and she managed my anxieties expertly. Thanks also to meticulous copyeditor Anne Nissen. Many thanks to the Kellogg Foundation for their generous support of this book and for helping its human and policy stories reach far and wide.

In the spring of 2017, I had the great fortune to spend five very productive weeks at the Carey Institute for Global Good in Rensselaerville, New York as part of their Logan Nonfiction Program. Thanks to Gareth Crawford, Sue Shufelt, Carly Willsie, Tom Jennings, Josh Friedman, Carol Ash, Mark Kramer, Tim and the crew at the restaurant, and all who fund and support the program. My book also benefited from the stimulating conversation and critical feedback of the other fellows: Joanne Drayton, Katherine Reynolds Lewis, Cath Collins, Erin Banco, Gian Cassini, Irene Chidinma Nwoye, May Jeong, Anastasia Taylor-Lind, Michael Scott Moore, M.T. Connelly, Raphael Minder, Saumya Roy, Taran Khan, Sylvia Harvey, Anastasia Taylor-Lind, Adrian LeBlanc, Rasha Elass, and Kenneth Rosen. Thanks also to Bruce Wallace, who alerted me to the residency. Bruce is a deft journalist and treasured friend whose creativity, talent, and doggedness inspire me. Thanks to Caroline and Brent for recommendations.

One of the best things about writing a book is spending time in libraries and archives. Thank you to Rob Schoeberlein and Ed Papenfuse for your tenacity at the Baltimore City Archives; University of Baltimore Special Collections staff, including Aiden Faust, Benjamin Blake, Fatemah Rezaei, Adele Marley, and Angela Rodgers-KouKoui; Robin Emrich at the Columbia Archives for chasing down threads about James Rouse; Alan Holdsmith at the Enoch Pratt Central Library; Joe Tropea at the Maryland Historical Society for guiding me toward the amazing Jonestown photo collection and his colleague Debbie Harner for helping me dig through the boxes; and Lorie Rombro and the Jewish Museum of Maryland staff for pulling out exactly the files I needed about the Baltimore Jewish Council. The Enoch Pratt Free Library has an amazing Central Branch, but I also adore the library for its online resources. I downloaded hundreds of *Baltimore Sun* articles going back to 1859.

Thanks to Social Security Administration historian Eric DeLisle for finding a newsletter article about the 1970 U.S. Commission on Civil Rights hearing. Thanks to Joannie Barth, assistant to Philip Yancey, for finding and scanning an article from the May 1975 issue of *Campus Life*. Thanks to Dot Boersma for details about Tenth Presbyterian Church. Thanks to Kay Owens, Kerry Regester, and Jacob Harner at the U.S. District Courthouse clerk's office in downtown Baltimore. They wheeled out cart after cart of filings and transcripts during my many visits.

Many people at government agencies responded to requests for data and documents, including Tania Baker, Marlon Blue, Gerson Gomez, Ralph Matos, Thomas Elder, Sara Luell, Amy Grasso, Cindy Mumby, Meaghan Alegi, Joanne Gray, Christina Belcastro, James Massey, and Kelly Cimino.

Thank you to Amtrak Police Officer Nathaniel Rufful for getting my stolen laptop back; thanks also to Amtrak Officer Ted Oliver and Boston Police Detective Paul Joyce. Thanks to Puru Pokharel at Apple Repair Club in Manhattan for data recovery. Thanks to Dr. John M. Perkins for driving me to Walmart to buy clothes after I discovered a bedbug in my Jackson, Mississippi, hotel room.

How deep my gratitude is for the sources in this book. There are too many to thank each individually. Thank you, Antoine Bennett, for being so welcoming when I started reporting this book. Mark and Betty Lange welcomed me into their home and into their lives many, many times, as did Nicole Smith, her son Joe, and her mother Melinda. They gave me so much, with me offering in return only an aspirational notion that telling their stories would matter somehow. I will never be able to express enough gratitude to them. The same goes for Barbara Samuels. Barbara did not want this book to be about her, and she was reluctant to participate. Ultimately, she devoted countless hours to my interviews and requests for minute details. She does, as her colleagues told me, have a mind like a steel trap.

That all seems insufficient—let me repeat my gratitude for my sources and all of the time and effort they gave me. Thank you also to the many people and institutions that are eluding my memory at this given moment.

And now for friends, neighbors, and family. My family has a wonderful, sustaining community in Northeast Baltimore. Here's a shout out to everyone in our world here, especially those who pitched in to watch my children when tight deadlines tied me up.

Thank you to my in-laws for their support and for the satellite office in Quincy, Illinois. Thank you to N. Charles Emil, a generous educator I wish I had met. Thank you, Eric Appleton and Alex Cuervo, for your encouragement and your inordinate hospitality at Casa Cuerppleton in New York City.

I am fortunate that my sisters and their children still live in the region. Their encouragement means more than they probably realize. My parents—Mary Elise Lanahan and Lawrence S. Lanahan Jr.—still live nearby. Their love and encouragement are the foundation of anything worthwhile I've ever done, including this book (presuming it is worthwhile).

When I started working on this book, my youngest son, Theodore, was a newborn, and his brother Emil was two. The satisfaction of finishing a book is nothing compared to the joy of watching these energetic, funny, and loving children grow. They make every day sacred. I love you, Emil and Theo.

I burst with gratitude for my wife, Andrea Appleton. My three-plus years of madly scrambling to complete this book repeatedly interrupted the time and concentration necessary for her own writing. Andrea took care of our children for five weeks while I attended a writing residency in upstate New York. Andrea's patient love pulled me through several difficult years, and her mind pushed me forward. She consistently inspires me to new insights, encourages intellectual honesty in my long-held ideas, and exactingly edits much of what I write. She also cracks me up. I am lucky that my eyes open to her beauty each morning. I love you, *a chuisle mo chroí.*

NOTES

Prologue

1   **Murphy Homes** Katie Gunther, "High-rises Denounced: New Public Housing Demanded by Groups," *Baltimore Sun*, August 3, 1983, F14.

2   **"Formstone"** Kenneth D. Durr, *Behind the Backlash: White Working Class Politics in Baltimore, 1940–1980* (Chapel Hill: University of North Carolina Press, 2003), 73.

2   **fatally shot in the head** *Baltimore Sun*, 2007. Date withheld to mask the exact location of the shooting.

3   **rental in the private market** The government also ran a "Project-Based Section 8" program that kept private dwelling units reserved for Section 8 tenants. Charles L. Edson, "Affordable Housing: An Intimate History," *The Legal Guide to Affordable Housing Development* (Chicago: American Bar Association Forum on Affordable Housing and Community Development, 2011), 9.

4   **waiting list** Housing Authority of Baltimore City, "Moving to Work Plans, FY2007 and FY2008," www.hud.gov/sites/documents/DOC_10257.PDF.

5   **houses there** "Riverside, 1,400-Acre Planned Community, Is Now Open in Harford," *Baltimore Sun*, September 27, 1981, F1.

One: One Region, Two Worlds

11   **"dangerous for white school children"** Housing Authority of Baltimore City, "Annual Report," 1939, 14–15; also, Peter H. Henderson, "Local Deals and the New Deal State: Implementing Federal Public Housing in Baltimore, 1933–1968" (PhD diss., Johns Hopkins University, 1993), 214.

11   **lived all over the city** Kenneth D. Durr, *Behind the Backlash: White Working Class Politics in Baltimore, 1940–1980* (Chapel Hill: University of North Carolina Press, 2003), 9, 11; also, Hayward Farrar, *The Baltimore Afro-American, 1892–1950* (Westport, Connecticut: Greenwood Press, 1998), 101.

12   **substandard alley houses** Elizabeth Nix, "Divided Baltimore" (lecture, University of Baltimore, Baltimore, MD, August 31, 2015), https://ubalt.hosted.panopto .com/Panopto/Pages/Viewer.aspx?id=fed42ab1-b1c4-4f63-be2b-0079fc103f08.

12   **ordinance prohibiting** Garrett Power, "Apartheid Baltimore Style: the Residential Segregation Ordinances of 1910–1913," *Maryland Law Review* 42:2 (1983),

http://digitalcommons.law.umaryland.edu/mlr/vol42/iss2/4; also, Rhonda Y. Williams, *The Politics of Public Housing: Black Women's Struggles* (New York: Oxford University Press, 2005), 58; also, Mary Ellen Hayward, *Baltimore's Alley Houses: Homes for Working People since the 1780s* (Baltimore: Johns Hopkins University Press, 2008), 235; also, Campbell Gibson and Kay Jung, "Historical Census Statistics On Population Totals By Race, 1790 to 1990, and By Hispanic Origin, 1970 to 1990, For Large Cities And Other Urban Places In The United States," Population Division Working Paper No. 76, U.S. Census Bureau, Washington, DC, February 2005.

12   **just as much about** Power.

12   **segregation ordinances** *Buchanan v. Warley*, 245 U.S. 60 (1917).

12   **white power structure became** James R. Cohen, "Abandoned Housing: Exploring Lessons from Baltimore," *Housing Policy Debate*, 12:3 (2001).

12   **sniffing for code violations** Power, "Apartheid Baltimore Style."

12   **ostracized agents** U.S. Commission on Civil Rights (USCCR). Transcript: Hearing Held in Baltimore, Maryland, August 17–19, 1970, 94.

12   **covenants barring owners** Antero Pietila, *Not in My Neighborhood: How Bigotry Shaped a Great American City* (Chicago: Ivan R. Dee, 2010), 48–49.

12   **residential security maps** Amy Hillier, "Redlining and the Homeowners' Loan Corporation," *Journal of Urban History* 29:4 (2003), 394–420.

12   **insure home loans disproportionately** Hillier, 394–420; also, Elizabeth Nix, email message to author, September 9, 2015.

12   **housing authority placed** United States Department of the Interior, National Park Service, National Register of Historic Places registration form, "Gilmor Homes, Baltimore City, MD," July 1992.

12   **the border** Power, "Apartheid Baltimore Style"; also, Pietila, *Not in My Neighborhood*; also, Williams, *Politics of Public Housing*, 58.

12   **"self-respecting families"** The editor, Clark Hobbs, saw "no point in tearing down good houses merely to replace them with other good houses." Peter H. Henderson, "Local Deals and the New Deal State: Implementing Federal Public Housing in Baltimore, 1933–1968" (PhD diss., Johns Hopkins University, 1993), 215.

12   *faced* **strategically** Williams, *Politics of Public Housing*, 57–58.

12   **idea animating these placements** Mary Ellen Hayward and Charles Belfoure, *The Baltimore Rowhouse* (New York: Princeton Architectural Press, 1999), 173; also, Memorandum from W.E. Trevett to E.H. Klaber, Trip to Baltimore on March 31, 1934, Baltimore Regional Studies Archives Repository, American Civil Liberties Union of Maryland Records, *Thompson v. HUD*, Plaintiff's Exhibits, Exhibit 83, University of Baltimore. More on "projects as racial barriers" can be found in Marc L. Silver and Martin Melkonian, eds., *Contested Terrain: Power, Politics, and Participation in Suburbia* (Westport, CT: Greenwood Press, 1995), 204; and "Report of the Joint Committee on Housing in Baltimore," *Baltimore Engineer* 8:7 (1934).

15   **Home Owners Loan Corporation** Home Owners Loan Corporation, "Area Description" for Area D1 (east Baltimore), May 1937, https://dsl.richmond.edu/panorama/redlining/#loc=13/39.2931/-76.6334&opacity=0.8&city=baltimore-md&area=D1&adview=full&adimage=3/75/-120.

15   **"clearance and containment"** Power, "Apartheid Baltimore Style," 316.

15   **housing authority opened** Housing Authority of Baltimore City, "Celebrating 75 Years!" www.baltimorehousing.org/75th_timeline.

15   **Brooklyn Homes** *Carmen Thompson, et al. v. United States Department of Housing and Urban Development et al.*, 348 F. Supp. 2d 398 (D. Md. 2005).

15   **shipyards** Roderick N. Ryan, "When Baltimore's War Effort Tripped Over Race," *Baltimore Sun*, August 11, 1993, http://articles.baltimoresun.com/1993-08-11 /news/1993223043_1_riveters-shipyards-seams.

15   *de jure* **white project** *Thompson v. HUD*, 348 F. Supp. 2d 398 (D. Md. 2005).

15   **white war workers** Durr, *Behind the Backlash*, 309.

15   **white residents objected** "Baltimore Housing Authority Yields to Racial Opposition," *Baltimore Afro-American*, March 27, 1943, A1.

15   **Robert Jackson** "Negro Housing Held Health Menace Here: Colored Doctor Tells Plan," *Baltimore Sun*, October 3, 1941, 34.

15   **black war workers** Durr, *Behind the Backlash*, 309; also, Williams, *Politics of Public Housing*, 56.

15   **privileging "seniority"** Ryan, "Baltimore's War Effort Tripped"; also, Durr, 16, 26–27.

15   **only permanent black war housing** *Thompson v. HUD*, 348 F. Supp. 2d 398 (D. Md. 2005).

15   **Key Highway shipyard** Durr, *Behind the Backlash*, 309.

16   **married** "Weddings of Interest Announced," *Baltimore Sun*, August 1, 1954, 113.

16   **ended segregation** "Background Notes on Desegregation Policy for Use in Planning and Executing Training Program to Be Conducted as Part of Applying Policy," Housing Authority of Baltimore City memo, 1954, ACLU–Maryland Records, Local Defendant's Exhibit 420.

16   **in 1962** Arnold Hirsch, "Public Policy and Residential Segregation, 1900–1968," ACLU–Maryland Records, Plaintiff's Exhibit 3.

16   **opened that year** John C. Schmidt, "Ten Years in the Making: $68 Million Beltway Opens Today," *Baltimore Sun*, July 1, 1962, BF1.

16   **Interstate 83** "Expressway Section Open: Jones Falls Road Finished All the Way to Beltway," *Baltimore Sun*, November 3, 1962, 4.

16   **growing suburbs** Kenneth Jackson, *Crabgrass Frontier: The Suburbanization of the United States* (New York: Oxford University Press, 1985).

17   **three days of vandalism** "Suburban Integration," newsletter of Baltimore Neighborhoods, Inc., 1:1 (June 1962), 4.

17   **discourage agents from using racial designations** "Racial Designations," newsletter of Baltimore Neighborhoods, Inc., 1:1 (June 1962), 1. Realtors sometimes used this designation for listings in neighborhoods that were still substantially white, part of a phenomenon called blockbusting. This hastened the racial turnover of the neighborhood, allowing agents to buy low from fleeing whites and sell high to black families who'd long aspired to homeownership but faced a restricted housing supply.

17   **executive order** Executive Order no. 11063, *Code of Federal Regulations*, title 3, 652 (1959–1963), www.presidency.ucsb.edu/ws/index.php?pid=59002.

17   **FHA's practices** Jackson, *Crabgrass Frontier*, 206.

17   **overall population** United States Commission on Civil Rights. *Staff Report: Demographic, Economic, Social, and Political Characteristics of Baltimore City and Baltimore County*, 1970.

17   **as was Chadwick Manor** Black homebuyers in the Baltimore region at that time knew that homes listed in the "suburban" section of the newspaper classifieds weren't open to them. USCCR Transcript (August 17–19, 1970), 98.

17   **pioneer the integration** "The Social Security Administration and Information Technology-Special Report, OTA-CIT-311," U.S. Congress, Office of Technology Assessment, (Washington, DC: U.S. Government Printing Office, October 1986), 93.

17   **banned discrimination in the federal defense workforce** Executive Order no. 8802, *Code of Federal Regulations*, title 3, 957 (1938–1943), www.presidency.ucsb.edu /ws/index.php?pid=59002.

18   **commuted from the city** USCCR Transcript (August 17–19, 1970).

18   **Between 1960 and 1970** Dickens Warfield and George B. Laurent. "A Study of the Economic Potential of Baltimore Black Families for Living in the Suburban Baltimore Area," Baltimore Neighborhoods, Inc., Appendix G (June 1972).

18   **hearing** Frederic B. Hill, "Civil Rights Hearings Set: U.S. Commission to Look at City, County Actions," *Baltimore Sun*, August 16, 1970, 16.

18   **Hesburgh** Frederic B. Hill, "Urban-Crisis Apathy Criticized: Panel Studying County Finds Government, People 'Not Serious,'" *Baltimore Sun*, August 20, 1970, A1.

19   **audience** Bettye Moss, "If YOU Ask ME: People, Places and Things," *Baltimore Afro-American*, September 5, 1970, 5.

19   **Hesburgh said** Unless otherwise noted, dialogue from the hearing comes from USCCR Transcript (August 17–19, 1970).

19   **"one way street"** Alvin P. Sanoff, "Embry Hints Low-Income Housing Curb: City-Resident Priority Would Effectively Bar County Influx," *Baltimore Sun*, January 7, 1971, D20.

19   **gaining 94,000 black residents** Dickens Warfield and George B. Laurent. "A Study of the Economic Potential of Baltimore Black Families for Living in the Suburban Baltimore Area," Baltimore Neighborhoods, Inc., Appendix G (June 1972).

20   **days of testimony** Johnny Bowles, "Dale Anderson Talks to Commission; Promise to Build Low-cost Homes," *Baltimore Afro-American*, August 22, 1970, 1.

21   **"affirmatively to further"** "Report from the Maryland Advisory Committee to the U.S. Commission on Civil Rights," ACLU–Maryland Records, Local Defendant's Exhibit 419, 10.

21   **need to do one** "Report from the Maryland Advisory Committee to the U.S. Commission on Civil Rights."

22   **pull themselves up** "Economic mobility," Anderson said, was the path to "alternative residential environments." "Report from the Maryland Advisory Committee to the U.S. Commission on Civil Rights."

22 **report** U.S. Commission on Civil Rights. *Equal Opportunity in Suburbia.* Washington, DC, 1974.

26 **more than 35,000 people** Eileen Canzian, "Baltimore Finds Integrating Public Housing an Elusive Goal," *Baltimore Sun*, July 2, 1985, 1D; also, Eileen Canzian, "Housing in the City: For Many, There's No Place to Go: Subsidized Housing Units," *Baltimore Sun*, August 17, 1986, 1.

26 **Federal investigators pinned** "Stanfield and Boardley Investigations," Bureau of Justice Assistance, National Criminal Justice Reference Service, www.ncjrs.gov /html/bja/gang/bja4.html.

27 **he shot a man** Allegra Bennett, "Stanfield Said to Kill Man for Not Showing Respect," *Baltimore Sun*, January 6, 1987, 1B.

27 **January 1987 report** David Simon, "Heroin Trade Enlists Ever-younger Killers for Reign by Bloodletting," *Baltimore Sun*, January 13, 1987, 1B. Barksdale pleaded guilty and received a fifteen-year sentence. The names Barksdale and Stanfield may sound familiar; Simon later used them in HBO's *The Wire.* Simon's report describes Barksdale burning a woman's face with a curling iron and stabbing her in the breasts, then trying to slice off her companion's ear.

27 **change their circumstances** Milford Prewitt, "Project's Drug Woes: Lasting Cure Sought," *Baltimore Sun*, April 1, 1983, D3; "Violence: The Community," *Baltimore Sun*, February 28, 1982, VM20; Katie Gunther, "City Facing Rent Strike Despite Fix-up," *Baltimore Sun*, December 8, 1983, D1; Katie Gunther, "Most Rent Strikers Drop Protest of Public High-rises," *Baltimore Sun*, January 3, 1984, D1; Amy Goldstein, "Judge Tells 8 Tenants to Halt Rent Strike," *Baltimore Sun*, January 7, 1984, B1.

27 **They felt** "Violence: The Community," VM20.

27 **organized to demand** Katie Gunther, "High-rises Denounced: New Public Housing Demanded by Groups," *Baltimore Sun*, August 3, 1983, F14.

27 **rent strike** Goldstein, "Judge Tells 8."

29 **"Fine with me"** Melinda kept her word; she never lived in public housing again.

29 **Joe Miller called Game 5** "1983 Season Highlights Orioles WFBR," www .youtube.com/watch?v=6WpEdjecU3U.

29 **Miller's shouting** "1983 Season Highlights."

29 **canneries and tin decorating plants** Deborah Rudicille, *Roots of Steel: Boom and Bust in an American Mill Town* (New York: Anchor Books, 2010), 55.

29 **hoping to renovate** Katie Gunther, "Growth Plan Drafted for Waterfront Areas," *Baltimore Sun*, January 11, 1984, F1.

29 **American Can Company** Andrew Merrifield, "The Struggle over Place: Redeveloping American Can in Southeast Baltimore," *Transactions of the Institute of British Geographers* 18:1 (1993), 110.

29 **$160,000** Tom Horton, "Tour Finds Comeback in Canton," *Baltimore Sun*, June 17, 1984, C1.

29 **more than double** "New Home Sales Drop 5.1%," *Baltimore Sun*, October 1, 1983, C13.

29   **At a dive** Patrick A. McGuire, "In City's Streets, Bars, Fans Cheer Their Champions," *Baltimore Sun*, October 17, 1983, A1.

30   **not the burgeoning** Merrifield, "Struggle over Place," 102.

30   **blacktop "cuts"** Peter Hermann and Tim Craig, "Drugs and Violence Claim Their Own Turf," *Baltimore Sun*, December 12, 1999, http://articles.baltimoresun.com /1999-12-12/news/9912110095_1_o-donnell-heights-heights-home-army-barracks.

30   **built in 1942** HABC, "Celebrating 75 Years!"

30   **twelve years after** Arnold Hirsch, "Public Policy and Residential Segregation, 1900–1968."

30   **more than three-quarters white** Eileen Canzian, "Elusive Goal."

30   **O'Donnell Heights** Tracie Rozhos, "O'Donnell Heights 'Like Concentration Camp'," *Baltimore Sun*, October 2, 1978, A1.

30   **angry with the housing authority** Tracie Rozhos, "O'Donnell Heights: The City's Forgotten Edge," *Baltimore Sun*, October 1, 1978, A1.

30   **exposed wires** Tracie Rozhos, "City Construction Team to Check O'Donnell Heights Homes," *Baltimore Sun*, October 16, 1978, C1.

30   **rent strike** "Tenants Begin Rent Strike at Fairfield, O'Donnell," *Baltimore Sun*, December 1, 1978, C4; also, Williams, *Politics of Public Housing*, 222.

31   **turning back over to market rate** Eileen Canzian, "State Faces Loss of Housing for Poor, Elderly," *Baltimore Sun*, October 7, 1988, 1E.

31   **commission claimed** President's Commission on Housing, "The Report of the President's Commission on Housing," Washington, DC: 1982, www.huduser.gov /portal//Publications/pdf/HUD-2460.pdf.

31   **Section 8 program** Charles L. Edson, "Affordable Housing: An Intimate History," *The Legal Guide to Affordable Housing Development* (Chicago: American Bar Association Forum on Affordable Housing and Community Development, 2011), 10; also, President's Commission on Housing, "Report," 10.

31   **Federal funding** Nancy J. Schwerzler, "Reagan's HUD: Where Politics Ruled: Zealous Appointees Sought to Curtail Federal Housing Role," *Baltimore Sun*, June 18, 1989, 1A.

31   **piece of concrete fell** Roger Twigg, "Failing Concrete Kills Boy at W. Baltimore High-rise," *Baltimore Sun*, June 7, 1989, 3D.

32   **Raymond Toulson's father** Rafael Alvarez, "Guard Killed, Several Hurt in Pen Fracas," *Baltimore Sun*, October 7, 1984, 1A.

32   **Tragedy** Twigg, "Failing Concrete."

32   **incision in a larger block** Marilyn McCraven, "Preserving History Is Down Her Alley; Survey: The thousands of tiny rowhouses along Baltimore alleys are threatened with extinction. Meanwhile, Mary Ellen Hayward is documenting this little-known part of urban history," *Baltimore Sun*, February 15, 1997, 1A; also, Philip C. LaCombe, "Life in a Small Street in Baltimore: One Hundred Fifty Years of an Evolving, Unique Urban Landscape" (master's thesis, University of Maryland, College Park, 2012). These so-called "alley streets" are one of Baltimore City's great charms. Their diminutive houses provided the city's original affordable housing for African Americans and immigrants from Germany, Ireland, and other European countries. Despite decades of

efforts to demolish them, by the 1990s there remained several thousand houses along 750 blocks of alley streets. One researcher found in the 1990s that many residents were fond of their little tucked-away communities. Children could play safely away from traffic; neighbors knew each other well and kept an eye on each other's homes.

33   **Harlem Park** James Bock, "Blacks Less Eager for Housing Integration, Equal Opportunity Is More Important Series: Race and Housing: Barriers Fall, but Patterns Endure," *Baltimore Sun*, July 7, 1991, 1A.

33   **residents** "Neighborhoods Moving Up: What Baltimore Can Learn from Its Own Improving Neighborhoods," Institute for Policy Studies, Johns Hopkins University, 2001.

35   **James Rouse** Joshua Olsen, *Better Places, Better Lives: A Biography of James Rouse* (Washington, DC: Urban Land Institute, 2003), 5.

35   **By twenty-one** Olsen, 12.

35   **charm** Olsen, 19.

35   **documentary** Olsen, Chapter 2; *The Baltimore Plan*, Encyclopaedia Brittanica Films, Inc., 1953.

36   **Congress included** Olsen, Chapter 2, 45–46. The law reflected Rouse's preference for rehabilitation over "slum clearance," but in practice, urban renewal earned a reputation for rapacious demolition and was referred to derisively as "Negro removal."

36   **used restrictive covenants** The Roland Park area is described as "well restricted" here: Home Owners Loan Corporation, "Area Description" for Area B1 (Roland Park), May 1937, https://dsl.richmond.edu/panorama/redlining/#loc=14/39.3526/-76.6415&opacity=0.8&city=baltimore-md&area=B1&adimage=3/80/-120.

36   **Jews and African Americans** Elizabeth Evitts Dickinson, "Roland Park: One of America's First Garden Suburbs, and Built for Whites Only," *Johns Hopkins Magazine*, Fall 2014, https://hub.jhu.edu/magazine/2014/fall/roland-park-papers-archives; also, Jim Holechek, *Baltimore's Two Cross Keys Villages: One Black. One White.* (Lincoln, NE: iUniverse, Inc., 2003), 107; also, Paige Glotzer, "Legacy of Exclusion: Roland Park Co. and the Segregated City" (lecture, Johns Hopkins University, Baltimore, MD, October 27, 2016); according to Glotzer, the Roland Park Company followed its lawyers' advice to omit language banning sales or rentals to "Negroes" from its covenants in the Roland Park neighborhood, but allowed such passages for deeds in the Guilford neighborhood; also, Paige Glotzer, email messages to author, October 29, 2016, and April 26, 2018; also, Pietila, *Not in My Neighborhood*, 35–36.

36   ***Shelley v. Kraemer***, *Shelley v. Kraemer*, 334 U.S. 1 (1948), https://caselaw.findlaw.com/us-supreme-court/334/1.html.

36   **accused Rouse of maintaining a quota** Chronology of BJC negotiations with Marylander Apartments, no date, Baltimore Jewish Council Collection, Jewish Museum of Maryland, Baltimore; also, Letter from James Rouse to Leon Sachs, August 7, 1951, Baltimore Jewish Council Collection, Jewish Museum of Maryland, Baltimore. The council claimed Rouse admitted to a "flexible" 10 percent quota. Rouse denied an "antisemitic" policy, saying that his group simply monitored the proportion of Jewish tenants and considered new applications "in terms of these . . . proportions looking to the goal of 'harmonious and compatible living' in a mixed apartment in a previously non-mixed community."

36 **consultant's warning** Paul Marx, *Jim Rouse: Capitalist/Idealist* (Lanham, MD: University Press of America, 2008), 66–67. The black families moving toward the development, Rouse wrote to a partner, "are largely home owners who have paid $7,500 and $15,000 and up for their houses." Rouse may have resisted the consultant's objection, but his own reasoning was objectionable: "The noticeable improvement in recent years in the living habits of the higher-income Negroes and the strong trend against racial segregation may make this part of the walk-in market more acceptable."

36 **1959** Olsen, *Better Places, Better Lives*, 92–93.

36 **advocated for racial integration** Olsen, 127–128; also, "BNI Was Maryland's First Fair Housing Organization," BNI's History, Baltimore Neighborhoods, Inc., www.bni-maryland.org/history.

36 **mixed-use development** Olsen, 128.

36 **touting Cross Keys** Olsen, 129.

36 **whip up us-versus-them** Holechek, *Baltimore's Two Cross Keys Villages*, 101; also, Olsen, 129.

36 **backed his zoning request** Olsen, 129.

36 **Roland Park got behind** Charles V. Flowers, "Apartments Get Conditional O.K.: Two 10-story Buildings Set in Village," *Baltimore Sun*, August 26, 1964, 42.

36 **created shell companies** Olsen, *Better Places, Better Lives*, 144.

36 **fourteen-member "Non-Physical Planning" team** Olsen, 151, 161; also, Adam Sachs, "More Is at Stake Than Just Sandtown, Rouse Says; Columbia's Founder on Hope for Poor," *Baltimore Sun*, July 23, 1995, http://articles.baltimoresun.com/1995 -07-23/news/1995204018_1_rouse-sandtown-enterprise-foundation; also, USCCR Transcript (August 17–19, 1970), 462.

37 **"encourage human growth"** Olsen, 164.

37 **not to tell anyone the race** USCCR Transcript (August 17–19, 1970).

37 **Columbia's first residents** Olsen, *Better Places, Better Lives*, 195–197.

37 **child** Lisa Leff, "'Everybody Is the Same in Columbia,'" *Washington Post*, July 5, 1987, www.washingtonpost.com/archive/politics/1987/07/05/everybody-is-the -same-in-columbia/329385a5-cd61-485d-a026-f2ae9c5c2e1c; "Community Q&A," *Baltimore Sun*, April 3, 2005, http://articles.baltimoresun.com/2005-04-03/news /0504040244_1_barbara-russell-columbia-biracial-baby.

37 **hearing on suburban housing discrimination** Unless otherwise indicated, actual excerpts from Rouse's testimony, as well as descriptions of his testimony, are based upon the USCCR Transcript (August 17–19, 1970), 448–465.

37 **fallen short of a goal** Columbia, Rouse had said, should be home to the "company president" and the "janitor." When the chance first came to use a government program for subsidized rental housing, Rouse demurred. Under the "221(d)(3)" program, the federal government bought loans from lenders whose customers promised to keep rents in their developments below certain levels set by HUD. When Rouse bought the land that would become Columbia, there were already a dozen existing subdivisions, and he wasn't willing to spook the residents there. "If we had gone in with a 221(d)(3) project alongside of any one of those subdivisions," he testified, "it would have received the same kind of fear and opposition that it would receive any-

where else." Charles J. Orlebeke, "The Evolution of Low-Income Housing Policy, 1949 to 1999," *Housing Policy Debate* 11:2 (2000), 493–494.

37   **proportion three times the average** USCCR Transcript (August 17–19, 1970), 451; also, Gibson and Jung, "Historical Census Statistics."

38   **Rabin's 1970 report** Yale Rabin, "The Effects of Development Control on Housing Opportunities for Black Households in Baltimore County, Maryland: A Report to the U.S. Commission on Civil Rights," U.S. Commission on Civil Rights Hearing Held in Baltimore, Maryland, August 17–19, 1970, Exhibits Entered Into the Hearing Record, 724–725.

39   **Cockburn described the world as** Bruce Cockburn, "Broken Wheel," *Inner City Front*, True North Productions, © 1981 Golden Mountain Music Corp. (SOCAN), http://brucecockburn.com/discography/inner-city-front.

39   *The God Who Is There* Francis Schaeffer, *The God Who Is There* (Westmont, IL: Intervarsity Press, 1968).

40   **can't be a true Christian without** John Gerstner, "Reformation: The Impact of Revival," audio recording of lecture presented to the Philadelphia Conference on Reformed Theology, April 1982, Alliance of Confessing Evangelicals, mp3.

41   **little church** "Minutes from July 10, 2008 meeting," Baltimore County Landmarks Preservation Commission, 3, http://kingsville-md.us/docs/LPCMinutes/2008 /071008minutes.pdf.

41   **historic railroad town** Lauren Loricchio, "Relay's History Topic of Talk at Arbutus Senior Center," *Baltimore Sun*, August 20, 2014, www.baltimoresun.com /news/maryland/baltimore-county/arbutus-lansdowne/ph-at-history-of-relay-0820 -20140820-story.html.

42   **four-lane highway** Patrick J. LaForge, "Dryness Speeds Job on Route 24 Bypass," *Baltimore Sun*, August 17, 1986, 294.

42   **in 1946** John and Vera May Perkins Foundation Legacy Timeline, https://docs .google.com/spreadsheets/d/16sstm6FDIskez-v4xTh58m0LUO3vS0d1rUVa5S7Akgk /edit#gid=0.

42   **marshal had roughed up** Philip Yancey, "Mississippi Ambush," *Campus Life* 32:10 (May 1975); also, Electronic Army Serial Number Merged File, ca. 1938–1946 (Enlistment Records), World War II Army Enlistment Records, created 6/1/2002 - 9/30/2002, documenting the period ca. 1938–1946, National Archives and Records Administration, Office of Records Services—Washington, DC. Modern Records Programs, Electronic and Special Media Records Services Division.

42   **ordained** "Biography of Dr. John M. Perkins," http://boazandruth.com/friendly .cfm/topic/perkins.

42   **social ministry** Charles Marsh, *Beloved Community: How Faith Shapes Social Justice from the Civil Rights Movement to Today* (New York: Basic Books, 2005), 167.

43   **Then they'll listen** Marsh, 154.

43   **specter of white hatred** Yancey, "Mississippi Ambush."

43   **inaction of white Christians** In his 1976 autobiography, *Let Justice Roll Down*, Perkins wrote, "It's the system, the whole structure of economic and social cages that have neatly boxed the black man in so that 'nice' people can join the oppression

without getting their hands dirty—just by letting things run along." John M. Perkins, *Let Justice Roll Down* (Grand Rapids, MI: Baker Books, 1976).

43   **other emerging black leaders** Philip Yancey, *Soul Survivor: How Thirteen Unlikely Mentors Helped My Faith Survive the Church* (New York: Galilee, 2001); also, Yancey, "Mississippi Ambush."

43   **washed my hatred away** Yancey, "Mississippi Ambush."

43   **In 1972** "Biography of Dr. John M. Perkins," http://boazandruth.com/friendly .cfm/topic/perkins; also, Yancey, "Mississippi Ambush."

44   *With Justice for All* John Perkins, *With Justice for All: A Strategy for Community Development* (Grand Rapids, MI: Baker Books, 1982), 88.

44   **pamphlet** Stephen E. Berk, "From Proclamation to Community: The Work of John Perkins," *Transformation* 6:4 (1989).

44   **in 1984** Marsh, *Beloved Community*, 190.

46   **sawed-off shotgun** Mark Bomster, "Fear vs. the Schools; A Violent Few Keep the 'Good Kids' from Learning; Can the System Create a Climate Free of Menace?" Series: Bright Faces, Fading Dreams. Second in a series, *Baltimore Sun*, June 8, 1992, 1A.

46   **stabbed** Michael Fletcher, "Cleaning Woman Slain at Calverton School," *Baltimore Sun*, November 1, 1992, 2B.

46   **ranked 194th** Joan Jacobson, "Targeted Schools Question State's Aim: School Reform Controversy," *Baltimore Sun*, February 2, 1995, 17A.

46   **a "dumping ground"** Bomster, "Fear vs. the Schools," 1A.

46   **state superintendent of schools ordered** Jacobson, "Targeted Schools."

47   **turned over** Jacobson.

47   **killed the girl** Peter Hermann and Robert Hilson Jr., "Girl, 12, Is Shot and Killed; 18-year-old Man Charged," *Baltimore Sun*, December 3, 1994, 1A.

48   **school Nicole was zoned to attend** Liz Bowie, "Taking Back a School; Order: The Principal at Frederick Douglass High School Uses Discipline and Shared Responsibility to Keep Her Students Under Control," *Baltimore Sun*, December 3, 1997, 1A.

48   **offering to sell her** According to Melinda Smith's recollection.

48   **social club** Brittany Britto, "Over a Century Old, Arch Social Club Preserves Particular Vision of Black Masculinity," *Baltimore Sun*, April 15, 2016, www .baltimoresun.com/features/bs-ae-arch-social-club-20160414-story.html.

49   **average at the time** "National Average Contract Mortgage Rate History for the Purchase of Previously Occupied Homes," Federal Housing Finance Agency, www .fhfa.gov/DataTools/Downloads/Pages/National-Average-Contract-Mortgage-Rate -History.aspx#2017.

49   *Rich Christians* Ronald Sider, *Rich Christians in an Age of Hunger* (Nashville, TN: Thomas Nelson, 1978).

49   **won an award** "Belmar Homes Wins 4 Design Awards," *Baltimore Sun*, April 5, 1987, 26.

50   **nearly all-black neighborhood** "Map: Black Population by Census Tract (as a percent of all persons), Baltimore City, 1990 Census," University of Baltimore, Baltimore Regional Studies Archives, Citizens Planning and Housing Association Records, Programs 1940–2009, Housing 1940–2008.

51 **showed up** Wayne Gordon and John M. Perkins with Randall Frame, *Making Neighborhoods Whole: A Handbook for Christian Community Development* (Downers Grove, IL: IVP Books, 2013), 34–35; also, Pamela Toussaint, "CCDA's Beginnings," *Christian Community Development Association* (blog), September 14, 2010, http://web.archive.org/web/20160913064514/http://www.ccda.org/blog/12-blog/138-ccdas -beginnings; also, "CCDA's Beginnings," *Christian Community Development Association* (blog), September 13, 2011, https://ccda.org/ccdas-beginnings.

51 **first annual conference** Mark R. Gornik and Noel Castellanos, "How to Start a Christian Community Development Ministry," in *Restoring At-Risk Communities: Doing It Together and Doing It Right*, John M. Perkins, ed. (Grand Rapids, MI: Baker Books, 1995); also, Toussaint, "CCDA's Beginnings."

52 **Sandtown's population** Edward Gunts, "Home Sweet First Home: How the Enterprise Foundation Is Helping the Working Poor Buy Homes and Save Their Neighborhoods in the Process," *Baltimore Sun*, July 21, 1991, 9; also, Guy Gugliotta, "Rebuilding a Community from the Ground Up," *Baltimore Sun*, January 4, 1993; also, Stefanie DeLuca and Peter Rosenblatt, "Sandtown-Winchester—Baltimore's Daring Experiment in Urban Renewal: 20 Years Later, What Are the Lessons Learned?," *The Abell Report* 26:8 (November 2013); also, "An Economic Model for the Transformation of Sandtown, Summary Report," The Enterprise Foundation, 1996; also, Katie Gunther, "Vacant House Ills Tied to Small Owners: Most Are Not Out-of-towners," *Baltimore Sun*, July 31, 1983, B1; also, Prudence Brown, Benjamin Butler, and Ralph Hamilton, "The Sandtown-Winchester Neighborhood Transformation Initiative: Lessons Learned About Community Building and Implementation," The Annie E. Casey Foundation and The Enterprise Foundation, 2001; also, Edward G. Goetz, "Sandtown-Winchester, Baltimore: Housing as Community Development," in *Affordable Housing and Urban Redevelopment in the United States: Learning from Failure and Success*, ed. Willem van Vliet (London: Sage Publications, 1996).

52 **many families remained** Gunts, "Home Sweet First Home."

52 **when African Americans of all professions** "Black History's Future on Pennsylvania Avenue," *Maryland Morning with Sheilah Kast*, WYPR-FM, Baltimore, MD, February 28, 2011, https://mdmorn.wordpress.com/2011/02/28/0228112; also, Reginald Fields, "At 83, 'Shoe Shine King' Still Polishing His Craft: King's Still Shining After a Long, Polished Career," *Baltimore Sun*, February 18, 2003, http://articles .baltimoresun.com/2003-02-18/news/0302180010_1_shine-craig-works-butch; also, James Brown, *Pure Dynamite!* (recorded at Royal Theater, Baltimore), © 1964 Universal Japan; also, Sidney Levy, "Lost City: Baltimore's Grand Theatres," *Underbelly*, Maryland Historical Society, April 14, 2016, www.mdhs.org/underbelly/2016/04/14 /lost-city-baltimores-grand-theatres; also, Otis Williams with Patricia Romanowski, *Temptations* (New York: Cooper Square Press, 1988), 66.

52 **accepted him** Mark R. Gornik, *To Live in Peace: Biblical Faith and the Changing Inner City* (Grand Rapids, MI: William B. Eerdmans Publishing Company, 2002).

52 **In 1989** Gornik; also, Mark Gornik, personal communication, May 19, 2018.

52 **threw his support behind** Gornik, *To Live in Peace*.

52 **the dedication** Drew Bailey, "Church Dedication Merges Cultures," *Baltimore Evening Sun*, November 12, 1990.

53 **1886** Gornik, *To Live in Peace*; also, S.M. Khalid, "Neighborhood Celebrates New Use for Old Convent," *Baltimore Sun*, November 12, 1990, 2D.

53   **convent for the Sisters of Mercy** *The Catholic Church in the United States of America, Vol. III* (New York: The Catholic Editing Company, 1914), 66.

53   **community** Gornik, *To Live in Peace*; also, Khalid, "Neighborhood Celebrates"; also, Bailey, "Church Dedication."

53   **Nehemiah** Audrey Haar, "Nehemiah Homes Attract Eager First-time Buyers," *Baltimore Sun*, April 28, 1991, http://articles.baltimoresun.com/1991-04-28/business /1991118169_1_nehemiah-mortgage-houses-in-baltimore.

53   **Schmoke told the crowd** Khalid, "Neighborhood Celebrates."

53   **money was there** Brown, Butler, and Hamilton, "The Sandtown-Winchester Neighborhood Transformation Initiative."

53   **Enterprise Foundation document** "An Economic Model for the Transformation of Sandtown, Summary Report," The Enterprise Foundation, 1996.

54   **the cover** Olsen, *Better Places, Better Lives*, 1; also, *Time*, August 24, 1981.

54   **downtown Baltimore's metamorphosis** My mother had a cousin named Rusty who knew some of the captains in the inner harbor. When she was young, Rusty would take her along for dinner with the captains. The wharf, she confirms, was smelly. "Your mileage may vary" on how "telegenic" it is these days. Mary Elise Lanahan, a.k.a., "Mom," personal communication.

      Rouse overcame significant opposition to get Harborplace built. The project, which planned to snatch up one of the few parcels of open space left along the Inner Harbor, was controversial enough to land on the 1978 ballot. The support of an important alliance of religious leaders brought out the black vote for Harborplace, and a *Baltimore Afro-American* post-election survey found that "black Baltimoreans were more enthusiastic about the Harborplace concept than any other single voting bloc." The overall vote was 58 percent in favor. Olsen, 285–286; also, "Harborplace," *Baltimore Afro-American*, November 11, 1978, 4; also, C. Fraser Smith, "Voters O.K. Waterfront Pavilions: Binding Arbitration for Firemen Backed by Nearly 2 to 1," *Baltimore Sun*, November 8, 1978, A1.

54   **African Americans voted for** "Harborplace," *Afro*; also, Smith.

54   **Rouse resolved to help house the poor** Olsen, *Better Places, Better Lives*, 298.

54   **Enterprise Foundation** Olsen, 297–300.

54   **Reagan administration task force** Olsen, 310.

54   **"depreciation"** Olsen, 322–323.

54   **Rouse packaged** Olsen, 323–324.

55   **bill included** Olsen, 324–325; also, David E. Rosenbaum, "A Tax Bill for the Textbooks," *New York Times*, October 23, 1986, D16, www.nytimes.com/1986/10/23 /business/tax-reform-act-1986-measure-came-together-tax-bill-for-textbooks.html.

55   **permission to enforce** Olsen, 341–342.

55   **never fully got off the ground** Olsen, 342–343.

55   **solve all the problems** Olsen, 350.

55   **self-sufficient community** Gunts, "Home Sweet First Home." Schmoke says someone at the Baltimore Jewish Council told him about the project.

55 **transform Sandtown** Olsen, *Better Places, Better Lives*, 351–352.

56 **overall goals** Diana A. Meyer, Jennifer L. Blake, Henrique Caine, and Beth Williams Pryor, "Community Building in Partnership, Baltimore, MD," in *On the Ground with Comprehensive Community Initiatives*, ed. Diana A. Meyer (The Enterprise Foundation, 2000); also, Harold McDougall, *Black Baltimore: A New Theory of Community* (Philadelphia: Temple University Press, 1993); also, Goetz, "Sandtown-Winchester, Baltimore: Housing as Community Development"; also, "An Economic Model for the Transformation of Sandtown, Summary Report," The Enterprise Foundation, 1996.

56 **added 227 homes** James Bock, "Hard Part Still Ahead for 'Urban Lab' Sandtown: Hope on the Horizon," *Baltimore Sun*, November 23, 1993, 1A.

56 **modernization program brought** Tania Baker, spokesperson for Housing Authority of Baltimore City, email to author, November 9, 2015.

56 **Habitat for Humanity's campaign** James Bock, "Reclamation Battle Line Drawn in W. Baltimore," *Baltimore Sun*, March 27, 1992, 1A.

56 **Community Building in Partnership** Bock, "Hard Part Still Ahead"; also, James Bock, "Sandtown Blueprint Drafted; Big Changes for Better Foreseen," *Baltimore Sun*, May 9, 1993, 1B; also, Barry Yeoman, "Left Behind in Sandtown," *City Limits*, January 1, 1998, https://citylimits.org/1998/01/01/left-behind-in-sandtown; also, McDougall, *Black Baltimore*.

56 **employed neighborhood residents** Meyer, Blake, Caine, and Pryor, "Community Building in Partnership, Baltimore, MD"; also, Goetz, "Sandtown-Winchester, Baltimore: Housing as Community Development."

56 **public-private partnership** Gornik, *To Live in Peace*; also, Brown, Butler, and Hamilton, "The Sandtown-Winchester Neighborhood Transformation Initiative."

56 **daycare center** Brown, Butler, and Hamilton, 19, 41.

56 **"place-based" campaign** Bock, "Hard Part Still Ahead."

57 **number of vacant units** "Notes from meeting with Housing Authority on Vacant Units," December 31, 1992, Citizens Planning and Housing Association (CPHA) Records.

57 **federal modernization funds becoming available** Michael J. Kelly to Thomas Hobbs, letter, January 4, 1990, CPHA Records; also, "Housing Authority of Baltimore City's Four Family High-Rise Developments."

57 **what to do** Kelly to Hobbs, letter, January 4, 1990; also, "The Housing Authority of Baltimore City's Four Family High-Rise Developments," December 1, 1989 (updated February 1990), CPHA Records.

57 **consider** Kelly to Hobbs, letter, January 4, 1990; also, "Housing Authority of Baltimore City's Four Family High-Rise Developments."

57 **"ring of absurdity"** "Minutes of the Family High-Rise Modernization Task Force, Baltimore City Housing Authority," March 23, 1990, CPHA Records.

57 **stopped short of recommending demolition** Ginger Thompson, "Getting Rid of High-rise Projects?" *Baltimore Sun*, December 2, 1990, 1D.

57 **how to get families out** "Demolishing the High-rises," *Baltimore Sun*, December 28, 1991, A6.

57   **one-for-one replacement** Michael H. Schill and Susan M. Wachter, "The Spatial Bias of Federal Housing Law and Policy: Concentrated Poverty in Urban America," *University of Pennsylvania Law Review* 143 (1985), 1285–1342.

57   **funding for new construction** Joan Jacobson, "Crime-ridden High-rises on City's Demolition List; 5 New Low-rises Would Replace Them," *Baltimore Sun*, January 22, 1992, D1.

57   **use modernization money for new** Thompson, "Getting Rid of High-rise Projects?"

57   **a new agenda** "Strategy for Public High-rises for Families, Draft #2," Citizens Planning and Housing Association Housing Committee," January 14, 1992, CPHA Records.

58   **January 1992** Hathaway Ferebee to Citizens Housing and Planning Association Executive Committee, memo, January 13, 1992, CPHA Records.

58   **two-story apartments** Jacobson, "Crime-ridden High-rises."

58   **collaborate** "Minutes of Meeting with HABC Staff February 21, 1992," February 25, 1992, CPHA Records.

58   **252 units that required replacements** "Public Housing Meeting Minutes," April 30, 1992, CPHA Records.

58   *Gautreaux* Alex Polikoff, *Waiting for Gautreaux: A Story of Segregation, Housing, and the Black Ghetto* (Evanston, IL: Northwestern University Press, 2006), 48.

58   **blocked attempts** Polikoff, 30.

58   **more projects in black neighborhoods** Polikoff, 46.

58   **group of public interest lawyers** Polikoff, xv.

58   **thirty-nine-year-old named Alex Polikoff** Polikoff, 7, 23.

58   **claimed a violation** Polikoff, 48–49.

58   **filed a complaint in federal court** Polikoff, 48.

58   **special Section 8 certificates** Polikoff, 231. When the *Gautreaux* remedy launched, Section 8 certificates were valid only within the jurisdiction of the housing authority that distributed them.

58   **7,100 families** Polikoff, 243–244.

58   **gains** Polikoff, 250.

59   **opened in 1942** HABC, "Celebrating 75 Years!"

59   **Fairfield Homes** Martin C. Evans, "Fairfield Tenants Face Move out of Danger Area," *Baltimore Sun*, January 31, 1988, 1B; also, David Brown, "Life in Wagners Point: Cut Off but Happy," *Baltimore Sun*, December 26, 1982, B1; also, John Schidlovsky, "Old Fairfield Worries About Community's Future," *Baltimore Sun*, October 29, 1979, C1; also, Joe Mathews, "City Quietly Begins Buyout in Fairfield; Chemical Companies and Government Make Competing Offers," *Baltimore Sun*, June 23, 1999, 3B; also, David Brown, "Neighbors in Hawkins Point Get Together One Last Time," *Baltimore Sun*, August 15, 1982, C1; also, Philip Diamond, "An Environmental History of Fairfield/Wagner Point," University of Baltimore School of Law, 1998; also, Joe Mathews, "Goodbye to Wagner's Point," *Baltimore Sun*, April 1, 1999, 1A; also, Heather Dewar and Joe Mathews, "Residents Want Out of Industrial Ghetto," *Baltimore Sun*, April 19, 1998, 1A; also, Martin C. Evans, "Fairfield Tenants Face Move out of Danger Area," *Baltimore Sun*, January 31, 1988, 1B.

59   **three more years before** Amended and Class Action Complaint, *Thompson v. HUD* (D. Md. 1995).

59   **She argued instead** Barbara Samuels to Vera Hall, letter, March 25, 1992, CPHA Records.

59   **grant to fund** Citizens Planning and Housing Association, "Ensuring Opportunities for Public Housing Families: A Proposal to the Abell Foundation," May 1, 1992, CPHA Records.

59   **continued to pressure the city** Hathaway Ferebee to Juanita Harris, January 31, 1992, CPHA Records; also, Hathaway Ferebee to Juanita Harris, February 26, 1992, CPHA Records; also, Jane Conover to Vera Hall, March 25, 1992, CPHA Records; also, Hathaway Ferebee to Maxine Saunders, March 31, 1992, CPHA Records; also, "Public Housing Meeting Minutes," Citizens Planning and Housing Association, April 29, 1992, CPHA Records; also, Hathaway Ferebee and Jane Conover to Carol Beck, June 3, 1993, CPHA Records; also, Hathaway Ferebee and Jane Conover, Invitation to "A New Look at Public Housing," City Series Forum, May 19, 1992, CPHA Records.

59   **forged connections** Ferebee and Conover, Invitation; Hathaway Ferebee to Juanita Harris, July 2, 1992, CPHA Records.

59   **spoke about Moving to Opportunity** Hathaway Ferebee and Jane Conover, Invitation to "A New Look at Public Housing," City Series Forum, May 19, 1992, CPHA Records.

59   **helped craft the legislative language** Polikoff, 262.

59   **housing authority staffer committed to apply** Hathaway Ferebee and Jane Conover to Daniel Henson, June 11, 1993, CPHA Records.

60   **had yet to create any** Robert W. Hearn to Joseph G. Schiff, September 8, 1992, ACLU–Maryland Records, Plaintiff's Exhibit 310.

60   **plans to convert a former public school** Robert W. Hearn to Joseph G. Schiff, September 8, 1992, ACLU–Maryland Records, Plaintiff's Exhibit 310.

60   **smaller proportion of minority population** Declaration of William D. Tamburrino, *Thompson v. HUD* (D. Md. 1995), December 5, 2001.

60   **the flier** "City wants to build 'High Rise Projects' in HIGHLANDTOWN!!," ACLU–Maryland Records, Local Defendant's Exhibit 423.

60   **meeting ended quickly** Jacqueline Watts, "School #47 Housing Proposal Roundly Rejected," *East Baltimore Guide*, August 13, 1992, 1, 3.

60   **asked HUD to waive** Eric Siegel, "Move Is Focus of Public Housing Case," *Baltimore Sun*, December 14, 2003, http://articles.baltimoresun.com/2003-12-14/news /0312140241_1_public-housing-housing-residents-city-officials.

60   **"Whether we like it or not"** Robert W. Hearn to Joseph G. Schiff, September 8, 1992, ACLU–Maryland Records, Plaintiff's Exhibit 310. Hearn said he would "continue to pursue" non-impacted sites.

60   **replace the Canton plans** Memorandum from Michael A. Smerconish to Joseph G. Schiff, "Fairfield Homes Replacement Housing, Baltimore, Maryland," October 27, 1992, ACLU–Maryland Records, Plaintiff's Exhibit 311.

61   **CPHA wrote** "Jane M. Conover to Carol Beck, November 2, 1992, CPHA Records."

61   **Conover invited** Jane M. Conover to Carol Beck, November 2, 1992, CPHA Records; also, Jane Conover to Barbara Samuels, December 28, 1992, CPHA Records.

62   **residential patterns** A *New York Times* data mapping project provides a stunning visual of the racial divides along individual streets like York Road: "Mapping America: Every City, Every Block," *New York Times*, data from U.S. Census, American Community Survey 2005–2009, www.nytimes.com/projects/census/2010 /explorer.html.

62   **write up proposals** "Second Quarter Abell Foundation Report," February 2, 1993, CPHA Records.

62   **Hearn announced the closure** Housing Authority of Baltimore City, "Executive Director Hearn Announces New Strategy for Fixing-Up a Public Housing Development, Lexington Terrace to Undergo $500,000 Restoration," press release, January 1993, CPHA Records.

62   **Conover fired off a memo** Jane Conover to Joyce Knox, January 14, 1993, CPHA Records.

62   **livid** Melody Simmons, "Many Shun High-rise Vacancies; Families Repelled by Vandalism, Crime," *Baltimore Sun*, January 13, 1993, http://articles.baltimoresun .com/1993-01-13/news/1993013035_1_housing-authority-public-housing -demolition.

62   **might be ignoring** Simmons.

62   **Complaints** Melody Simmons, "No Teary Goodbyes as Tenants Leave Building 734," *Baltimore Sun*, March 19, 1993, 1C.

62   **stuck in an elevator** Simmons, "No Teary Goodbyes."

62   **Schmoke replaced** DeWayne Wickham, "Baltimore: Where Black Politicians Got In On Urban Renewal," *Black Enterprise* (August 1978); also, Michael A. Fletcher, "Housing Commissioner Operates by His rules; Blunt, Savvy Henson Rejuvenates Agency," *Baltimore Sun*, October 3, 1993, 1B; also, Laura Lippman, "City's 'Mother Teresa' Fails on Finances," *Baltimore Sun*, May 29, 1994, 1B.

62   **Henson and Schmoke invited** "Memorandum from Daniel P. Henson, III to Elizabeth Wright," November 9, 1993, CPHA Records.

62   **archival document** Housing Authority of Baltimore City (HABC), Division of Public Relations, Research and Special Studies, "Effects of the Post-War Program on Negro Housing," September 25, 1945, ACLU–Maryland Records, Plaintiff's Exhibit 113.

63   **"substandard"** Cleveland R. Bealmear, Housing Authority of Baltimore City, "Post-War Housing Program for Baltimore: General Statement," January 1944, ACLU–Maryland Records, Plaintiff's Exhibit 112.

63   **"pay a profitable rent"** HABC, "Effects of the Post-War Program on Negro Housing."

63   **"important causes of blight"** HABC.

63   **"the major cause"** HABC.

64   **"shoot or poison the slum dweller"** "Bealmear, 'Post-War Housing Program for Baltimore.'"

64   **filed *Walker v. HUD***   Daniel and Beshara, P.C., "Walker v. HUD," www
.danielbesharalawfirm.com/walker-v-hud.

64   **"evidence of past and present purposeful racial segregation"**   Elizabeth K.
Julian and Michael M. Daniel, "Separate and Unequal: The Root and Branch of Public
Housing Segregation," *Clearinghouse Review* (October 1989), 670.

64   **"Now is the time"**   Hathaway Ferebee and Jane Conover to Daniel Henson,
June 11, 1993, CPHA Records.

64   **leaned heavily on housing mobility**   "Initial Proposal to the Replacement
Housing Task Force: Results of discussions between residents of Lafayette Courts and
housing advocates representing ACLU, Baltimore Neighborhoods, Inc., Community
Law Center, and CPHA," July 1993, CPHA Records.

64   **application to the Abell Foundation**   Stuart Comstock-Gay, Susan Goering,
"Proposal to the Abell Foundation for Funding to Prepare the Legal Basis for Ensuring
Residential Choice for the City's Public Housing Residents," American Civil Liberties
Union of Maryland, June 1, 1993, CPHA Records. Daniel Henson had taken an interest
in *Gautreaux* early in his tenure and even invited Alex Polikoff to town. He believed any
such program would need to be done under cover of a court order, and he was willing
to be a "friendly defendant." But he was also skeptical. When Polikoff came to town,
Henson got the sense that Polikoff had been making a living from *Gautreaux* for two
decades, and he suspected fair housing lawyers in Baltimore of seeing the prospect of a
similar court battle as a potential golden goose. Henson also believed integration efforts
would prove elusive; in his experience in the Baltimore area, when black people moved
in, white people moved out. Daniel Henson, personal communication, May 7, 2018; also,
Declaration of Daniel Henson, *Thompson v. HUD* (D. Md. 1995).

65   **plan to demolish**   Melody Simmons, "HUD to Help Replace City High-rise
Projects, State Contribution Spurs U.S. Aid," *Baltimore Sun*, October 13, 1993, 1A;
also, Eric Siegel and Melody Simmons, "State, City Worked Together to Develop
Housing Plan," *Baltimore Sun*, October 14, 1993, 1B; also, "CPHA Options for Public
Housing," October 1993, CPHA Records. The state and city funding was subject to
legislative approval, and the city would have to compete for the HUD dollars, but
if the money came through, it would go toward demolition of Flag House Courts,
Lafayette Courts, Murphy Homes, and Lexington Terrace, as well as construction of
low-rise units on the same sites. Only 60 percent of the units would be replaced on site,
so the Housing Authority would use some of the funding to settle hundreds of families somewhere else. HUD funding for replacement units—about $17 million—would
require placement in non-impacted areas, but the $71 million in state and city money
was likely to be used only within the city.

65   **The day after**   Barbara Samuels, email message to author, October 11, 2016.

65   **a draft**   "Memorandum from Daniel P. Henson III to Elizabeth Wright,"
November 9, 1993, CPHA Records.

65   **Hathaway Ferebee and Jane Conover wrote back**   Hathaway Ferebee and Jane
Conover to Daniel P. Henson III, letter, November 12, 1993, CPHA Records.

65   **They got to work**   Barbara Samuels and Susan Goering to Roberta Achtenberg,
November 16, 1993, CPHA Records; also, Melody Simmons, "Public Housing Resident
to Join Board Governing City Agency," *Baltimore Sun*, April 13, 1993, 12B; also, "Members of the Citizens Task Force on Metropolitan Housing Agreement," CPHA Records.

65 **"statement of purpose"** Citizens Task Force on Metropolitan Housing, "Statement of Purpose," November 1993, CPHA Records; also, Citizens Task Force on Metropolitan Housing, "Draft Agenda" and "Presentation on Recent Developments," November 19, 1993, CPHA Records.

65 **Lafayette Courts demolition and rebuilding plan** Michael A. Fletcher, "Rebuilding Public Housing Project," *Baltimore Sun*, December 4, 1993, 1B.

65 **They floated criteria** Citizens Task Force on Metropolitan Housing, Meeting notes: December 6, 1993, and January 10, January 26, and February 16, 1994, CPHA Records.

65 **city had less than two months** Citizens Task Force on Metropolitan Housing, Meeting notes, February 16, 1994, CPHA Records.

65 **proposed Fairfield replacement sites** "Fairfield Replacement Housing," Baltimore ACLU–Maryland Records, Plaintiff's Exhibit 282.

65 **passed it on** Citizens Task Force on Metropolitan Housing, Meeting notes, February 16, 1994, CPHA Records.

66 **"non-minority" sites** Memorandum, "Inhouse Site Analysis—Fairfield," from Harold S. Jackson to Candace S. Simms, ACLU–Maryland Records, Plaintiff's Exhibit 285.

66 **"impacted" sites** "Fairfield Replacement Housing," ACLU–Maryland Records, Plaintiff's Exhibit 282.

66 **criteria** Citizens Task Force on Metropolitan Housing, Meeting notes: January 26, February 16, and March 16, 1994, CPHA Records.

66 **Given the barriers** Citizens Task Force on Metropolitan Housing, Meeting notes, January 26 and February 16, 1994, CPHA Records.

66 **Notes from the meeting** Citizens Task Force on Metropolitan Housing, Meeting notes, February 16, 1994, CPHA Records. Henson says metropolitan replacements had his blessing, and that it would have been county officials, not him, who would have found it challenging to place subsidized housing in "non-impacted" areas. He'd learned from his own experience in the few non-impacted areas within city borders. Henson says he had staff look for apartments to buy in places like Mt. Washington, but developers didn't want to sell to the housing authority. Daniel Henson, personal communication, May 7, 2018.

66 **letter to Mayor Schmoke** Hathaway Ferebee and Matthews Wright to Kurt Schmoke, March 17, 1994, CPHA Records.

66 **voted at a May 1994 meeting** Citizens Task Force on Metropolitan Housing, Meeting notes, January 26 and May 12, 1994, CPHA Records. Twelve days later, the housing authority produced a draft of a revised replacement policy. Little had changed. Housing Authority of Baltimore City, "Replacement Housing Policy: Draft for Discussion Purposes Only," May 25, 1994, CPHA Records.

67 **task force planned** Citizens Task Force on Metropolitan Housing, Meeting notes, January 26 and June 29, 1994, CPHA Records.

67 **"HEAR US SHOUT"** Xavier de Souza Briggs, Susan J. Popkin, and John Goering, *Moving to Opportunity: The Story of an American Experiment to Fight Ghetto Poverty* (New York: Oxford University Press, 2010), 61.

67 **flier went up** Ed Brandt, "Scare Tactics Bring Down Federal Housing Program," *Baltimore Sun*, October 30, 1994, 1B.

67   **between 1980 and 1990** Briggs, Popkin, and Goering, *Moving to Opportunity*, 61; also, Polikoff, *Waiting for Gautreaux*, 265.

67   **opened in 1976** HABC, "Celebrating 75 Years!"

67   **city applied** Citizens Task Force on Metropolitan Housing, "Statement of Purpose," November 1993, CPHA Records; also, Citizens Task Force on Metropolitan Housing, "Draft Agenda" and "Presentation on Recent Developments," November 19, 1993, CPHA Records.

67   **state legislator got his hands on** Ed Brandt, "Scare Tactics Bring Down Federal Housing Program," *Baltimore Sun*, October 30, 1994, 1B.

67   **passing the documents around** Larry Carson, "Dundalk Councilman Won't Seek Re-election," *Baltimore Sun*, February 2, 1994, 4B.

67   **HUD chose Baltimore** Ed Brandt, "City's Poor to Get Help Relocating," *Baltimore Sun*, June 13, 1994, 1B.

68   **opposition quickly mounted** Larry Carson and Pat Gilbert, "Plan to Relocate Families from Inner City Fuels Fears," *Baltimore Sun*, July 31, 1994, 1B.

68   **their own flier** Citizens Task Force on Metropolitan Housing, Meeting minutes: April 27, 1994, CPHA Records.

68   **"What is the grand agenda?"** Brandt, "Scare Tactics."

68   **primary election** Larry Carson, "Balto. Co.'s 7th Council District: DePazzo vs. Political Novice Jung," *Baltimore Sun*, August 17, 1994, 2B.

68   **"must be taught to bathe"** Larry Carson and Pat Gilbert, "Plan to Relocate Families from Inner City Fuels Fears," *Baltimore Sun*, July 31, 1994, 1B.

68   **where opposition was loudest** Briggs, Popkin, and Goering, *Moving to Opportunity*, 62.

68   **Moving to Opportunity families** Michael A. Fletcher, "Mikulski, Champion of Liberal Causes, Led Fight to Kill MTO," *Baltimore Sun*, September 25, 1994, 4E.

68   **"free-for-all"** Carson and Gilbert, "Plan to Relocate Families."

68   **ambitious "longer term" strategies** Citizens Task Force on Metropolitan Housing, "Position Paper on Providing Metropolitan Housing Choices for Residents of Public Housing," June 1, 1994, CPHA Records.

69   **the end of Moving to Opportunity** Fletcher, "Mikulski, Champion of Liberal Causes."

69   **Mikulski claimed** Brandt, "Scare Tactics."

69   **announced** JoAnna Daemmrich, "6 Public High-rises to Be Demolished," *Baltimore Sun*, December 21, 1994, 1B.

69   **new 196-unit building** Tanya Jones, "Lafayette High-rises to Be Replaced," *Baltimore Sun*, October 22, 1994.

69   **class action complaint** Class Action Complaint, *Thompson v. HUD* (D. Md. 1995).

69   ***Carmen Thompson et al. v. U.S. Department of Housing and Urban Development et al.*** *Thompson v. HUD*, 348 F. Supp. 2d 398 (D. Md. 2005); also, James Bock, "'Apartheid, Baltimore Style' City Housing Suit and History of Bias," *Baltimore Sun*, February 5, 1995.

69   **the complaint read** Class Action Complaint, *Thompson v. HUD*.

Two: In Search of Home

71   **logged 321 murders** Michael James, "A Deadly Year on the Streets of Balti-more: Drugs, Violence, and Death," *Baltimore Sun*, January 8, 1995, http://articles.baltimoresun.com/1995-01-08/news/1995008010_1_violence-baltimore-slayings.

71   **city had handed over** Mark Bomster, "Minn. Firm to Run 9 City Public Schools: Move Called Bid to Improve System," *Baltimore Sun*, June 10, 1992, 1A.

72   **New Song Academy** Eric Siegel, "Small School's Big Successes; Education: New Song Academy, Chosen Yesterday to Join the Public System, Rewrites the Tradi-tional Rules to Teach Its 25 Students," *Baltimore Sun*, January 24, 1997, 1A.

72   **attended New Song Academy year-round** Brown, Butler, and Hamilton, "The Sandtown-Winchester Neighborhood Transformation Initiative."

72   **school was run** Prudence Brown and Leila Fiester, "New Song Academy," Annie E. Casey Foundation, 2003.

73   **health center** Gornik, *To Live in Peace.*

73   **"church planting"** Presbyterian Church in America, Mission to North Amer-ica, "Church Planting," https://pcamna.org/church-planting.

73   **didn't allow women to preach** Sarah Eekhoff Zylstra, "PCA Goes Back to Where It Started: Women's Ordination," *Christianity Today*, June 28, 2016, www.christianitytoday.com/news/2016/june/pca-goes-back-to-where-it-started-womens-ordination.html.

73   **stated objective of Community Building in Partnership** McDougall, *Black Baltimore*, 150.

74   **major source of tension** Susan Middaugh and Prentice Bowsher, *Sandtown-Winchester: Managing Large-Scale Housing Developments* (Columbia, MD: The Enter-prise Foundation, Inc., 1997–2002).

74   **under pressure** McDougall, *Black Baltimore*, 154–155.

74   **"blueprint"** James Bock, "Sandtown Blueprint Drafted; Big Changes for Better Foreseen," *Baltimore Sun*, May 9, 1993, 1B.

74   **started to fall behind** McDougall, *Black Baltimore*, 153.

74   **"urban lab"** Bock, "Hard Part Still Ahead."

75   **$60 million** Bock, "Hard Part Still Ahead."

75   **$100 million** Eric Siegel, "Mayor Picks Hitchcock as the $100 Million Man," *Baltimore Sun*, January 6, 1995, A1.

75   **By 1995** Brown, Butler, and Hamilton, "The Sandtown-Winchester Neighbor-hood Transformation Initiative."

75   **Call to Commitment** Elizabeth O'Connor, *Call to Commitment: The Story of the Church of the Saviour, Washington, D.C.* (New York: Harper and Row, 1963).

75   **Church of the Saviour** Lily Percy, "Pastor, Mentor and Social Activist: Remem-bering Gordon Cosby," *All Things Considered*, National Public Radio, April 14, 2013, www.npr.org/2013/04/14/177218091/pastor-mentor-and-social-activist-remembering-gordon-cosby; also, Church of the Saviour, "Origins," http://inwardoutward.org/origins.

75   **Community development** Olsen, *Better Places, Better Lives*, 172.

76 **article about Costigan's departure** James Bock, "Revival Project's Guard Changes; N.Y. Transit Official to Run Sandtown Effort," *Baltimore Sun*, August 5, 1996, 1B.

76 **Gornik announced his departure** James Bock, "For 9 Years, Clergyman Enriches Poor Neighborhood, Shining 'Light'; Departing Minister Helped Sandtown to Achieve a Vision," *Baltimore Sun*, November 27, 1995.

76 **land in between** Phillip McGowan, "Putting a Face on a Center's Fight Against Addiction; Mosaic Mural Illustrates One Woman's Success," *Baltimore Sun*, September 29, 2003, 3B.

76 **at New Song Academy** Eric Siegel, "Small School's Big Successes; Education: New Song Academy, Chosen Yesterday to Join the Public System, Rewrites the Traditional Rules to Teach Its 25 Students," *Baltimore Sun*, January 24, 1997, 1A.

76 **joined the city's public school system** Jean Thompson, "City Looks to Privatize 9 Schools; Nonprofits' Plans for Management Due for Approval Today; In Search of Improvement; Chosen Operators Will Take Control Starting in September," *Baltimore Sun*, January 23, 1997, 1A; also, Siegel; also, Lincoln Taylor, "Rallying Around the New Schools; Public-private Effort Scrambling to Get Ready for Year's First Bell," *Baltimore Sun*, August 9, 1997, 2B; also, Brown and Fiester, "New Song Academy."

77 **Harris remained on the board** Jim Haner, "Last Resort Rends Lives; Homes: The Thousands of Evictions Ordered Each Year in Baltimore Are Anything but Routine to the Tenants," *Baltimore Sun*, May 27, 1999, 1B.

77 **groundbreaking** Douglas Birch, "Mayor Begins to Make Rounds; Groundbreaking for Center, Temple Visit Part of His Full Day," *Baltimore Sun*, December 12, 1999, 1B.

77 **lent his expertise** Zach Sparks, "Pastor Wins Award for Efforts to Restore City," *Baltimore Sun*, May 27, 2013, A2.

77 **mayor of Baltimore picked up a golden shovel** Birch, "Mayor Begins to Make Rounds."

79 **zoned school** Liz Bowie, "Taking Back a School; Order: The Principal at Frederick Douglass High School Uses Discipline and Shared Responsibility to Keep Her Students Under Control," *Baltimore Sun*, December 3, 1997, 1A.

79 **more flight than integration** Howell S. Baum, *"Brown" in Baltimore: School Desegregation and the Limits of Liberalism* (Ithaca, NY: Cornell University Press, 2010).

79 **only constitutional if** Howell Baum and Ray Winbush, "The Lines Between Us, Episode 42: *Brown v. Board*'s Legacy," *Maryland Morning with Sheilah Kast*, WYPR 88.1 FM, July 26, 2013.

79 **that was that** Baum, *"Brown" in Baltimore*.

79 **factors that limit educational opportunity** Gary Orfield, John Kucsera, and Genevieve Siegel-Hawley, "E Pluribus . . . Separation Deepening, Double Segregation for More Students," The Civil Rights Project, Harvard University, September 2012.

79 **highest degree of racial isolation** Erica Frankenberg and Chungmei Lee, "Race in American Public Schools: Rapidly Resegregating School Districts," The Civil Rights Project, Harvard University, August 2002.

80   **African Americans who later came to prominence** United States Department of the Interior, National Park Service, National Register of Historic Places registration form, "Frederick Douglass High School," July 1989.

80   **pained its distinguished alumni** Gary Gately, "Douglass Troubles Cloud Anniversary; Alumni Recall Past Glories, Offer Help to Students," *Baltimore Sun*, October 29, 1993, 1A.

80   **closed it for two days** Gately, "Douglass to Close."

80   **possible takeover** Gary Gately, "2 Schools Targeted for State Takeover," *Baltimore Sun*, January 8, 1994, 1A.

80   **new principal** Gary Gately, "Principal Readies Ultimatum for Troublemakers," *Baltimore Sun*, March 7, 1994, 1B.

80   **state backed off** Gary Gately, "State Won't Take Control of Douglass High," *Baltimore Sun*, April 20, 1994, 1A.

80   **series of lawsuits** Jean Thompson, "In Schools Case, Unlikely Partners; 3 Merged Lawsuits Unite Two Judges with Formidable Strengths," *Baltimore Sun*, November 11, 1996, 1B.

80   **threatened** JoAnna Daemmrich and John Rivera, "Baltimore Is Told to Reform 35 Schools or Turn Them Over; Schmoke Negotiating with State Officials over Final List," *Baltimore Sun*, January 24, 1996, 1A.

80   **withholding $24 million in state aid** "IT WAS NOT a Good Legislative Session in Annapolis For," *Baltimore Sun*, April 20, 1996, 10A.

80   **dispute** Saunders, "Settling Without 'Settling.'"

80   **rallied** Marilyn McCraven, "Rally Organizers Say State's Bid to Reform City Schools Will Fail; 14 Groups to Sponsor Protest on Sept. 19 at Douglass High School," *Baltimore Sun*, September 10, 1996, 3B.

80   **Maryland has never funded** John Rivera, "200 at City Rally Protest Possible School Takeover; Leaders Also Seek Release of Withheld $30 Million," *Baltimore Sun*, September 20, 1996, 3B.

81   **settlement** Saunders, "Settling Without 'Settling.'"

81   **three former guards** Scott Wilson, "Ex-Nation of Islam Guards Working at Douglass High; 3 Hired as Mentors, Monitors at City School," *Baltimore Sun*, February 3, 1996, 1B.

81   **Backus-Davis's tenure** Bowie, "Taking Back a School."

81   **earned plaudits** Bowie.

83   **West Virginia State** Samuel Speciale, "WV State University Marks 125 Years," *Charleston Gazette-Mail*, March 15, 2016, www.wvgazettemail.com/news/education/wv-state-university-marks-years/article_2a24d5c4-d751-593a-9c9d-3e2604c0eeb0.html; also, West Virginia State University, "Our History Runs Deep," www.wvstateu.edu/About/History-and-Traditions.aspx; also, Shereen Marisol Meraji, "The Whitest Historically Black College in America," *Morning Edition*, National Public Radio, October 18, 2013, www.npr.org/sections/codeswitch/2013/10/18/236345546/the-whitest-historically-black-college-in-america.

85   **he shot someone half a block up** "Evangelical Movement Targets Poverty," *Al Jazeera America*, April 16, 2015, http://america.aljazeera.com/watch/shows/live-news/2015/4/evangelical-movement-targets-poverty.html.

86 **June 2000** Sandtown Habitat for Humanity newsletter, Spring 2000, 1.

88 **candidates** Tim Craig, "Housing Case May Hamper Ehrlich," *Baltimore Sun*, July 22, 2002; also, Robert L. Ehrlich Jr. to Henry G. Cisneros, October 27, 1995, Robert L. Ehrlich Jr. Collection for Public Leadership Studies, Towson University.

88 **November 1994** Adam Clymer, "The 1994 Elections: Congress, the Overview; G.O.P. Celebrates Its Sweep to Power," *New York Times*, November 10, 1994, 1A.

89 **"abolish HUD tomorrow"** Kenneth J. Cooper, "Gingrich Pledges Major Package of Spending Cuts Early Next Year," *Washington Post*, December 13, 1994, www.washingtonpost.com/archive/politics/1994/12/13/gingrich-pledges-major -package-of-spending-cuts-early-next-year/bba4244a-6494-4d73-8aa6-9591a83825a6.

89 **the motion** Motion for preliminary injunction, March 24, 1995, *Thompson v. HUD* (D. Md. 1995); also, Michael James, "ACLU Seeks to Stop Plan for Housing," *Baltimore Sun*, March 25, 1995, http://articles.baltimoresun.com/1995-03-25/news /1995084040_1_public-housing-housing-opportunities-housing-officials.

89 **Census tracts** U.S. Census Bureau, "Geographic Terms and Concepts—Census Tract," www.census.gov/geo/reference/gtc/gtc_ct.html.

89 **second motion for injunction** Motion for preliminary injunction, June 13, 1995, *Thompson v. HUD* (D. Md. 1995).

89 **demolition of the high-rises** JoAnna Daemmrich, "Lafayette Courts Ends in 20 Seconds of Explosions, Cheers, Tears," *Baltimore Sun*, August 20, 1995.

89 **pile of rubble** "Largest US High Rise Estate Is Demolished," *Associated Press TV*, August 19, 1995, www.aparchive.com/metadata/youtube/3a04a44e710df72afe1d 01e0dfa8bfa4.

91 **wasn't easy to find** Robin E. Smith, "Housing Choice for HOPE VI Relocatees: Final Report," The Urban Institute, Washington, DC, April 2002.

91 **hardly any were leaving the city** Daniel P. Henson III, to Ed Rutkowski, June 24, 1996, CPHA Archives.

91 **pressure built on the agency to stop the flow** Michael Olesker, "Couple Tapes Collapse of Neighborhood," *Baltimore Sun*, April 18, 1996, 1B; also, Jim Haner, "Poverty Surges Are Called Common Citywide Problem, Civic Groups, Officials Say," *Baltimore Sun*, November 29, 1995.

91 **neighborhood leaders blamed** Robert C. Embry, Jr., to Daniel P. Henson, November 8, 1995, CPHA Archives.

91 **O'Malley wrote** Martin O'Malley to Daniel Henson, November 2, 1995, ACLU–Maryland Records, Plaintiff's Exhibit 611. In an incredible marriage of brevity and insolence, O'Malley concluded the letter, "Thank you for reading this. Please shock me with a response."

91 **mostly defined the terms of a settlement** Elizabeth K. Julian to Nelson A. Diaz, June 12, 1996, CPHA Archives.

92 **article** JoAnna Daemmrich, "Public Housing Suit Tentatively Settled; City–ACLU Accord Would Give Thousand Rental Certificates," *Baltimore Sun*, October 13, 1995.

92 **Ruppersberger** Patrick Gilbert and Will Englund, "HUD Urged to Kill Plan for Housing; Cardin, Ehrlich Join Balt. County's Protest of City Suit Settlement," *Baltimore Sun*, October 14, 1995.

92   **hired a Washington, DC, law firm** John Mercurio, "Baltimore County Fights Housing Plan," *Baltimore Times*, October 26, 1995, A1.

92   **might pursue litigation** Gilbert and Englund, "HUD Urged to Kill Plan."

92   **now had to present** Larry Carson, "Housing Battle May Land in Court; County, ACLU Still Far Apart on Relocating Families," *Baltimore Sun*, November 18, 1995.

92   **his own county had** Anthony W. McCarthy, "City, Baltimore County at Odds over Housing," *Baltimore Afro-American*, October 28, 1995, A1.

92   **met in the Maryland state capital** Larry Carson, "County Talks Tough in Housing Battle; Legal Weapons Ready, Ruppersberger Says," *Baltimore Sun*, December 7, 1995.

92   **law journal article** Julian and Daniel, "Separate and Unequal: The Root and Branch of Public Housing Segregation."

92   **limiting the ages of children** Marina Sarris, "Cisneros Won't Halt Shift of City Poor; HUD Chief Envisions Screening, Counseling Those Leaving Projects," *Baltimore Sun*, December 2, 1995.

92   **made some concessions** Larry Carson, "Housing Talks Resume amid Confusion; Baltimore County Says Issue Isn't Settled; City Says It Is," *Baltimore Sun*, December 14, 1995; also, Larry Carson, "Ruppersberger Shows He Can Play Tough, Too," *Baltimore Sun*, December 15, 1995.

93   **U.S. Department of Justice for review** JoAnna Daemmrich and Eric Siegel, "Baltimore County to Get Fewer Poor; Federal Officials, City, ACLU Revise Bias Suit Settlement," *Baltimore Sun*, December 13, 1995.

93   **mobility counseling** James Bock, "City to Get $300 Million for Housing," *Baltimore Sun*, April 8, 1996, 1A.

93   **benefited from the firepower** In particular, Barbara considered attorneys Don Verrilli and Susan Podolsky integral to the negotiations.

93   **HUD promised** Bock, "City to Get $300 Million."

93   **"partial consent decree"** The decree was "partial" because it covered only claims related to Fairfield Homes and the four high-rise projects. Claims regarding HABC's other low-rise projects remained open to litigation.

93   **non-impacted areas** Non-impacted indicates a low minority population and a relative dearth of subsidized housing.

94   **outside of Baltimore City** Partial consent decree, April 8, 1996, *Thompson v. HUD* (D. Md. 1995); also, Bock, "City to get $300 million."

94   **reserved the right** Partial consent decree, *Thompson v. HUD*, 47–48.

94   **surrounding counties expressed acceptance** Larry Carson, "Baltimore County Says It Won Better Deal in Housing Bias Suit; Court Intervention Could Have Cost Millions," *Baltimore Sun*, April 10, 1996, 4B.

94   **keep trying to defund** Bock, "City to Get $300 Million."

94   **op-ed** Robert L. Ehrlich, "Rep. Ehrlich Explains His Position," *Baltimore Sun*, April 25, 1996, 22A.

94   **"Communities of opportunity and hope"** "Public Housing Renewal," C-SPAN, July 27, 1996, www.c-span.org/video/?73976-1/public-housing-renewal.

94 **demolition began on Fairfield Homes** Marilyn McCraven, "City Begins Demolishing Huge Fairfield Homes Public Housing Complex; Workers Clearing Site for Use by Light Industry," *Baltimore Sun*, January 26, 1997, 3B.

94 **relocate its residents** Martin C. Evans, "Fairfield Tenants Face Move out of Danger Area," *Baltimore Sun*, January 31, 1988, 1B.

94 **demolition of Murphy Homes** Sarah Pekkanen and Zerline A. Hughes, "After 36 Years, a Pile of Memories; Murphy Homes High-rises, Once Home to Hundreds, Imploded in W. Baltimore," *Baltimore Sun*, July 4, 1999.

94 **Flag House Courts** Local defendants' amended report under section 14.2 of the Partial Consent Decree: 1/1/00 to 6/30/00, *Thompson v. HUD* (D. Md. 1995).

95 **housing authority signed a contract** Local defendants' amended report under section 14.2 of the Partial Consent Decree: 7/1/98 to 12/31/98, August 13, 1997, *Thompson v. HUD* (D. Md. 1995).

95 **thought the certificates were useless** Declaration of Daniel Henson, *Thompson v. HUD* (D. Md. 1995).

95 **At the end of 1998** Local defendants' amended report under section 14.2 of the Partial Consent Decree: 7/1/98 to 12/31/98, August 13, 1997, *Thompson v. HUD* (D. Md. 1995).

95 **only sixty-seven families had been awarded certificates** Local defendants' amended report under section 14.2 of the Partial Consent Decree: 1/1/99 to 6/30/99, *Thompson v. HUD* (D. Md. 1995).

95 **actions of the plaintiffs' counsel** This is plain in the docket for *Thompson v. HUD*. I went through all of the hard copy filings on file at the U.S. District Courthouse in Baltimore.

95 **Martin O'Malley** Douglas Birch, "Mayor Begins to Make Rounds," *Baltimore Sun*, December 12, 1999, 1B.

95 **would not reappoint Henson** Gerard Shields, "O'Malley Appoints Housing Commissioner; Patricia Payne Served in State Cabinet; Wants to Increase Homeownership," *Baltimore Sun*, February 2, 2000, 3B.

96 **They handed her** Mary Otto, "Public Housing Strategy Riles Baltimore Neighbors," *Washington Post*, November 9, 2000, www.washingtonpost.com/archive/politics/2000/11/09/public-housing-strategy-riles-baltimore-neighbors/c4851d93-196f-4825-9f85-fcbc98109b10 .

96 **Dixon pushed the housing authority** Gerard Shields, "City's Plan on Housing Is Attacked; ACLU Lawsuit Result to Put Poor Residents into Neighborhoods," *Baltimore Sun*, September 21, 2000, 1B.

96 **residents** M. Dion Thompson and Gerard Shields, "O'Malley Pledges to Seek New Plan for Housing Poor; Mayor Quiets Crowd Irate over Proposal for Neighborhoods," *Baltimore Sun*, October 4, 2000, 1A.

96 **meeting for October 2** Otto, "Public Housing Strategy Riles."

96 **crowding at the front door** "Videotape of newscasts relating to the 40 Hamilton units," ACLU–Maryland Records, Plaintiff's Exhibit 412, 6:10.

96 **demanding entry** Gerard Shields, "Public Housing Meeting Canceled; Size of Crowd Forces Police to Reschedule at Larger Hamilton Site," *Baltimore Sun*, October 3, 2000, 1B.

96 **"not gonna endanger the safety"** "Videotape of newscasts," 6:19.

96 **man in a floppy fishing hat** "Videotape of newscasts," 9:20, 0:55.

96 **"that's what we moved away from"** "Videotape of newscasts," 2:10.

97 **"Let! Us! In!"** "Videotape of newscasts," 23:49.

97 **mostly white crowd** Plaintiffs' Reply to Defendants' Oppositions to Motion for Finding of Violations of Partial Consent Decree and for Relief and Memorandum in Support of Motion to Show Cause, March 10, 2004, 27, *Thompson v. HUD* (D. Md. 1995).

97 **fanned their faces with signs** "Videotape of newscasts."

97 **glum-looking group** "Videotape of newscasts," 19:57.

97 **crowd roared** "Videotape of newscasts," 22:15.

97 **she placidly noted** Todd Richissin, "Advocate for Poor Stays Her Course; Relocation Foes Miss Point, She Says," *Baltimore Sun*, October 6, 2000, 1B.

97 **crime and "drug families"** Otto, "Public Housing Strategy Riles."

97 **"a mistake"** "Videotape of newscasts," 15:59.

97 **he told the crowd, grasping** "Videotape of newscasts," 21:02.

97 **resignation** Shields and Thompson, "City's Housing Director to Resign," 1A.

97 **October 11 meeting** "Northeast Baltimore Group: Notes from 10/11/00 meeting," NEGN Files.

98 **he had already begun backtracking** Eric Siegel, "City's Plan for Housing Is Revised; New Approach Aims to Help the Poor Buy Middle-class Homes," *Baltimore Sun*, January 7, 2001, 1B.

98 **Some had witnessed** Email message, Leslie F. Miller to Jeff Sattler, August 21, 2002, NEGN Files.

99 **getting by with old kitchen cabinets** Michael Anft, "Poor Relations: In Northeast Baltimore, Neighbors Divide Over the Prospect of Public Housing," *Baltimore City Paper*, December 13, 2000.

99 **the proposal** Caroline Queale to Martin O'Malley, "Northeast Good Neighbors: Proposal for 40 Homes for Public Housing Families in Non-Traditional Areas of Baltimore City," July 23, 2001, NEGN Files.

99 **Graziano wrote to Queale** Paul T. Graziano to Caroline Queale, August 21, 2001, ACLU–Maryland Records, Plaintiff's Exhibit 514.

99 **deadline** Eric Siegel, "City Selects Housing Sites; Decree Calls for 40 Units Outside Poor Areas," *Baltimore Sun*, August 16, 2002, 1B.

99 **summer of 2002** Plaintiffs' Reply to Defendants' Oppositions to Motion for Finding of Violations of Partial Consent Decree and for Relief and Memorandum in Support of Motion to Show Cause, May 10, 2004, *Thompson v. HUD* (D. Md. 1995).

99 **picked twelve addresses** Siegel, "City Selects Housing Sites."

99 **couldn't meet the goals** Housing Authority of Baltimore City, "5 Year Plan for Fiscal Years 2000–2004; Annual Plan for Fiscal Year 2000"; also, Local defendants' amended report under section 14.2 of the Partial Consent Decree: 1/1/00 to 6/30/00, *Carmen Thompson v. HUD* (D. Md. 1995).

99 **HABC had terminated** Local defendants' amended report under section 14.2 of the Partial Consent Decree: 7/1/00 to 6/30/01, *Thompson v. HUD* (D. Md. 1995).

100 **"extremely slow"** Plaintiffs' Reply to Defendants' Oppositions to Motion for Finding of Violations of Partial Consent Decree and for Relief and Memorandum in Support of Motion to Show Cause, May 10, 2004, *Thompson v. HUD* (D. Md. 1995).

100 **Garbis expressed disappointment** Marvin J. Garnis, October 7, 2002, *Thompson v. HUD* (D. Md. 1995).

100 **assigned the case** Marvin J. Garbis to James Bredar, May 25, 2001, *Thompson v. HUD* (D. Md. 1995).

100 **settlement conferences** James Bredar, January 28, 2003, *Thompson v. HUD* (D. Md. 1995).

100 **Bredar told the** *Baltimore Sun* Eric Siegel, "Trial Set on Segregation Claims Against City Housing Authority," *Baltimore Sun*, November 29, 2003, 1A.

Three: Crossing the Lines

101 **"so many things I've got to tell you"** Musiq Soulchild, "Love," Aijuswanaseing, The Island Def Jam Music Group, © 2000 Mercury Records Limited.

102 **concentrated in the city** Baltimore City Department of Housing and Community Development, "The City of Baltimore: Comprehensive Housing Affordability Strategy, 1994–1998," December 30, 1993, 3, 5.

102 **March 2001 audit** Daniel G. Temme to William D. Tamburrino, "Housing Authority of Baltimore City, Section 8 Certificate and Voucher Programs, Baltimore, Maryland, 2001-PH-1003," March 28, 2001, Washington, DC, Office of Inspector General, U.S. Department of Housing and Urban Development, ACLU–Maryland Records, Plaintiff's Exhibit 401.

102 **"barely functional"** Caitlin Francke, "Appeal for Housing Aid Stretches into 10 Years; Woman Is Stymied by Agency's Errors," *Baltimore Sun*, January 31, 2002, 1B.

102 **panic over the Y2K bug** "A Housing Mess on O'Malley's Steps; Computers Failed, Apartments Were Abandoned While City Went After Snazzy Projects," *Baltimore Sun*, May 7, 2000, 2C.

102 **vouchers sitting on the shelf** Temme to Tamburrino, "Housing Authority of Baltimore City, Section 8 Certificate and Voucher Programs."

102 **private rental market** Baltimore Metropolitan Council, "Baltimore Regional Fair Housing Action Plan 2002," ACLU–Maryland Records, Plaintiff's Exhibit 475.

102 **sending even more vouchers** Kurt Streeter, "City Will Aid Stranded Families; 8 Households Moving from Flag House, Broadway Projects," *Baltimore Sun*, June 21, 2000, 1B.

102 **Section 8–friendly landlords** Deirdre Shesgreen and Van Smith, "Blockbuster," *Baltimore City Paper*, April 5, 1995.

102 **two to four months** Tania Baker, spokesperson for Housing Authority of Baltimore City, email to author, October 8, 2018.

102 **only a few dozen families had moved** Temme to Tamburrino, "Housing Authority of Baltimore City, Section 8 Certificate and Voucher Programs."

102 **only increased to** Local defendants' report under section 14.2 of the Partial Consent Decree for the Period July 1, 2003 through June 30, 2004, August 16, 2004, *Thompson v. HUD.*

103 **scattered site houses** "Who Will House Baltimore's Poor? Housing Authority: Despite Long Waiting Lists, Half of 2,800 Scattered-site Public Housing Units Are Vacant," *Baltimore Sun,* November 24, 2001, 12A.

103 **tended to live scattered** Myron Orfield, "Racial Integration and Community Revitalization: Applying the Fair Housing Act to the Low Income Housing Tax Credit," *Vanderbilt Law Review,* 58:6 (2005); also, Henry G. Cisneros, "Regionalism: The New Geography of Opportunity," U.S. Department of Housing and Urban Development, Washington, DC, March 1995, 9, ACLU–Maryland Records, Plaintiff's Exhibit 152.

103 **biggest housing discrimination trial** Philip Tegeler, email message to author, March 31, 2017.

104 **heroin ring** Gail Gibson, "Leaders of Rap Label to Stand Trial Today; Duo Accused of Using Studio as Front in Drug Ring," *Baltimore Sun,* December 1, 2003, 3B.

104 **the judge said** ". . . with professionalism." Unless otherwise noted, quotations from the December 2003 *Thompson v. HUD* liability trial come from the transcript provided by the clerk's office at the U.S. District Courthouse in Baltimore. The format will be *date, transcript page number*; in this case, 12/1/03, at 4.

104 **"two kinds of claims"** 12/1/03, at 5.

104 **"Duties were established"** 12/1/03, at 6.

104 **"three interrelated tools"** 12/1/03, at 10.

104 **"litigate the past . . . Demographic changes and individual choices,"** 12/1/03, at 22–28.

105 **"make sure the record reflects . . . suffered through its own racial issues,"** 12/1/03, at 34–35.

106 **higher than the median sale price** Stefanie DeLuca and Peter Rosenblatt, "Sandtown-Winchester—Baltimore's Daring Experiment in Urban Renewal: 20 Years Later, What Are the Lessons Learned?", *The Abell Report* 26:8 (November 2013).

106 **"dollar house" program** Barbara Pash, "Two $1 Houses Become One Home," *Baltimore Sun,* September 19, 1982, SM42.

107 **spell the word "multicollinearity" out loud** 12/2/03 at 411.

107 **research reports** Karl Taeuber, "Public Housing and Racial Segregation in Baltimore," April 29, 2003, ACLU–Maryland Records, Plaintiff's Exhibit 2; also, Rolf Pendall, "The Ghettoization of HABC-Assisted Tenants in Baltimore City," April 21, 2003, ACLU–Maryland Records, Plaintiff's Exhibit 5.

107 **present-day effects** Lawrence Hurley, "Debate in Public Housing Trial Turns to Demographics," *The Daily Record,* December 3, 2003.

107 **the role of race** Eric Siegel, "Race Determined Housing Sites, Researcher Testifies; Predominantly Black Areas Targeted, Professor Says," *Baltimore Sun,* December 3, 2003, 3B.

107 **Barkoff asked Pendall** Siegel, 3B.

107 ***Making the Second Ghetto*** Arnold Hirsch, *Making the Second Ghetto: Race and Housing in Chicago, 1940–1960* (Chicago: University of Chicago Press, 1998).

107 **"Slum clearance, public housing"** Arnold Hirsch, "Public Policy and Residen-

tial Segregation in Baltimore, 1900–1968," May 3, 2003, ACLU–Maryland Records, Plaintiffs' Exhibit 3.

108 **report** Hirsch, "Public Policy and Residential Segregation."

108 **"It marks a turning point. . . 'more as privilege than a problem by each of you'"** 12/5/03, at 1103–1107.

108 **"Have you ever heard . . . Sondheim . . . Watts . . . civic figures"** 12/5/03, at 1136, 1140, 1141.

108 **"history's judgment"** 12/5/03, at 1147–1149.

109 **1101 N. Monroe Street** 12/9/03, at 1566.

109 **Bryant wept . . . Bryant replied** 12/9/03, at 1572.

110 **"Do you know . . . moved to Columbia"** 12/9/03, at 1576 to 1577.

110 **Ralph fondly remembered** 12/9/03, at 1580.

110 **Sandtown** In a prime example of what residents called "Smalltimore," Ralph Moore was on a list of witnesses that plaintiffs' counsel intended to call. Dana Petersen Moore had shrieked when she'd seen it. To the relief of his wife, plaintiffs never called Ralph Moore to the stand.

110 **"Would you like to see . . . vacant houses and lots"** 12/9/03, at 1583.

112 **"I guess the thumbnail sketch . . . system as applied"** 12/22/03, at 4383.

112 **"If the system in place . . . It's both"** 12/22/03, at 4403.

112 **"That was the position of the department . . . we had a responsibility to do something about it"** 12/1/03, at 152.

112 **"resolve cases"** 12/1/03, at 151.

112 **"defend the indefensible"** 12/1/03, at 157.

112 **direct examination** 12/4/03.

112 **Tamburrino threatened** Eric Siegel, "Housing Program May Face Takeover; City's Section 8 Rentals Have Deadline of June 30, HUD Official Says in Court," *Baltimore Sun*, December 5, 2003, 3B; also, 12/4/03, at 977 to 979.

113 **mismanaged waiting list** Lawrence Hurley, "Housing Policy Not Properly Implemented, Official Alleges at Trial," *The Daily Record*, December 5, 2003; also, 12/4/03, at 853 to 876.

113 **process for assigning tenants** Siegel, "Housing Program May Face Takeover," 3B; also, 12/4/03, at 853 to 876.

113 **He and his colleagues . . . unequivocally rejected the request** 12/4/03, at 897 to 912.

113 **"I perceived that that practice was not appropriate"** 12/4/03, at 984.

113 **she grilled him about HUD's oversight** 12/8/03, at 1255–1270.

113 **100 percent white** Hirsch, 67; also, Taeuber.

113 **east quadrant contained** Van Story Branch to R.C. Embry, Jr., October 16, 1968, ACLU–Maryland Records, Plaintiff's Exhibit 152.

113 **both of those projects remained** Taeuber, "Public Housing and Racial Segregation in Baltimore," T-4 1981.

113 **letter** Thomas R. Hobbs to Michael J. Kelly, June 30, 1981, ACLU-Maryland Records, Plaintiff's Exhibit 164.

113 **could have exacerbated segregation** 12/8/03, at 1258–1259.

114 **1989** Memorandum from Jack Kemp to All Regional Administrators - Regional Housing Commissioners, "Elimination of PHA Project and Locational Preferences," ACLU–Maryland Records, Plaintiff's Exhibit 46.

114 **1992** 12/8/03, at 1263.

114 **1995, 1997, and 2003** 12/8/03, at 1264–1271.

114 **Tamburrino made one qualification along the way** 12/8/03, at 1271.

115 **"give her another hand"** Nicole Smith, videotape of "DRU/Mondawmin Healthy Families Graduation Ceremony," June 24, 2005.

115 **Robert Fishman** Robert Fishman, "Public Housing Policy for Baltimore and the Nation, 1937–74," October 2003, ACLU–Maryland Records, Federal Defendant's Exhibit 590.

115 **"a better historian of Chicago"** 12/9/03, at 1609.

115 **"terrible weight"** 12/9/03, at 1603.

115 **like James Rouse's Baltimore Plan** 12/9/03, at 1656.

115 **"Baltimore is remarkable among American cities"** 12/9/03, at 1610.

115 **only 6 percent of public housing** 12/10/03 at 1766; also, Shelley Lapkoff, "Demographic Analysis of Baltimore and Its Federally-Assisted Housing," October 1, 2003, 29, ACLU–Maryland Records, Federal Defendant's Exhibit 591.

115 **at the time their sites were chosen** Lawrence Hurley, "HUD's Figures Paint a Different Picture of Baltimore's Housing Projects," *The Daily Record*, December 11, 2003.

116 **where the vacant houses were** Lapkoff, "Demographic Analysis," ii, 29.

116 **Rohe's report** William Rohe, "The Siting of Public Housing Developments in Baltimore," September 30, 2003, 19, ACLU–Maryland Records, Federal Defendant's Exhibit 592.

116 **Nothing the government did . . . "patterns that we see"** 12/17/03, at 3101.

117 **"Mr. Henson"** 12/17, at 3136–3137.

117 **first time he'd left West Baltimore** 12/23/03, at 4676.

117 **"Living around me"** 12/17, at 3163.

117 **"And I felt that in the mixed income environment"** 12/17, at 3164.

117 **"Does race play . . . building the house"** 12/17, at 3165.

118 **HOPE VI program** U.S. Department of Housing and Urban Development, "About HOPE VI," www.hud.gov/program_offices/public_indian_housing/programs/ph/hope6/about.

118 **the replacements** Local defendants' report under section 14.2 of the Partial Consent Decree for the Period July 1, 2005 through June 30, 2006, August 14, 2006, *Thompson v. HUD* (D. Md. 1995).

118 **"Was it possible" . . . economic diversity** 12/17 at 3165–3166.

118 **played up their witness's local roots** 12/18, at 3377–3378.

118 **City College High School** There are a couple of high schools called colleges around Baltimore because . . . well, because Baltimore has to make everything difficult.

118 **"And I understand . . . that's true"** 12/18, at 3377–3378

118 **"Did you have any intent" . . . parks or even new housing in their place?** 12/18, at 3399–3400.

118 **"viewed by the community"** 12/18 at 3404.

118 **Schmoke said he heard no racial animus expressed** 12/18, at 3421.

119 **"Is it a fair summary"** 12/18, at 3488.

119 **"net positive for the city"** 12/18, at 3490.

119 **Canton got a playground** 12/18, at 3489, 3401–3404.

119 **"Ridiculous"** 12/17, at 3203.

119 **"We thought doing"** 12/17, at 3284–3285.

119 **"the human infrastructure of a community"** 12/17, at 3190.

119 **"Poor people aren't stupid"** 12/17, at 3192.

119 **"What we were looking for was decent, safe housing for people"** 12/17, at 3178.

120 **solicited a proposal from Quadel** Local defendants' amended report under section 14.2 of the Partial Consent Decree: 7/1/00 to 6/30/01, *Thompson v. HUD* (D. Md. 1995).

120 **be allowed to administer** Local defendants' report under section 14.2 of the Partial Consent Decree: 7/1/01 to 6/30/02, *Thompson v. HUD* (D. Md. 1995).

120 **moved 586 families** Local defendants' report under section 14.2 of the Partial Consent Decree for the period July 1, 2005 through June 30, 2006, *Thompson v. HUD* (D. Md. 1995).

121 **helped James Rouse found** John E. Woodruff, "40 Years of Renewing a City," *Baltimore Sun*, January 12, 1995, http://articles.baltimoresun.com/1995-01-12 /business/1995012082_1_rouse-greater-baltimore-committee-revitalize -downtown.

121 **1955** Gary Gately, "Walter Sondheim Jr., 98, Leader in Baltimore Renewal, Dies," *New York Times*, February 16, 2007, www.nytimes.com/2007/02/16/us /16sondheim.html.

121 **ear of every mayor** "Walter Sondheim Sets Standard for Civic Duty," October 10, 1999, *Baltimore Sun*, http://articles.baltimoresun.com/1999-10-10/news/9910 -090363_1_sondheim-charles-center-public-housing.

121 **"consummate public servant"** Patrick A. McGuire, "The Consummate Public Servant," *Baltimore Sun*, August 6, 1989, SM14.

121 **chairman of the housing authority's board of commissioners** Walter Sondheim Jr., Papers, Additional Description, Biographical Note, Baltimore Regional Studies Archives, University of Baltimore, https://archivesspace.ubalt.edu/repositories /2/resources/110.

121 **service on the city's school board** "Walter Sondheim Sets Standard for Civic Duty," October 10, 1999, *Baltimore Sun*, http://articles.baltimoresun.com/1999-10-10/ news/9910090363_1_sondheim-charles-center-public-housing; also, Transcripts, 12/19, at 4079.

121 **this challenge** Aaron M. Glazer, "Course Correction," *Baltimore City Paper*, September 5, 2001; also, Roszel C. Thomsen, "The Integration of Baltimore's

Polytechnic Institute: A Reminiscence," *Maryland Historical Magazine* 79:3 (Fall 1984), 238; also, Transcripts, 12/19, at 4080.

121 **"The Urban League"** Transcripts, 12/19, at 4080, 4081.

121 **Judge Garbis pointed** Transcripts, 12/19, at 4080, 4081.

121 **a portrait** "Roszel C. Thomsen, United States District Judge, 1954–1992," United States District Court, District of Maryland, Historical Society, Portraits, "1931–1966," www.mdd.uscourts.gov/content/1931-1966.

121 **"There he is"** Transcripts, 12/19, at 4080, 4081.

121 **"Judge Thomsen was president"** 12/19, at 4081.

122 **voted to admit** Aaron M. Glazer, "Course Correction," *Baltimore City Paper*, September 5, 2001.

122 **very same week** Transcripts, 12/19 at 4082.

122 **Sondheim brought** Reginald Fields, "'Inherently Unequal,'" *Baltimore Sun*, May 16, 2004, www.baltimoresun.com/news/opinion/oped/bal-pe.md.history16may 16-story.html.

122 **June 3, 1954** "Board Votes Ban on Pupil Race Curbs: Negro, White Children to Attend Classes in Same Institutions," *Baltimore Sun*, June 4, 1954, 1.

122 **the Supreme Court ruling** Oliver L. Winston, "Desegregation Policy: An Address to All Employees of the Housing Authority of Baltimore City," June 30, 1954, ACLU–Maryland Records, Plaintiff's Exhibit 137.

122 **voted unanimously to desegregate** "Board Votes Ban on Pupil Race Curbs," 1.

122 **burned a cross on Sondheim's lawn** Transcripts, 12/19, at 4084.

122 **"One could say"** 12/19, at 4087; also helpful in this section was this long interview with Sondheim: "Reflections on *Brown*," *Inside Maryland Humanities* (Winter 2004), 4–9, http://msa.maryland.gov/megafile/msa/speccol/sc5300/sc5339/000113/002000 /002941/unrestricted/20052430e.pdf.

123 **"unusual"** 12/22/2003, at 4174.

123 **"free-swinging barroom kind of conversation"** 12/22/2003, at 4245.

123 **assumed the case would be appealed** 12/23/2003, at 4785.

123 **"some, but relatively little attention"** 12/22/2003, at 4222–4223.

123 **"the power and duty . . . within Baltimore City"** 12/22/2003, at 4233.

124 **statement of facts** Plaintiffs' statement of material facts submitted in support of their pre-trial memorandum, *Thompson v. HUD* (D. Md. 1995).

124 **"Do you understand, Ms. Samuels . . . wherever it is they should choose to live"** Transcripts, 12/22/2003, at 4238.

124 **"Her solution is [to] take money"** 12/22/2003, at 4241.

124 **The idea, Barbara countered, was balance** 12/22/2003, at 4247–4248.

124 **"We're going to move to the merits"** 12/22/2003, at 4249.

124 **Susan Podolsky started . . . Judge Garbis acceded** 12/22/2003, at 4254

124 **He also went for her throat . . . "are as follows"** 12/22/2003, at 4256–4259.

125 **Podolsky ticked off her list . . . sharpen their arguments** 12/22/2003, at 4259–4264.

125 **erection of the Hollander Ridge fence** 12/22/2003, at 4265.

126 **"I mean if you and the Rosedale people"** 12/22/2003, at 4281.

126 **"those projects were integrated"** 12/22/2003, at 4384.

126 **"The argument I think against you"** 12/22/2003, at 4391.

126 **"By the early 90s . . . caused you to finally wake up and do the right thing"** 12/22/2003, at 4392–4393.

126 **"3608 is a lot more wide open" . . .** HUD counsel fully admitted that the statute applied to them 12/23/2003, at 4735.

126 **"We believe the Supreme Court"** 12/23/2003, at 4769–4770.

127 **Susan Podolsky cited a long list of those sins** 12/23/2003, at 4746–4751.

127 **Subar argued . . . forced the city into over the waiting list** 12/23/2003, at 4752.

127 **Plaintiffs' counsel Chris Brown questioned** 12/23/2003, at 4777.

127 **Brown called for tightening up** 12/23/2003, at 4778.

127 **Subar implied** 12/23/2003, at 4779.

127 **qualified her for a voucher** Metropolitan Baltimore Quadel, "The Special Mobility Housing Choice Voucher Program," brochure.

128 **Maryland's list of "failing schools"** Walker Childs, "Local Schools Get Mixture in Test Results; 3 Dropped, 3 Added on List of Troubled Schools," *Baltimore Sun*, June 30, 2004, 1B.

128 **mortgage rates never went higher** "HSH's National Monthly Mortgage Statistics: 1986 to 2016," HSH.com, www.hsh.com/monthly-mortgage-rates.html.

129 **number of foreclosures in Maryland** "Foreclosure Prevention in Maryland Becomes More Urgent," *Maryland Morning with Sheilah Kast*, WYPR-FM, Baltimore, MD, January 25, 2010, https://mdmorn.wordpress.com/2010/01/25/foreclosure-prevention-in-maryland-becomes-more-urgent.

129 **court statement estimated** Maryland Judiciary Case Search, http://casesearch.courts.state.md.us/casesearch/inquiry-index.jsp.

129 **"All right . . . Thank you"** Transcripts, 12/23/2003, at 4784–4785.

129 ***Baltimore Sun* wrote** Michael Hill, "Decades After Injustices Were Exposed by the Civil Rights Movement, Sentiment Keeps Blacks and Whites Living Apart," *Baltimore Sun*, January 18, 2004, 1C.

130 ***Restoring At-Risk Communities*** John M. Perkins, *Restoring At-Risk Communities: Doing It Together and Doing It Right* (Grand Rapids, MI: Baker Books, 1995).

130 **Spencer Perkins** Spencer Perkins was the son who invited John Perkins to Sunday School in the late 1950s. He died of heart failure two years after the publication of *Restoring At-Risk Communities*.

130 **Rice was shocked** Perkins, *Restoring At-Risk Communities*, 115.

130 **"pretty reliable rule of thumb"** Perkins, 119.

130 **"'What a wonderful place!'"** Perkins, 127.

131 **"Thompson" had already earned a place alongside** Rhonda Y. Williams, "Race, Dismantling the 'Ghetto,' and National Housing Mobility: Considering the

Polikoff Proposal," *Northwestern Journal of Law & Social Policy* 1:1 (Summer 2006); also, Florence Wagman Roisman, "Long Overdue: Desegregation Litigation and Next Steps to End Discrimination and Segregation in the Public Housing and Section 8 Existing Source," *Cityscape* 4:3 (1999); also, Poverty & Race Research Action Council, "An Analysis of the *Thompson v. HUD* Decision," February 2005, Washington, DC.

131 **partial consent decree** Partial consent decree, April 8, 1996, *Thompson v. HUD* (D. Md. 1995), 1.

131 **short windows** *Thompson v. HUD*, 348 F. Supp. 2d 398 (D. Md. 2005), 8–9.

131 **racially neutral on their face** Just because a policy is racially neutral on its face doesn't mean that a policymaker hasn't successfully hidden an intent to discriminate. In fact, investigations by reporters like Nikole Hannah-Jones have ferreted out discriminatory intent in so-called neutral policies.

131 **future civil rights cases might lean** Philip Tegeler, email message to author, March 22, 2017.

132 **ruling** *Thompson v. HUD*, 348 F. Supp. 2d 398 (D. Md. 2005).

132 **"Plaintiffs have not proven"** "Baltimore Is Not 'A Container for All of the Poor of a Contiguous Region'—Excerpts from the Decision," *Baltimore Sun*, January 7, 2005, 10A.

132 **"But I think"** "Baltimore Is Not a Container."

132 **argued intent claims** Transcripts, 12/22/2003 at 4259–4264.

132 **become too overwhelmingly black** *Thompson v. HUD*, 348 F. Supp. 2d 398 (D. Md. 2005), 92–93.

133 **"Baltimore is a city"** *Thompson v. HUD*, 348 F. Supp. 2d 398 (D. Md. 2005), 132–133.

133 **Guilford and Mount Washington** *Thompson v. HUD*, 348 F. Supp. 2d 398 (D. Md. 2005), 108.

133 **selling off city-owned plots** *Thompson v. HUD*, 348 F. Supp. 2d 398 (D. Md. 2005), 95–96.

133 **even contribute to revitalization** *Thompson v. HUD*, 348 F. Supp. 2d 398 (D. Md. 2005), 97, 106–108, 135.

133 **Baltimore faced a "tension"** *Thompson v. HUD*, 348 F. Supp. 2d 398 (D. Md. 2005), 107.

133 **took "justified and acceptable measures to rectify"** *Thompson v. HUD*, 348 F. Supp. 2d 398 (D. Md. 2005), 103.

133 **CNNMoney.com headline** David Goldman, "Housing Prices to Free Fall in 2008–Merrill," *CNNMoney.com*, January 23, 2008, http://money.cnn.com/2008/01/23/real_estate/merrill_forecast/?postversion=2008012317.

134 **orientation** Lora Engdahl, *New Homes, New Neighborhoods, New Schools: A Progress Report on the Baltimore Housing Mobility Program*, Poverty and Race Research Action Council and Baltimore Regional Housing Campaign, October 2009.

134 **"Section 3608(e)(5)"** *Thompson v. HUD*, 348 F. Supp. 2d 398 (D. Md. 2005), 11.

134 **parameters of the "affirmatively further" duty** *Thompson v. HUD*, 348 F. Supp. 2d 398 (D. Md. 2005), 33; also, *Otero v. New York City housing Authority*, 484

F.2d 1122 (2d Cir. 1973); also, Lynette Rawlings, Margery Turner, and Susan J. Popkin, *Public Housing and the Legacy of Segregation* (Washington, DC: Urban Institute Press, 2009); also, Samuel Leiter and William M. Leiter, *Affirmative Action in Antidiscrimination Law and Policy: An Overview and Synthesis* (Albany, NY: SUNY Press, 2011).

135 **"island reservation for use as a container"** *Thompson v. HUD*, 348 F. Supp. 2d 398 (D. Md. 2005), 11.

135 **told the crowded courtroom** Eric Siegel, "Judge Criticizes Pooling Poor in City; Court Says HUD Violated Housing Law by Failing to Take a Regional Approach," *Baltimore Sun*, January 7, 2005, 1A.

135 **"effectively wearing blinders"** Lawrence Hurley, "Former Baltimore Mayor Welcomes Return to Regional Approach to Housing," *The Daily Record*, January 11, 2005.

135 **lived up to the affirmative duty** Doug Donovan, "From High-rise to 'A Heavenly Place' in Mount Washington; Transplanted Tenants," *Baltimore Sun*, January 7, 2005.

135 **failed to achieve significant desegregation** *Thompson v. HUD*, 348 F. Supp. 2d 398 (D. Md. 2005), 151.

135 **"'regional magnet'"** *Thompson v. HUD*, 348 F. Supp. 2d 398 (D. Md. 2005), 266.

135 **regionalization** *Thompson v. HUD*, 348 F. Supp. 2d 398 (D. Md. 2005), 151.

135 **"beyond the boundaries of Baltimore City"** *Thompson v. HUD*, 348 F. Supp. 2d 398 (D. Md. 2005), 152.

135 **"virtually no evidence"** *Thompson v. HUD*, 348 F. Supp. 2d 398 (D. Md. 2005), 155.

135 **left open the question** *Thompson v. HUD*, 348 F. Supp. 2d 398 (D. Md. 2005), 12, 102, 103, 123–124, 160. Garbis's ruling took as a premise that there was intentional discrimination before the open period. That meant that a finding of constitutional liability could hang on a failure during the open period to disestablish the harm from previous intent. Maryland at a Glance, 28.

135 **final score** *Thompson v. HUD*, 348 F. Supp. 2d 398 (D. Md. 2005), 10.

135 **First** *Thompson v. HUD*, 348 F. Supp. 2d 398 (D. Md. 2005), 123–124.

135 **Second** *Thompson v. HUD*, 348 F. Supp. 2d 398 (D. Md. 2005), 156.

135 **hope for a settlement** Donovan, "From High-rise to 'A heavenly place.'"

136 **tight and expensive housing market** *Thompson v. HUD*, 348 F. Supp. 2d 398 (D. Md. 2005), 119, 146, 147.

136 **Robert Ehrlich** In the 2002 election, Ehrlich took Howard County by a margin of 11 percentage points, Baltimore County by 23 points, Anne Arundel County by 30 points, Harford County by 49 points, and Carroll County by 59 points.

136 **"we're all together"** "Baltimore Is Not 'A Container.'"

136 **lawyers had some comments** This section comes from Gregory Countess, Sarah Glorian, Philip Tegeler, and Jonathan P. Hooks to Patricia Rynn Sylvester, letter, February 14, 2005.

137 **unemployment rate** Bureau of Labor Statistics, "Labor Force Statistics from the Current Population Survey," https://data.bls.gov/timeseries/LNS14000000; also, Federal Reserve Bank of St. Louis, Unemployment Rate in Maryland, https://fred .stlouisfed.org/series/MDUR.

Four: One Region, New Worlds

140 **newsletters** New Song Urban Ministries, newsletter, February 2005, May/June 2005.

140 **church's community work** New Song Urban Ministries, newsletter, Fall 2006.

140 **A newsletter entry** New Song Urban Ministries, newsletter, May/June 2005.

141 **"they would have done so"** Patrick M. Costigan, "A Comprehensive Approach to Rebuilding Poor Neighborhoods," *Georgia Academy Journal* 7:1 (Summer 1999), 16–24. Costigan listed accomplishments: the renovation of hundreds of vacant houses (and over 200 more built from scratch), a 19 percent drop in violent crime, the recruitment of 100 block captains, job placement or training for hundreds of residents, free primary health care, a decrease in infant mortality, referrals for treatment to 700 addicts, new management and fresh produce for a "dilapidated municipal market," the registration of 1,700 new voters, and the transformation of a vacant school into a community center.

141 **pour out grievances** Barry Yeoman, "Left Behind in Sandtown," *City Limits*, 1998, http://barryyeoman.com/1998/01/left-behind-in-sandtown-baltimore.

141 **Enterprise Homes continued building** Edward Gunts, "The Rowhouse Is Reborn in Sandtown," *Baltimore Sun*, October 15, 2000, http://articles.baltimoresun .com/2000-10-15/entertainment/0010230263_1_sandtown-rowhouse-development -team.

141 **just a $40,000 mortgage . . . people making 60 percent or less** Gunts; also, Chickie Grayson, personal communication.

141 **of around $50,000** Anne Arundel County, "GDP Background Report: Demographic and Economic Characteristics," January 2008, www.aacounty.org /departments/planning-and-zoning/long-range-planning/general-development -plan/forms-and-publications/GDP_Background_Demo.pdf; also, Center for Urban Environmental Research and Education and Maryland Institute for Policy Analysis Research, University of Maryland, Baltimore County, "The State of the Baltimore Region: A Baseline Report for a New Century," October 2002, https://cfpub.epa.gov /ncer_abstracts/index.cfm/fuseaction/display.files/fileID/13337.

141 **that number dropped** Community Building in Partnership, Inc., IRS Form 990, Return of Organization Exempt from Income Tax, accessed via Guidestar.org.

142 **real estate bubble** The axiomatic statement "Housing Prices Can Go Down" qualified to be a CNN headline in September 2005, and a CNN headline just two months later read "Home Price Increases May Have Flattened." [Note: the headlines in the text are as they appeared in Google News]. Les Christie, "Real Estate: When Booms Go Bust," September 19, 2005, CNNMoney.com, http://money.cnn.com/2005 /09/19/real_estate/buying_selling/price_declines/index.htm; also, Les Christie, "Outlook Sours for Real Estate," CNNMoney.com, November 15, 2005, http://money.cnn .com/2005/11/14/real_estate/buying_selling/prices_going_south/index.htm.

144 **homicides had jumped 14 percent** Lawrence Lanahan, "Secrets of the City," *Columbia Journalism Review*, January/February 2008, https://archives.cjr.org /cover_story/secrets_of_the_city.php.

145 **Perkins had helped spark** Longtime New Song leaders had also discussed such a project earlier.

145 **"own the pond"** New Song Community Church, "Economic Development," http://web.archive.org/web/20070626225933/http://www.nsc-church.org/Ownership .htm.

145 **New Song Worship and Arts Center** New Song converted this former Boys' Club building at 1601 N. Calhoun Street that the church had bought in 2001 for more worship and office space. By April 2007, church services had gotten so crowded there that worship moved into the New Song Academy's gymnasium in the new building at Presstman and Gilmor. New Song Community Church, "News Items," http://web.archive.org/web/20160215032829/http://nsc-church.org/events.htm; also, New Song Community Learning Center, "Welcome," http://web.archive.org/web /20080807163600/http://www.newsonglc.org/main.htm.

145 **Christian coffee shop** Georgia Pabst, "Church Finds Peace in Coffee," *Journal Sentinel*, September 13, 2008, http://archive.jsonline.com/entertainment/dining /32537969.html.

146 **balloons** My description of this scene comes from several interviews and a video recording, Steven Holloway, dir., *Stores of Hope*, 2011, New Song Urban Ministries, www.imdb.com/title/tt2137299/?ref_=nm_flmg_cin_6.

148 **shot him in the chest** Incident report, Baltimore Police Department.

150 **free and reduced-price meals** Maryland State Department of Education, "Howard County, Running Brook Elementary, Students Receiving Special Services," 2017 Maryland Report Card, http://reportcard.msde.maryland.gov/SpecialServices .aspx?PV=36:E:13:0515:3:N:0:14:1:1:1:1:1:3.

150 **94 percent of the students had qualified** Maryland State Department of Education, "Baltimore City, Westside Elementary, 1999 to 2011 Students Receiving Special Services for Elementary Students by Special Service," 2011 Maryland Report Card, http://msp2011.msde.state.md.us/SpecialServices.aspx?PV=36:E:30:0024:1:N:0:14:1:1 :1:1:1:1:3.

150 **students of all colors attended** Nicole Smith, "The Lines Between Us, Episode 5: Public Housing in Baltimore," *Maryland Morning with Sheilah Kast*, WYPR 88.1 FM, October 26, 2012, www.linesbetweenus.org/sites/linesbetweenus.org/files/audio /nicoles_story.mp3; also, transcript of fairness hearing before the honorable Marvin J. Garbis, United States Senior District Judge, November 20, 2012, *Thompson v. HUD* (D. Md. 1995), 39.

151 **nearly half of the 1,342** Local defendants' report under section 14.2 of the Partial Consent Decree for the Period July 1, 2005 through June 30, 2006, August 14, 2006, *Thompson v. HUD* (D. Md. 1995).

152 **nine thousand housing units materialize** Plaintiffs' proposed remedial order, May 31, 2006, *Thompson v. HUD* (D. Md. 1995). Units created under the partial consent decree counted toward this goal, but even with all of those in place, the proposed remedy called for over 6,700 new units.

152 **an index** Remedial Phase Expert Report Of john powell, August 19, 2005, *Thompson v. HUD* (D. Md. 1995). john a. powell was the executive director of Ohio State University's Kirwan Institute for the Study of Race and Ethnicity. According to the communications office at University of California Berkeley, powell uses the lowercase "in the belief that we should be 'part of the universe, not over it, as capitals signify.'"

152 **promised HUD an opportunity** *Thompson v. HUD*, 348 F. Supp. 2d 398 (D. Md. 2005).

152 **made a lengthy argument** Federal Defendants' post-trial reply brief, June 30, 2006, *Thompson v. HUD* (D. Md. 1995); also, Memorandum and order, January 10, 2006, *Thompson v. HUD* (D. Md. 1995).

152 **more affordable housing in "communities of high opportunity"** Michael Sarbanes, testimony, remedial trial, 457, 459, *Thompson v. HUD* (D. Md. 1995).

152 **Trudy McFall** In the 1970s, McFall ran a metropolitan subsidized housing program in the Twin Cities region that was hailed as a national model, then worked with Robert Embry at HUD. In the 1980s, she worked for the Community Development Administration, which handled Low-Income Housing Tax Credit applications for Maryland's housing department. In 1994, McFall cofounded a nonprofit development company called Homes for America. McFall also worked under contract for the Citizens Planning and Housing Association in the mid-1990s to identify rental opportunities for low-income families in the counties surrounding Baltimore City, and she testified during the liability trial in *Thompson v. HUD*. Ernest Holsendolph, "Minneapolis Area Begins Rent Plan," *New York Times*, November 23, 1975; also, "Solutions: Challenge Is Great, Solutions Difficult," *Star-Democrat*, December 28, 1984, 57.

152 **lobbied for inclusionary housing laws** Engdahl, *New Homes, New Neighborhoods, New Schools*.

153 **reduce prices** "Requirements for the Moderately Priced Housing Program," Executive Regulation 75-92, Montgomery County, Maryland; also, Aron Trombka, Michael Faden, Sonya Healy, Marlene Michaelson, Ralph Wilson, and Sally Roman, "Strengthening the Moderately Priced Dwelling Unit Program: A 30 Year Review, A Report to the Montgomery County Council on Future Program and Policy Options," February 2004.

153 **their units** In addition, the county's housing authority reserved the right to buy one-third of the discounted units for use as public housing.

153 **city and counties join forces** "Greater Baltimore Committee Weighs In on Segregation," *The Daily Record*, April 5, 2006.

153 **city council passed** Jill Rosen, "Affordable Housing Bill Passes; Developers Who Receive City Aid Must Provide Low-Cost Options," *Baltimore Sun*, June 12, 2007, 1A.

153 **required developments** *Baltimore City Code*, Article 13, § 2B (June 19, 2007). The law's 100 amendments were indicative of the compromises it took to get the bill passed. Under the law, the city would draw on an "Inclusionary Housing Offset Fund" to compensate developers for the cost of reducing rents. Rosen, "Affordable Housing Bill Passes."

153 **academic journal published a proposal** Alexander Polikoff, "Racial Inequality and the Black Ghetto," *Northwestern Journal of Law & Social Policy* 1:1 (Summer 2006).

153 **a response** Rhonda Y. Williams, "Race, Dismantling the 'Ghetto,' and National Housing Mobility: Considering the Polikoff Proposal," *Northwestern Journal of Law & Social Policy 1:1* (Summer 2006)

153 **Derided at first** Janet Stearns, "The Low-Income Housing Tax Credit: A Poor Solution to the Housing Crisis," *Yale Law & Policy Review* 6:1 (1998), 213.

153 **the tax credit had produced** Jill Khadduri, Larry Buron, and Ken Lam, "LIHTC and Mixed Income Housing: Enabling Families with Children to Live in Low Poverty Neighborhoods?," paper prepared for presentation at The Association of Public Policy and Management 26th Annual Research Conference, October 30, 2004.

153 **no other government program produced more** U.S. General Accounting Office, *Opportunities to Improve Oversight of the Low-Income Housing Program: Report to the Chairman, Committee on Ways and Means; and the Chairman, Subcommittee on Oversight, Committee on Ways and Means, House of Representatives*, Washington, DC: 1997.

153 **HUD report** Carissa Climaco, Meryl Finkel, Sandra Nolden, and Karen Rich, *Updating the Low Income Housing Tax Credit (LIHTC) Database: Projects Placed in Service Through 2002*, U.S. Department of Housing and Urban Development, Office of Policy Development and Research, December 2004.

154 **Roisman** Florence Wagman Roisman, "Mandates Unsatisfied: The Low Income Housing Tax Credit Program and the Civil Rights Laws," *University of Miami Law Review* 52 (1998).

154 **prohibiting landlords from denying** Low-income housing credit, 26 U.S. Code, § 42(h)(6)(B)(iv). Given the comparative reticence of suburban landlords to accept Section 8 vouchers, this provision makes LIHTC developments particularly valuable to mobility advocates.

154 **Orfield laid out the damage** Myron Orfield, "Racial Integration and Community Revitalization: Applying the Fair Housing Act to the Low Income Housing Tax Credit," *Vanderbilt Law Review*, 58:6 (2005).

154 **depleting home equity** "The American Middle Class Is Losing Ground: Wealth Gap Between Middle-income and Upper-income Families Reaches Record High," Pew Research Center, December 9, 2015, www.pewsocialtrends.org/2015/12/09/5-wealth-gap-between-middle-income-and-upper-income-families-reaches-record-high/.

154 **poor whites "live more dispersed"** Orfield, "Racial Integration."

154 **schools** David Rusk, author of a 1995 report on the shared destiny of Baltimore's urban and suburban communities called *Baltimore Unbound: A Strategy for Regional Renewal*, called this phenomenon a "segregation tax." David Rusk, "The 'Segregation Tax' The Cost of Racial Segregation to Black Homeowners," The Brookings Institution, Center on Urban & Metropolitan Policy, October 2001, www.brookings.edu/wp-content/uploads/2016/06/rusk.pdf.

154 **"virtually the only capital available"** Orfield, "Racial Integration."

154 **helped Section 8 families in Dallas** Michael M. Daniel and Laura B. Beshara to Commissioner of Internal Revenue, "Petition for rulemaking involving 26 C.F.R. § 1.42-17 Qualified Action Plan," March 12, 2008.

154 **perpetuation of racial segregation** Complaint, March 28, 2008, *Inclusive Communities Project, Inc., v. The Texas Department of Housing and Community Affairs* (N.D. Tex. 2008).

155 **two of the most seemingly straightforward sections** *Fair Housing Act of 1968*, 42 U.S. Code § 3604, 3605.

155 **3604(a) and 3605(a)** The former of those two passages makes it illegal to "refuse to sell or rent after the making of a bona fide offer, or to refuse to negotiate for the sale or rental of, or otherwise make unavailable or deny, a dwelling to any person because of race." The latter outlaws racial discrimination in any "residential real estate-related transactions."

155 **"history of deliberate segregation"** "MEMORANDUM OPINION–WALKER III: JOINDER OF THE CITY OF DALLAS AS A DEFENDANT SUBJECT TO THE CONSENT DECREE," August 4, 1989 (revised September 22, 1989), *Debra Walker, et al. v. U.S. Department of Housing and Urban Development, U.S. Department of Justice, et al.* (N.D. Tex.), https://law.justia.com/cases/federal/district-courts/FSupp/734/1289 /1461714.

155 **disproportionately harmed a protected class** "Implementation of the Fair Housing Act's Discriminatory Effects Standard," proposed rule, *Federal Register* 76, no. 221 (November 16, 2011): 70921–70922, www.federalregister.gov/documents /2011/11/16/2011-29515/implementation-of-the-fair-housing-acts-discriminatory -effects-standard; also, Lawrence Lanahan, "Who Gets to Live Where?: The Battle over Affordable Housing," *Al Jazeera America*, January 18, 2015, http://america .aljazeera.com/articles/2015/1/18/fair-housing-battle.html. Inclusive Communities interpreted Sections 3604(a) and 3605(a) as outlawing practices with discriminatory *effects*, not just intent, and they had plenty of precedent behind them. HUD's administrative judges routinely accepted complaints about what the agency termed "facially neutral practices that have a disparate impact on protected classes," and nearly every federal appeals court had interpreted the Fair Housing Act to apply to practices with a disparate impact. The language in the Fair Housing Act regarding discrimination was vague enough to brook disagreement over its applicability to disparate impact, but advocates considered it one of the most powerful tools in the fair housing toolbox.

155 **LIHTC tax credits** Using "tax credits" after an abbreviation for Low-Income Housing Tax Credits is redundant, but we have chosen it for the sake of simplicity.

155 **local approval provision intact** Maryland Department of Housing and Community Development, Maryland Low Income Housing Tax Credit Program: 2009 Qualified Allocation Plan, October 24, 2008, www.novoco.com/sites/default/files /atoms/files/maryland_final_09.pdf; also, Maryland Department of Housing and Community Development, Multifamily Housing Notice: 08-13, November 6, 2008, http://dhcd.maryland.gov/HousingDevelopment/RHF%20Current%20Notices /Notice%2008-13%20110308.pdf.

156 **September 2009** Plaintiffs' Unopposed Motion for Approval of Settlement of Attorneys' Fees and Expenses, January 23, 2014, *Thompson v. HUD* (D. Md. 1995), 2.

156 **began** National Low Income Housing Coalition, Resource Library, "Settlement Proposed for Baltimore Public Housing Fair Housing Case, Thompson v. HUD," August 31, 2012, http://web.archive.org/web/20171108044545/http://nlihc.org/article /settlement-proposed-baltimore-public-housing-fair-housing-case-thompson -v-hud.

156 **"balance revitalization with de-concentration and desegregation"** Mullin & Lonergan Associates, "Analysis of Impediments to Fair Housing Choice (AI)," presentation for public hearing, January 18, 2012.

156 **the same tension** Did the Obama administration's tough talk on fair housing catalyze this new movement on fair housing in the Baltimore region? Either way, some credit must go to the Clinton and Bush administrations. HUD had complained repeatedly during the late 1990s and early 2000s about the Baltimore region's inaction on fair housing impediments. HUD specifically objected to a lack of follow-up on the region's 1996 analysis of impediments, asking several times for a new one. The Baltimore Metropolitan Council helped the city and counties produce a "Baltimore Regional Fair Housing Action Plan" in 2002, but several years later HUD was still documenting its displeasure with local governments for failing to take sufficient action.

156 **progress report** Lora Engdahl, *New Homes, New Neighborhoods, New Schools: A Progress Report on the Baltimore Housing Mobility Program*, October 2009, Poverty and Race Research Action Council and Baltimore Regional Housing Campaign.

156 **Baltimore Housing Mobility Program demonstrated better numbers** Engdahl, *New Homes, New Neighborhoods, New Schools*.

156 **distinction between elderly and family** Barbara A. Samuels to Patricia Ryan Sylvester, December 15, 2010.

156 **Nationwide** Carissa Climaco, Meryl Finkel, Bulbul Kaul, Ken Lam, and Chris Rodger, *Updating the Low Income Housing Tax Credit (LIHTC) Database: Projects Placed in Service Through 2006*, U.S. Department of Housing and Urban Development, Office of Policy Development and Research, January 2009.

157 **Maryland** Samuels to Sylvester.

157 **Qualified Allocation Plan** Maryland Department of Housing and Community Development, Maryland Low Income Housing Tax Credit Program: 2011 Qualified Allocation Plan, January 24, 2011, www.novoco.com/sites/default/files/atoms/files/maryland_final_11.pdf; also, Maryland Department of Housing and Community Development, Multifamily Housing Notice: 11-02, February 4, 2011, http://dhcd.maryland.gov/HousingDevelopment/RHF%20Current%20Notices/Multifamily%20Housing%20Notice%2011-02%20--%20Final%20QAP%20Funding%20Round%20Staff%20Web.pdf.

157 **co-counsel for plaintiffs in a suit against Westchester** Michael Allen, "HUD's New AFFH Rule: The Importance of the Ground Game," *The Dream Revisited*, NYU Furman Center, September 2015, http://furmancenter.org/research/iri/essay/huds-new-affh-rule-the-importance-of-the-ground-game.

157 **lawsuit against Wells Fargo** *City of Baltimore v. Wells Fargo* (D. Md. 2008).

157 **the complaint** Housing Discrimination Complaint, *Baltimore Regional Housing Campaign v. State of Maryland and Raymond A. Skinner, Secretary of the Department of Housing and Community Development of the State of Maryland*, August 30, 2011.

157 **another major housing discrimination complaint** Housing Discrimination Complaint, *Baltimore Neighborhoods, Inc., et al. v. Baltimore County*, Maryland, September 30, 2011.

158 **afoul of its civil rights obligations** Housing Discrimination Complaint, September 30, 2011.

159 **adopted an inclusionary housing law** Julie Scharper, "Affordable Housing Law Extension Passes Key Hurdle; Committee Approves Indefinite Extension; Rawlings-Blake Backs 2020 Sunset," *Baltimore Sun*, June 8, 2011, http://articles.baltimoresun.com/2011-06-08/news/bs-md-ci-affordable-housing-20110608_1_housing-market-mel-freeman-council-members.

159 **Howard County** Howard County Housing and Community Development director Kelly Cimino, personal communication, September 15, 2016.

159 **banning discrimination based on one's source of income** Howard County Council, Bill no. 68, adopted September 26, 1992, *Howard County Code of Ordinances*, §12.207(1)(a).

159 **draft analyses of impediments** "Notice of Release of, and Public Hearing On, Draft Baltimore Metropolitan Region's Analysis of Impediments to Fair Housing Choice"; also, Citizens Planning and Housing Association, "Support Bold Steps Toward Fair Housing," December 21, 2011, www.cphabaltimore.org/2011/12/support -bold-steps-toward-fair-housing.

159 **draft for the region** Baltimore Regional Housing Campaign, "A New Regional Fair Housing Plan," December 16, 2011, www.baltimoreregionalhousing.org/2011/12 /16/a-new-regional-fair-housing-plan.

159 **The local approval provision** "Analysis of Impediments to Fair Housing Choice, Baltimore Metropolitan Region, October 2011," Mullin & Lonergan Associates for the Baltimore Metropolitan Council.

159 **criticism** "Analysis of Impediments . . . October 2011."

159 **John Greiner pushed back** "Notice of Release of, and Public Hearing On, Draft Baltimore Metropolitan Region's Analysis of Impediments to Fair Housing Choice"; also, Citizens Planning and Housing Association, "Support Bold Steps Toward Fair Housing," December 21, 2011, www.cphabaltimore.org/2011/12/support-bold-steps -toward-fair-housing; also, John Greiner to Elizabeth Glenn, January 21, 2012, in "Analysis of Impediments to Fair Housing Choice, Baltimore Metropolitan Region, February 2012," Mullin & Lonergan Associates for the Baltimore Metropolitan Council.

160 **May 28, 2010** "A Celebration of Life: Allan Mark Tibbels, March 18, 1955– June 3, 2010," funeral program, June 14, 2010.

161 **infection** "Celebration of Life."

161 **June 3** Jacques Kelly and Erica L. Green, "Agent for Change on a Mission in the City: Allan Tibbels 1955-2010; Force Behind Sandtown Habitat for Humanity Helped Boost Homeownership in Neighborhood," *Baltimore Sun*, June 4, 2010, A1.

162 **one thousand people had come to say good-bye** Jason DeParle, "Wheelchair Missionary," *New York Times*, December 21, 2010, http://archive.nytimes.com /www.nytimes.com/interactive/2010/12/26/magazine/2010lives.html#view=allan _tibbels.

162 **sounds of Bruce Cockburn** "Celebration of Life."

162 **U2** DeParle, "Wheelchair Missionary."

162 **"I can hear Allan saying"** Erica L. Green, "Hundreds Bid Farewell to Sandtown Leader; Funeral Service for Allan Tibbels a Celebration of Life, and a Call to Action," *Baltimore Sun*, June 15, 2010.

162 **his eightieth birthday** John and Vera May Perkins Foundation Legacy Timeline, https://docs.google.com/spreadsheets/d/16sstm6FDIskez-v4xTh58m0LUO 3vS0d1rUVa5S7Akgk/edit#gid=0.

162 **eulogy** Green, "Hundreds Bid Farewell."

163 **built toward an associate's degree** Howard Community College, Catalog 2012–2013, June 2012.

163 **closed it for underperforming** Sarah Fisher, "7 City Schools to Shut, 3 Grow: Alonso Reorganization Plan Includes Closings for Chronic Low Performance; 3 Schools Relocating," *Baltimore Sun*, July 28, 2009, A3.

165 **part of the final settlement** Settlement agreement, September 13, 2012, *Thompson v. HUD* (D. Md. 1995).

165 **1,800 families who had been offered** Transcript of fairness hearing before the honorable Marvin J. Garbis, United States Senior District Judge, November 20, 2012, *Thompson v. HUD* (D. Md. 1995), 11.

165 **Nearly three hundred people** Docket, *Carmen Thompson, et al. v. United States Department of Housing and Urban Development, et al.* (D. Md. 1995), www .plainsite.org/dockets/index.html?id=282398&start=0; also, Transcript of fairness hearing before the honorable Marvin J. Garbis, United States Senior District Judge, November 20, 2012, *Thompson v. HUD* (D. Md. 1995), 20, 33.

165 **Garbis addressed the crowd** Unless otherwise noted, quotations from the November 20, 2012, fairness hearing in front of Judge Marvin J. Garbis regarding the final settlement of *Thompson v. HUD* come from the transcript provided by the clerk's office at the U.S. District Courthouse in Baltimore. The format will be *date, transcript page number*; in this case, November 20, 2012 at 3.

166 **"Having practiced law in the city"** November 20, 2012 at 25.

166 **to thank her** November 20, 2012 at 27.

166 **"forced to reside in one of his units"** November 20, 2012 at 29.

166 **"I sort of echo what Bill said"** November 20, 2012 at 30.

167 **"That's it," Nicole said** November 20, 2012 at 36–39.

167 **"HUD is a political organization"** November 20, 2012 at 47–52.

167 **reelected** David A. Fahrenthold, "Obama Reelected as President," *Washington Post*, November 7, 2012, www.washingtonpost.com/politics/decision2012/after -grueling-campaign-polls-open-for-election-day-2012/2012/11/06/d1c24c98-2802 -11e2-b4e0-346287b7e56c_story.html.

168 **"could have been impeached"** November 20, 2012 at 52–53.

168 **embezzlement conviction** Julie Bykowicz and Annie Linskey, "Dixon Convicted of Embezzlement," *Baltimore Sun*, December 1, 2009, http://articles.baltimoresun .com/2009-12-01/news/bal-dixon-trial1201_1_felony-theft-partial-verdict-count-of -fraudulent-misappropriation.

168 **"It is approved, and I thank you"** November 20, 2012 at 53–54.

168 **eighty employees** New Song Urban Ministries, home page, http://web.archive .org/web/20080315002445/http://www.nsum.org:80.

168 **Sandtown Habitat** Sandtown Habitat claimed to have brought $20 million in housing investment into the neighborhood. Sandtown Habitat for Humanity, "About Us," http://web.archive.org/web/20111001041314/http://www.sandtownhabitat.org/ about_us.htm.

168 **He attended** Thurman Williams, presentation, annual meeting of the Christian Community Development Association, Indianapolis, October 12, 2011, www.youtube.com/watch?v=mm5YzlmQHlM&t=797s.

169 **titles of some of his sermons** New Song Community Church, "Sermons," www.nsc-church.org/sermons.htm.

169 **belonged** New Song Community Church, home page, www.nsc-church.org.

170 **long a self-described "community church"** New Song Community Church, "Keeping it Real: Lived Theology," http://web.archive.org/web/20080509141714/http://www.nsc-church.org/Real.htm.

170 **"community-based" church** New Song Community Church, "Our Ministries and Partnerships," www.nsc-church.org/aboutus.htm.

171 **both resigned** Prasada-Rao moved to Chicago to take a position with the Christian Community Development Association. In November 2012, Antoine Bennett received an eighteen-month, $60,000 "community fellowship" from Open Society Institute–Baltimore for a ministry called Men of Valuable Action. Open Society Institute–Baltimore, "Antoine Bennett," www.osibaltimore.org/author/antoinebennett/?profile=true.

171 **small businesses** One of the contributors to Dr. Perkins's 1996 book *Restoring At-Risk Communities* discussed the movement's history of launching businesses in struggling neighborhoods in a section called "A Word of Caution": "As some of the seasoned Christian Community Development Association members and advisors reflected on their varied experiences with economic development and redistribution, it was clear that, in terms of making a profit, there were more failures in CCD-operated profit-making enterprises than there were successes. We care more about developing people than about creating wealth or producing a product. While we don't want to dampen attempts to be creative and start businesses, the collective feeling was that in all such ventures we should concentrate more on our strength—developing people." *Restoring At-Risk Communities: Doing It Together and Doing It Right*, John M. Perkins, ed. (Grand Rapids, MI: Baker Books, 1995), 151–152.

171 **failed within two years** Small Business Administration, "Do Economic or Industry Factors Affect Business Survival?", Small Business Facts, June 2012, www.sba.gov/sites/default/files/Business-Survival.pdf.

171 **half went under** Small Business Administration, "Frequently Asked Questions," September 2012, www.sba.gov/sites/default/files/FAQ_Sept_2012.pdf.

173 **Gornik considered her** Gornik, *To Live in Peace*.

173 **state housing officials were holding** Listening session in the matter of LIHTC Qualified Allocation Plan and Guide, August 24, 2012, Maryland Department of Housing and Community Development, Crownsville, MD.

173 **guidelines** Maryland Department of Housing and Community Development, Multifamily Housing Notice 12-09, August 14, 2012.

173 **"This is the first time"** Unless otherwise noted, quotations from listening sessions in the matter of the LIHTC Qualified Allocation Plan and Guide come from the transcripts compiled by Gore Brothers Reporting and Videoconferencing on August 24, 2012, September 14, 2012, February 26, 2013, and April 26, 2013. The format will be *QAP session, date, transcript page number*; in this case, QAP session, August 24, 2012, 4.

173 **she felt contributed to segregation** QAP session, August 24, 2012, 23–29.

173 **aggressively defended urban tax-credit developments** QAP session, August 24, 2012, 41–47.

174 **"increase the pie"** QAP session, August 24, 2012, 57–62.

174 **"beyond me"** QAP session, August 24, 2012, 100–102.

174 **"love to see if we can expand"** QAP session, August 24, 2012, 114–116.

174 **codified the process** "Implementation of the Fair Housing Act's Discriminatory Effects Standard," final rule, *Federal Register* 78, no. 32 (February 15, 2013): 11460–11482.

174 **criticized the Obama administration** Poverty and Race Research Action Council, "Affirmatively Furthering Fair Housing at HUD: A First Term Report Card," Part I (January 2013), Part II (March 2013), Washington, DC.

175 **increased scrutiny of analyses of impediments** Poverty and Race Research Action Council.

175 **analyses were outdated** U.S. Government Accountability Office, *Housing and Community Grants: HUD Needs to Enhance Its Requirements and Oversight of Jurisdictions' Fair Housing Plans*, Washington, DC, September 2010.

175 **Westchester County** Elizabeth Ganga, "Westchester Loses $5 Million More in HUD Grants," *Journal News*, September 30, 2014, www.lohud.com/story/news/local/westchester/2014/09/30/westchester-loses-million-hud-grants/16500049.

175 **"long history" of watering down enforcement** Nikole Hannah-Jones, "Soft on Segregation: How the Feds Failed to Integrate Westchester County," *ProPublica*, November 2, 2012, www.propublica.org/article/soft-on-segregation-how-the-feds-failed-to-integrate-westchester-county.

175 **"major piece of unfinished business"** Poverty and Race Research Action Council, Part I, Part II.

176 **opened its doors to introduce a new draft** QAP session, February 26, 2013.

176 **"The lawyers wouldn't let you?"** QAP session, February 26, 2013.

176 **response** Anthony J. Mohan, Response to Comments Regarding the Local Approval Requirement and its Applicability to the Tax Credit Program and Multifamily Loan Programs, April 18, 2013.

176 **cited a Maryland Court of Special Appeals decision** Office of the Maryland Attorney General, Opinions of the Attorney General of Maryland, Constitutional Law–Separation of Powers–Federal Preemption–Whether "Local Approval" Requirement Implemented by Department Of Housing and Community Development Violates Separation of Powers Principle of State Constitution or Federal Low Income Housing Tax Credit Law, 96-OAG-17, April 13, 2011, https://msa.maryland.gov/megafile/msa/speccol/sc5300/sc5339/000113/014000/014773/unrestricted/20120609e-002.pdf; also, Plan approval process, *West's Annotated Code of Maryland*, Housing and Community Development, § 4-213; also, Maryland General Assembly, Multifamily Rental Housing Programs Efficiency Act, House Bill 453, Chapter 229, adopted April 14, 2014.

In the opinion, the Office of the Attorney General noted that the state's code required the Community Development Administration—a state housing office responsible for the Low-Income Housing Tax Credit program—to "work closely, consult, and cooperate with local elected officials" and "give primary consideration to local needs and desires." The Community Development Administration had "long required explicit approval of a project by the local governing body," the opinion read, and a Maryland Court of Special Appeals decision had interpreted that passage as requiring local approval. Given the code and the Court of Special Appeals ruling, the Attorney General's opinion called local approval an "implicit condition" for Low-Income Housing Tax Credit applications.

176   **announced a few more changes** QAP session, April 26, 2013, 22.

176   **a passage in state code** Maryland Attorney General, Whether "Local Approval" Requirement Implemented by Department Of Housing and Community Development Violates Separation of Powers Principle of State Constitution or Federal Low Income Housing Tax Credit Law, 96-OAG-17, April 13, 2011.

177   **again referred to the Court of Special Appeals ruling** QAP session, April 26, 2013, 23.

177   **"Is it just trying"** QAP session, April 26, 2013, 102.

177   **Donovan announced** Shaun Donovan, "Prepared Remarks of Secretary Shaun Donovan Before the NAACP's 104th Annual Convention," Orlando, Florida, July 16, 2013, https://archives.hud.gov/remarks/donovan/speeches/2013-07-16.cfm.

177   **included digital tools** "Affirmatively Furthering Fair Housing," proposed rule, *Federal Register* 78, no. 139 (July 19, 2013): 43710–43743.

177   **"most important" aspect** Donovan, "Prepared Remarks."

177   **Using HUD's powerful prototype map** Lawrence Lanahan, "Fighting Segregation in Housing: There's a Map for That," *Al Jazeera America*, February 5, 2014, http://america.aljazeera.com/articles/2014/2/5/fighting-segregationinhousingtheres amapforthat.html.

178   **published the draft rule** "Affirmatively Furthering Fair Housing," proposed rule, *Federal Register* 78, no. 139 (July 19, 2013): 43710–43743.

178   **final version of its 2013 Qualified Allocation Plan** Maryland Department of Housing and Community Development, "Maryland Qualified Allocation Plan for the Allocation of Federal Low Income Housing Tax Credits" and "Multifamily Rental Financing Program Guide," July 31, 2013.

178   **Baltimore County Council took up** Baltimore County Council, Resolution No. 114-13, November 4, 2013.

178   **Homes for America had applied** Baltimore County Council, Resolution No. 114-13, November 4, 2013.

178   **community association responded with a letter** Lionel Harris to Kathy Ebner, June 12, 2013.

178   **did not fall within a "community of opportunity"** Baltimore County Council, Resolution No. 114-13, November 4, 2013. It wouldn't have qualified for the *Thompson* final settlement, either, landing on john powell's map within a tract with "moderate" opportunity, not "high" or "very high."

178   **county council disapproved** Council Resolution 114-13.

178   **supported Bevins's resolution** Alison Knezevich, "Balto. Co. Council Rejects Low-income Housing Plan," *Baltimore Sun*, November 19, 2013, A2.

178   **only African American** Baltimore County Council, http://web.archive.org/web /20131104125657/http://www.baltimorecountymd.gov/countycouncil/index.html.

178   **In a letter to Maryland housing secretary Raymond Skinner** Barbara Samuels to Ray Skinner, November 22, 2013.

179   **legislative committee** Maryland Association of Counties, Legislative Tracking Database, www.ciclt.net/sn/clt/mdcounties/l_main.aspx?ClientCode=mdcounties&L _Session=&L_Prior=&L_State=sc&StateName=; also, Maryland Association of Counties, Legislative Committee, www.mdcounties.org/112/Legislative-Committee.

179 **scheduled** HB 453, History, http://mgaleg.maryland.gov/webmga/frmMain .aspx?pid=billpage&stab=01&id=hb0453&tab=subject3&ys=2014rs.

179 **February 5** Maryland Association of Counties, MACo Legislative Committee Meeting, February 5, 2014, www.mdcounties.org/Calendar.aspx?EID=168&day=5& month=2&year=2014&calType=0.

179 **storm** Scott Dance, "150,000 Lose Power, Look Ahead Nervously: Ice Causes Outages; More Wintry Weather Expected on Weekend," *Baltimore Sun*, February 6, 2014, A1.

179 **no position** Maryland Association of Counties, Legislative Tracking Database, www.ciclt.net/sn/clt/mdcounties/l_main.aspx?ClientCode=mdcounties&L_Ses sion=&L_Prior=&L_State=sc&StateName=; also, Maryland Association of Counties, Legislative Committee, www.mdcounties.org/112/Legislative-Committee.

179 **commissioner complained** "Official Minutes," Carroll County Planning and Zoning Commission, February 18, 2014.

179 **Hodge** Robert J. Hodge, Maryland Manual On-Line, https://msa.maryland .gov/msa/mdmanual/36loc/ce/leg/former/html/msa15098.html.

179 **late February work session** All dialogue from this meeting comes from "Worksession Meeting Agenda and Audio," Cecil County Council, February 25, 2014, www.ccgov.org/government/county-council/council-meeting-agendas-minutes -audio-recordings/work-session-meetings/2014/february-25-2014.

179 **council voted unanimously to support** "Work Session Minutes," County Council of Cecil County, February 25, 2014.

180 **testimony** Maryland General Assembly, Hearing on House Bill 453, House Environmental Matters committee, video, February 6, 2014, http://mgahouse .maryland.gov/mga/play/3b0a018a-3363-4017-8be3-423b8c1a9d0c/?catalog.

180 **came to the floor** HB 453, History.

180 **"Gentleman from Harford County"** Maryland General Assembly, Session #1, audio, February 18, 2014, http://mgaleg.maryland.gov/webmga/frmLegislation .aspx?id=2014rs_house_audio&stab=02&pid=legisnlist&tab=subject3&ys=2014rs.

180 **"Speak English!"** Michaelle Bond, "Delegate Seeks English-only Law in Md.," *Cecil Whig*, November 15, 2010, www.cecildaily.com/news/localnews/article _1580a5a4-f058-11df-8d6d-001cc4c002e0.html?mode=jqm_com.

180 **"calls on this legislation"** Maryland General Assembly, Session #1, audio, February 18, 2014.

180 **effectively stalled** Maryland General Assembly, Department of Legislative Services, "Legislative Lingo," http://mgaleg.maryland.gov/pubs-current/current -legislative-lingo.pdf; also, Maryland General Assembly, "Explanation of Floor Motions and Legislative Actions," http://mgaleg.maryland.gov/pubs-current/current -motions.pdf.

180 **House approved** HB 453, History.

180 **February 20** HB 453, History.

181 **Niemann said** Maryland General Assembly, Session #1, audio, February 20, 2014, http://mgaleg.maryland.gov/webmga/frmLegislation.aspx?id=2014rs_house _audio&stab=02&pid=legisnlist&tab=subject3&ys=2014rs.

181 **bill passed a final reading** HB 453, History.

181 **voted against** Maryland General Assembly, Multifamily Rental Housing Programs Efficiency Act, House Bill 453, Documents, 2014, http://mgaleg.maryland .gov/webmga/frmMain.aspx?pid=flrvotepage&tab=subject3&id=HB0453,h -0155&stab=02&ys=2014rs.

181 **hearing** Maryland General Assembly, Hearing on House Bill 453, Senate Education, Health, and Environmental Affairs committee, video, March 25, 2014, http:// mgahouse.maryland.gov/mga/play/fd537009-ff1e-406f-88c7-455bd59a9bb8/?catalog /03e481c7-8a42-4438-a7da-93ff74bdaa4c.

181 **signed it into law** HB 453, History.

181 **August 2012 remedial order** Opinion and order, August 7, 2012, *Inclusive Communities Project, Inc., v. The Texas Department of Housing and Community Affairs,* (N.D. Tex. 2008).

182 **published its final disparate impact rule** "Implementation of the Fair Housing Act's Discriminatory Effects Standard," proposed rule, *Federal Register* 78, no. 32 (February 15, 2013): 11460–11482.

182 **sent it back** *Inclusive Communities Project, Inc., v. The Texas Department of Housing and Community Affairs,* 747 F.3d 275 (5th Cir. 2014).

182 **"petition for a writ of *certiorari*"** Petition for a Writ of Certiorari, *ICP v. TDH-CA* (N.D. Tex. 2008). An order to review a lower court's ruling.

182 **just 1 or 2 percent** United States Courts, Supreme Court Procedures, www .uscourts.gov/about-federal-courts/educational-resources/about-educational -outreach/activity-resources/supreme-1.

182 **once in 2011** *Gallagher v. Magner,* 619 F.3d 823 (8th Cir. 2010), *cert. granted,* 132 S.Ct. 548 (2011).

182 **once in 2013** *Mt. Holly Gardens Citizens in Action, Inc. v. Township of Mount Holly,* 658 F.3d 375 (3d Cir. 2011), *cert. granted,* 133 S. Ct. 2824 (2013).

182 **had never had an opportunity** Amy Howe, "Will the Third Time Be the Charm for the Fair Housing Act and Disparate-impact Claims?", *SCOTUSblog,* January 6, 2015, www.scotusblog.com/2015/01/will-the-third-time-be-the-charm-for-the -fair-housing-act-and-disparate-impact-claims-in-plain-english.

182 **"The way to stop discrimination"** *Parents Involved in Community Schools v. Seattle School District No. 1,* et al., 551 U.S. 701 (2007).

183 **scrap a section of the Voting Rights Act** *Shelby County, Alabama v. Holder, Attorney General,* 570 U.S. 2 (2013).

183 **Shaw** "Taking Inequality to Court," *The Lines Between Us,* series, *Maryland Morning with Sheilah Kast,* WYPR-FM, Baltimore, MD, May 10, 2013.

183 **Johnson suggested** Olatunde C.A. Johnson, "The Agency Roots of Disparate Impact," *Harvard Civil Rights–Civil Liberties Law Review* 49 (2014), 125–154.

183 **agencies had expertise that the courts didn't** Johnson.

183 **"equality directives"** Olatunde C.A. Johnson, "Beyond the Private Attorney General: Equality Directives in American Law," *New York University Law Review* 87 (November 2012), 1339–1413.

183 **for someone to take inequality to court** James Rouse had touched on the idea back in 1970 when he testified to the U.S. Commission on Civil Rights. "If the govern-

ment really took its whole construct of leverage and said, 'We are just going to have an open housing market in America,'" Rouse had testified, "then we would have it." U.S. Commission on Civil Rights (USCCR). Transcript: Hearing Held in Baltimore, Maryland, August 17–19, 1970, 454.

183 **documented examples** Olatunde C. A. Johnson, "Disparity Rules," *Columbia Law Review* 107:2 (Mar., 2007), 374–425.

184 **consider just the petition's first question** Warren Richey, "Supreme Court: Texas Housing Case Could Prove Pivotal for Civil Rights," *Christian Science Monitor*, October 2, 2014, 17; also, Adam Liptak, "Justices Take Cases on Bias, Redistricting and Judicial Elections," *New York Times*, October 3, 2014, A12.; also, *ICP v. TDHCA*, 747 F.3d 275 (5th Cir. 2014), *cert. granted*, 135 S. Ct. 2507 (2015).

184 **dominated media coverage** The Opportunity Agenda, "Coverage of Inclusive Communities Supreme Court Argument: Media Analysis," 2015, https://opportunityagenda.org/explore/resources-publications/coverage-inclusive-communities-supreme-court-argument.

184 **takes four votes** United States Courts, Supreme Court Procedures, www.uscourts.gov/about-federal-courts/educational-resources/about-educational-outreach/activity-resources/supreme-1.

184 **Enterprise Homes applied** Sara Luell, email message to author, September 5, 2017.

184 **schools ranked** School Digger, www.schooldigger.com.

184 **bill allowed plots** Anne Arundel County Council, Bill No. 56-11, adopted October 12, 2011.

184 **passed 6 to 1** Anne Arundel County Council, 2011 Bill Log, www.aacounty.org/departments/county-council/forms-publications/Bills_2011.pdf.

184 **John Grasso** John J. Grasso, Maryland Manual On-Line, https://msa.maryland.gov/msa/mdmanual/36loc/an/leg/html/msa15355.html.

184 **working-class Glen Burnie** Durr, *Behind the Backlash*, 68.

185 **"What kind of a quality person"** Allison Bourg, "Marley Meadows Project One Step Closer—County Council Now Must Vote on Property Tax Break," *The Capital*, October 18, 2011.

185 **incensed** Zoe Read, "Proposed Pasadena Housing Project Panned," *Capital Gazette*, November 12, 2014.

185 **complain** Brandi Bottalico, "Earleigh Heights Development Takes Flak at Hearing," *Capital Gazette*, December 3, 2014; also, Read; also, Sparks, "Area Residents Voice Concerns."

185 **bill to roll back part** Anne Arundel County Council, Bill No. 82-14, adopted January 9, 2015.

185 **had enough words in it** Anne Arundel County, Bill 82–14.

185 **submitted testimony in opposition** Public hearing, Anne Arundel County Council, Annapolis, MD, January 5, 2015.

185 **Cimbolic wrote** Pete Cimbolic, "Testimony of ACLU of Maryland in Opposition to Council Bill 82–14," January 5, 2015.

185 **January 5 hearing** County Council of Anne Arundel County, Maryland, Minutes of Legislative Session 2015, Legislative Day No. 1, January 5, 2015.

185 **if they would testify against** Lanahan, "Who Gets to Live Where?"

185 **Fink took up** County Council of Anne Arundel County, Maryland, Legislative Session 2015, Legislative Day No. 1, January 5, 2015, video, www.youtube.com/watch?v=CQJOK4iDIIQ&index=13&list=PLFDsPtElNXo5OKvVop-vjZvq1hvgmdt8-.

185 **opened the floor** City Council of Anne Arundel County video. Former District 1 representative Daryl Jones—who sponsored the original workforce housing bill—pleaded guilty in 2011 to a charge of failing to file a tax return and spent part of 2012 locked up. Peter Smith replaced him, but the Maryland Court of Appeals nullified his ouster, and Smith offered Jones his seat back. Term limits kept Jones from pursuing the seat in the 2014 election; Smith ran unopposed in the primary and defeated his Republican opponent by a mere 288 votes. Pamela Wood, "For Daryl Jones, a Long Road Back to Arundel County Council," *Baltimore Sun*, November 18, 2013, http://articles.baltimoresun.com/2013-11-18/news/bs-md-ar-daryl-jones-returns-20131117_1_council-seat-law-license-prison-sentence; also, "Election Summary Report: Gubernatorial Primary Election, Anne Arundel County, Maryland, Tuesday, June 24, 2014," July 7, 2014, www.aacounty.org/boards-and-commissions/board-of-elections/forms-and-publications/years/GEMS%20OFFICIAL%20ELECTION%20SUMMARY%20REPORT%20070714.pdf; also, "Election Summary Report: Gubernatorial General Election, Anne Arundel County, Maryland, November 4, 2014," November 11, 2014, www.aacounty.org/boards-and-commissions/board-of-elections/forms-and-publications/years/Election_Summary_Report_Official_Results_111414.pdf.

185 **riverkeeper association** Magothy River Association Facebook page, January 6, 2015, www.facebook.com/permalink.php?id=22985569977&story_fbid=10150483450344978.

186 **Linda Schuett** County Council of Anne Arundel County, January 5, 2015, video. Schuett worked as a lobbyist for Enterprise Homes and had helped Daryl Jones draft the original workforce housing bill. She spoke in her capacity as vice chair of the Anne Arundel Affordable Housing Coalition.

187 **Keisha Scott** County Council of Anne Arundel County video.

187 **unimpressed** County Council of Anne Arundel County video.

187 **scowling back** County Council of Anne Arundel County video.

187 **voted for** Anne Arundel County Council, 2011 Bill Log, www.aacounty.org/departments/county-council/forms-publications/Bills_2011.pdf.

187 **rejected their application** Maryland Department of Housing and Community Development, "Fall 2014 Competitive Funding Round—Applicant Information," http://dhcd.maryland.gov/HousingDevelopment/Documents/rhf/Fall_2014_Round_Waiver.pdf.

187 **voted 4 to 3** Anne Arundel County Council, 2014 Bill Log, www.aacounty.org/departments/county-council/forms-publications/Bills_2014.pdf.

188 **Barbara Samuels took a seat** Litigants get a certain number of seats; Barbara came as a board member of Inclusive Communities Project.

188 **All around her** Supreme Court of the United States, About the Court, Building Features, www.supremecourt.gov/about/buildingfeatures.aspx.

188 **Keller said** Unless otherwise noted, quotations from oral arguments in this case come from the transcript of Oral arguments, January 21, 2015, *ICP v. TDHCA*, 747 F.3d 275 (5th Cir. 2014), *cert. granted*, 135 S. Ct. 2507 (2015). (Audio available at www.supremecourt.gov/oral_arguments/audio/2014/13-1371.) The format will be *Oral arguments, date, at transcript page number*; in this case, Oral arguments, January 21, 2015, at 3.

188 **"why doesn't that"** Oral arguments, January 21, 2015, at 3–10.

188 **Fair Housing Act amendments** *TDHCA v. ICP*, et al., 135 S.Ct. 2507 (2015).

188 **"prohibit something that doesn't exist"** Oral arguments, January 21, 2015, at 17.

188 **reliably liberal judges** Lee Epstein, Andrew D. Martin, Kevin M. Quinn, and Jeffrey A. Segal, "Ideological Drift Among Supreme Court Justices: Who, When, and How Important?", *Northwestern University Law Review* 101:4 (2007), 1483–1582.

188 **Ruth Bader Ginsburg** Oral arguments, January 21, 2015, at 32.

189 **Ginsburg asked** Oral arguments, January 21, 2015, at 32–33.

189 **"most clearly show"** Oral arguments, January 21, 2015, at 37.

189 ***Chevron*** Oral arguments, January 21, 2015, at 39.

189 **pushed courts to defer to agencies** Nina Totenberg, "Trump's Supreme Court Nominee Skeptical of Federal Agency Power," *Morning Edition*, National Public Radio, March 17, 2017, www.npr.org/2017/03/17/520310365/trumps-supreme-court -nominee-skeptical-of-federal-agency-power.

189 **Scalia was a big fan** Antonin Scalia, "Judicial Deference to Administrative Interpretations of Law," *Duke Law Journal* 1989:3 (June 1989), 511–521.

189 **Agency roll back regulations** Steven Davidoff Solomon, "Should Agencies Decide Law? Doctrine May Be Tested at Gorsuch Hearing," *New York Times*, March 14, 2017, www.nytimes.com/2017/03/14/business/dealbook/neil-gorsuch -chevron-deference.html?mcubz=1.

189 **"Which one gets credit?"** Oral arguments, January 21, 2015, at 39.

190 **"seems very odd to me"** Oral arguments, January 21, 2015, at 45.

190 **commencement** Howard Community College, "Howard Community College to Graduate Its Largest Class Ever on Tuesday, May 20," May 12, 2014, www .howardcc.edu/about-us/news-events/news/howard-community-college-to-graduate -its-largest-class-ever-on-tuesday-may-20; also, Howard Community College, "HCC Commencement 2014" [photograph], https://www.flickr.com/photos/howardcc /14273476703.

190 **commissioned by James Rouse** Rouse built Merriweather as a summer home for the National Symphony Orchestra, thinking a cultural center would help put his new city on the map. Financial reality quickly asserted itself, however, and soon "heads" from around the region were cramming onto the lawn section to smoke grass and watch bands like The Who and Procol Harum. (The author will never forget the evening in 1995 that he received a citation for underage drinking while "pre-gaming" in the Columbia Mall parking lot, and then, as he settled on the Merriweather lawn for an Allman Brothers concert, heard a deafening "*Wooooo!!!*" and turned to see a long-haired dude dressed like Superman who yelled, "I just got out of jail!" Beethoven's Fifth it wasn't—although fifths were not in short supply on the lawn that night.)

Kevin Leonard, "Merriweather: Birth of a Classic Music Venue," *Columbia Flier*, June 13, 2017, www.baltimoresun.com/news/maryland/howard/columbia/ph-ho-cf -history-merriweather-20170613-story.html.

191 **but not** In March 2018, Mimi Heimsoth said BCCC had finally joined the CCCPDF program.

192 **"apartheid" enrollment** The Civil Rights Project, "Report Finds Over Half of Maryland's Black Students Attend Intensely Segregated Schools," April 18, 2013, www .civilrightsproject.ucla.edu/news/press-releases/2013-press-releases/report-finds-over -half-of-maryland2019s-black-students-attend-intensely-segregated-schools.

192 **Wilde Lake Middle** Maryland State Department of Education, "Howard County, Wilde Lake Middle, 2011 to 2017 Enrollment for All Grades, Students by Race/Ethnicity," 2017 Maryland Report Card, http://reportcard.msde.maryland.gov /Enrollment.aspx?PV=34:17:13:0512:1:N:6:13:1:2:1:1:1:1:3.

192 **free or reduced-price lunch** Maryland State Department of Education, "Howard County, Wilde Lake Middle, 2004 to 2017 Students Receiving Special Services for Middle, Students by Special Service," 2017 Maryland Report Card, http://reportcard .msde.maryland.gov/SpecialServices.aspx?PV=36:M:13:0512:1:N:0:14:1:1:1:1:1:1:3.

192 **fifty families enrolled their children** Gady A. Epstein and Erika D. Peterman, "Columbia Parents Vote with Their Bus; Believing Older Schools Are Inferior, They Send Children to Newer One," *Baltimore Sun*, September 14, 1999.

192 **newspapers jumped on the story** For instance, Gady A. Epstein, "School Transfers Raise Issues of Equity, Policy; Howard County Mulls Ramifications of Open Enrollment," *Baltimore Sun*, September 15, 1999, 1B.

192 **wrote one reader** "Wilde Lake Parents Underestimated Their Children," *Baltimore Sun*, September 19, 1999, 6B.

192 **meeting in October 1999** Epstein, "PTAs May Contribute."

192 **citizen's committee on school equity** Larry Carson, "School Equity Panel Created in Howard; 23-member Committee Will Attack Problems of Polarization," *Baltimore Sun*, October 29, 1999, 1C.

193 **"all-white, all-black or all-Hispanic"** Larry Carson, "Older Schools Show Rise in Black Pupils; White Enrollment in Some Elementaries in Columbia Down; Local Officials Puzzled; Racial Trend Noted as Panel Investigates Quality Concerns," *Baltimore Sun*, December 19, 1999, 1B.

193 **committee called for** Jamie Smith Hopkins, "Panel Urges School System Redistricting; Equity Committee Says Open-enrollment Freeze Should Follow; 47-page Report Presented; 70 Proposals Made; Robey Believes Cost Would Be 'Millions'," *Baltimore Sun*, March 14, 2000, 1B.

193 **moratorium** Tanika White, "Open Policy on Enrolling Put on Hold; No Additional Students May Switch Schools for 1 Year, Board Decides; 'Creates Instability'; Moratorium Called to Gauge How Practice Affects Neighborhoods," *Baltimore Sun*, May 1, 2000, 1B.

193 **more than five years** "Howard Week," *Baltimore Sun*, February 13, 2005, 2B.

193 **improved Wilde Lake Middle** Tanika White, "Bused Columbia Pupils Finish

Middle School; Wilde Lake Parents Sent Children to Lime Kiln; Action Spurred System Change; Bused Columbia Pupils Finish Middle School," *Baltimore Sun*, June 11, 2002, 1B.

193 **new white students enrolled** Larry Carson, "Schools' Racial Makeup Changes; White Enrollment Drops in Columbia, North Laurel Over Five-year Period; Wilde Lake Is an Exception; 16 County Schools Have Mainly Minority Students," *Baltimore Sun*, February 8, 2004, 1B.

193 **an "exception"** Carson.

193 **the percentage** Maryland State Department of Education, "Howard County, Wilde Lake Middle, 2011 to 2017 Enrollment for All Grades, Students by Race/Ethnicity," 2017 Maryland Report Card, http://reportcard.msde.maryland.gov/Enrollment .aspx?PV=34:17:13:0512:1:N:6:13:1:2:1:1:1:1:3.

194 **network of half-acre farms** Jonathan Pitts, "Planting a New Farm in Baltimore: Private Firm, Nonprofit Aim to Create Jobs and Sell Crops," *Baltimore Sun*, December 1, 2012, A1.

194 **Sandtown had an acre and a half** Alia Malek, "Urban Green: Hoop Houses Replace Rowhouses in Baltimore's Sandtown," *Al Jazeera America*, May 18, 2014, http://america.aljazeera.com/articles/2014/5/18/urban-green-hoophousesreplace rowhousesinbaltimoreassandtown.html.

194 **five-year lease** Pitts, "Planting a New Farm"; also, Malek.

195 **agreed to buy everything** Malek.

195 **workers broke ground** Pitts, "Planting a New Farm."

195 **"support system"** Strength to Love II, "Support System," http://s2l2.inter sectionofchange.org/support-system.

195 **four sermons in 2014** New Song Community Church, "2014 Sermon Archive," www.nsc-church.org/2014%20Sermons/2014sermons.htm.

195 **"community fellowship" from Open Society Institute–Baltimore** Open Society Institute–Baltimore, "Antoine Bennett," www.osibaltimore.org/author/antoine bennett/?profile=true.

196 **church also had** New Song Community Church, "About Us," http://web .archive.org/web/20141006030729/http://www.nsc-church.org:80/aboutus.htm.

196 **merge** Habitat for Humanity of the Chesapeake, "Habitat for Humanity of the Chesapeake and Sandtown Habitat for Humanity Announce Merger," press release, July 30, 2014, www.habitatchesapeake.org/file/16/HabitatMergerMediaKit.pdf.

196 **"Boundary Block Party"** "No Boundaries," *Maryland Morning with Sheilah Kast*, WYPR-FM, Baltimore, MD, May 6, 2011, https://mdmorn.wordpress.com/2011 /05/06/56112-no-boundaries.

196 **mission statement** No Boundaries Coalition of Central West Baltimore, "Mission," www.noboundariescoalition.com/about/mission.

196 **Kelly excoriated the department** Ray C. Kelly, "More Visibility Than They Ever Imagined," *Neighbors in the Hood* (blog), May 30, 2014, https://trueurbanadvocacy .wordpress.com/2014/05/30/more-visibility-than-they-ever-imagined.

197 **Kelly wrote** Ray C. Kelly, "Open Letter to Mayor and Police Department," No Boundaries Coalition, News, December 11, 2014, www.noboundariescoalition.com /open-letter-to-mayor-and-police-department.

197 **voters elected Marilyn Mosby** Maryland State Board of Elections, "Official 2014 Gubernatorial General Election results for Baltimore City," https://elections.maryland .gov/elections/2014/results/General/gen_results_2014_2_by_county_030.html.

197 **who'd served the city** Mark Reutter, "Analysis: How to Defeat an Incumbent State's Attorney? Take Lessons from His 2010 Win," *Baltimore Brew*, June 25, 2014, www.baltimorebrew.com/2014/06/25/analysis-how-to-defeat-an-incumbent-states -attorney-take-lessons-from-his-2010-win.

197 **upset the incumbent** "Mosby Defeats Bernstein in Baltimore Prosecutor's Primary," *The Daily Record*, June 25, 2014, https://thedailyrecord.com/2014/06/25/mosby -defeats-bernstein-in-baltimore-prosecutors-primary.

197 **Larry Hogan** John Wagner and Jenna Johnson, "Republican Larry Hogan Wins Md. Governor's Race in Stunning Upset," *Washington Post*, November 5, 2014, www .washingtonpost.com/local/md-politics/republican-larry-hogan-wins-md-governors -race-in-stunning-upset/2014/11/05/9eb8bf46-60ac-11e4-8b9e-2ccdac31a031_story .html; also, Maryland State Board of Elections, "Official 2014 Gubernatorial General Election Results for Baltimore City," https://elections.maryland.gov/elections/2014 /results/General/gen_results_2014_2_by_county_030.html.

197 **after the election** Maryland State Board of Elections, "Election Dates," https://elections.maryland.gov/elections/2014/index.html;   also,   New   Song Community Church Facebook page, November 10, 2014, www.facebook.com /NSCChurch/posts/10152752205156355%20;   also,   New   Song   Community Church Facebook page, November 19, 2014, www.facebook.com/NSCChurch /posts/10152769162346355.

197 **two guest sermons** New Song Community Church, "2014 Sermon Archive," www.nsc-church.org/2014%20Sermons/2014sermons.htm.

197 **Wilson** New Song Community Church, "Meet Our Team: Dr. Louis Wilson," http://nscommunity.org/about/leadership/#wilson.

198 **Jubilee Arts announced** Jubilee Arts' Facebook page, April 9, 2015, https:// www.facebook.com/events/870849079649308/permalink/870867476314135.

198 **Boundary Block Party** Jubilee Arts Facebook page (event), "Boundary Block Party—8th Annual!," www.facebook.com/events/870849079649308.

199 **report** Report of the Inclusionary Housing Board, Submitted to City Council on November 28, 2014.

199 **singled out Sandtown for evaluation** Stefanie DeLuca and Peter Rosenblatt, "Sandtown-Winchester–Baltimore's Daring Experiment in Urban Renewal: 20 Years Later, What Are the Lessons Learned?," *The Abell Report* 26:8 (November 2013).

199 **DeLuca** DeLuca had also analyzed data for the 2009 report on the Baltimore Housing Mobility Program.

199 **public and private investment** DeLuca and Rosenblatt, "Sandtown -Winchester."

199 **2000** Chickie Grayson, whose Enterprise Homes built housing in Sandtown, claims only $60 million was spent on housing, and that no one really knows what the overall number is.

199 **both ways** DeLuca and Rosenblatt, "Sandtown-Winchester."

199 **"Undue Force"** Mark Puente, "Undue Force," *Baltimore Sun*, September 28, 2014, http://data.baltimoresun.com/news/police-settlements.

199 **Justice Policy Institute** Justice Policy Institute and Prison Policy Initiative, "The Right Investment? Corrections Spending in Baltimore City," February 2015, www.justicepolicy.org/uploads/justicepolicy/documents/rightinvestment_design_2 .23.15_final.pdf.

199 **the Baltimore region thrived** Opportunity Collaborative, "Baltimore Regional Plan for Sustainable Development," June 2015.

200 **mapped opportunity** From Gerrit Knapp to Nexus Committee of the Baltimore Regional Sustainable Communities Initiative, Memorandum, "Re: Technical Memorandum #2: Measures of Opportunity in the Baltimore Metropolitan Region," September 16, 2013.

200 **"Targeted law enforcement"** Opportunity Collaborative, "Strong Workforce, Strong Economy: Baltimore Regional Workforce Development Plan," March 2015.

200 **article on "hypersegregation"** Douglas S. Massey and Jonathan Tannen, "A Research Note on Trends in Black Hypersegregation," *Demography* 52:3 (June 2015), 1025–1034.

200 **"segregation created"** Douglas Massey and Nancy A. Denton, *American Apartheid: Segregation and the Making of the Underclass* (Cambridge, MA: Harvard University Press, 1993).

200 ***Great American City*** Robert Sampson, *Great American City: Chicago and the Enduring Neighborhood Effect* (Chicago: University of Chicago Press, 2012).

200 ***Stuck in Place*** Patrick Sharkey, *Stuck in Place: Urban Neighborhoods and the End of Progress Toward Racial Equality* (Chicago: University of Chicago Press, 2013).

200 **"from the same families"** Sharkey, 9.

200 **"the place itself"** Sampson and Sharkey both addressed mobility and place-based revitalization. Sharkey noted the success of some mobility programs, but argued that they must target the most concentrated disadvantage and could not be a "primary solution." He suggested "direct and sustained investments in poor urban neighborhoods." Sampson argued for "community-level intervention instead of individual-level escape hatches." Sharkey, 175, 179; also, Sampson, *Great American City*, 421.

201 **article** Douglas S. Massey and Jonathan Tannen, "A Research Note on Trends in Black Hypersegregation," *Demography* 52:3 (June 2015), 1025–1034.

201 **8:39 a.m.** Kevin Rector, "The 45-Minute Mystery of Freddie Gray's Death," *Baltimore Sun*, April 25, 2015, www.baltimoresun.com/news/maryland/freddie-gray /bs-md-gray-ticker-20150425-story.html.

201 **bright, cool morning** "Gilmor Homes Arrest Video: Citizen Video Taken April 12, 2015," *Baltimore Sun*, www.baltimoresun.com/news/maryland/crime /83290396-132.html; also, Weather Underground, History, www.wunderground.com/ history.

201 **halfway through** St. Peter Claver and St. Pius Catholic Church, www .josephites.org/parish/md/spc.

201 **about to start** Sharon Baptist Church of Baltimore Facebook page, "About," www.facebook.com/pg/sharonbaptistchurchbaltimore/about/?ref=page_internal.

201 **young black man in a black T-shirt** "New Video Shows Arrest of Freddie Gray in Baltimore," CNN, April 21, 2015, www.youtube.com/watch?v=7YV0EtkWyno&t=1s.

201 **corner of Presbury and N. Mount Streets** Adam Marton and Emma Patti Harris, "Freddie Gray Arrest Timeline," *Baltimore Sun*, April 21, 2015, www.baltimoresun.com/news/maryland/baltimore-city/bal-map-freddie-gray-arrest-timeline-20150421-htmlstory.html.

201 *"Ahhhngh!"* Descriptions in this scene are based on two videos filmed by bystanders. The *Baltimore Sun* interviewed one of the bystanders, Kevin Moore, and published his video—attributed to Baltimore's WJZ-TV—in this article: Catherine Rentz, "Videographer: Freddie Gray Was Folded like 'Origami'," *Baltimore Sun*, April 23, 2015, www.baltimoresun.com/news/maryland/freddie-gray/bs-md-gray-video-moore-20150423-story.html. The video from the other bystander, who was not named, appeared in this article: "Gilmor Homes Arrest Video: Citizen Video Taken April 12, 2015," *Baltimore Sun*, www.baltimoresun.com/news/maryland/crime/83290396-132.html.

202 **"they tased"** Police later said one officer pulled out a taser but did not use it.

202 **"tased yo like that"** Young Baltimoreans sometimes deploy "yo" as a "gender-neutral pronoun."

202 **Seven days later, he was dead** Rector, "The 45-Minute Mystery"; also, Marton and Harris, "Freddie Gray Arrest Timeline"; also, Natalie Sherman, Chris Kaltenbach, and Colin Campbell, "Freddie Gray Dies a Week After Being Injured During Arrest," *Baltimore Sun*, April 19, 2015, www.baltimoresun.com/news/maryland/freddie-gray/bs-md-freddie-gray-20150419-story.html.

Five: Spring 2015

203 **filming a video** Quotations from this passage come from the video. Kinetics Live, "A Word from Baltimore Activists on #FreddieGray Actions," YouTube video, April 23, 2015, www.youtube.com/watch?v=BX_URMZWBek.

203 **Brown, thirty-five** "Minister Heber Brown III Continues the Legacy of the Black Church," *The Spokesman*, March 4, 2013, http://themsuspokesman.com/686/alumni/minister-heber-brown-iii-continues-the-legacy-of-the-black-church.

203 **defer to those of us** KineticsLive.

203 **Brown and Love had helped lead a rally** Dayvon Love's Facebook page, March 12, 2015, www.facebook.com/photo.php?fbid=10102010447509055&set=a.10101162578844655.1073741829.18412299&type=3&theater; also, Heber Brown III's Facebook page, March 12, 2015, www.facebook.com/HeberBrown/posts/10153146124438610.

203 **nine hours' worth of testimony** Hearing on House Bill 968, House Judiciary Committee, March 12, 2015, http://mgahouse.maryland.gov/mga/play/d8890118-ee6c-4954-acc2-76c82f1f29e8/?catalog/03e481c7-8a42-4438-a7da-93ff74bdaa4c.

203 **testified in favor** Leaders of a Beautiful Struggle's Facebook page, March 12, 2015, www.facebook.com/LBSBaltimore/photos/a.170060463006184.40618.134910449854519/954788271200062/?type=3&theater; also, Maryland General Assembly, Law Enforcement Officers' Bill of Rights—Alterations, House Bill 968, 2015, http://mgaleg.maryland.gov/webmga/frmMain.aspx?pid=billpage&stab=02&id=hb0968&tab=subject3&ys=2015rs.

203 **legislative session ended** Maryland Manual On-Line, General Assembly, Legislative Sessions: 2015, https://msa.maryland.gov/msa/mdmanual/07leg/html/sessions/2015.html.

203 **only three of the seventeen bills** Lawrence Lanahan, "Before Freddie Gray's Death, a Failed Attempt at Police Reform," *Al Jazeera America*, April 28, 2015, http://america.aljazeera.com/articles/2015/4/28/Maryland-failed-attempt-at-police-reform-before-freddie-gray-death.html.

204 **died six days later** Sherman, Kaltenbach, and Campbell, "Freddie Gray Dies a Week After Being Injured."

204 **protests spread** Evan Serpick, Baynard Woods, Brandon Soderberg, and Caitlin Goldblatt, "The Fight for Freddie Gray: Dispatches from Last Week's Protests," *Baltimore City Paper*, April 28, 2015, www.citypaper.com/bcpnews-the-fight-for-freddie-gray-20150428-story.html.

204 **as did Malik Shabazz** Jonathan Pitts, "Shabazz Plans Rally for Thousands Saturday: Group's Protest to Address 'The Burn Behind the Burn,'" *Baltimore Sun*, April 29, 2015, A8.

204 **the video** *Baltimore United for Change* (blog), "A Word from Baltimore Activists on #FreddieGray Actions," April 25, 2015, http://bmoreunited.org/2015/04/a-word-from-baltimore-activists-on-freddiegray-actions.

204 **to serve as a hub** KineticsLive.com, "About Us," http://kineticslive.com/about-us/; also, Baltimore United for Change, http://bmoreunited.org.

204 **"This is a moment"** KineticsLive, "A Word."

205 **"Shut it down!"** Sheryl Gay Stolberg and Stephen Babcock, "Scenes of Chaos in Baltimore as Thousands Protest Freddie Gray's Death," *New York Times*, April 25, 2015, www.nytimes.com/2015/04/26/us/baltimore-crowd-swells-in-protest-of-freddie-grays-death.html#.

205 **scheduled 7:05 p.m.** "Boston Red Sox at Baltimore Orioles Box Score, April 25, 2015," Baseball Reference, www.baseball-reference.com/boxes/BAL/BAL201504250.shtml.

205 **ran toward each other** SelkieKezia, "Baltimore Freddie Gray Rioting at Camden Yards 4/25/15," YouTube video, April 26, 2015, www.youtube.com/watch?v=9qVF5_4FPls.

205 **smashing storefront windows** Mike Thomas, "4/25/2015 Freddie Gray Protest in Baltimore's Camden Yards," YouTube video, April 26, 2015, www.youtube.com/watch?v=mZFYGKALiuo.

206 **"so adorable!"** William Scipio Facebook page, video, April 25, 2015, www.facebook.com/100006179656794/videos/1610037605878879.

206 **message on the Jumbotron** Eduardo A. Encina, Twitter post, April 25, 2015, 9:40 p.m., https://twitter.com/EddieInTheYard/status/592141068583497728.

206 **Orioles won** "Boston Red Sox at Baltimore Orioles Box Score, April 25, 2015," Baseball Reference, www.baseball-reference.com/boxes/BAL/BAL201504250.shtml.

206 **Baltimore was safe** Dan Connolly, Twitter posts, April 25, 2015, 10:05 p.m., https://twitter.com/danconnolly2016/status/592147012193247232 and https://twitter.com/danconnolly2016/status/592147114681049088; also, Baltimore OEM, Twitter post, 10:08 p.m., https://twitter.com/BaltimoreOEM/status/592148088887840768.

206 **Wilson grasped the edges** Descriptions in this scene are based on video of Dr. Wilson's April 26, 2015, sermon: New Song, "20150426 sermon," YouTube video, April 26, 2015, www.youtube.com/watch?v=icfWnhj7L4g.

207 **the response of the "black church"** Jonathan Pitts, "Voices of Local Pastors Shape Calls for Justice: As Angry Protesters Take to the Streets, Members of the Clergy Offer Their Support, Leadership and Wisdom," *Baltimore Sun*, April 25, 2015, A1.

209 **schoolchildren converging on the mall** Damien Cave, "Explaining 'The Purge'"; Ron Nixon, "Area of 'Purge' Is Regular Transfer Point for Students Returning from School"; also, Micheal Cieply, "Hollywood Film Linked to Riots," *New York Times*, April 28, 2015, www.nytimes.com/live/confrontation-in-baltimore/explaining-the-purge/?mcubz=1.

209 **one of the city's biggest transit hubs** Maryland Transit Administration, "MTA Regional Transit Map," http://web.archive.org/web/20150504160916/http://mta.maryland.gov/sites/default/files/MTA-Regional-Transit_0.pdf.

209 **yellow buses** Baltimore City Public Schools, "Transportation," www.baltimorecityschools.org/transportation; also, Sonja Brookins Santelises, J. Keith Scroggins, John M. Land, and Jacinta Hughes, "Transportation Update: Presentation to the Baltimore City Board of School Commissioners, September 19, 2017."

209 **schools within a mile of Mondawmin** Marlon D. Blue, "SY 14-15 Schools near Mondawmin," email message to author, June 25, 2018.

209 **1,083-student** Maryland State Department of Education, "Baltimore City, Frederick Douglass High, 1993 to 2017 Enrollment for All Grades: All Students," 2017 Maryland Report Card, http://reportcard.msde.maryland.gov/Enrollment.aspx?PV=34:17:30:0450:1:N:0:13:1:2:1:1:1:1:3.

209 **as schools were letting out** Baltimore Mayor's Office of Emergency Magagement, "Timeline of Events," 10; also, Justin Fenton and Erica L. Green, "Baltimore Rioting Kicked Off with Rumors of 'Purge,'" *Baltimore Sun*, April 27, 2015, www.baltimoresun.com/news/maryland/freddie-gray/bs-md-ci-freddie-gray-violence-chronology-20150427-story.html; also, Kevin Rector, Scott Dance, and Luke Broadwater, "Riots Erupt: Baltimore Descends into Chaos, Violence, Looting," *Baltimore Sun*, April 28, 2015, www.baltimoresun.com/news/maryland/freddie-gray/bs-md-ci-police-student-violence-20150427-story.html.

210 **"I just pray"** I interviewed George and his wife for a November 2015 *Urbanite* story. Most of the details in this passage come from video's George posted on Facebook. Lawrence Lanahan, "Who Can Save Sandtown," *Urbanite*, November 2015, www.urbanitebaltimore.com/100/who-can-save-sandtown/; also, George Hop Norfleet's Facebook page, April 26, 2015, www.facebook.com/photo.php?fbid=10206670544672374.

210 **posted the video** Norfleet Facebook, April 27, 2015, www.facebook.com/george.h.norfleet/videos/10206677582328311.

210 **"When it get dark"** Norfleet Facebook, April 27, 2015, www.facebook.com/george.h.norfleet/posts/10206677728531966.

210 **"They coming"** Norfleet Facebook, April 27, 2015, www.facebook.com/george.h.norfleet/posts/10206677838814723.

210 **said his wife** Norfleet Facebook, April 27, 2015, www.facebook.com/george.h.norfleet/videos/10206678182063304.

210 **longest average commute** Lawrence Lanahan, "Who Can Save Sandtown?," *Urbanite*, November 2015, www.urbanitebaltimore.com/100/who-can-save-sandtown.

210 **"it's gonna get"** Norfleet Facebook, April 27, 2015, www.facebook.com/george.h.norfleet/videos/10206678182063304.

211 **sound of smashing glass** Norfleet Facebook, April 27, 2015, www.facebook.com/george.h.norfleet/videos/10206679339452238.

211 **"Next to the organic garden"** Norfleet Facebook, April 27, 2015, www.facebook.com/george.h.norfleet/videos/10206678708316460.

211 **"that's the farm!"** Lawrence Lanahan, "A Baltimore Neighborhood Takes Care of Its Own as It Recovers from Unrest," *Al Jazeera America*, April 29, 2015, http://america.aljazeera.com/articles/2015/4/29/a-baltimore-neighborhood-takes-care-of-its-own-as-it-recovers-from-unrest.html.

211 **Pennsylvania Triangle Park** Baltimore City Recreation and Parks Department, "Baltimore City Land Preservation, Parks and Recreation Plan, 2017–2022," http://dnr.maryland.gov/land/Documents/Stewardship/BaltimoreCity_2017-LPPRP-Draft.pdf.

212 **center for children with developmental disabilities** Kennedy Krieger Institute, "About Us," www.kennedykrieger.org/overview/about-us.

212 **"Baltimore clean-up effort"** "Baltimore clean-up effort," Facebook event, April 28, 2015, www.facebook.com/events/7572493743883320.

212 **take cleaning supplies** Neil Sanzgiri, post to "Baltimore clean-up effort," April 27, 2015, www.facebook.com/events/1575563112714557/permalink/1575582736045928/?ref=1&action_history=null.

213 **wrote another** Comment on "Baltimore clean-up effort," April 28, 2015, www.facebook.com/events/757249374388332/permalink/757476251032311/?ref=1&action_history=null.

213 **event page's organizers** Post to "Baltimore clean-up effort," April 28, 2015, www.facebook.com/events/1575563112714557/permalink/1575815879355947/?ref=1&action_history=null.

213 **with the No Boundaries Coalition** Comment to "Baltimore clean-up effort," April 28, 2015, www.facebook.com/events/757249374388332/permalink/757476251032311.

214 **Despite the cleanup** Lawrence Lanahan, Twitter post, May 2, 2015, 12:47 p.m., https://twitter.com/llanahan/status/594543796043575296.

215 **Mary Harvin Center** Donna Kimura, "The Woda Group Doubles Down," *Affordable Housing Finance*, April 18, 2016, www.housingfinance.com/management-operations/the-woda-group-doubles-down_o.

215 **heap of rubble and ash** "3-alarm Fire Fully Engulfs East Baltimore Building," WBAL-TV, Baltimore, MD, April 28, 2015, www.wbaltv.com/article/3-alarm-fire-fully-engulfs-east-baltimore-building/7093242.

215 **Bell called Reverend Donte Hickman** Adam Bednar, "Destroyed Seniors' Center, Symbol of Riot's Damage, Set to Rise Again," *The Daily Record*, May 4, 2015, https://thedailyrecord.com/2015/05/04/construction-to-begin-on-seniors-housing-burned-in-east-baltimore.

215 **pastor** Southern Baptist Church, "Pastor," www.southernbaptistchurch.org /index.php?option=com_content&view=article&id=3&Itemid=3.

215 **three-alarm blaze** WBAL-TV.

215 **disheartening** Ray Sanchez, "Baltimore Riots: Catalyst for Rebuilding Burned Down," CNN, April 29, 2015, www.cnn.com/2015/04/28/us/baltimore-community -center-fire/index.html.

215 **"We're not leaving"** Kimura, "Woda Group Doubles Down."

216 **Scipio and Kelly wrote** William Scipio and Ray Kelly, "Please Do With and Not For," No Boundaries Coalition, News, April 30, 2015, www.noboundariescoalition .com/please-do-with-and-not-for.

217 **police had wound yellow tape** Edwin Torres, "State of Emergency," *ProPublica*, July 28, 2015, www.propublica.org/article/baltimore-freddie-gray-protest-photos.

217 **water and food** Darcy Spencer, Twitter post, May 2, 2015, 9:39 p.m., https:// twitter.com/darcyspencer/status/594677573994426368.

217 **emergency curfew** Baltimore City, Office of the Mayor, "Executive Order: State of Emergency," April 27, 2015, www.baltimorecity.gov/emergency-curfew-20150427.

217 **Three days later** "Read the Transcript of Marilyn J. Mosby's Statement on Freddie Gray," *Time*, May 1, 2015, http://time.com/3843870/marilyn-mosby-transcript -freddie-gray.

217 **rumor had spread** deray, Twitter post, May 2, 2015, 9:08 p.m., https://twitter .com/deray/status/594669835134590976.

217 **break the curfew as a show of defiance** deray, Twitter post, May 2, 2015, 11:12 p.m., https://twitter.com/deray/status/594700938725699584.

217 **amplified the repressive policing and policymaking** deray, Twitter post, May 2, 2015, 9:56 p.m., https://twitter.com/deray/status/594681897902542848.

217 **"scholactivist"** Twitter feed, Brittany Cooper, http://archive.is/HkUml. In the archive of Cooper's feed, it shows Cooper following Brown, whose bio at the time contains the term "scholactivist."

217 **Men and Families Center** Men and Families Center, Inc., "Home," www .menandfamiliescenter.org.

217 **redevelopment around Johns Hopkins Hospital** *The Lines Between Us* keeps mostly to the west side, city-wise. But someone could write a book about East Baltimore. In fact, Marisela Gomez did. *Race, Class, Power, and Organizing in East Baltimore* gives a detailed account of Baltimore, inequality, organizing, segregation, Johns Hopkins's long history of urban renewal in East Baltimore, and Baltimore's dependence on foundations and anchor institutions. It is doubly interesting for being told by someone who not only helped residents organize, but also worked on the Hopkins medical campus for fourteen years as a "student, research fellow, medical resident, and instructor." Marisela Gomez, *Race, Class, Power, and Organizing: Rebuilding Abandoned Communities in America* (Lanham, MD: Lexington Books, 2012).

217 **a series of articles** Lawrence Brown, "Change the Game: Creating a Better Baltimore in Light of Lessons from The Wire," *Indypendent Reader*, May 13, 2013,

https://indyreader.org/content/change-game-creating-better-baltimore-light-lessons
-wire; also, Lawrence Brown, "Avarice and Avatar in Charm City: Stepping Up the
Fight Against Displacement and Dispossession," *Indypendent Reader*, June 17, 2013,
https://indyreader.org/content/avarice-and-avatar-charm-city-stepping-fight-against
-displacement-and-dispossession; also, Lawrence Brown, "A Discussion About
Gentrification and Displacement in Baltimore," *Indypendent Reader*, June 24, 2013,
https://indyreader.org/content/discussion-about-gentrification-and-displacement
-baltimore; also, Lawrence Brown, "In Charm City, Plutocratic Pimpin' Is Easy,"
Indypendent Reader, August 12, 2013, https://indyreader.org/content/charm-city
-plutocratic-pimpin%E2%80%99-easy.

217 **grand jury declined** "Ferguson Cop Darren Wilson Not Indicted in Shooting of Michael Brown," *NBC News*, November 24, 2014, www.nbcnews.com/storyline
/michael-brown-shooting/ferguson-cop-darren-wilson-not-indicted-shooting
-michael-brown-n255391.

217 **posting frequently** BmoreDoc's Twitter feed, November 24, 2014 through
March 31, 2015, https://twitter.com/search?f=tweets&q=from%3Abmoredoc%20since
%3A2014-11-24%20until%3A2015-3-31&src=typd&lang=en.

217 **"Until We Tackle"** Lawrence Brown, "Until We Tackle Segregation, White
Cops Will Keep Shooting Black People," *Talking Points Memo*, April 9, 2015, https://
talkingpointsmemo.com/cafe/segregation-is-a-root-cause-of-cop-shootings.

218 **excessive force complaints correlating with levels of residential segregation**
Brad W. Smith and Malcolm D. Holmes, "Police Use of Excessive Force in Minority
Communities: A Test of the Minority Threat, Place, and Community Accountability
Hypotheses," *Social Problems* 61:1 (February 2014), 83–104.

218 **Brown wrote** Brown, "Until We Tackle."

218 **Brown tweeted** BmoreDoc, Twitter post, May 1, 2015, 1:52 p.m., https://twitter
.com/BmoreDoc/status/594197713165557761.

218 **white protesters** deray, Twitter post, May 2, 2015, 9:58 p.m., https://twitter
.com/deray/status/594682518139490305.

218 **Neighborhood Services Unit** Baltimore Police Department, "Northern District," www.baltimorepolice.org/districts/northern-district.

218 **they'd get another warning** deray, Twitter post, May 2, 2015, 10:00 p.m., https:
//twitter.com/deray/status/594682931844624385.

218 **the protester said** deray, Twitter post, May 2, 2015, 10:06 p.m., https://twitter
.com/deray/status/594684373485678592.

218 **"your second warning"** deray, Twitter post, May 2, 2015, 10:09 p.m., https://
twitter.com/deray/status/594685093777670144.

219 **Gibson said** deray, Twitter post, May 2, 2015, 10:12 p.m., https://twitter.com
/deray/status/594685998719770624.

219 **officers rushed toward the crowd** Kevin Rector, "Lawsuit Alleges Police Brutality, Unlawful Arrests During Baltimore Unrest," *Baltimore Sun*, April 20, 2016,
www.baltimoresun.com/news/maryland/freddie-gray/bs-md-ci-unrest-lawsuit
-20160420-story.html. [Video credit to WPTV, West Palm Beach, FL.]

219 **prostrate man** RT, "Baltimore Clashes: Cops Pepper-spray Protester in Face at Point Blank Range," YouTube video, May 3, 2015, www.youtube.com/watch?v= e1gXqrUsZYM&feature=youtu.be; also, Robert Brune Social Justice Journalist, "#BaltimoreUprising Larry Lomax Hosed w/ Pepper Spray 05.02," YouTube video, May 3, 2015, www.youtube.com/watch?v=xmgpPB0F-Z8.

219 **Darcy Spencer did** Darcy Spencer, Twitter post, May 2, 2015, 10:09 p.m., https://twitter.com/darcyspencer/status/594685192377212928.

219 **Brown retweeted** BmoreDoc, Twitter post, May 2, 2015, 10:28 p.m., https://twitter.com/BmoreDoc/status/594689998290604033.

220 **looks like** Joel Landau, "Baltimore Protester Wearing 'F--- THE POLICE' Shirt Pepper Sprayed by Police (WARNING: GRAPHIC CONTENT)," *New York Daily News*, May 3, 2015, www.nydailynews.com/news/crime/baltimore-protestor -wearing-f-police-shirt-arrested-article-1.2208530; also, L'Instant—Paris Match's Facebook page, May 4, 2015, www.facebook.com/instant.parismatch/photos/pb .286711201413197.-2207520000.1457401147./835506343200344/?type=3&theater.

220 **Stolarik's caption** Robert Stolarik, No. 05145117, Polaris Images, www .polarisimages.com/webgate/index.php?UURL=3a37cc93811de0ede200c6f94cccc0cf &SEARCHSHOWTAB=1&TABLIGHTBOX=RESULT&TABNAV=SEARCH.

220 **relieve his pain** "Raw: Man Pepper-Sprayed, Detained in Baltimore," Associated Press, YouTube video, May 2, 2015, www.youtube.com/watch?time _continue=34&v=zkehS8HPRHA.

220 **the narrative** Not everyone bought that narrative. It was an "entirely false comparison," according to a blogger with the pseudonym Baltimore Chop. "The idea was to hold quiet neighborhoods up to the yardstick of Penn North and Gilmor Homes," the blogger wrote, "but to compare enforcement you'd have to go to quiet black neighborhoods as well. Did anyone in the media or social media go to Cedonia to check the state of enforcement?" Regardless, the simultaneous Hampden/Penn North curfew protests went down as a "told you so" moment. "Baltimore's Golden Rules and Hampden's Curfew Protest," *The Baltimore Chop* (blog), May 4, 2015, http://thebaltimorechop.com/2015/05/04/baltimores-golden-rules-and-hamdens-curfew -protest-2.

220 **"time to get something done"** Descriptions in this scene are based on video of Dr. Wilson's May 3, 2015, sermon: New Song, "20150503 sermon," YouTube video, May 3, 2015, www.youtube.com/watch?v=6y2tBPvchqA.

221 **"how many of us"** Those outraged at "black-on-black" crime must account for the fact that Sandtown's population is black-on-black-on-black-on-black-on-black. There's hardly anyone else to commit a crime against. Also, the rates of "white-on-white" violent crime are only slightly lower than those for "black-on-black" violent crime, and both rates declined almost equally—a 79 percent decline for white-on-white, and a 78 percent decline for black-on-black—between 1993 and 2015. Rachel E. Morgan, "Race and Hispanic Origin of Victims and Offenders, 2012–2015," U.S. Department of Justice, Bureau of Justice Statistics, October 2017, www.bjs.gov/content/pub/pdf /rhov01215.pdf. There are plenty of criticisms of the focus on "black-on-black" crime, including the one found here: Michael Harriot, "Why We Never Talk About Black-on-black Crime: An Answer to White America's Most Pressing Question," *The Root*,

October 3, 2017, www.theroot.com/why-we-never-talk-about-black-on-black-crime
-an-answer-1819092337.

222 **hadn't gotten a badge** Dr. Wilson told me in an interview, "Fifteen books mention New Song; the ethnicity of all the authors is white." I thought, "I guess I'm making
it sixteen."

223 **"for the wrong reason"** Reverend Louis Wilson, "Godly Principle & Precepts
Before Projects" (audio), sermon, February 8, 2015, http://nscommunity.org/sermon
-archive-2015/#audio147.

223 **six police officers** Alan Blinder and Richard Pérez-Peñamay, "6 Baltimore
Police Officers Charged in Freddie Gray Death," *New York Times*, May 1, 2015,
www.nytimes.com/2015/05/02/us/freddie-gray-autopsy-report-given-to-baltimore
-prosecutors.html.

224 **a clear day** Photograph, *Duluth News Tribune*, May 3, 2015, www
.duluthnewstribune.com/sites/default/files/styles/16x9_620/public/field/image
/2015-05-03T213235Z_1276221380_GF10000083021_RTRMADP_3_USA-POLICE
-BALTIMORE.JPG?itok=jXqPIYZ7.

224 **conventional wisdom** Thomas B. Edsall, "Does Moving Poor People Work?"
New York Times, September 16, 2014, www.nytimes.com/2014/09/17/opinion/does
-moving-poor-people-work.html.

224 ***Washington Post*** Emily Badger, "How Baltimore and Cities like It Hold
Back Poor Black Children as They Grow Up," *Washington Post*, May 6, 2015, www
.washingtonpost.com/news/wonk/wp/2015/05/06/how-baltimore-and-cities-like-it
-hold-back-poor-black-children-as-they-grow-up/?utm_term=.77e11d32b73a.

224 **two headlines** David Leonhardt, Amanda Cox, and Claire Cain Miller, "An
Atlas of Upward Mobility Shows Paths out of Poverty," *New York Times*, May 4, 2015,
www.nytimes.com/2015/05/04/upshot/an-atlas-of-upward-mobility-shows-paths-out
-of-poverty.html; also, Justin Wolfers, "Why the New Research on Mobility Matters:
An Economist's View," *New York Times*, May 4, 2015, www.nytimes.com/2015/05/05
/upshot/why-the-new-research-on-mobility-matters-an-economists-view.html.

224 **bold conclusion** Raj Chetty, Nathaniel Hendren, and Lawrence Katz, "The
Effects of Exposure to Better Neighborhoods on Children: New Evidence from the
Moving to Opportunity Experiment, Executive Summary," May 2015; published in
full for the National Bureau of Economic Research in August 2015.

224 **They found** Raj Chetty and Nathaniel Hendren, "The Impacts of Neighborhoods on Intergenerational Mobility: Childhood Exposure Effects and County-Level
Estimates, Executive Summary," April 2015; published in full for the National Bureau
of Economic Research in May 2015.

225 **improving childhood environments** Chetty and Hendren, "The Effects of
Exposure to Better Neighborhoods on Children," May 2015.

225 **they did argue for "policies"** Chetty, Hendren, and Katz, "The Effects of Exposure to Better Neighborhoods on Children"; also, Chetty and Hendren, "The Impacts
of Neighborhoods on Intergenerational Mobility."

225 ***Atlantic, New York Times,* and *Washington Post*** David Leonhardt, Amanda
Cox and Claire Cain Miller, "An Atlas"; also, Justin Wolfers, "Why the New Research";

also, Derek Thompson, "The Curse of Segregation," *The Atlantic*, May 5, 2015, www
.theatlantic.com/business/archive/2015/05/the-curse-of-segregation/392321;   also,
Emily Badger, "How Baltimore and Cities Like It Hold Back Poor Black Children
as They Grow Up," *Washington Post*, May 6, 2015, www.washingtonpost.com/news
/wonk/wp/2015/05/06/how-baltimore-and-cities-like-it-hold-back-poor-black
-children-as-they-grow-up; also, "The Best and Worst Places to Grow Up: How Your
Area Compares," *New York Times*, May 4, 2015, www.nytimes.com/interactive/2015
/05/03/upshot/the-best-and-worst-places-to-grow-up-how-your-area-compares.html.

225 **editorial** "The Urban Agenda: Our View: Presidential Candidates Must
Address 'Inequality of Opportunity' That Underlies Baltimore's Recent Unrest and
Plagues Many Other U.S. Cities," *Baltimore Sun*, May 6, 2015, A22.

225 **op-ed** Jonah Goldberg, "To Break the Cycle of Poverty in Baltimore, Fix the
Culture of Poverty," *Baltimore Sun*, May 10, 2015, A23.

225 **Rodricks** Dan Rodricks, "City Had Lots of Warning Before Unrest: Rusk's
Book on Baltimore's Decline, Housing Lawsuit Focused on Central Problem of Poverty," *Baltimore Sun*, May 12, 2015, A3; also, Dan Rodricks, "Not Too Late to Do Right
by City's Poorest: 20 Years After a Program to Help Families Escape Poverty Was Shot
Down, We Can Still Act," *Baltimore Sun*, May 24, 2015, A3; also, Dan Rodricks, "How
History and Voters Will Judge: Hogan and Rawlings-Blake Are Being Handed a Blueprint for the Baltimore Region's Big Fix," *Baltimore Sun*, June 7, 2015, A3.

225 **"Baltimore Regional Plan for Sustainable Development"** Opportunity Collaborative, "Baltimore Regional Plan for Sustainable Development," June 2015.

226 **come to be known around Baltimore as the "White L"** Jenna McLaughlin,
"Ride, Respect, and Revelry: For the Creator of the Baltimore Bike Party, It's Not
Actually About the Bikes," *Baltimore City Paper*, July 24, 2013, http://web.archive
.org/web/20130727000022/http://www.citypaper.com/news/ride-respect-and-revelry
-1.1524717; also, Baltimore City Paper, Twitter post, July 25, 2013, 10:17 a.m., https:
//twitter.com/city_paper/status/360403375369621505; also, Andrew Zaleski, "Real
News Network Plants Roots—and Tackles the 'Media Desert'—in Baltimore," *Baltimore City Paper*, May 28, 2014, www.citypaper.com/bcp-cms-1-1693114-migrated
-story-cp-20140528-featu-20140528-story.html; also, Klaus Philipsen, "Are Cities Becoming Less Authentic?", *Community Architect* (blog), April 17, 2015, http://
archplanbaltimore.blogspot.com/2015/04/are-cities-becoming-less-authentic.html;
also, "On the Myth of Baltimore as a Cheap Place to Live," *The Baltimore Chop* (blog),
April 5, 2015, http://thebaltimorechop.com/2015/04/05/on-the-myth-of-baltimore-as
-a-cheap-place-to-live.

Six: If Not Now, When?

229 **planned to issue opinions** David S. Cohen, "It's Justice Kennedy's World,
and We're All Just Living in It," *Rolling Stone*, June 30, 2015, www.rollingstone.com
/politics/news/its-justice-kennedys-world-and-were-all-just-living-in-it-20150630;
also, U.S. Supreme Court, "Opinions of the Court—2014," www.supremecourt.gov
/opinions/slipopinion/14.

229 **Rothstein** Richard Rothstein, "From Ferguson to Baltimore: The Fruits of
Government-Sponsored Segregation," *Working Economics Blog*, Economic Policy

Institute, April 29, 2015, www.epi.org/blog/from-ferguson-to-baltimore-the-fruits-of
-government-sponsored-segregation.

229 **Kerner Commission** *Report of the National Advisory Commission on Civil Disorders* (New York: Bantam Books, 1968), xvi, 1.

229 **on white society** "White society is deeply implicated in the ghetto," the report said. "White institutions created it, white institutions maintain it, and white society condones it." *Report of the National Advisory Commission (1968).*

229 **similar one about Ferguson** Richard Rothstein, "The Making of Ferguson," *Economic Policy Institute*, October 15, 2014, www.epi.org/publication/making
-ferguson.

230 **He wrote that the law's language** Kennedy also referred to the 1988 amendment to the Fair Housing Act that listed specific conditions in which disparate impact claims were not valid. If the statute didn't allow disparate impact claims in the first place, he wrote, those exemptions would be "superfluous."

230 **in response to the riots** U.S. Department of Housing and Urban Development, "History of Fair Housing," www.hud.gov/program_offices/fair_housing_equal_opp
/aboutfheo/history.

230 **insisting that the Act must help prevent** *TDHCA v. ICP*, et al., 135 S.Ct. 2507 (2015).

231 **state would not build** "Excerpts from Md. Gov. Larry Hogan's Transportation Announcement," *Washington Post*, June 26, 2015, www.washingtonpost.com/local/md
-politics/excerpts-from-md-gov-larry-hogans-transportation-announcement/2015
/06/26/06eab61a-1b9b-11e5-bd7f-4611a60dd8e5_story.html?noredirect=on&utm
_term=.f42cd342eeb3; also, Television newscast, Christian Schaffer, WMAR Channel 2, Baltimore, MD, YouTube video, June 25, 2015, www.youtube.com/watch
?v=z0n2y4yCmDY.

231 **rule** "Affirmatively Furthering Fair Housing," final rule, *Federal Register* 80, no. 136 (July 16, 2015): 42272–42371.

231 **HUD secretary Julian Castro told reporters** Julian Castro, telephone press conference, July 8, 2015.

231 **HUD supported "a balanced approach"** "Affirmatively Furthering Fair Housing," final rule.

231 **hiding the story** Stanley Kurtz, "AFFH: Admission of Stealth Caught on Video," *National Review*, June 15, 2015, www.nationalreview.com/corner/affh-admission
-stealth-caught-video-stanley-kurtz.

232 **Carson wrote** Ben Carson, "Experimenting with Failed Socialism Again: Obama's New Housing Rules Try to Accomplish What Busing Could Not," *Washington Times*, July 23, 2015, www.washingtontimes.com/news/2015/jul/23/ben-carson
-obamas-housing-rules-try-to-accomplish-.

232 **Carson led** Mark Murray, "NBC/WSJ Poll: Carson Surges Into Lead of National GOP Race," *NBC News*, November 4, 2015, www.nbcnews.com/politics/2016-election
/nbc-wsj-poll-carson-surges-lead-national-gop-race-n456006; also, WSJ Graphics, Twitter post, November 3, 2015, 12:41 p.m., https://twitter.com/WSJGraphics/status
/661599053780795392.

232 **homicides spiked** Justin Fenton, Twitter post, November 22, 2015, 7:39 p.m., https://twitter.com/justin_fenton/status/668589648671875072.

232 **feeling less safe** "Rash of Homicides in West Baltimore Have Residents Asking: Where Are Police?," Associated Press, May 28, 2015, www.cbsnews.com/news /rash-of-homicides-in-west-baltimore-have-residents-asking-where-are-police/; also, Richard A. Oppel Jr., "West Baltimore's Police Presence Drops, and Murders Soar," *New York Times*, June 12, 2015, www.nytimes.com/2015/06/13/us/after-freddie-gray -death-west-baltimores-police-presence-drops-and-murders-soar.html.

232 **"no police"** "Rash of Homicides," AP.

232 **dropped 43 percent** "Rash of Homicides," AP.

232 **60 percent** Justin George, "Western District Leaders Try to Make Connections with the Residents as They Fight an Uptick in Crime," *Baltimore Sun*, June 21, 2015, A1.

232 **Batts told the *Baltimore Sun*** Justin George and Justin Fenton, "Police Struggling in West Baltimore: Officers Face Hostility, Crowds, Cameras amid Gray Fallout," *Baltimore Sun*, May 21, 2015: A1.

232 **department ordered** George, "Western District Leaders."

232 **Rawlings-Blake fired** "City Leaders Firing Back After Comments Made by Former Police Commissioner," CBS Baltimore, September 3, 2015, http://baltimore .cbslocal.com/2015/09/03/ex-baltimore-police-commissioner-discusses-tenure -firing.

232 **stunned the region** Colin Campbell, "Anthony Batts Says Police 'Took a Knee' After Baltimore Riots," *Baltimore Sun*, September 2, 2015, www.baltimoresun.com /news/maryland/freddie-gray/bs-md-batts-panel-20150902-story.html.

232 **homicide count** Justin Fenton, Twitter post, October 1, 2015, 7:58 a.m., https: //twitter.com/justin_fenton/status/649599278101434368; also, Justin Fenton, Twitter post, November 15, 2015, 3:58 p.m., https://twitter.com/justin_fenton/status /666042510322610176; also, Paul Gessler, "City's First Two Homicides of 2017 in Violent Western District," Fox 45 News, January 3, 2017, http://foxbaltimore.com/news /local/citys-first-two-homicides-of-2017-in-violent-western-district.

232 **demanded "sexual *quid pro quo*"** Second Amended Complaint, Class Action Claims and Jury Demand, *Nicole Andrea Smith, et al., v. Housing Authority of Baltimore City, et al.* (D. Md. 2015), www.scribd.com/document/289597389/Second -Amended-Complaint.

232 **310 murders** Justin Fenton, Twitter post, November 28, 2015, 6:06 a.m., https: //twitter.com/justin_fenton/status/670604737746739201.

232 **record per-capita murder rate** Justin Fenton, Twitter post, November 17, 2015, 12:55 p.m., https://twitter.com/justin_fenton/status/666721256935419904.

232 **new organization** Donald Morton Glover Facebook page, November 29, 2015, www.facebook.com/TheGloverReport/posts/1663978987212010; also, Donald Morton Glover Facebook page, October 27, 2015, www.facebook.com/TheGloverReport /posts/1655551334721442; also, Donald Morton Glover Facebook page, October 20, 2015, www.facebook.com/TheGloverReport/posts/1653741574902418.

232 **meetings** Doni Glover's Facebook page, August 1, 2015, www.facebook
.com/doni.glover/photos/a.1415340985390766.1073741828.1415338302057701
/1626206694304193/?type=3&theater.

232 **No Boundaries Coalition** No Boundaries Coalition's Facebook page, May 15,
2015, www.facebook.com/NoBoundariesCoalition/photos/a.412923568755205.94959
.412916495422579/901536473227243/?type=3&theater.

232 **Commission on Police Misconduct** The West Baltimore Commission on
Police Misconduct and the No Boundaries Coalition, "Over-policed, Yet Underserved:
The People's Findings Regarding Police Misconduct in West Baltimore," 2016, www
.noboundariescoalition.com/wp-content/uploads/2016/03/No-Boundaries-Layout
-Web-1.pdf.

232 **police misconduct allegations** No Boundaries Coalition's Facebook page,
May 27, 2015, www.facebook.com/NoBoundariesCoalition/posts/906607269386830.

233 **argue for more civilian oversight** No Boundaries Coalition, "Safety," www
.noboundariescoalition.com/safety/.

233 **scheduled for December 1** Kevin Rector and Justin Fenton, "Trial of First Officer in Freddie Gray Case Set to Begin Wednesday," *Baltimore Sun*, December 1, 2015,
www.baltimoresun.com/news/maryland/freddie-gray/bs-md-ci-freddie-gray-porter
-trial-20151201-story.html.

233 **primary election** Yvonne Wenger, "Baltimore Mayor Stephanie Rawlings-
Blake Won't Seek Re-election," *Baltimore Sun*, September 11, 2015, www.baltimoresun
.com/news/opinion/editorial/bs-md-ci-rawlings-blake-20150911-story.html.

233 **declined to run** Wenger.

233 **every city council seat** Maryland State Board of Elections, Official 2016 Presidential Primary Election results for Baltimore City, https://elections.maryland.gov
/elections/2016/results/primary/gen_results_2016_3_by_county_030.html.

233 *Not in My Neighborhood* Antero Pietila, *Not in My Neighborhood: How Bigotry Shaped a Great American City* (Chicago: Ivan R. Dee, 2010).

233 **the ad** Pamela Wood, "Ad Campaign Urges Baltimore to Consider 'Structural Racism,'" *Baltimore Sun*, September 18, 2015, www.baltimoresun.com/news
/maryland/baltimore-city/bs-md-activist-ad-20150917-story.html.

233 **for-credit course** "Divided Baltimore: How Did We Get Here, Where Do We
Go? A Course and a Community Discussion from The University of Baltimore," *University of Baltimore* (blog), https://blogs.ubalt.edu/dividedbaltimore.

233 **"Where Do We Go?"** Disclosure: I attended the Aspen work group's three-day
seminar in 2011 and attended several meetings through 2015. After I began writing the
book, I temporarily withdrew from the group. I also taught a section of the University
of Baltimore's "Divided Baltimore" course and was a featured speaker at one session.

234 **Ayira warned** A. Adar Ayira, lecture, University of Baltimore, October 26,
2015, video archived at https://ubalt.hosted.panopto.com/Panopto/Pages/Viewer
.aspx?id=691fb747-24ba-48a1-88fe-842417bcf1fb.

234 **editorial** "Seeds of Hope: Our View: A Year After the Unrest Sparked by Freddie Gray's Death, Youthful Activists Are Reframing the Context of the Struggle for
Social Justice in Baltimore," *Baltimore Sun*, April 24, 2016, A18.

234 **Leaders of a Beautiful Struggle** Lawrence Grandpre, "Leaders of a Beautiful Struggle Public Speaking Profile," Academia.edu, www.academia.edu/5766457/Leaders_of_a_Beautiful_Struggle_Public_Speaking_Profile.

234 **"potential of 'people power'"** "Seeds of Hope."

234 **a bright afternoon** Weather Underground, "History," www.wunderground.com/history.

234 **scheduled a final vote** Luke Broadwater and Kevin Rector, "City Council Confirms Kevin Davis as Police Chief," *Baltimore Sun*, October 19, 2015, www.baltimoresun.com/news/maryland/baltimore-city/bs-md-ci-kevin-davis-vote-20151019-story.html.

234 **hearing on Davis's appointment five nights earlier** Edward Ericson Jr., "This is what democracy looks like": The Scene Inside City Hall at Kevin Davis' Confirmation Hearing," *Baltimore City Paper*, October 19, 2015, www.citypaper.com/blogs/the-news-hole/bcpnews-this-is-what-democracy-looks-like-the-scene-inside-city-hall-at-kevin-davis-confirmation-hearing-20151019-story.html.

235 **City Bloc** Danielle Sweeney, "Removal of City College Student Group's Fliers Raises Questions," *Baltimore Brew*, September 15, 2015, www.baltimorebrew.com/2015/09/15/principal-smacks-down-student-political-org/.

235 **Baltimore City College** Again, this is a high school, not a college, despite its name. Your guess is as good as mine.

235 **wanted Commissioner Davis to agree** "Open Letter to Baltimore Police Dept. Concerning Peaceful Protesters," https://gallery.mailchimp.com/ecf8e6c8c23e30330f6713de8/files/BCC_Bloc_Letter.pdf.

235 **redirected toward community building** Dayvon Love, "Op-Ed: Setting the Record Straight on #CityHallShutDown Protests," *Leaders of a Beautiful Struggle* (blog), October 20, 2015, http://lbsbaltimore.com/setting-the-record-straight-on-city hallshutdown-protests.

235 **fire housing commissioner** Baltimore United for Change, "An Update on the City Hall Shutdown" (press release), October 19, 2015, https://us10.campaign-archive.com/?u=ecf8e6c8c23e30330f6713de8&id=35a7ff95de.

235 **failed to provide** Ralph F. Boyd, Jr. to Parris N. Glendening, 2002, www.justice.gov/crt/i-background-1.

235 **simply open more spots** Joe Tropea and Casey McKeel, "The Youth Jail: Tactics in Struggle," *Indypendent Reader*, November 19, 2012, https://indyreader.org/content/youth-jail-tactics-struggle.

235 **"strategic" alliance** Lawrence Grandpre and Dayvon Love, *The Black Book: Reflections from the Baltimore Grassroots* (Baltimore: Leaders of a Beautiful Struggle, 2014), 160–181.

235 **op-ed** Adam J. Jackson, "Op-Ed: What Was Wrong with the "Affirmative Opportunity" Rally Against the Youth Jail?," *Leaders of a Beautiful Struggle* (blog), November 12, 2012, http://lbsbaltimore.com/what-was-wrong-with-the-affirmative-opportunity-rally-against-the-youth-jail.

236 **Heber Brown wrote** Reverend Heber Brown III, "Free From The Inside Out:

A Cursory Examination of Racism's Reach Within Social Movements," *Indypendent Reader*, Spring 2011, https://indyreader.org/content/free-inside-out-cursory-examination-racisms-reach-within-social-movements.

236 **2013 essay** Dayvon Love, "Episode #38: 'Black Children, White Adults,'" *The Lines Between Us* (series), *Maryland Morning with Sheilah Kast*, WYPR-FM, Baltimore, MD, June 28, 2013, www.linesbetweenus.org/our-stories/episode-38-black-children-white-adults.html.

236 **WYPR** Disclosure: I commissioned Love's essay for WYPR's "The Lines Between Us" series on regional inequality. Love goes into much more detail about the youth jail campaign and his philosophy on community organizing and combatting white supremacy in his and Lawrence Grandpre's publication *The Black Book: Reflections from the Baltimore Grassroots*.

236 **Love wrote** Love, "Episode #38."

236 **state pulled the plug** Yvonne Wenger, "State Scraps Its Plans to Build a Youth Jail," *Baltimore Sun*, January 17, 2013, A1.

236 **city council voted** Broadwater and Rector, "City Council Confirms Kevin Davis."

236 **they took to the streets** "Activists Return to City Hall to Defend the Right to Protest," *The Real News*, YouTube video, October 19, 2015, www.youtube.com/watch?v=QYBLX1lsJ2Q.

236 **the killing** Gray was injured in police custody. "Killing" is accurate according to the state medical examiner, whose office ruled his death a homicide because of a failure to follow "established safety procedures." Sheryl Gay Stolberg, "Prompt Medical Care May Have Saved Freddie Gray, Experts Testify," *New York Times*, December 7, 2015, www.nytimes.com/2015/12/08/us/medical-examiner-questioned-on-homicide-ruling-in-freddie-grays-death.html.

236 **"Buy Where You Can Work" boycott** Andor Skotnes, "'Buy Where You Can Work': Boycotting for Jobs in African-American Baltimore, 1933–1934," *Journal of Social History* 27:4 (Summer, 1994), 735–761.

237 **organizing in Baltimore public housing** Williams, *Politics of Public Housing*.

237 **Occupy Baltimore** Jean Marbella, "Occupy Baltimore Seeks New Goals After Eviction," *Baltimore Sun*, December 13, 2011, www.baltimoresun.com/news/breaking/bs-md-occupy-next-day-20111213-story.html.

237 **Trayvon Martin** Childs Walker, "Trayvon Martin Case Strikes Deep Chord with Baltimoreans," *Baltimore Sun*, March 29, 2012, www.baltimoresun.com/news/breaking/bs-md-trayvon-martin-reaction-20120329-story.html.

237 **Anthony Anderson** Baltimore Bloc's Facebook page, "1 Year Anniversary of the Murder of Anthony Anderson," September 22, 2013, www.facebook.com/pg/bmorebloc/photos/?tab=album&album_id=547941928609363.

237 **Tyrone West** Baltimore Bloc's Facebook page, "Anti-Police Brutality Action for Tyrone West," July 23, 2013, www.facebook.com/pg/bmorebloc/photos/?tab=album&album_id=519560241447532.

237 **grand jury declined to indict** "Ferguson Cop Darren Wilson Not Indicted in Shooting of Michael Brown," *NBC News*, November 24, 2014, www.nbcnews .com/storyline/michael-brown-shooting/ferguson-cop-darren-wilson-not-indicted -shooting-michael-brown-n255391.

237 **Baltimore Bloc helped organize a march** Baltimore Bloc, Twitter post, November 25, 2014, 12:40 a.m., https://twitter.com/BmoreBloc/status/537118682791829504.

237 **blocked on-ramps** Justin George and Jessica Anderson, "Ferguson Protesters Take to Baltimore Streets," *Baltimore Sun*, November 25, 2014, www.baltimoresun .com/news/maryland/baltimore-city/bs-md-ci-ferguson-protests-20141125-story .html; also, Baltimore Bloc, Twitter post, November 26, 2014, 9:26 p.m., https://twitter .com/BmoreBloc/status/537839965615710208.

237 **homeless evictions** Baltimore Bloc, Twitter post, August 5, 2013, 11:33 a.m., https://twitter.com/BmoreBloc/status/364408781725122561.

237 **government subsidies to developers** Baltimore Bloc's Facebook page, "MAR8 | Camp 83 Destroyed," March 9, 2013, www.facebook.com/pg/bmorebloc/photos /?tab=album&album_id=461056273964596; also, Baltimore Bloc's Facebook page, "Harbor Point Hearing at City Hall," July 17, 2013, www.facebook.com/pg/bmorebloc /photos/?tab=album&album_id=516630535073836.

237 **Baltimore Racial Justice Action** Baltimore Racial Justice Action, http:// bmoreantiracist.org.

237 **"white allyship" workshops** Love, "Episode #38."

237 **Showing Up for Racial Justice** SURJ Baltimore, www.baltimoresurj.com.

237 **white supremacy** In *The Black Book*, Dayvon Love defines white supremacy as "the social, political and economic domination of people of color by white people." Grandpre and Love, *The Black Book*.

237 **"accountability partners"** SURJ Baltimore, "Partner Organizations," www .baltimoresurj.com/partners.html.

238 *Urbanite* **magazine** "Fix the City," *Urbanite*, November 2015, www .urbanitebaltimore.com/100/fix-the-city/#sthash.XbS6p2p6.IWvNi1PX.dpbs.

238 **"Fix the City"** Disclosure: I wrote a feature about Sandtown and regional inequality for the issue.

238 **In less than five hundred words** "Fix the City."

238 **judge declared a mistrial** Justin Fenton and Kevin Rector, "Mistrial Declared in Trial of Officer William Porter in Death of Freddie Gray," *Baltimore Sun*, December 16, 2015, www.baltimoresun.com/news/maryland/freddie-gray/bs-md-porter -trial-jury-wednesday-20151216-story.html.

238 **celebrate with** New Song Community Church's Facebook page, December 23, 2015, www.facebook.com/NSCChurch/videos/10153648120981355.

239 **block of N. Stricker Street** Maryland GovPics Flickr page, "Project C.O.R.E.," June 14, 2016, www.flickr.com/photos/mdgovpics/27687252115/in/photostream.

239 **not one occupied** I determined this using a September 2014 version of Google Maps. Of the few houses that did not display as boarded up on Google Maps, all were in the technical possession of the mayor and City Council of Baltimore by the time

of the governor's announcement that follows, according to the Maryland Department of Assessments and Taxation (https://sdat.dat.maryland.gov/RealProperty/Pages /default.aspx); also, Sara Luell, email message to author, June 15, 2018.

239 **Hogan announced** Office of Maryland Governor Larry Hogan, "Governor Hogan, Mayor Rawlings-Blake Partner to Address Blight in Baltimore City, Announce State Project" (press release), January 5, 2016.

239 **Hogan and other elected officials surrounded** Maryland Housing, Twitter post, January 5, 2016, 3:53 p.m., https://twitter.com/MDHousing/status/68447 7782492053504.

239 **plans to eliminate** Office of Maryland Governor Larry Hogan, "Governor Hogan, Mayor Rawlings-Blake Partner to Address Blight in Baltimore City, Announce State Project" (press release), January 5, 2016.

239 **Hogan** Luke Broadwater and Yvonne Wenger, "Gov. Hogan Announces $700M Plan to Target Urban Decay in Baltimore," *Baltimore Sun*, January 5, 2016, www.baltimoresun.com/news/maryland/politics/bs-md-ci-hogan-demolition -20160105-story.html; also, "Governor Larry Hogan: Creating Opportunities for Renewal and Enterprise," GovHogan, Youtube video, January 5, 2016, www.youtube .com/watch?v=0PkAu5fHmbo.

239 **excavator clawed** "Governor Larry Hogan: I'm a Guy on a Mission, Who Wants to Get Things Done," GovHogan, YouTube video, January 5, 2016, www.youtube.com /watch?v=K2ydFVnF9VE; also, Komatsu Hydraulic Excavator PC290LC-11, www .komatsuamerica.com/equipment/excavators/mid-size/pc290lc-11.

239 **250 people crammed** Fern Shen, "Personalities and Positions on Display at Mayoral Candidates' Forum," *Baltimore Brew*, January 28, 2016, www.baltimorebrew .com/2016/01/28/personalities-and-positions-on-display-at-mayoral-candidates -forum.

239 **slogged through** Impact Hub's Facebook page, February 3, 2016, www .facebook.com/impacthubbalt/photos/a.1890155364544234.1073741840.16683625 90056847/1890155391210898/?type=3&theater.

239 **record-setting** National Weather Service, "Snowfall and Cold," www.weather .gov/lwx/winter_storm-pr.

239 **Democratic candidates** Impact Hub Baltimore's Facebook page, "Mayoral Candidate Forum @ Impact Hub Baltimore" (event), www.facebook.com/events /926503440778768.

240 **"in the next five years?"** Descriptions in this scene are based on video from Impact Hub's January 27, 2016, Mayoral Candidate Forum, and on my experience as a co-moderator of the forum. "Mayoral Candidate Forum at Impact Hub Baltimore Jan 2016," CityExplainer, YouTube video, January 28, 2016, www.youtube.com /watch?v=MWT47Iq2aNE.

240 **Catherine Pugh** Amy Mulvihill, "The Lady in Waiting," *Baltimore Magazine*, January 2017, www.baltimoremagazine.com/2017/1/9/the-lady-in-waiting -mayor-catherine-pugh-lands-her-dream-job.

240 **who'd served** Maryland Manual On-line, Catherine E. Pugh, https://msa .maryland.gov/msa/mdmanual/05sen/html/msa14413.html.

240 **#mayoralforumIHB** Twitter hashtag "#MayoralForumIHB," https://twitter.com/hashtag/MayoralForumIHB?src=hash&lang=en.

240 **one user wrote** bilphena, Twitter post, January 27, 2016, 6:37 p.m., https://twitter.com/GoldWomyn/status/692491684924559361.

240 **candidate Joshua Harris** Lawrence Lanahan, "Does Baltimore Need DeRay Mckesson?," *Slate*, February 5, 2016, www.slate.com/articles/news_and_politics/metropolis/2016/02/deray_mckesson_will_make_baltimore_s_mayoral_race_crazier_and_maybe_better.html.

240 **TIFs** Baltimore Development Corporation, Tax Increment Financing (TIF), http://baltimoredevelopment.com/incentives/tif.

240 **TIF process** Board of Finance of Baltimore City, Baltimore City Department of Finance, and Baltimore City Bureau of Treasury Management, Tax Increment Financing Policy and Project Submission Requirements, January 23, 2012, https://board-of-finance.baltimorecity.gov/sites/default/files/Baltimore-Tax-Increment-Policy-FINAL.pdf.

240 **a better way to attract development** Baltimore Development Corporation, Tax Increment Financing (TIF).

241 **East Baltimore** East Baltimore Development Inc., "EBDI's Response to *The Daily Record* Series," February 9, 2011, www.ebdi.org/ebdi_response_to_the_daily_record; also, Melody Simmons and Joan Jacobson, "Baltimore Finds Funds for EBDI TIF," *The Daily Record*, September 18, 2011, https://thedailyrecord.com/2011/09/18/baltimore-finds-funds-for-ebdi-tif.

241 **community activist named J.C. Faulk** An End to Ignorance—Circles of Voices' Facebook page, "About," www.facebook.com/pg/anendtoignorance/about/?ref=page_internal.

241 **morning after** Public Justice Center, "Community + Land + Trust: Tools for Development Without Displacement" (press release), www.publicjustice.org/events/view/80.

241 **report** Peter Sabonis and Matt Hill, "Community + Land + Trust Tools for Development Without Displacement," Baltimore Housing Roundtable, 2016, https://d3n8a8pro7vhmx.cloudfront.net/unitedworkers/pages/239/attachments/original/1453986068/C_L_T_web.pdf?1453986068.

241 **Where, the authors wanted to know, was the plan to house them?** Sabonis and Hill.

242 **signed off on a settlement** "Conciliation agreement and Voluntary Compliance Agreement between the U.S. Department of Housing and Urban Development; and Baltimore County Branch of the NAACP, and Baltimore Neighborhoods, Inc.; and Baltimore County, Maryland," 2016.

242 **"unprecedented"** Doug Donovan, "Baltimore County to Curb Housing Segregation," *Baltimore Sun*, March 15, 2016, www.baltimoresun.com/news/maryland/baltimore-county/bs-md-hud-county-deal-20160315-story.html.

242 **one thousand "hard units"** Conciliation agreement, 2016.

242 **116 census tracts** The tracts were chosen from several opportunity maps, including those drawn by the state's housing department and the Opportunity Collaborative.

242 **eliminated** Conciliation agreement, 2016.

242 **veto** "Background on Conciliation Agreement and Voluntary Compliance Agreement with Baltimore Co. to End Housing Discrimination Against African Americans, Families with Children and People with Disabilities," American Civil Liberties Union of Maryland, 2016, www.aclu-md.org/uploaded_files/0000/0756/backgrounder_hud -baltimore_county_agreement.pdf.

242 **county specifically cited** Baltimore County Department of Planning, "HUD Conciliation Agreement: Frequently Asked Questions," www.baltimorecountymd .gov/Agencies/planning/fairhousing/hudconciliation.html; also, *Texas Department of Housing and Community Affairs et al., v. Inclusive Communities Project, Inc.*, et al., 135 S.Ct. 2507 (2015).

242 **Counties had banned** Pamela Wood, "Baltimore County Council Rejects Housing Anti-discrimination Bill," *Baltimore Sun*, August 1, 2016, www.baltimoresun .com/news/maryland/baltimore-county/bs-md-co-housing-policy-vote-20160801 -story.html.

242 **as had the cities** Poverty and Race Research Action Council, "Expanding Choice: Practical Strategies for Building a Successful Housing Mobility Program; APPENDIX B: State, Local, and Federal Laws Barring Source-of-Income Discrimination," updated May 2018, http://prrac.org/pdf/AppendixB.pdf.

242 **failed to pass a statewide ban** "Steve's 2012 End of Session Letter," *Steve Lafferty* (blog), April 16, 2012, http://delegatelafferty.com/p/salsa/web/news/public /?news_item_KEY=1429; also, Baltimore County HOME Act Coalition, "County Advocates Welcome Introduction of the HOME Act" (press release), July 5, 2016, https://hprplawblog.wordpress.com/2016/07/05/advocates-welcome-introduction -of-baltimore-co-home-act/; also, "Steve's News from Annapolis," *Steve Lafferty* (blog), March 27, 2017, http://delegatelafferty.com/p/salsa/web/news/public/?news _item_KEY=2244; also, General Assembly of Maryland, Legislation by Session, http://mgaleg.maryland.gov/webmga/frmLegislation.aspx?pid=legisnpage&tab =subject3.

242 **introduce legislation** Conciliation agreement, 2016.

242 **largest Tax Increment Financing package** Adam Marton, Natalie Sherman, and Caroline Pate, "Port Covington Redevelopment Examined," *Baltimore Sun*, http: //data.baltimoresun.com/news/port-covington.

242 **employed nearly two thousand** Rick Seltzer, "Under Armour Expects to Occupy Locust Point Headquarters for Another Decade," *Baltimore Business Journal*, April 28, 2016, www.bizjournals.com/baltimore/blog/real-estate/2016/04/under -armour-expects-to-occupy-locust-point.html.

243 **sponsored athletes** Opendorse, "Top 100 Highest-Paid Athlete Endorsers of 2016," http://opendorse.com/blog/2016-highest-paid-athlete-endorsers.

243 **Bryce Harper** Darren Rovell, "Source: Bryce Harper Signs Biggest Endorsement Deal for MLB Player," ESPN, May 4, 2016, www.espn.com/mlb/story/_/id/15451591 /washington-nationals-star-bryce-harper-gets-new-deal-armour.

243 **purchased 160 acres** Natalie Sherman, "Port Covington Developer Asks City for $535 Million in Support," *Baltimore Sun*, March 9, 2016.

243 **Sagamore Development planned** Sagamore Development Company, LLC,

Port Covington Tax Increment Financing Application, May 23, 2016, http://board
-of-finance.baltimorecity.gov/sites/default/files/Port%20Covington%20TIF%20
Application%205.23.16.pdf.

243 **supported** Sherman, "Port Covington Developer Asks."

243 **well over 1,000** Pete Cimbolic, email to author, October 24, 2018.

243 **93 percent white** 2010 U.S. Census Data, prepared by Baltimore Neighborhood Indicators Alliance, Jacob France Institute, University of Baltimore, accessed at
The Lines Between Us, WYPR-FM, Baltimore, MD, www.linesbetweenus.org/seeing
-inequality/interactive-inequality-map-baltimore.html.

243 **30 percent white city** Maryland Department of Planning, "Race Profile 1:
Detailed Race by Hispanic/Latino Ethnicity, with Total Tallies," U.S. Census 2010,
Summary File 1, http://web.archive.org/web/20171010134933/planning.maryland.gov
/msdc/census/cen2010/SF1/RaceProf/Race_baci.pdf.

243 **"certain to prove substantially different"** "City Council Endorsements: Districts 1-5," *Baltimore Sun*, April 18, 2016, www.baltimoresun.com/news/opinion/
editorial/bs-ed-council-endorse-20160418-story.html.

244 **shuttles to early voting stations** No Boundaries Coalition, "9th Annual
Boundary Block Party" (advertisement), https://trueurbanadvocacy.files.wordpress
.com/2016/03/no-bounderies-color_final-jpg.jpeg.

245 ***Post* reporter** Steve Hendrix, "In Baltimore, a Battered City Seeks a New Mayor
Who Can Heal Its Wounds," *Washington Post*, April 24, 2016, www.washingtonpost
.com/local/in-baltimore-a-battered-city-seeks-a-new-mayor-who-can-heal-its
-wounds/2016/04/24/c4d85cca-07dd-11e6-b283-e79d81c63c1b_story.html.

245 **attracting several** Google search, "Clyde Harris Sandtown roof."

245 **candidates** "City Council Endorsements."

245 **Pugh looked to be in the lead** Hendrix, "In Baltimore, A Battered City
Seeks"; also, Sam Fossum, "Pugh Leads Race for Baltimore Mayor," Johns Hopkins
News-Letter, April 21, 2016, www.jhunewsletter.com/article/2016/04/pugh-leads-race
-for-baltimore-mayor.

245 **"Public Safety and Policing Work Group"** Maryland Manual On-line,
"General Assembly, Defunct Legislative Committees, Commissions, Task Forces, &
Work Groups, Public Safety & Policing Work Group," https://msa.maryland.gov/msa
/mdmanual/07leg/html/com/defunct/spublicsafety.html.

245 **recommended** Erin Cox, "Maryland Task Force Recommends 22 Police
Reforms," *Baltimore Sun*, January 11, 2016, www.baltimoresun.com/news/maryland
/politics/bs-md-policing-group-20160111-story.html.

245 ***possible*** David Collins, "Criminal Justice Reforms Pass, Income Tax Relief
Fails in General Assembly," WBAL-TV Channel 11, April 12, 2016, www.wbaltv.com
/article/criminal-justice-reforms-pass-income-tax-relief-fails-in-general-assembly
/7100029.

245 **three officers** Michael Dresser and Pamela Wood, "City Senators Push for
Civilians on Police Trial Boards," *Baltimore Sun*, March 25, 2016, www.baltimoresun
.com/news/maryland/politics/bs-md-police-boards-20160325-story.html.

245 **after negotiations** Justin Fenton, "Citizens to Gain Peek at Police Discipline, but Not Full View," *Baltimore Sun*, April 17, 2016, www.baltimoresun.com/news /maryland/crime/bs-md-police-accountability-bills-20160417-story.html.

245 **sure to oppose** Jayne Miller, "Police Contract Negotiations Exposes Hole in Reform Law," WBAL-TV Channel 11, June 8, 2016, www.wbaltv.com/article/police -contract-negotiations-exposes-hole-in-reform-law/6950476.

245 **rally at city hall** Leaders of a Beautiful Struggle, "Don't Sit on the Sidelines!" (press release), https://us3.campaign-archive.com/?u=666dcba8cc07fd7bdbd79512e& id=07bd47f228.

245 **another rally in Annapolis** Baltimore United for Change's Facebook page, "#BaltimoreStillRising" (event), www.facebook.com/events/182339972152518/?active _tab=discussion.

245 **Harriet Tubman** Harriet Tubman Underground Railroad Byway, "About Harriet Tubman," http://harriettubmanbyway.org/harriet-tubman/#_about.

246 **Brion Gill** Open Society Institute–Baltimore, "Brion Gill," www.osibaltimore .org/author/brion-gill.

246 **government study of syphilis** Vann R. Newkirk II, "New Research Suggests a Strong Link Between the Public Revelation of the Tuskegee Study and Poor Health Outcomes for Black Men," *The Atlantic*, June 17, 2016, www.theatlantic.com/politics/ archive/2016/06/tuskegee-study-medical-distrust-research/487439.

246 **refused treatment** "AP Was There: Black Men Untreated in Tuskegee Syphilis Study," Associated Press, May 16, 1997, https://apnews.com/e9dd07eaa4e74052878 -a68132cd3803a/AP-WAS-THERE:-Black-men-untreated-in-Tuskegee-Syphilis -StudyP.

246 **"Vacants to Value"** Catherine Rentz, "Activist 'Squatters' Take Over Home near Gray's Arrest a Year Later," *Baltimore Sun*, April 13, 2016, www.baltimoresun .com/news/maryland/freddie-gray/bs-md-gilmor-area-changemakers-20160419 -story.html.

246 **reporter** Another disclosure: That reporter was me. Sorry for all the endnotes. I'm trying to keep myself out of the story, but I was around for a lot of what I'm writing about.

247 **April 19** Luminous Intervention's Facebook page, "Community Gathering at Tubman House on 1st Anniversary of Freddie Gray's Death" (event), www.facebook .com/events/1550266755273176.

247 **balloons** Coalition of Friends/Tubman House's Facebook page, April 19, 2016, www.facebook.com/CoalitionofFriends/photos/pcb.267684916908786/267684710 242140/?type=3&theater.

247 **thirty-five years old or younger** Yvonne Wenger and Luke Broadwater, "8 Newcomers Replace Veterans; New Members Pledge to Push More Liberal Agenda; Young, Pratt Stay in Office," *Baltimore Sun*, November 9, 2016, A3.

247 **Polls** "Polls: 2016 Republican Presidential Nomination," *Real Clear Politics*, www.realclearpolitics.com/epolls/2016/president/us/2016_republican_presiden tial_nomination-3823.html.

247 **Clinton leading Trump** "Polls: General Election: Trump vs. Clinton (4-Way)," *Real Clear Politics*, www.realclearpolitics.com/epolls/2016/president/us/general_election_trump_vs_clinton-5491.html#polls.

248 **Howard County had preserved** Howard County Government, "Preservation Easements" (interactive map), https://data.howardcountymd.gov/InteractiveMapV3.html?Workspace=Preservation#tab8.

250 **blizzard** "Storm Slams into Eastern U.S. with Wet Snow, Strong Gales," *Baltimore Sun*, January 23, 2016, www.baltimoresun.com/news/nation-world/ct-east-coast-snow-storm-20160122-story.html.

252 **fall of 2014** "Fall 2015 Report," Little Falls Friends Meeting Interchange Reports, Baltimore Yearly Meeting of the Religious Society of Friends, www.bym-rsf.org/who_we_are/meetings/md_meetings/littlefalls/littlefallsinch.html.

252 **Conway maintained his innocence** Justin Fenton, Ian Duncan, and Justin George, "Black Panther Leader, Convicted of Killing Cop, Released from Prison," *Baltimore Sun*, March 4, 2014, www.baltimoresun.com/news/maryland/crime/bs-md-ci-eddie-conway-black-panther-released-20140304-story.html.

252 **FBI was infiltrating the Panthers** "A Huey P. Newton Story," PBS, www.pbs.org/hueypnewton/actions/actions_cointelpro.html.

252 **opening of Tubman House** Rentz, "Activist 'Squatters' Take Over Home."

254 **ban source-of-income discrimination** Julian E. Jones Jr. and Stephen W. Lafferty, "Baltimore County Bill Would End Income Discrimination Against Renters," *Baltimore Sun*, July 20, 2016, www.baltimoresun.com/news/opinion/oped/bs-ed-home-act-20160720-story.html.

254 **Van Arsdale** Plaintiffs had filed the complaint against Van Arsdale and former housing office administrator Lois Cramer, but Van Arsdale supported the bill.

256 **1,400 petitions** Pamela Wood, Twitter post, July 21, 2016, 5:12 p.m., https://twitter.com/pwoodreporter/status/756235394761494528.

256 **a stellar school** "Atholton High School Profile, 2017–18," www.hcpss.org/f/schools/profiles/prof_hs_atholton.pdf.

257 **Baltimore Development Corporation** They did so with little transparency; in fact, a state board ruled that the BDC had violated a state "open meetings" law when it shut reporters out of two March 2016 meetings where the Sagamore development was discussed. "BDC Violated Open Meetings Law by Shutting Out Reporters, Board Rules," *Baltimore Brew*, May 23, 2016, www.baltimorebrew.com/2016/05/23/bdc-violated-open-meetings-law-by-shutting-out-reporters-board-rules.

257 **a master plan** Melody Simmons, "Port Covington Master Plan Wins Approval from City Planning Commission," *Baltimore Business Journal*, June 23, 2016, www.bizjournals.com/baltimore/blog/real-estate/2016/06/port-covington-master-plans-wins-approval-from.html.

257 **new zoning** "Port Covington Master Plan (draft)," June 16, 2016.

257 **waiver** Board of Estimates of Baltimore City, Minutes, April 20, 2016.

257 **10 percent affordable housing** Natalie Sherman, "City Panel OKs Port Covington Tax Deal; Board of Finance Moves Along Record $535 Million Public Financing Package," *Baltimore Sun*, April 26, 2016, A1.

259 **community benefits agreement** Luke Broadwater, "Developers to Pay Millions to Neighboring Communities; Port Covington Agreement to Boost South Baltimore," *Baltimore Sun*, July 15, 2016, A1.

259 **potential** Mark Reutter, "Analysis: Benefits Appear Limited in Community Pact with Sagamore," *Baltimore Brew*, July 15, 2016, www.baltimorebrew.com/2016/07/15/analysis-benefits-appear-limited-in-community-pact-with-sagamore.

259 **advocates and community groups** Port3 Coalition, "PORT3 Coalition Decries Sagamore's Affordable Housing Offer, Calls on Company to Do More Than the Bare Minimum" (press release), September 2, 2016, www.marylandconsumers.org/penn_station/folders/press/statements_and_comments/PORT3Statement.pdf.

259 **in a pair of photochromic glasses** Fern Shen, "Critics: Port Covington Deal Financially Risky, Worsens Segregation," *Baltimore Brew*, July 27, 2016, www.baltimorebrew.com/2016/07/27/critics-port-covington-deal-financially-risky-worsens-segregation.

259 **comments for the city's planning director** Barbara A. Samuels, C. Matthew Hill, Monisha Cherayil, and D'Sean Williams-Brown to Thomas J. Stosur, June 16, 2016.

259 **city council president** Barbara A. Samuels and D'Sean Williams-Brown to Jack Young, July 27, 2016.

259 **could eventually lead to cuts** Samuels, Hill, Cherayil, and Williams-Brown to Thomas J. Stosur.

259 **one-third of jobs** Samuels, Hill, Cherayil, and Williams-Brown.

259 **5,329** Sagamore Development Company, LLC, Port Covington Tax Increment Financing Application, May 23, 2016, http://board-of-finance.baltimorecity.gov/sites/default/files/Port%20Covington%20TIF%20Application%205.23.16.pdf.

259 **7,500** Marton, Sherman and Pate, "Port Covington Redevelopment Examined."

259 **14,000** Fern Shen, "A Pep Rally for Port Covington," *Baltimore Brew*, June 3, 2016, www.baltimorebrew.com/2016/06/03/a-pep-rally-for-port-covington.

259 **"live-work-play environment"** Sagamore Development, TIF Application, 43.

260 **market analysis** Battelle Technology Partnership Practice, "Regional Economic and Demographic Market Analysis and Economic Impact Assessment of the Port Covington Project/Under Armour Headquarters Project," December 2015.

260 **pop urbanist Richard Florida** Richard Florida, "Cities and the Creative Class," *City & Community* 2:1 (March 2003), 3–19.

260 **just 8.5 percent** Richard Florida, "The Racial Divide in the Creative Economy," *CityLab*, May 9, 2016, www.citylab.com/life/2016/05/creative-class-race-black-white-divide/481749.

260 **88 percent white, 2 percent black** "South Baltimore," Baltimore Neighborhood Indicators Alliance, Jacob France Institute, University of Baltimore, https://bniajfi.org/community/South%2520Baltimore.

261 **mistrial for the third** Fenton and Rector, "Mistrial Declared in Trial"; also,

Kevin Rector, "Charges Dropped, Freddie Gray Case Concludes with Zero Convictions Against Officers," *Baltimore Sun*, July 27, 2016, www.baltimoresun.com/news /maryland/freddie-gray/bs-md-ci-miller-pretrial-motions-20160727-story.html.

261 **the same corner** Kevin Richardson, "Transcript: State's Attorney Marilyn Mosby on the Dropped Charges" (video), *Baltimore Sun*, July 27, 2016, www.baltimoresun .com/news/maryland/freddie-gray/bal-transcript-state-s-attorney-marilyn-mosby -on-the-dropped-charges-20160727-story.html.

261 **she would drop charges** Vanessa Herring, Twitter post, July 27, 2016, 11:01 a.m., https://twitter.com/VanessaWBAL/status/758316284618629120.

261 **smaller hall** Liam Davis, Twitter post, July 27, 2016, 5:18 p.m., https://twitter .com/LiamFD/status/758411167240974341.

262 **Word spread** Liam Davis, Twitter post, July 27, 2016, 5:18 p.m., https://twitter .com/LiamFD/status/758411167240974341.

263 **sat behind a long table** CharmTV Citizens' Hub, "City Council Hearing: Port Covington; July 27, 2016," YouTube video, August 5, 2016, www.youtube.com /watch?v=puUiu0R-KmE.

264 **boos** CharmTV Citizens' Hub.

266 **Fifty years earlier** Scott Sullivan, "Foes of Bill on Housing Boo Cardinal: City Council Shocked at Hearing on Open Occupancy Plan," *Baltimore Sun*, January 14, 1966, C24.

266 **flood** Ovetta Wiggins, Mary Hui, and John Woodrow Cox, "Two Dead After Severe Flash Flood in Maryland," *Washington Post*, July 31, 2016, www.washingtonpost .com/local/severe-flash-flood-strikes-ellicott-city-overturning-cars-and-destroying -businesses/2016/07/31/a8e50184-5720-11e6-831d-0324760ca856_story.html.

266 **6:00 p.m. meeting** Baltimore County Council Agenda, August 1, 2016. www.wadekach.com/baltimore-county-council-agendas/baltimore-county-council -agenda-ws-july-21-2016-ls-august-1-2016.

266 **Korryn Gaines** Alison Knezevich and Kevin Rector, "Investigative Files Provide New Insights into Korryn Gaines' 6-hour Standoff with Baltimore County Police," *Baltimore Sun*, November 5, 2016, www.baltimoresun.com/news/maryland /investigations/bs-md-co-korryn-gaines-timeline-20161103-story.html.

267 **conciliation agreement** Conciliation agreement, 2016; also, Matt Hill, email message to author, June 12, 2018.

267 **South Baltimore** Doug Donovan, "City Board of Estimates Approves Sale of Land to Aquarium; Parcel on Middle Branch Would Be Second Campus; Board Approves Sale of Waterfront Site to National Aquarium," *Baltimore Sun*, December 23, 2004, 1B.

267 **Sagamore got its hands on** Scott Dance, "Sagamore Announces More Tenants for City Garage," *Baltimore Sun*, October 1, 2015, www.baltimoresun.com/business /under-armour-blog/bs-bz-sagamore-city-garage-20151001-story.html.

267 **start-up companies** "Daily Briefing," *Baltimore Sun*, June 6, 2015, A10.

267 **Stokes was notably absent** Lawrence Lanahan, Twitter post, September 8, 2016, 5:08 p.m., https://twitter.com/llanahan/status/773991363700547584.

268 **T-shirts that displayed the Under Armour logo** Fern Shen, "BUILD Asks Young to Pull Port Covington Vote from Committee," *Baltimore Brew*, September 9, 2016, www.baltimorebrew.com/2016/09/09/build-asks-young-to-pull-port-covington -vote-from-committee.

269 **had walked away** Fern Shen, "Groups Reject Port Covington Developer's Final Offer, Calling It 'Empty'," *Baltimore Brew*, September 3, 2016, www.baltimorebrew .com/2016/09/03/groups-reject-port-covington-developers-final-offer-calling-it -empty.

269—**Committee convened** CharmTV Citizens' Hub, "City Council Work Session—Port Covington; September 08, 2016," YouTube video, September 9, 2016, www .youtube.com/watch?v=xgKUhzlpQ5s.

269 **special taxing** Baltimore City Council, Council Bill 16-0671, adopted October 24, 2016.

269 **development** Baltimore City Council, Council Bill 16-0669, adopted October 24, 2016.

269 **issue the bonds** Baltimore City Council, Council Bill 16-0670, adopted October 24, 2016.

269 **sale would fund** Fern Shen, "Echoes of Harbor Point Process as Stokes Halts Port Covington Voting," *Baltimore Brew*, September 9, 2016, www.baltimorebrew.com /2016/09/09/echoes-of-harbor-point-process-as-stokes-halts-port-covington-voting.

270 **If the third bill made it** Luke Broadwater, "Council Advances Port Covington Deal; Final Vote on Public Financing, Community Benefits Likely Next Week," *Baltimore Sun*, September 13, 2016, A1; also, Luke Broadwater, "Port Covington Deal OK'd in 12-1 Vote, City Council Approves $660 Million Public Financing Package for Under Armour," *Baltimore Sun*, September 20, 2016, A1; also, Yvonne Wenger, "Rawlings-Blake Signs Off on Port Covington's Public Financing; $660 Million in Bonds to Go Toward Infrastructure Work," *Baltimore Sun*, September 29, 2016, A2.

271 **moved it to a final vote** Broadwater, "Council Advances."

271 **unanimously approved** Luke Broadwater, "Community Benefit Deal OK'd for Port Covington; Board of Estimates Approves $100 Million Plan That Includes Training and Loans," *Baltimore Sun*, September 15, 2016, A2.

271 **approved it** Broadwater, "Port Covington Deal OK'd."

271 **mayor signed** Wenger, "Rawlings-Blake Signs Off."

271 **26-point margin** Maryland State Board of Elections, "Official 2016 Presidential General Election Results for President and Vice President of the United States," https:// elections.maryland.gov/elections/2016/results/general/gen_results_2016_4_001-.html.

271 **Clinton took just three precincts** Ryne Rohla, "Creating a National Precinct Map," *Decision Desk HQ*, March 30, 2017, https://decisiondeskhq.com/data-dives/ creating-a-national-precinct-map.

271 **supporters openly made racist comments** Brandon Soderberg, "Notes from a Donald Trump Rally One Year Ago Today in Berlin, MD on Hitler's Birthday," *Baltimore City Paper*, April 20, 2017, www.citypaper.com/blogs/the-news-hole/bcpnews-notes -from-a-donald-trump-rally-one-year-ago-today-in-berlin-md-on-hitler-s-birthday -20170420-story.html; also, Ashley Parker, Nick Corasaniti, and Erica Berenstein,

"Voices from Donald Trump's Rallies, Uncensored," *New York Times*, August 3, 2016, www.nytimes.com/2016/08/04/us/politics/donald-trump-supporters.html.

272 **"might have to kill'm"** Television newscast, WNCN Channel 17, Raleigh, NC, YouTube video, March 10, 2016, www.youtube.com/watch?v=bfw7LSdJI3U&feature=youtu.be.

272 **having groomed themselves** Anna Silman, "For the Alt-Right, Dapper Suits Are a Propaganda Tool," *The Cut, New York Magazine*, November 23, 2016, www.thecut.com/2016/11/how-the-alt-right-uses-style-as-a-propaganda-tool.html.

272 **"What the hell do you have to lose?"** Andrew Rafferty, "Trump to African-American Voters: 'What the Hell Do You Have to Lose?'," August 19, 2016, *NBC News*, www.nbcnews.com/card/trump-african-american-voters-what-do-you-have-lose-n634756.

272 **spike in incidents** Eyder Peralta, "Threats and Intimidation Against Minorities Reported Nationwide," *All Things Considered*, National Public Radio, November 13, 2016, www.npr.org/2016/11/13/501935930/threats-and-intimidation-against-minorities-reported-nationwide.

272 **building plans of his own** Camessia Johnson, "The Fan | Vision Package," November 27, 2017, https://issuu.com/camessiajohnson/docs/the_fan_25_pages.

272 **complex** "Upton / Sandtown Site Beautification Day!," (press release), AIA Baltimore, www.aiabaltimore.org/upton-sandtown-site-beautification-day.

273 **shot his own father** Tim Prudente and Justin George, "Police Investigating Shooting at New Song Church in West Baltimore," *Baltimore Sun*, June 7, 2016, www.baltimoresun.com/news/maryland/crime/bs-md-ci-church-shooting-20160607-story.html.

274 **someone shot** Edward Ericson Jr., "Murder Ink 11/23/16: 9 Murders This Week; 280 Murders This Year," *Baltimore City Paper*, November 22, 2016, www.citypaper.com/news/murderink/bcp-112316-murderink-20161122-story.html.

274 **joint statement** U.S. Department of Housing and Urban Development and U.S. Department of Justice, "Joint Statement of the Department of Housing and Urban Development and the Department of Justice: State and Local Land Use Laws and Practices and the Application of the Fair Housing Act," November 10, 2016, Washington, DC.

274 **disparate impact counted** U.S. Department of Housing and Urban Development and U.S. Department of Justice, "Joint Statement."

274 **Kennedy's opinion** TDHCA v. ICP., et al., 135 S.Ct. 2507 (2015).

274 **selected Ben Carson** Trip Gabriel, "Trump Chooses Ben Carson to Lead HUD," *New York Times*, December 5, 2016, www.nytimes.com/2016/12/05/us/politics/ben-carson-housing-urban-development-trump.html.

274 **IRS statement** U.S. Department of the Treasury, Internal Revenue Service, "Revenue Ruling 2016-29," *Internal Revenue Bulletin: 2016-52*, December 27, 2016, www.irs.gov/irb/2016-52_IRB.

275 **"without regard" to the presence** U.S. Department of the Treasury, Internal Revenue Service, "Notice 2016-77," *Internal Revenue Bulletin: 2016-52*, December 27, 2016, www.irs.gov/irb/2016-52_IRB.

275 **regional voucher program** Baltimore Metropolitan Council, Request for Proposals: Baltimore Regional Project-Based Voucher (PBV) Program, July 21, 2016, http://baltometro.org/our-work/baltimore-regional-project-based-voucher-program.

275 **attached Housing Choice Vouchers** Baltimore Metropolitan Council (PBV).

275 **the pilot** Baltimore Metropolitan Council, "New Opportunity for Property Owners & Developers," www.baltometro.org/phocadownload/Publications/Socioeconomic_Trends/RegionalPBV_170607_2-Pager.pdf.

275 **developments in opportunity areas** Baltimore Metropolitan Council, "Baltimore Regional Project-Based Voucher Program," www.baltometro.org/community-planning/baltimore-regional-project-based-voucher-program.

275 **No complex would be allowed** Baltimore Metropolitan Council.

275 **Black Lives Matter sign** WBFF Fox 45's Facebook page, November 21, 2016, www.facebook.com/FOXBaltimore/posts/10154100426774607; also, Paul Gessler, "Towson Church's 'Black Lives Matter' Sign Vandalized Again," *Fox 45 News*, November 20, 2016, http://foxbaltimore.com/news/local/towson-churchs-black-lives-matter-sign-vandalized-again.

275 **caption** Fatimah Waseem, "Racial Tensions Rock Two Howard Schools," *Howard County Times*, November 16, 2016.

275 **a cadet** Nick Perlin, "Opinion: Atholton Steps Up: Atholton Moves Forward After a Leaked Photo with a Caption Using a Racial Slur," *The Raider Review*, December 9, 2016, https://ahsraiderreview.com/2016/12/09/opinion-atholton-steps-up.

275 **teacher** Erica L. Green, "Baltimore Teacher Caught on Video Using 'N' Word as She Berates Black Students," *Baltimore Sun*, November 17, 2016, www.baltimoresun.com/news/maryland/education/bs-md-ci-teacher-video-20161117-story.html.

275 **double homicide** Edward Ericson Jr., "Murder Ink: 2016 Ends with 318 Murders; New Year Starts with Three," *Baltimore City Paper*, January 4, 2017, www.citypaper.com/news/murderink/bcpnews-murder-ink-20170104-story.html.

275 **sixty-eight-year-old man** Colin Campbell, "Two Killed in West Baltimore Double Shooting, One of Them 68 Years Old," *Baltimore Sun*, December 19, 2016, www.baltimoresun.com/news/maryland/crime/bs-md-ci-homicides-20161219-story.html.

276 **highest had come in 2015** Kevin Rector, "Baltimore's Homicide Rate Is Down from 2015—But Up over Every Other Year on Record," *Baltimore Sun*, December 21, 2016, www.baltimoresun.com/news/maryland/crime/bs-md-ci-homicides-shootings-20161221-story.html.

276 **stunning 163-page report** U.S. Department of Justice, Civil Rights Division, *Investigation of the Baltimore City Police Department*, August 10, 2016, Washington, DC, www.justice.gov/crt/file/883296/download.

276 **arrests, excessive force, and "severe and unjustified disparities"** U.S. Department of Justice, Civil Rights Division, *Investigation of the Baltimore City Police Department*, 3.

276 **"in two small, predominantly African-American districts"** U.S. Department of Justice, Civil Rights Division, *Investigation of the Baltimore City Police Department*, 6.

276 **"undermines community trust"** U.S. Department of Justice, Civil Rights Division, *Investigation of the Baltimore City Police Department*, 73.

276 **city and the U.S. Department of Justice** Camila Domonoske, "Baltimore, DOJ Reach Agreement on Consent Decree for Baltimore Police," *The Two-Way*, National Public Radio, January 12, 2017, www.npr.org/sections/thetwo-way/2017/01 /12/509479934/baltimore-doj-reach-agreement-on-consent-decree-for-baltimore -police.

276 **reform its practices** Consent Decree, *United States of America v. Police Department of Baltimore City, et al.*, January 12, 2017, www.justice.gov/opa/file/925056 /download.

276 **indictment of seven Baltimore police officers** Justin Fenton and Kevin Rector, "Seven Baltimore Police Officers Indicted on Federal Racketeering Charges," *Baltimore Sun*, March 1, 2017, www.baltimoresun.com/news/maryland/crime/bs-md-ci -baltimore-police-indicted-20170301-story.html.

276 **over $200,000** U.S. Department of Justice, U.S. Attorney's Office District of Maryland, "Seven Baltimore City Police Officers Arrested for Abusing Power in Federal Racketeering Conspiracy" (press release), March 1, 2017, www.justice.gov /usao-md/pr/seven-baltimore-city-police-officers-arrested-abusing-power-federal -racketeering.

276 **One of the white officers was the brother of a man** Mike Hellgren, "Death Threats and Retaliation: New Fallout from Officer Indictments," *CBS Baltimore*, March 7, 2017, https://baltimore.cbslocal.com/2017/03/07/death-threats-and-retalia tion-new-fallout-from-officer-indictments; also, Mike Hellgren, "Brother of Indicted Officer: 'The Charges Are Bogus,'" *CBS Baltimore*, March 5, 2017, https: //baltimore.cbslocal.com/2017/03/05/brother-of-indicted-officer-the-charges-are -bogus; also, Paul Gessler, "Hersl's Brother Calls Federal Charges 'Bogus,' Politically Motivated," *Fox 45 News*, March 6, 2017, https://foxbaltimore.com/news/local /hersls-brother-calls-federal-charges-bogus-politically-motivated; also, Larry Carson, "Activists Fight County for Accepting Funding for Housing People with AIDS," *Baltimore Sun*, January 29, 1995, http://articles.baltimoresun.com/1995-01-29/news /1995029045_1_money-for-aids-people-with-aids-aids-victims; also, Ed Brandt, "Relocation Program Won't Grow," *Baltimore Sun*, September 10, 1994, http://articles .baltimoresun.com/1994-09-10/news/1994253038_1_mto-program-public-housing -relocation-program; also, Lori Montgomery, "Where Should Poor Families Live?," Knight-Ridder Newspapers, July 23, 1994, www.chicagotribune.com/news/ct-xpm -1994-07-23-9407230027-story.html; also, Karen De Witt, "Housing Voucher Test in Maryland Is Scuttled by a Political Firestorm," *New York Times*, March 28, 1995, www.nytimes.com/1995/03/28/us/housing-voucher-test-in-maryland-is-scuttled -by-a-political-firestorm.html.

277 **Dylann Storm Roof** Doug Stanglin, "Dylann Roof Attacked Next to Jail Shower," *USA Today*, August 4, 2016, www.usatoday.com/story/news/2016/08/04 /charleston-church-shooter-attacked-jail-shower/88073180.

277 **manifesto** Frances Robles, "Dylann Roof Photos and a Manifesto Are Posted on Website," *New York Times*, June 20, 2015, www.nytimes.com/2015/06/21/us/dylann -storm-roof-photos-website-charleston-church-shooting.html.

277 **trailer park** Rachel Kaadzi Ghansah, "A Most American Terrorist: The Making of Dylann Roof," *GQ*, August 21, 2017, www.gq.com/story/dylann-roof-making-of -an-american-terrorist.

277 **Manufacturing Jobs Initiative** White House, "President Trump Announces Manufacturing Jobs Initiative" (press release), January 27, 2017, www.whitehouse .gov/briefings-statements/president-trump-announces-manufacturing-jobs -initiative.

277 **Dorsey posted** Ryan Dorsey, comment on Baltimore City Voters' Facebook page, January 30, 2017, www.facebook.com/groups/baltimoreelection2016/permalink /401207920214126/?comment_id=401341113534140&comment_tracking=%257 B%2522tn%2522%253A%2522R6%2522%257D.

277 **"holding our City back"** Ryan Dorsey, Baltimore City Voters' Facebook page, January 30, 2017.

277 **Timothy Caughman** Jim Dwyer, "Another Murderer Crazed by Color, This Time Met by Silence," *New York Times*, March 23, 2017, www.nytimes.com/2017/03/23 /nyregion/james-harris-jackson-timothy-caughman-murder.html.

277 **racist manifesto** Ashley Southall, "Suspect in Manhattan Killing Hated Black Men, Police Say," *New York Times*, March 22, 2017, www.nytimes.com/2017/03/22 /nyregion/manhattan-nyc-james-harris-jackson-hate-crime.html.

277 *Baltimore Sun* **profile** Marbella, "A Baltimore Man's Inexplicable Path."

278 **vigil** Sarah Rice's Facebook page, "Vigil for Timothy Caughman and Hate-Free Hampden" (event), March 25, 2017, www.facebook.com/events/581512282056900.

278 **sign with a red heart** Tedd Henn, "Vigil for Timothy Caughman and Hate-Free Hampden in Photos," *Baltimore City Paper*, www.citypaper.com/bcpnews-vigil -for-timothy-caughman-and-hate-free-hampden-in-photos-20170327-photogallery .html.

278 **reporter approached Ralph Moore** Devin Bartolotta, "Hampden Community Holds Vigil for New York Man Killed by Baltimore Man," WJZ-TV Channel 13, Baltimore, MD, YouTube video, March 25, 2017, www.youtube.com/watch?v=Rjib7f_r3eE.

278 **Klan held ceremonies** Andrew Holter, "Our Town: What the Rise of Nazism Looked Like in Baltimore During the 1930s," *Baltimore City Paper*, February 15, 2017, www.citypaper.com/news/features/bcpnews-our-town-what-the-rise-of-nazism -looked-like-in-baltimore-during-the-1930s-20170214-htmlstory.html; also, "Klan Joins 14 Orders in Rites in Clubhouse Despite Ban," *Baltimore Sun*, November 30, 1925, 22; also, "Klan Closes Carnival in Hampden with Parade," *Baltimore Sun*, July 1, 1928, 3.

278 **christened a baby** "Klan Kiddie Khristened K. K. K.," *Baltimore Sun*, September 5, 1927, 18.

278 **"over 870 members"** Luther Butler, interview by Susan Hawes, August 3, 1979, transcript, Baltimore Neighborhood Heritage Project, transcribed and edited by John Brockenwitch, ANTH 640, University of Maryland, October 2005.

278 **vacated a house in Hampden** Jane A. Smith, "Black Family Decides to Leave Hampden: Harassment Ends as Police Move In," *Baltimore Sun*, May 26, 1988, 1D.

278 **openly recruited** Mark Bomster, "Skinheads Called 'Street Warriors for the Klan Groups' in U.S.; 'State Director' of Skinhead Group Has Ties to Known Md. Klan Official," *Baltimore Sun*, February 14, 1991, http://articles.baltimoresun.com/1991-02 -14/news/1991045138_1_skinhead-groups-klan-ku-klux.

278 **all kinds of trouble** Mark Bomster, "Racial Tension Persists at School in Hampden; Skinhead Outsiders Blamed for Trouble at Poole Middle School," *Baltimore Sun*, February 14, 1991, http://articles.baltimoresun.com/1991-02-14/news /1991045204_1_hampden-black-students-ku-klux.

278 **$50,000** Live Baltimore, "Average Home Sales by Neighborhood—Baltimore City 1998–2000," November 1, 2006, http://web.archive.org/web/20111203070158/ http://www.livebaltimore.com:80/UploadedFiles/resources/stats/salesbyneighborhood /NeighAvgs_2000-1998_zips_printable.pdf.

279 **$225,000** Live Baltimore, "Hampden," https://livebaltimore.com/neighbor hoods/hampden/#.WxGI_pM-eY1.

279 **oyster restaurant** Suzanne Loudermilk, "Dining Review: Dylan's Oyster Cellar Shows Passion for Seafood," *Baltimore Sun*, February 2, 2017, www.baltimoresun .com/entertainment/dining/bs-fo-dylans-oyster-cellar-20170202-story.html.

279 **"teaching kitchen"** Anna Walsh, "Where to Learn How to Cook," *Baltimore City Paper*, February 24, 2016, www.citypaper.com/special/eat/2016/bcpnews-where -to-learn-how-to-cook-20160224-story.html.

Epilogue

281 **"Rejoice in the Lord"** Israel Houghton and Aaron Lindsey, "Again I Say Rejoice," © 2004 Integrity's Praise! Music/BMI, Sound of the New Breed Publishing.

281 **"New Song Cares" ministry** New Song Community Church, "Searching for Employment Opportunities? New Song Cares," http://nscommunity.org/ministries /new-song-cares.

282 **who had taught middle-school science at New Song Academy** New Song Community Learning Center, "Staff," http://web.archive.org/web/20161107030211 /newsonglearningcenter.org/about-us-2/staff/.

282 **"Draw Me Close"** Donnie McClurkin, "Draw Me Close," *Psalms, Hymns & Spiritual Songs*, (BMI), Sony Legacy, 2005.

Afterword

288 **In a video** Steve McIntire, "Unaccountable Ideologues" (video), McIntire4MD Facebook page, May 16, 2018, https://www.facebook.com/McIntire4MD/videos /313458165854260.

288 **Adam Jackson** In August 2018, the *Baltimore Afro-American* reported that a woman had anonymously accused Jackson of rape and that black women activists had accused him of intimidating behavior. Jackson called the allegations "patently FALSE" and "a political takedown on the work I'm doing in Baltimore." Two prominent black women known as leaders in the community defended Jackson in the article.

Lisa Snowden-McCray, "Baltimore Grassroots Leader Facing Rape Allegations," *Baltimore Afro-American*, August 16, 2018, www.afro.com/leaders-of-the-beautiful -struggle-ceo-faces-abuse-and-harassment-allegations; also, Adam J. Jackson Facebook page, "Truth and Transparency: Part 1," August 14, 2018, www.facebook.com/ notes/adam-j-jackson/truth-transparency-part-1/10155618460462541.

289 **prosecutors charged him** Ian Duncan, Kevin Rector, and Tim Prudente, "Baltimore Police Chief De Sousa Charged with Failing to File Taxes, but Mayor Expresses Confidence in Him," *Baltimore Sun*, May 10, 2018.

290 **publicly condemned** Felicia Sonmex, "House Republican Campaign Chairman Rebukes Rep. Steve King for 'Completely Inappropriate' Comments on White Nationalism," *Washington Post*, October 30, 2018.

SELECTED BIBLIOGRAPHY

Bloom, Nicholas Dagen. *Merchant of Illusion: James Rouse, America's Salesman of the Businessman's Utopia.* Columbus: Ohio State University Press, 2004.

Bonilla-Silva, Eduardo. *Racism without Racists: Color-Blind Racism and the Persistence of Racial Inequality in America.* Lanham, MD: Rowman & Littlefield, 2003.

Brown, Prudence, Benjamin Butler, and Ralph Hamilton. "The Sandtown-Winchester Neighborhood Transformation Initiative: Lessons Learned about Community Building and Implementation." The Annie E. Casey Foundation and The Enterprise Foundation, 2001.

Durr, Kenneth D. *Behind the Backlash: White Working Class Politics in Baltimore, 1940–1980.* Chapel Hill: University of North Carolina Press, 2003.

Gomez, Marisela. *Race, Class, Power, and Organizing: Rebuilding Abandoned Communities in America.* Lanham, MD: Lexington Books, 2012.

Gordon, Wayne, and John M. Perkins with Randall Frame. *Making Neighborhoods Whole: A Handbook for Christian Community Development.* Downers Grove, IL: IVP Books, 2013.

Gornik, Mark R. *To Live in Peace: Biblical Faith and the Changing Inner City.* Grand Rapids, MI: William B. Eerdmans Publishing Company, 2002.

Grandpre, Lawrence, and Dayvon Love. *The Black Book: Reflections from the Baltimore Grassroots.* Baltimore: Leaders of a Beautiful Struggle, 2014.

Harris, Fredrick C., and Robert C. Lieberman (eds.). *Beyond Discrimination: Racial Inequality in a Postracist Era.* New York: Russell Sage Foundation, 2013.

Hirsch, Arnold. *Making the Second Ghetto: Race and Housing in Chicago, 1940–1960.* Chicago: University of Chicago Press, 1998.

Jackson, Kenneth. *Crabgrass Frontier: The Suburbanization of the United States.* New York: Oxford University Press, 1985.

Katznelson, Ira. *When Affirmative Action Was White: An Untold History of Racial Inequality in the Twentieth Century.* New York: W.W. Norton & Company, 2005.

Marsh, Charles. *Beloved Community: How Faith Shapes Social Justice from the Civil Rights Movement to Today.* New York: Basic Books, 2005.

Marx, Paul. *Jim Rouse: Capitalist/Idealist.* Lanham, MD: University Press of America, 2008.

Massey, Douglas, and Nancy A. Denton. *American Apartheid: Segregation and the Making of the Underclass.* Cambridge, MA: Harvard University Press, 1993.

McDougall, Harold. *Black Baltimore: A New Theory of Community*. Philadelphia: Temple University Press, 1993.

Olsen, Joshua. *Better Places, Better Lives: A Biography of James Rouse*. Washington, DC: Urban Land Institute, 2003.

Orser, Edward. *Blockbusting in Baltimore: The Edmondson Village Story*. Lexington: University Press of Kentucky, 1994.

Painter, Nell Irvin. *The History of White People*. New York: W.W. Norton & Company, 2010.

Perkins, John M. *Let Justice Roll Down*. Grand Rapids, MI: Baker Books, 1976.

Perkins, John M., ed. *Restoring At-Risk Communities: Doing It Together and Doing It Right*. Grand Rapids, MI: Baker Books, 1995.

Perkins, John. *With Justice for All: A Strategy for Community Development*. Grand Rapids, MI: Baker Books, 1982.

Pietila, Antero. *Not in My Neighborhood: How Bigotry Shaped a Great American City*. Chicago: Ivan R. Dee, 2010.

Polikoff, Alex. *Waiting for Gautreaux: A Story of Segregation, Housing, and the Black Ghetto*. Evanston, IL: Northwestern University Press, 2006.

powell, john a. *Racing to Justice: Transforming Our Conceptions of Self and Other to Build an Inclusive Society*. Bloomington: Indiana University Press, 2012.

Rabin, Yale. "The Effects of Development Control on Housing Opportunities for Black Households in Baltimore County, Maryland: A Report to the U.S. Commission on Civil Rights." U.S. Commission on Civil Rights Hearing Held in Baltimore, Maryland, August 17–19, 1970, Exhibits Entered Into the Hearing Record.

Report of the National Advisory Commission on Civil Disorders. New York: Bantam Books, 1968.

Rusk, David. *Baltimore Unbound: A Strategy for Regional Renewal*. Baltimore: Johns Hopkins University Press, 1995.

Sampson, Robert. *Great American City: Chicago and the Enduring Neighborhood Effect*. Chicago: University of Chicago Press, 2012.

Satter, Beryl. *Family Properties: Race, Real Estate, and the Exploitation of Black America*. New York: Metropolitan Books, 2009.

Sharkey, Patrick. *Stuck in Place: Urban Neighborhoods and the End of Progress Toward Racial Equality*. Chicago: University of Chicago Press, 2013.

Spence, Lester. *Knocking the Hustle: Against the Neoliberal Turn in Black Politics*. Brooklyn, NY: Punctum Books, 2015.

Sugrue, Thomas. *The Origins of the Urban Crisis: Race and Inequality in Postwar Detroit*. Princeton: Princeton University Press, 1996.

U.S. Commission on Civil Rights. *Equal Opportunity in Suburbia*. Washington, DC, 1974.

Williams, Rhonda Y. *The Politics of Public Housing: Black Women's Struggles*. New York: Oxford University Press, 2005.

INDEX

ABOUT THE AUTHOR

Lawrence Lanahan's writing and reporting has been published by the *New York Times*, Al Jazeera America, *Columbia Journalism Review*, *Slate*, NPR's *Morning Edition*, and *Colorlines*. *The Lines Between Us*, a fifty-episode radio series that Lanahan produced for Baltimore's WYPR, won Columbia University's duPont Award. He is a recipient of the Carey Institute's Logan Nonfiction Fellowship and lives in Baltimore.

PUBLISHING IN THE PUBLIC INTEREST

Thank you for reading this book published by The New Press. The New Press is a nonprofit, public interest publisher. New Press books and authors play a crucial role in sparking conversations about the key political and social issues of our day.

We hope you enjoyed this book and that you will stay in touch with The New Press. Here are a few ways to stay up to date with our books, events, and the issues we cover:

- Sign up at www.thenewpress.com/subscribe to receive updates on New Press authors and issues and to be notified about local events
- Like us on Facebook: www.facebook.com/newpressbooks
- Follow us on Twitter: www.twitter.com/thenewpress

Please consider buying New Press books for yourself; for friends and family; or to donate to schools, libraries, community centers, prison libraries, and other organizations involved with the issues our authors write about.

The New Press is a 501(c)(3) nonprofit organization. You can also support our work with a tax-deductible gift by visiting www.thenewpress.com /donate.

THE STUDS AND IDA TERKEL AWARD

On the occasion of his ninetieth birthday, Studs Terkel and his son, Dan, announced the creation of the Studs and Ida Terkel Author Fund. The Fund is devoted to supporting the work of promising authors in a range of fields who share Studs's fascination with the many dimensions of everyday life in America and who, like Studs, are committed to exploring aspects of America that are not adequately represented by the mainstream media. The Terkel Fund furnishes authors with the vital support they need to conduct their research and writing, providing a new generation of writers the freedom to experiment and innovate in the spirit of Studs's own work.

Studs and Ida Terkel Award Winners

Janet Dewart Bell, *Lighting the Fires of Freedom: African American Women in the Civil Rights Movement*

David Dayen, *Chain of Title: How Three Ordinary Americans Uncovered Wall Street's Great Foreclosure Fraud*

Aaron Swartz, *The Boy Who Could Change the World: The Writings of Aaron Swartz* (awarded posthumously)

Beth Zasloff and Joshua Steckel, *Hold Fast to Dreams: A College Guidance Counselor, His Students, and the Vision of a Life Beyond Poverty*

Barbara J. Miner, *Lessons from the Heartland: A Turbulent Half-Century of Public Education in an Iconic American City*

Lynn Powell, *Framing Innocence: A Mother's Photographs, a Prosecutor's Zeal, and a Small Town's Response*

Lauri Lebo, *The Devil in Dover: An Insider's Story of Dogma v. Darwin in Small-Town America*